Fourth Edition

100
BEST
CRUISE VACATIONS

THE TOP CRUISES
THROUGHOUT THE WORLD FOR
ALL INTERESTS AND BUDGETS

THEODORE W. SCULL

The
Globe
Pequot
Press

The schedules and rates listed in this guidebook were confirmed at press time. We recommend, however, that you call before traveling to obtain current information.

To buy books in quantity for corporate use or incentives, call **(800) 962–0973, ext. 4551,** or e-mail **premiums@GlobePequot.com.**

Text design by Nancy Freeborn

ISSN 1546-0789
ISBN 0-7627-3862-6

Manufactured in the United States of America
Fourth Edition/First Printing

3 9547 00293 7204

TO MY DEAR WIFE, SUELLYN,
WHO HAS ALSO TAKEN A COTTON TO CRUISING.
—TWS

Fourth Edition

100

B E S T

CRUISE VACATIONS

a photo essay

Regatta and *Insignia*

 River Explorer

Tobermory on the
Isle of Mull/
Hebridean Princess

 Seabourn Pride

Sun Boat III

 Star Flyer

Queen of the West

 National Geographic
Endeavour

Reef Endeavour

 Excelsior

Grande Caribe

 Queen Elizabeth 2

Sea Cloud

 Martha's Vineyard/
American Eagle

Clipper Adventurer

 *Crystal Symphony*

Viking Neptune

 *Queen Mary 2*

Oriana

 *SuperFast IX*

Spirit of '98

Photo credits: p. i © Oceania Cruises; p. iii courtesy of R/B River Explorer—Barging Through America®; p. iv–v courtesy of Hebridean Island Cruises; p. vi (top) courtesy of The Yachts of Seabourn; (bottom) courtesy of Abercrombie & Kent; p. vii (top) © Tim Thompson/Star Clippers; (bottom) courtesy of American West Steamboat Company; p. viii (top) photo by Ralph Lee Hopkins/Lindblad Expeditions; (bottom) MV *Reef Endeavour* courtesy of Captain Cook Cruises; p. ix (top) © William Mayes; (bottom) courtesy of American Canadian Caribbean Line; p. x (top) courtesy of Cunard Line; (bottom) courtesy of Sea Cloud Cruises; p. xi (top) © 2005 American Cruise Lines Inc.; (bottom) courtesy of Clipper Cruise Line; p. xii (top) © Crystal Cruises; (bottom) © Viking River Cruises; p. xiii (top) courtesy of Cunard Line; (bottom) © William Mayes; p. xiv (top) © William Mayes; (bottom) © Cruise West; p. 1 courtesy of American West Steamboat Company; p. 77 courtesy of Cunard Line; p. 91 © Princess Cruises; p. 121 © Crystal Cruises; p. 151 courtesy of Hebridean Island Cruises; p. 215 MV *Reef Endeavour* courtesy of Captain Cook Cruises; p. 227 courtesy of Abercrombie & Kent; p. 233 © Tim Thompson/Star Clippers; p. 241 photo by Ralph Lee Hopkins/Lindblad Expeditions; p. 247 © Discovery World Cruises; p. 271 courtesy of the author.

CONTENTS

NORTH AMERICA

EAST COAST—UNITED STATES AND CANADA

WEST COAST—ALASKA AND CANADA

U.S AND CANADIAN COASTAL RIVERS, LAKES, AND CANALS

ATLANTIC OCEAN

THE BAHAMAS AND
CARIBBEAN ISLANDS

THE BAHAMAS

CARIBBEAN ISLANDS

LATIN AMERICA

EUROPE

EUROPEAN RIVERS AND CANALS

MEDITERRANEAN SEA

PACIFIC OCEAN

AUSTRALIA AND NEW ZEALAND

HAWAIIAN ISLANDS

SOUTH PACIFIC

AFRICA AND
THE MIDDLE EAST

AFRICA

THE MIDDLE EAST

SOUTHEAST ASIA AND THE FAR EAST

POLAR REGIONS

CIRCUMNAVIGATIONS AND LONG VOYAGES

ACKNOWLEDGMENTS

100 Best Cruise Vacations has now arrived in a new fourth edition. With the ever-expanding range of terrific cruise opportunities, adding, deleting, and revising is a highly pleasurable and daunting task, one that requires the help of others updating the entries I would like to keep and finding new ships and itineraries. It could not be accomplished without these friends and fellow cruisers who suggested and wrote up their favorite shipboard experiences.

Bill Mayes, passionate sea traveler and generous B&B provider during my stays in England, wrote up the P&O's classic *Oriana,* Superfast's sleek new overnight cruise ferries from Scotland to the Netherlands, and a second highly recommended seaway from Genoa to the island of Sicily. He then updated chapters on four additional European ferry cruises, so this category now has numerous choices. Ben Lyons, U.S. merchant marine officer, contributed Lindblad Expeditions' Galápagos experience and tiny Glacier Bay Cruiselines' *Wilderness Adventurer* in Alaska. He also lent a fresh look at the venerable sailing yacht *Sea Cloud,* as well as updating several other entries. Andy Kilk, who spends months of his time moving from ship to ship all around the world, added the *Sapphire Princess*'s big-ship Mexican Riviera cruise and Royal Caribbean's *Vision of the Seas'* Pacific Coast positioning voyage. Charles Zuckerman reported on Oceana's *Insignia* transatlantic crossing. Cruise writer Heidi Sarna, both colleague and friend, provided invaluable help based on her considerable knowledge and the changing ways cruise lines are appealing to an even wider range of passengers.

Finally, my dear wife Suellyn has accompanied me on many cruises now with perhaps the most memorable, the wonderful tandem crossing of the *Queen Elizabeth 2* and *Queen Mary 2,* sailing over on the former and back on the latter. Many thanks to Lynn Zelem at The Globe Pequot Press for editing this latest edition.

—Theodore W. Scull, New York

INTRODUCTION

The popularity of cruise vacations has increased more than 300 percent in the last ten years. By the end of 2004, 10.5 million passengers had embarked on ships catering to the North American market, and more than eleven million are expected by the end of 2005. Cruises are increasingly seen as affordable, great fun, romantic, and a relaxing, hassle-free way to visit many parts of the world. To both meet and fuel the demand for cruise vacations, a score of large cruise ships are on order for completion between 2005 and 2007, joining the several hundred oceangoing ships that currently sail the high seas. Additional fleets of coastal and inland-waterway vessels, with many more under construction, explore inshore waters, rivers, and canals.

A traveler's cruising options have become mind-boggling, with so many different lines and respective reputations. The multitudinous decisions to be made include the specific type of cruise, itinerary, optimum ship size, whether it's a brand-new one or a fast disappearing classic liner, how much to spend on a cabin (and if to pay extra for a private veranda), the best time to go, and the relative personal importance attached to food, service, entertainment, and activities. Who are the other passengers going to be, mostly Americans? Or will there be persons of several nationalities aboard? What's the age range? And is this a cruise for children?

100 Best Cruise Vacations will help sort out the options by selecting the top ships, taking into account a fair balance between a ship's particular ambience, standards, and itineraries. Some of my choices will be obvious, and others may seem quirky or head scratchers.

Oceangoing ships come in sizes from 150,000 gross tons down to a little more than 2,000 tons, with passenger lists from less than one hundred to more than three thousand. The very largest may qualify as destinations themselves, where the itinerary is secondary to the rich shipboard experience, whereas others may offer a new port every day. Some people like lots of time at sea, so perhaps a voyage with ports spaced out every few days or a transocean crossing will fill the bill.

Enrichment cruises accompanied by top lecturers in a variety of fields may take in the great sites of the ancient world, while expedition-style voyages explore remote regions with a team of naturalists to lead passengers ashore. Some of the latter take you to places that may be hard, even impossible, to get to any other way, such as remote sections of Australia's Great Barrier Reef, South Pacific, the Galápagos Islands, Chilean fjords, and the white continent of Antarctica. Voyaging under sail through the Greek islands and along the Turkish coast or among the Caribbean's Leeward and Windward Islands may seem a romantic concept, and terrific choices are happily expanding. If you like water sports, some ships fold out their own marinas, with all sorts of boating, snorkeling, and diving equipment available for use.

To celebrate Americana, listen to great jazz and big-band sounds, and dine on Southern and Cajun cuisine, board a sternwheeler for a river cruise in the antebellum South, along the Upper Mississippi, or the Ohio up past Cincinnati. European river journeys ply the Rhine, Moselle, Elbe, and Danube to visit timeless medieval towns, hunting castles, and great Romanesque and Gothic cathedrals; and exotic inland trips penetrate deep into the Amazon Basin or into the heart of China. The pokiest cruises are aboard luxury barges, where the distance covered takes second place to savoring the passing countryside, biking into a nearby village, and sharing wonderful food and wines with a passenger complement of two dozen or fewer.

A cruise can be as short as an overnight crossing between the Scandinavian capitals, but more typically lasts a week to ten days. Vacationers with time and money can sail for several weeks around the bottom of South America or along the African coast, or go all the way, taking three to four months to circumnavigate the globe. Anyone remotely interested in taking a cruise vacation, or looking for something different, will find several that should appeal.

In this book, the cruise vacations are grouped into logical geographical regions beginning in North America and then casting a wider net overseas.

Defining the Best

What is terrific to one person may not appeal to someone else, and I am sure there will be lots of agreement and disagreement about the ships and the cruise itineraries I have chosen. Right up front, each cruise is entirely my own selection. After spending more than four years at sea since I made my first crossing to Europe as a teenager aboard the dear-departed French Line, I have come to thrive on the increasing diversity of available cruise experiences. I can be equally happy crossing the Atlantic, cruising around Britain, navigating Alaska's Inside Passage, exploring the Upper Amazon, or transiting the Panama Canal. For me the cover has long since blown off such clichés that cruises attract only old people, are nonstop drinking parties, or that they are stuffy, regimented, dull, crowded, and claustrophobic.

The best cruise vacation might imply the most expensive, and although some of the highest-rated boutique ships can cost upward of $500 to $1,000 a day per person, this need not be the case at all because there are excellent cruises at a third of that price and great values for even less. You will find itineraries at all fare levels.

The best cruises may involve the tangible and intangible features of a particular ship. The biggest ships on the high seas have always had a following, and I have picked those that truly excel in design and layout, have a pleasing or delightfully offbeat decor, provide lots of things to do aboard all day and well into the night, and have sound reputations for serving, feeding, and handling a small city of passengers and crew. If a midsize ship is more appealing, I have chosen these on the same but scaled-down basis. Remember, this is a selective guide, not inclusive of every best cruise vacation on the high seas, so if your favorite is not listed here, you already know about it.

Many of the finest ships, in terms of food and service, have passenger capacities that range from one hundred to about four hundred, and some cruisers choose the ship first, then one of several itineraries, and return again and again to the same ship or sistership.

The itinerary may be paramount. For the popular Panama Canal cruise, I offer several choices with different Caribbean and Pacific ports and a variety of onboard lifestyles and prices. Alaska and the Mediterranean also offer several alternatives.

Not all cruises should stand alone as the total travel experience, so for the islands north of Scotland, the Inside Passage of Alaska, and others, I have suggested land extensions.

I happen to be partial to older liners, and, in some cases, knowledgeable cruisers will wonder why I have included an over-the-hill ship, but she may offer something unique, giving readers the chance to sample what sea travel used to be like, before it's too late. It is fading fast.

The Itinerary

Some Caribbean ships may cruise year-round to the same set of ports, whereas others move seasonally to the Mediterranean or Alaska from late spring to early fall. I might suggest a ship for one itinerary and then make reference to another region where the same ship or a fleet mate cruises. Remember also, many ships form part of a series, so if the *Ryndam* substitutes for the *Maasdam,* the experience will remain much the same. Several top ships may get more than one full entry, as they cruise in many different parts of the world during one calendar year. A few ships may not repeat itineraries from one year to the next, and a set of ports for one Mediterranean or South American cruise might change the following year. While this muddies the waters, if the ship seems attractive to you, there will likely be some draw for a different itinerary. Cruise lines typically announce their schedules a year in advance, but then a ship gets sold or transferred elsewhere and another ship comes on line to take its place. Cruising is always in a state of flux, especially in uncertain times, so please don't expect to be able to exactly duplicate every cruise vacation

listed here. Rather use this book, literally, as a guide to what's out there—then get the latest news from your travel agent, the Internet, or the cruise line.

Every chapter will have a reference section that lists the following useful information:

Address/Phone: This listing includes the line's name and address, phone numbers, fax number, e-mail addresses, and Web sites, when available. Some lines do not take direct bookings because they sell cabins only through travel agents, tour companies, or over the Internet, so the phone numbers may be for information and brochures only. Cruise-line Web sites vary from excellent to you-wonder-why-they-bother because the information is so thin or out of date.

The Ship: The vital statistics are the year of build and previous names, if any; gross tonnage and length to give an indication of size; and draft (how deep in the water the ship sits), with a larger figure generally indicating more stability in heavy seas when matched with tonnage. Coastal ships and riverboats naturally have shallow drafts, so an exact figure is not always important, but it is likely to be 8 feet or less.

Passengers: This figure is usually for double occupancy, two to a cabin, whereas the maximum capacity may be higher as some cabins have third and fourth beds, perhaps a sofa bed or upper foldaway berths. The average age and nationality of one's fellow passengers are key points of information. Generally, the shorter the cruise, the younger the passenger, and average age increases markedly when the cruise begins to exceed a week. You can enrich the experience by sailing with Europeans or South Americans, or you may prefer to keep it simple and travel with passengers from your own country.

Dress: As most people increasingly seem to balk at getting dressed up, it is important to note what a line suggests for a particular evening, hoping that most passengers will comply to maintain the ambience. A little dressing up is part of the cruise experience for special occasions. I have used male evening dress codes, as they tend to be less understood and they can act also as a guide for women. "Formal" here means a tuxedo, dinner jacket, or a dark suit for men; "informal" means jacket with or without a tie; and "casual" means collared shirt and long pants. Daytime wear is even more casual. For women formal would be a gown or cocktail dress; informal, a dress or pants suit; and casual, a skirt or pants. You will not find me using terms such as "casually elegant" and telling people no T-shirts or tank tops in the dining room. If this is your style when the suggested dress at dinner is otherwise, you're on your own.

Officers/Crew: Some ships trade on the nationality of their officers and crew, so here we find out who's in charge and who does the serving.

Cabins: In addition to the accommodation information in the text, the number of cabins is listed, plus the number that are outside (with portholes or windows) and the availability of verandas, those private cabin balconies that let you step outside, found on most of the newer and largest ships. Few ships have dedicated single cabins, but if they do, this information is listed.

Fare: The $ signs are designed to give approximations for comparative purposes and are cruise brochure rates per person, double occupancy, per day for a standard outside cabin: $ = $100–$149; $$ = $150–$249; $$$ = $250–$399; $$$$ = $400– $599; $$$$$ = $600 upward.

Cruise-line fares are all over the map, even with the same ship on different itineraries. It's really no different from the yield management of the airlines. An empty cabin is lost revenue not only for its fare but also for what passengers will spend for shore excursions, drinks, shopping, gambling, spa treatments, and so on. Except for some small expedition ships and riverboats, the brochure rate is usually only the starting point for determining what you will ultimately pay. Nearly all lines have early booking discounts and may offer deals for departures selling poorly, which could occur months out or announced just before sailing. There are many ways to find the best-value fare, and it may be through a travel agent, a cruise-only specialist, a newspaper ad, the Internet, or directly from the line.

What's included: The $ to $$$$$ is based on what's normally included. A separate listing for what's not included specifies the extras. Most fares are cruise only, but sometimes the port charges are bundled into the fare. When they appear as a separate line item, they may add $100 to $200 to a typical seven-day cruise. Airfare to and from the ship is usually not included, but the line may have special add-on rates that are less than you can get on your own. Remember, if the line books the air travel, they can route you any way they want, but they are more likely to help you catch up to the ship if the flights are delayed or cancelled than if you have made your own arrangements, including the use of frequent-flyer mileage. With so many ships now departing U.S. and Canadian ports, there may be no need to fly, so you might consider taking a train or bus or drive to your next cruise. Some expedition cruises include shore excursions in the cruise fare, but most lines do not. A few upscale lines offer complimentary wine with meals, and fewer still include drinks and stocked mini-bars. For most lines tipping is your responsibility, but they will also almost always tell you what's expected, usually about $10 to $13 per day per person. The bottom line is to see what's included and what's not—the $ to $$$$$ may be skewed upward for a few lines because so much is already built into the fare.

Highlights: A summary of what makes this ship and/or cruise worth writing home about.

Other itineraries: If you like what you read but want to take a particular ship or the cruise line somewhere else, you will find references to other itineraries.

Ships Have Personalities

Some ships come from the same mold, but as they mature, they begin to show distinctive characteristics and differences from those of their fleet mates. Hundreds of passengers and crew help make a ship a living, breathing, seagoing community. A few ships have souls, and this special aspect will usually come across whether you are looking for it or not. All ships have personalities, and the best ones are happy ships, important not only to you as a paying passenger but also to the officers and crew who live aboard for months on end. Their time onboard may eventually add up to years, more than they spend ashore.

I hope you find your ship. I have, and it is present in these pages in great variety.

NORTH AMERICA

CRYSTAL CRUISES'
Crystal Symphony
New York via New England to the St. Lawrence and Montreal

Upscale, classy, and much larger than all other high-end cruise ships, the *Crystal Symphony* and larger and newer *Crystal Serenity* provide lots of space, amenities, and activities for Crystal's far-ranging itineraries. During a relatively short fall season, the *Crystal Symphony* visits New York, New England, and eastern Canada.

Crystal Cruises, owned by Japan's NYK Line, offers European-style service to a largely American clientele. The *Crystal Symphony,* built in Finland, is designed for worldwide cruising and spending happy days at sea. The second ship of the line, the *Crystal Serenity,* was completed at a French yard in 2003.

The primarily European and Filipino hotel and dining staff provides top service throughout the ship in the restaurants, bars, lounges, and on deck. The most popular gathering spot is the Palm Court, on this ship, one large wraparound room that serves as the venue for sightseeing in cool northern climes, reading, and enjoying formal afternoon tea and drinks before and after dinner. On this same Lido Deck, there's an outdoor lap pool, a second indoor-outdoor pool, adjoining Jacuzzis, lots of deck chairs in a wide variety of groupings, a snack and ice-cream bar, and indoor-outdoor buffet. The deck above has one of the largest oceanview spas at sea with an elaborate fitness center, saunas, steam rooms, aerobics, and body treatments, plus a paddle tennis court, golf driving range, and putting green. The jogging/walking teak deck at the promenade level runs the full length of the superstructure, and you can walk the perimeter of the Sun Deck.

Tiffany Deck 6 houses most of the public rooms radiating off the two-deck-high central atrium, understated compared to the Caribbean megaships. Aft of the all-the-way-forward Galaxy Show Lounge, for large-scale shows that are not a feature of the smaller upscale ships, are a large casino, a proper cinema for screening films and hosting lectures on theme cruises, several boutiques surrounding the atrium, the Bistro for coffee and pastries, a nightclub, library, computer center, and card room.

Dining is a delight, and the two special dinner options by reservation are Prego, a smartly decorated Italian restaurant, and the Jade Garden, Chinese/French fusion. The main dining room has two seatings, unusual for a ship of this caliber, but the food is excellent and the wine list, emphasizing California, is fairly priced. The Crystal Cove is a popular rendezvous for drinks outside the Crystal Dining Room.

All cabins are outside with well over half having private verandas, and the vast majority are laid out the full lengths of Decks 7 to 10. Amenities include sitting area, queen or twin beds, desk, TVs and VCR or DVD player, Internet access, refrigerator, safe, and bathrooms with stall showers and tubs, some not full length in lower categories. Room service from an extensive menu is available twenty-four hours, and penthouses have butlers in attendance.

The Itinerary

Following a summer season in Europe, the *Crystal Symphony* comes to New York for a brief series of seven- and eleven-day New England and Canada cruises. The short ones are round-trips from New York while the more lengthy voyages are one-way, originating either in New York or Montreal.

The cruise featured here departs from the Big Apple for Montreal, and as the ship progresses northward to the Canadian Maritimes and the St. Lawrence Valley, the autumn colors will dramatically change. Sailing from **New York** is always a treat with its majestic skyline, the Statue of Liberty, the passage beneath the Verrazano-Narrows Bridge, and ultimately out to sea.

The next morning the ship anchors off **Newport, Rhode Island,** and you can explore the elegant "summer cottages" along the Cliff Walk or stroll downtown Newport, a major East Coast sailing center. Be sure to go inland beyond the tourist shops along Thames Street to historic Newport, established well before the late-nineteenth-century new rich came to show off their wealth along Bellevue Avenue.

The *Symphony* exits Narragansett Bay and skirts Cape Cod to approach **Boston** through its harbor islands. From the Black Falcon Cruise Terminal, good walkers can reach the center of the city in about twenty minutes and access the T to take you by subway and trolley to wherever you wish to go—Boston Common, Beacon Hill, Faneuil Hall and Quincy Market, Back Bay, Cambridge, or the museums. Salem and its Witch Museum is less than an hour away. Then it's an overnight sail to **Bar Harbor, Maine,** for another look at an upscale summer resort, a lobster bake, and a great view of the surrounding seascape from atop Cadillac Mountain in **Acadia National Park.** Then after a full day at sea, the call at **Halifax** provides a visit to Canada's immigration depot museum at Pier 21, the lively waterfront attractions, and a drive down the scenic coastline via the Lighthouse Route to **Peggy's Cove** and Lunenburg.

The *Symphony* then leaves the North Atlantic and passes into the mouth of the St. Lawrence where the river is at first too broad to see the opposite shores. En route to **Quebec City,** the river becomes more defined, and it is possible to see whales, especially at the mouth of the Saguenay River. Docking beneath the Citadel, again you can tour on your own, first in the lower older city, then by funicular or on foot to the upper city. Have a drink and a great view at the Marine Bar in the Chateau Frontenac, one of the great castle-style hotels built by the Canadian Pacific Railway. The city has a distinctive French flavor, and with an overnight stay you can enjoy dinner out on the town in an atmosphere not unlike that of a Paris bistro.

The St. Lawrence narrows considerably when approaching **Montreal,** and the *Symphony* will tie up overnight opposite Old Montreal, another fine historic district to explore on foot with a walking tour map and to have a meal out at numerous restaurants within easy distance of the ship. The city's Metro is simple to use for reaching the commercial and shopping centers and perhaps for the gentle climb up through wooded Mont Royal Park.

This cruise also operates from Montreal to similar ports, and often adds Halifax, noted for its maritime flavor and coastal drives. A waterfront path connects the cruise terminal and the immigration museum with the attractions of the city's center.

Address/Phone: Crystal Cruises, 2049 Century Park East, Suite 1400, Los Angeles, CA 90067; (866) 446–6625 or (310) 785–9300; fax: (310) 785–0011; www.crystalcruises.com

The Ship: *Crystal Symphony* was built in 1995, has a gross tonnage of 51,044, a length of 781 feet, and a draft of 25 feet.

Passengers: 940 double occupancy; mostly North Americans fifty-five plus

Dress: Fit to kill. Formal nights, jackets and ties on informal nights

Officers/Crew: Norwegian and Japanese officers and European and Filipino crew

Cabins: 470 cabins, all outside, and 276 with private verandas

Fare: $$$$

What's included: Cruise fare, port charges, bottled water, soft drinks, specialty coffees

What's not included: Airfare, alcoholic drinks, shore excursions, tips

Highlights: Alternative Chinese/French fusion and Italian restaurants, excellent waiter/bar service, lots of onboard amenities

Other itineraries: In addition to these seven- and eleven-day New England and Canada cruises, which operate from late September to early November, the *Crystal Symphony* and *Crystal Serenity* make Panama Canal trips and cruise northern Europe, the Mediterranean, and, indeed, cruise most of the world.

PRINCESS CRUISES'
Star Princess
Big Ship Bound for Landscapes and Fall Foliage

The *Star Princess* entered service in February 2002 as the newest triplet to the *Golden Princess* and *Grand Princess,* and all three have cruised New England and Canada.

With a service speed of 22.5 knots and an overall length of 935 feet, the *Star Princess* is huge, and the long treks between cabin, lounges, restaurants, and outside decks constantly remind one of her mass. Yet within she seems smaller, because the scale of public rooms aims not to overwhelm.

The 2,600-plus passengers hail mostly from North America with a growing number coming from Britain to cruise where sister company London-based P&O does not. This ship, registered in Bermuda, is crewed with British and Italian officers and an international staff, largely European and Filipino.

Unless you delight in bounding up and down scores of steps, the elevators linking the fourteen passenger decks will see lots of use, and it is worth experimenting to find the best routes to avoid lengthy waits. The elegant and understated three-story atrium has attractive metal work covering the lift shafts and balconies for looking into the well and enjoying the quartet that fills the void with music.

The three main restaurants, Amalfi, Capri, and Portofino, offer both traditional reserved tables at two seatings and restaurant-style seating where at dinner passengers may request a table between 5:30 P.M. and midnight. In the catering department the food is good standard fare in the main dining rooms, but something rather special is offered in the theme restaurants. At Sabatini's Trattoria, the Italian staff hopes you will arrive hungry and with time on your hands because the multicourse Italian tasting menu includes eight antipasti; four kinds of pizza; minestrone; salad; three pastas; a choice of six entrees such as tiger prawns, sea scallops, or veal chop; and four desserts. They don't take kindly to—or even begin to understand—"No thank you, I am full."

The Sterling Steakhouse is the second extra-tariff restaurant, and the waiter brings the prime cuts, including a 22-ounce porterhouse to the table. The selections are then prepared in the open kitchen. Both restaurants require reservations and levy an extra charge, and it's worth it.

High up on Lido Deck 14, Horizon Court is open twenty-four hours, and late at night one section becomes a wait-served bistro, a feature on all Princess ships. The pool area has a grill for hamburgers and hot dogs and a second counter for pizza by the slice. Sundaes and scoops of ice cream come with land-side prices.

Three entertainment lounges include the two-level Princess Theater for the lavish shows; the smaller Vista Show Lounge for singers, comedians, and lecturers; and Explorer's Lounge, featuring a band playing amidst Egyptian, Moroccan, and wild animals of the jungle tropical decor.

Clubby and sedate, the dark-paneled Wheelhouse Bar is a pre-dinner gathering place enveloped in P&O maritime art, ship models, and photographs, making up an attractive collection touting the company's 170-year history trading to the British Empire. Other public spaces include the vast Atlantis Casino, attractive open-plan lounge bars facing the atrium, and Skywalkers, a lofty perch ensconced within a tubular glass pod suspended 155 feet above the foaming wake. By swiveling 180 degrees, the entire length of the *Star Princess* stretches away toward the horizon. The space-age capsule provides a quiet lounge during the day and a pulsating disco at night.

One of four widely separated main pools is positioned under an all-weather retractable glass roof, making it useable on this cool-weather itinerary. The large-windowed spa is sited forward on Sun Deck 15 and offers aerobics, steam rooms, saunas, massage, a beauty parlor, and the full range of treatments, plus a moderate-size gym. Some say it could be larger. For active out-of-doors types, there is a golf simulator, 9-hole miniature golf course, paddle tennis court, basketball, and volleyball. Constitutional walkers can completely circumnavigate the ship from the pointy end to the flat transom. For circumnavigators, the forward end of the Promenade Deck has steps that lead up to Emerald Deck and a covered walkway located below the mooring deck. By standing at the very bow, you can be the first to arrive in port, and the first to leave.

The huge high-tech, virtual-reality game room, Voyage of Discovery, creatively entertains the young and young at heart. However, children do not come on this cruise in any significant numbers.

Of the 1,301 earth-tone paneled and light-hued cabins, 711 have private verandas. Outside rooms with balconies measure 215–255 square feet. Standard outside cabins measure 165–210 square feet, and inside rooms, 160. The lounge sections have only a desk-cum-vanity and chair and curiously no room for a sofa. The tiered balcony design allows those above to lord over their neighbors dwelling below.

All cabins have refrigerators; TVs that bring in CNN, ESPN, TNT, and the BBC; phones; safes; hair dryers; cloth robes; and adequate storage in open closets. The twenty-five suites and 180 minisuites have sitting areas with sofa beds, two TVs, and tubs, with whirlpools added to the full-suite accommodations. Many cabins on Emerald Deck 8 have views blocked by lifeboats, and these are marked on the plans. Twenty-eight cabins, eighteen outside and ten inside, are wheelchair accessible.

The *Star Princess* offers a big-ship cruise for those who want their conveyance to be a destination, at least equal to the ports of call. But megaship size does not necessarily mean being part of the crowd. Passengers are well distributed, and quiet retreats can be found all over the ship. Mine is Skywalkers.

The Itinerary

Slightly more than twenty years ago, cruises from New York to New England and Canada were few and far between. Today, cruising up north extends from May to late October, with the greatest concentration coming during the fall foliage season. No region tops New England for the autumn colors, and having lived in the Northeast virtually all my life, I never tire of the grand spectacle. To witness peak fall foliage, the window is fairly wide with the earliest period for parts of Canada coming in September then extending into mid-November for the New York region. Colorful leaves are not by any means the only draw for these cruises.

Think French-speaking Acadians in Nova Scotia and New Brunswick; Pilgrims and Puritans in New England; whaling and fishing industries; spectacular coastlines; state and national parks; picture postcard towns; sailing, kayaking, cycling, and hiking; clam bakes and steamed Maine lobsters; and culture, art, and music in the bigger cities.

On my one-week New England–Canada round voyage aboard the 109,000-ton *Star Princess*, we boarded in New York on a Sunday afternoon, had two nights and a full day to settle in, then hit five consecutive ports—Halifax, Saint John, Bar Harbor, Boston, and Newport—all offering something different and in some cases, a mind-boggling array of tour choices. The order of port calls varies from one year to the next.

Princess Cruises has mounted an excellent Web site that allows one to study the options and pre-book all shore excursions. With the *Star Princess*'s large passenger capacity of 2,600, the result is a huge choice—motorcoach tours, hikes, town walks, carriage rides, cycling, kayaking, rafting, amphibious vehicles, and boat excursions, or doing it on your own on foot or in a rented car. By registering in advance, tour tickets arrive at the cabin door and you avoid queues and booked-up trips.

No departure tops a sail away from **New York** past the Manhattan skyline, Ellis Island and the Statue of Liberty, then out to sea beneath the graceful Verrazano-Narrows Bridge. For Sun Belt denizens, Northeastern autumn temperatures, ranging between 50 and 70 degrees, may be a bit nippy, more so on the ocean than ashore.

After a full day at sea and sailing into **Halifax** on the second morning, the pier is conveniently within easy walking distance of the city center, the active waterfront, the maritime museum, and the lovely nineteenth-century Public Gardens. The cemetery, where many *Titanic* disaster victims are buried, is located just outside town and best reached by taxi.

My favorite destination is Pier 21, Canada's superb immigration museum, located alongside the ship and loaded with artifacts, photographs, and memorabilia. Immigrants, war brides, and returning soldiers tell their poignant stories in videos and on tape. The most popular bus excursions head down the coast to **Peggy's Cove** and to historic and hilly Lunenburg.

At **Saint John, New Brunswick,** it is best to venture out into the countryside, such as on the ninety-minute drive to **St. Andrews,** an attractive waterside town that developed into a resort anchored by the venerable turn-of-the-last-century Algonquin Hotel, built by the mighty Canadian Pacific Railway and now part of the Fairmont chain. The residential streets, planted with a variety of trees introduced over the last one hundred years, are awash with displays of reds, yellows, oranges, and lingering greens. An alternate short trip takes to the rapids, including a raft ride, at the Reversing Falls.

Bar Harbor provides the best autumn foliage as Mount Desert Island is almost completely forested, and the island's towns have specifically planted deciduous trees exhibiting excellent color. Some passengers go cycling or take the full-day tour to Bar Harbor, Northeast Harbor, Somesville, and a drive up Cadillac Mountain rising out of **Acadia National Park** for 360-degree views including down on the ship at anchor in Frenchmen Bay. Lunch features steamed Maine lobster, tasty clam chowder, potato salad, corn on the cob, and fresh blueberry pie.

During the call at **Boston,** consider a leisurely all-day walk along the Freedom Trail, its route marked by a red line in the sidewalk that starts at the gold dome State House on Beacon Hill facing Boston Common and the Public Garden and leads to virtually everything of historic interest in the city, including Quincy Market, Fanueil Hall, the Old North Church, Charlestown Navy Yard, and the Italian North End.

Anchoring off **Newport, Rhode Island,** the resort city's diversions are plentiful whether on tour or on foot. Energetic walkers will find the lesser known eighteenth- and nineteenth-century historic district, just in from the tender landing, displaying an attractive low-key lifestyle contrasting sharply with Bellevue Avenue's extravagant so-called summer cottages. In addition to the organized tours, a seaside Cliff Walk passes in front of many of the mansions. It was a favorite Sunday picnic outing when I attended boarding school located on the next rise about one mile away.

Arriving back in New York harbor on the final morning, the Hudson River's Palisades had almost reached their peak of color, a spectacle readily accessible for those who purchase a post-cruise package. Additionally, nearby Central Park and Brooklyn's Botanic Garden provide a riot of colors, just a walk or subway ride away.

Address/Phone: Princess Cruises, 24305 Town Center Drive, Santa Clarita, CA 91355; (800) PRINCESS or (661) 753–0000; fax: (661) 259–3108; www.princess.com

The Ship: *Star Princess* was completed in 2002 and has a gross tonnage of 109,000, a length of 951 feet, and a draft of 26 feet.

Passengers: 2,600; mostly Americans, some British, in their thirties to seventies

Dress: Suits or tuxedos for the two formal nights and slacks and collared shirts for casual nights

Officers/Crew: British and Italian officers; international crew

Cabins: 1,300; 928 outside and 710 with verandas

Fare: $$

What's included: Cruise fare only

What's not included: Transportation to and from ship, port charges, shore excursions, drinks, lots of onboard extras

Highlights: Big-ship amenities, many public rooms, Sterling Steakhouse, fall foliage itinerary

Other itineraries: In addition to this New England–Canada cruise operating in the fall, Princess Cruises' large fleet offers worldwide itineraries.

HOLLAND AMERICA LINE'S

Maasdam

New England and Canada from Boston

Holland America, one of the world's oldest shipping companies, has long had a solid reputation of friendly service and beautiful, well-run ships. The 55,451-ton *Maasdam,* built in 1993, is the second ship in the *Statendam*-class series.

Two levels of public rooms, punctuated by a glass sculpture rising dramatically through the three-deck atrium, run the length of the ship along Promenade and Upper Promenade Decks, creating a rhythmic flow as passengers seek out their favorite spots and pass to and from the two-story dining room. An impressive double staircase links the two levels, and a Filipino orchestra serenades diners from a raised platform, with sound quality well distributed. HAL perpetuates its tradition of good, uncomplicated food and service by an attentive Filipino and Indonesian staff. A Pinnacle Grill has been added to the ship (and now the entire fleet), featuring a Pacific Northwest theme admirably suited to this East Coast itinerary and which includes salmon and crab cakes as well as steaks and chicken dishes. For informal dining, the well-laid-out lido restaurant has picture windows and seating inside and under cover near the pool, and it gets dressed up for dinner at night.

The bi-level show lounge, designed with good views except from the rear balcony, presents elaborate Broadway-style entertainment. A band plays for listening and dancing in the attractive Ocean Bar, the ship's principal social center. The Crow's Nest provides an indoor perch for viewing the coastal scenery, afternoon tea service, and a disco at night.

The roof of the central pool retracts in good weather, and sandwiches, pizza, and satay are informally served here. A gym, massage and steam rooms, saunas, and a juice bar look over the stubby bow, and a jogging track encircles the mezzanine above the lido. Constitutional walkers will enjoy circuits of the Lower Promenade Deck, also a favorite spot for stretching out in a wooden deck chair.

Cabins are arranged over five decks, with those on the topmost two having verandas. To provide as many outside cabins as possible, the rooms tend to be long and narrow, with small sitting areas, TVs, VCRs, and minibars.

The Itinerary

Sail from **Boston** from May to October on this one-week, one-way, five-port cruise via the Maritimes and the St. Lawrence River to Quebec City and Montreal, or do it in reverse. Departing from Boston's Black Falcon Terminal, located within sight of downtown, the *Maasdam* slides past the end of the main runway at Logan Airport and out through the Harbor Islands into the Atlantic on an overnight run up the coast to **Bar Harbor.**

Anchoring off the main town on **Mount Desert Island,** Bar Harbor once boasted some of the grandest summer homes on the East Coast, but many were destroyed in a great fire in the late 1940s. Today's town is more down to earth and geared to tourists, while Northeast Harbor has gained ascendancy but never showed off in the Newport sort of way that Bar Harbor did. A drive around the island perimeter is revealing of the multi-levels of summer residential life with the quietest places being Somesville and Southwest Harbor.

On a clear summer or autumn day, Cadillac Mountain, set in deeply wooded **Acadia National Park,** offers a delightful view of the nearby islands, coastline, and your ship, looking like a toy from such a height. For excursions, there are bus trips, lobster bakes, some strenuous biking, and gentle hiking.

Sailing north along the Nova Scotia coast, **Halifax** is a walkers' paradise. The waterside path leads straight from the cruise terminal, and the superb Pier 21 immigration museum, to the downtown waterfront for its great fish restaurants and Maritime Museum of the Atlantic. Exhibits include the *Titanic* disaster and salvaged items and the Halifax Explosion that leveled much of the city during World War I. Walk up a steep hill to the Citadel and stroll through the pretty adjacent Public Gardens and upscale leafy residential neighborhood. A taxi is advisable for a visit to the cemetery where 150 of *Titanic*'s passengers and crew are buried. A car rental agency on the pier is available for independent touring south along the rugged Lighthouse Route in the direction of **Peggy's Cove,** a tiny picture postcard fishing port.

Sailing up the Nova Scotian coast, the call at **Sydney** gives access to the 184-mile **Cabot Trail** that skirts the shoreline and passes through tiny communities that had Irish, English, and French Canadian origins. Alexander Graham Bell, who owned a mansion on Bras D'Or Lakes (also an excursion), considered the landscape to be more beautiful than the Rockies, Andes, or Alps. Hopefully a sunny day will show the region to its best and then let you decide. Another excursion visits Louisbourg, Parks Canada's top restoration, a fortified community that reflects the year 1744 and includes military reenactments and a tour to Chateau St. Louis to see the fabulous collection of furnishings, tapestries, and paintings.

A less frequented stop is **Charlottetown,** the low-key capital of Prince Edward Island, for its Victorian houses seen by double-decker bus or on out to the farmlands, forests, and seascapes. There are bus and bike tours; the latter uses a Rails to Trails project called the Confederation Trail and because of its original use, offers a flat ride.

Now the cruise enters the broad St. Lawrence Valley to cruise upriver to the mouth of the **Saguenay,** a fjord of outstanding beauty, and where the waters mix, there are likely to be whales feeding. Ever narrowing, the river route leads to **Quebec City,** a large slice of Old France in North America. Besides the city, at the waterline and atop the ramparts, there is a bus tour out to 272-foot Montmorency Falls, including a cable car ride for sweeping views of the St. Lawrence and the Ile D'Orleans. For cyclists, a nifty excursion starts with a ferry across to Levis on the south shore, then a rail trail ride along the banks for some 14 miles. You can get a great shot of the *Maasdam* from the ferry or the far shore, set against the Citadel and the Chateau Frontenac.

Then it's overnight to **Montreal** for disembarkation. Consider spending a night or two to take in the largest French-speaking city outside of France, the historic buildings, restaurants, cafes, and nightlife of Old Montreal and the urban residential and commercial district below leafy Mont-Royal, itself worth the short climb.

Address/Phone: Holland America Line, 300 Elliott Avenue West, Seattle, WA 98119; (800) 426–0327; fax: (206) 281–7110; www.hollandamerica.com

The Ship: *Maasdam* was built in 1993, has a gross tonnage of 55,451, a length of 719 feet, and a draft of 25 feet.

Passengers: 1,266 passengers, double occupancy; mostly Americans forty-five and up on these short cruises

Dress: Formal, informal, and casual nights

Officers/Crew: Dutch officers and Indonesian and Filipino crew

Cabins: 632, of which 502 are outside and 150 have verandas

Fare: $$$

What's included: Cruise only

What's not included: Airfare, port charges, shore excursions, drinks, tips

Highlights: A port-intensive itinerary available for the complete season, and convenient Boston embarkation for New Englanders

Other itineraries: In addition to these one-week New England and Canada cruises, which operate from May through October, the large Holland America fleet makes cruises in the Caribbean, South America, through the Panama Canal, to Hawaii and Alaska, Europe, and around the world.

NORWEGIAN CRUISE LINE'S
Norwegian Dawn
Year-round Cruising from New York to the Sun

Breaking the mold once again, Norwegian Cruise Line has tarted up one of its newest ships to catch the eye, with portraits of a dolphin playing in Technicolor waves on one side of the hull and a depiction of the Statue of Liberty and signatures of Impressionist artists on the other. The colorful artwork calls attention to the *Norwegian Dawn*'s innovative year-round operations between New York, Florida, and the Bahamas, and longer itineraries into the Caribbean.

Completed in late 2002, the 91,740-gross-ton giant offers cruisers every imaginable attraction to please the young and young at heart. For the active, facilities include a combination basketball and volleyball court, a golf driving range, gym and spa, swimming pools, Jacuzzis, a kids' wading pool, and jogging track. For entertainment, the list includes a three-level show lounge for major productions, sports bar, video arcade, Internet center, casino, a

disco for adults and another for teens, and fanciful play areas for young children. For a cluster of quiet retreats, high up there's a library, separate reading and writing room, and a card room.

Cabins range from inexpensive insides and lots of oceanview cabins with private balconies up to NCL's signature garden villas. The pair of three-bedroom, 5,350-square-foot suites boasts a living room furnished with a grand piano, an entertainment center, a kitchen, butler and concierge services, an outdoor dining area, a private Italian garden for relaxing, a Jacuzzi, and a roof terrace. Some families and friends move into one of these extravaganzas and disappear for the whole week.

Aboard the big new NCL ships, it's the dining options that set them well apart from other popularly priced lines. For foodies and those who like to sample as many new venues as possible, this ship has got what you want. Some eateries are open only for dinner but with extended hours—5:30 P.M. to midnight. A few have a cover charge or a la carte menu, but most come with no additional charge at all.

The three main dining rooms are Aqua, a modern restaurant with a healthy and light contemporary menu; the traditional, European-style Venetian with arrival via a grand staircase and big windows facing aft; and Impressions, offering a varied menu in a sophisticated Paris circa 1900 setting with Impressionist painting reproductions on walls of burl-wood paneling.

Three restaurants carry cover charges that range from $10 to about $25 per person. Le Bistro, a signature French restaurant, serves both traditional French and nouvelle cuisine in a formal yet colorful setting enhanced by original Impressionist paintings from four artists—Matisse, Monet, Renoir, and van Gogh. The adjacent Wine Cellar is an annex for Le Bistro that also hosts wine tastings.

Bamboo, a sprawling Asian restaurant, has three sections: a sushi, sashimi, and sake bar where the plates arrive on a conveyor belt; an eighteen-place Japanese teppanyaki room, where diners watch the food being prepared; and the main dining area with a long Chinese-Japanese-Thai menu.

The third, Cagney's, well away from the others on Deck 13, is an open-kitchen steakhouse serving sumptuous Angus beef for prime ribs and filet mignon, lamb, fish, and grilled chicken in a setting of wood and brick–style walls and newspaper wall clippings.

The most casual dining takes place at Salsa, a Tex-Mex-Tapas-Spanish-Middle Eastern–style restaurant overlooking the central atrium that also serves sangria and chips for those listening to the house band; diner-style Blue Lagoon, serving fish and chips, hamburgers, stir fries, and snacks round the clock; and the Garden Café for typical buffet food at breakfast and lunch, such as omelets, pastas, soups, and salads. One section, which gets a bit more ethnically dressed up in the evening as La Trattoria, offers pastas, pizzas, Italian desserts, and espresso. The bar here has a great beer selection from England, Scotland, and Australia. Lastly, the Bimini Bar & Grill dishes up simple fare such as hot dogs, burgers, and fries all day long.

The Itinerary

The *Norwegian Dawn* began offering year-round itineraries from **New York** in May 2003, the first ship to do so in many years. The upside for many Northeasterners is not having to fly to meet the ship, and instead being able to drive or take the train or a bus to New York or directly to the pier. The downside for some in winter might be the cool, even cold, and sometimes rough weather conditions for the first twenty-four hours after leaving New York, but with so much going on inside the ship, the fast passage into warmer weather should seem a relatively brief one. And the sail away from Manhattan cannot be topped.

On the seven-day cruises, two nights and a day after leaving New York, the ship will dock at **Port Canaveral, Florida,** and the long port call permits ample time to tour the nearby Kennedy Space Center or travel one hour inland to spend the day at **Walt Disney World** for the Magic Kingdom, Epcot, Disney-MGM Studios, and Animal Kingdom or visit its rival, **Universal Orlando,** with working motion-picture and TV studios and a theme park for thrilling roller-coaster rides and waterslides.

Following a South Beach disco party and an overnight sail to **Miami,** many will head to South Beach's art deco district for a walking tour, a meal, or just to ogle the local characters who flock here. For a visit to a flamboyant villa, Vizcaya Museum and Gardens is a spectacular Italian Renaissance–style mansion. Kids will want to go to the Miami Seaquarium to watch Flipper, the TV dolphin, and Lolita the killer whale perform, plus see sea lions, manatees, and sharks feeding. At the Monkey Jungle, it's the performing primates that roam free while the visiting humans walk through caged passages.

Arriving in **Nassau** in the morning, you can travel by foot, horse-drawn carriage, jitney, taxi, moped, scooter, rental car, or ferry for a day at the beach, snorkeling, or scuba diving; take a historic tour to the Queen's Staircase to see upscale houses; visit Paradise Island for a tour of the Cloister and Versailles Gardens; head out to Crystal Cay for the aquariums and underwater observation towers; or just hang around town and explore the British colonial connections and modern shopping district.

For the last call, spend the morning and early afternoon at NCL's private Bahamian island of **Great Stirrup Cay,** a tranquil palm-fringed beachfront that turns into an all-day party when passengers disembark. Facilities include barbecues and bar with live or broadcast music, volleyball, hammocks for a read or snooze, massage treatments, and water activities such as paddleboats, Sunfish, parasailing, banana boats, and snorkeling. Leaving the NCL playground, the *Norwegian Dawn* turns northward for New York with two nights and a day to make the final rounds of favorite or not-yet-sampled restaurants.

Address/Phone: Norwegian Cruise Line, 7665 Corporate Center Drive, Miami, FL 33126; (800) 327–7030 or (305) 436–4000; fax: (305) 436–4126; www.ncl.com

The Ship: *Norwegian Dawn,* built in 2002, has a gross tonnage of 91,740, a length of 965 feet, and a draft of 27 feet.

Passengers: 2,224, mostly American of all ages, especially during school holiday sailings

Dress: Casual or as you wish

Officers/Crew: Officers are European and the crew international

Cabins: 1,112, of which 759 are outside, and 509 have balconies

Fare: $$

What's included: Cruise fare

What's not included: Airfare, port charges, excursions, drinks, some alternative dining, tips

Highlights: For New York region residents, a year-round cruise option without the need to fly; a ship with ten dining choices

Other itineraries: Besides this weekly cruise by the *Norwegian Dawn* that operates much of the year from New York, the *Dawn* will offer several longer wintertime ten- and eleven-day sailings from New York to the deep Caribbean; a sample itinerary includes calls at St. Thomas, Tortola, St. Maarten, San Juan, and Great Stirrup Cay. Another cruises to the Western Caribbean. NCL ships cruise from many U.S. ports to Canada and New England, Bermuda, the Caribbean, South America, the Panama Canal, Alaska, Hawaii, and in Europe.

HOLLAND AMERICA LINE'S
Ryndam and *Statendam*
Alaska's Glacier Discovery Cruises and Alaska/Yukon Land Tours

Holland America Line dates back to 1873, operating transatlantic passenger service for the first hundred years. Now owned by the Carnival Corporation, Holland America runs one of the largest and most modern fleets, combining classical interiors with up-to-date amenities.

The *Statendam,* the first in the new series, and the *Ryndam,* the third, both offer ten decks of accommodations for 1,266 passengers. The Crow's Nest on Sports Deck is a delightful sightseeing lounge during the day and an intimate nightclub in the evening. The Lido Deck offers health and fitness facilities and a large pool area that can be covered by a retractable dome during Alaska's cooler weather.

The buffet restaurant amidships is designed to keep the queues short and provides a great selection at both breakfast and lunch and a semi-served buffet dinner. The aft dining room's two-level space offers decent food in a beautiful setting, with such regional specialties as baked Alaska, cod fillet, steamed king crab legs, and sesame-roasted king salmon fillet. For an extra charge, the Pinnacle Grill features a Pacific Northwest menu, including Dungeness crab cakes, seared duck breast, and Washington and Oregon wines. The show lounge has both balcony and orchestra levels for cruise-ship-style extravaganzas. The Ocean Bar, a Holland America Line trademark, is the social center for drinks and dancing, while the Explorer's Lounge provides a quieter venue. Both ships have attractive, understated three-story atriums that lead to the Java Café and the Wajang theater as well as to the

lower level of the show room forward and the dining room aft.

The 633 cabins and suites range from 187-square-foot inside cabins to four-room penthouse suites measuring 1,126 square feet. Avoid cabins above the theater if you retire early. Both ships have lots of open deck space for viewing the scenery, and the Lower Promenade is fully teaked for the constitutional walkers.

The Cruise Itinerary

Holland America offers more than one hundred departures each season with eight ships, and presented here will be a one-week northbound cruise embarking at **Vancouver.** The ports will vary slightly depending on the departure.

Following two nights and a day cruising between Vancouver Island and the mountainous British Columbia coast, the *Ryndam* or *Statendam* will call at **Ketchikan,** where the active might kayak the fishing harbor's waterfront or take a drive out to see the world's largest collection of totems depicting legends of Native Alaskans. Next, at **Juneau,** you can see the Mendenhall Glacier from the road or a small plane, or by helicopter that lands on the glacier. The capital is worth a look on foot as is the once raucous, now tame Red Dog Saloon, Alaska's most famous entertainment bar. Pay a visit to the Alaska State Museum for exhibits on the state's history, wildlife, and Native culture, or ride the Mount Roberts Tram for a 2,000-foot-high view.

At **Sitka,** passengers go ashore by tender, arriving within walking distance of many attractions. The New Archangel Dancers perform a show worth seeing in the Centennial

Hall, which also houses the visitor center. Nearby stands St. Michael's Russian Orthodox Cathedral, rebuilt after a fire in 1966. At the edge of town, the Sitka National Memorial Park has the most finely carved totems in the state.

Sailing across the Gulf of Alaska with the Wrangell–St. Elias National Park forming a backdrop, the ship turns to cruise up to the **Hubbard Glacier.** Enter **Prince William Sound** cruising **College Fjord,** with sixteen glaciers named after eastern colleges and universities, before sailing overnight to **Seward** for disembarkation. Some cruises spend a half day in Glacier Bay instead of visiting Hubbard Glacier.

The Land Itineraries

Holland America Westours provides nearly three dozen escorted pre- and post-cruise options. The following eight-day tour includes the most popular destinations, but there are shorter and less expensive offerings.

The tour begins with a scenic drive across the **Kenai Peninsula** to **Anchorage** for the night and a visit to the Alaska Native Heritage Center, followed by a rail cruise, including a full meal, aboard the **McKinley Explorer** dome cars, which seat sixty-six in a lounge and at tables. Overnight at a lodge on the Nenana River is followed by a drive into **Denali National Park** to look for caribou and grizzly bears beneath 20,320-foot Mount McKinley (Denali). Rejoin the McKinley Explorer for the rail trip to **Fairbanks.**

From Fairbanks there's a short river cruise, then a drive along the Alaska Highway to **Tok** for an overnight. The next day, a 102-mile **Yukon River** cruise from Eagle travels to the preserved former boomtown of **Dawson City.**

The motorcoach travels to the **Yukon Wildlife Preserve** for sightings of moose, musk oxen, caribou, and Dall sheep. Both Dawson City and **Whitehorse** provide spirited Follies-style entertainment. From Whitehorse, drive to the summit of the White Pass to join the **White Pass and Yukon Railroad** for a vintage train ride spiraling down along the Trail of '98 to **Skagway,** the main port of entry for the gold prospectors. The last stage is a daylight cruise along the Lynn Canal, a natural waterway leading to **Juneau** and flights south to the Lower 48.

Address/Phone: Holland America Line, 300 Elliott Avenue West, Seattle, WA 98119; (800) 426–0327; brochures: (800) 626–9900; fax: (206) 281–7110; www.hollandamerica.com

The Ship: *Statendam* was built in 1992 and the *Ryndam* in 1994, and they share a gross tonnage of 55,451, a length of 719 feet, and a draft of 25 feet.

Passengers: 1,266; mostly Americans, age fifty-five and up

Dress: Formal, informal, and casual nights

Officers/Crew: Dutch officers; Indonesian and Filipino crew

Cabins: 633; 502 outside and 150 with verandas

Fare: $$$

What's included: Cruise only unless a fly-cruise-land package is purchased

What's not included: Airfare, port charges, shore excursions, drinks, tips

Highlights: Most attractive ships on which to spend time at sea; lots to do on shore excursions during the cruise and on land tours in Alaska

Other itineraries: In addition to this seven-night Glacier Discovery cruise, which operates between early May and mid-September, there are seven-night Inside Passage cruises round-trip from Vancouver and Seattle. Holland America's large fleet pretty much covers the globe.

PRINCESS CRUISES'

Sapphire Princess

Big-Ship Cruising and Touring the Inside Passage, Gulf of Alaska, and National Parks

Princess Cruises operates a huge summer-in-Alaska program with one-way and round-trip cruises along the Inside Passage from Vancouver and Seattle that can be combined with land tours in British Columbia, Alaska, and the Yukon Territory. On the Vancouver, British Columbia, to Whittier, Alaska, run, the *Sapphire Princess* and her sistership, *Diamond Princess*, at 115,875 gross tons, are presently among the largest ships cruising the Pacific, and the sisters *Coral Princess* and *Diamond Princess* are slightly smaller at 91,637 tons. Here we will describe the *Sapphire Princess*.

While the ship is huge, she is easy to navigate, especially from the Grand Plaza, a three-deck-high atrium that serves as the heart. For vertical travel, three elevator banks and stair towers will connect you to all decks, and consider it healthy to have to walk from one end of the ship to the other.

Princess's Personal Choice dining provides traditional fixed seating in the aft International Dining Room or anytime from 6:00 to 10:00 P.M. in one of four restaurants on Decks 5 and 6 located aft of Grand Plaza. Pacific Moon serves Asian cuisine; Santa Fe, Mexican; Vivaldi, Italian; and Sterling, a variety of prime steaks. Sabatini's Trattoria, for an eight-course eating extravaganza, charges an extra tariff and requires reservations. For informal dining, the Horizon Court is open twenty-four hours a day high up on Lido Deck 14, and counters there and by the pools serve pizza, burgers, and sundaes.

Princess Theater, bi-level and forward on Decks 6 and 7, presents the main production shows, twice on one day with a third performance the following day. Explorer's Lounge, with its Middle Eastern and African decor, presents cabaret acts such as magicians and comedians, alternating with popular dancing sessions. Club Fusion serves multipurposes as a nightclub, cabaret room, and the platform for TV Trivia and game shows. For light entertainment and a drink before or after dinner, try the Wheelhouse Bar with a classy British pub atmosphere, a trio, and P&O Princess maritime memorabilia or Crooners Bar off the Grand Plaza featuring a pianist who encourages requests.

From 11:00 P.M. night owls flock to Skywalkers Night Club, perched high on Deck 18 just aft of the funnel, for a disco hosted by a DJ who manipulates the music, neon, strobes, moving lights, and interactive TVs. Skywalkers is a great location to watch the scenery if the weather outside is less than ideal for being on deck.

Forward on Sun Deck 15, the Lotus Spa houses the beauty parlor, massage rooms, gymnasium, a lap pool, aerobics classes, and fitness programs. Princess Links is a 9-hole golf putting green on Sports Deck 16 just forward of the funnel. Five swimming pools include the Calypso Pool and Bar enclosed under a glass dome, the outdoor Neptune's Reef, and a children's splash pool, plus eight whirlpools.

One thousand of the 1,337 cabins have ocean views, and 75 percent of these have balconies. All cabins have twin beds that can be made into queen-size, multifunction telephones, refrigerators, safes, hair dryers, and remote-control TV with CNN, TNT, CNBC, Discovery Channel, movies, special-interest lectures, and interviews. Minisuites and up have tub baths, robes, two TVs, and a separate sitting area with a sofa bed.

The Cruise Itinerary

Northbound the *Sapphire Princess* sails from **Vancouver** out under the Lion's Gate suspension bridge. Threading through the fast-flowing Seymour Narrows, the ship may encounter Pacific swells for several hours before returning to the protection provided by the Queen Charlotte Islands.

Ketchikan, reached on the second morning, was Alaska's salmon capital and is now oriented to tourism, especially along the once-bawdy Creek Street and at the two splendid totem pole parks. The active might canoe on a lake or go mountain biking or fly fishing. **Juneau,** the state capital, provides a walkable visit, although expect steep streets and steps, as the city is set against a mountainside. The Alaska State Museum is a good bet, and tours that drive and fly out to the **Mendenhall Glacier** include a guided alpine walk and sea kayaking in nearby Auke Bay. Departing late evening, the ship sails overnight to **Skagway,** a town that trades entirely on its historic link with the Klondike Gold Rush. The best excursion is on the White Pass and Yukon's vintage train that climbs out of Skagway to the top of the White Pass.

For many people **Glacier Bay** is the high point of the cruise, where the *Sapphire Princess* enters at about dawn to cruise amid floating ice. Mount Logan can be seen rising nearly 20,000 feet as the *Sapphire Princess* crosses the **Gulf of Alaska.** Twenty-four hours later, the ship passes through **Prince William Sound** to reach **College Fjord,** where sixteen long glacial tongues slide into the sea. The cruise ends at **Whittier,** where you can fly home from Anchorage or stay to enjoy one of the land extensions and board a train directly at the dock for Denali and Mount McKinley Princess Lodges.

The Land Itineraries

Three- to nine-night land tours are very popular before or after the week's cruise. They comprise several mix-and-match ingredients, lodge and hotel stays, train rides, river excursions, rafting, fishing, hiking, and flightseeing. Most tours begin with a drive or train ride from Whittier through the Kenai Mountains.

The **Midnight Sun Express,** using Princess Tours rail cars, provides a scenic daylight ride to **Denali National Park.** The bi-level dome cars offer lounge seating with bar service beneath glass windows on the upper level and a dining room and open platforms below. **Mount McKinley** (Denali), North America's highest peak at more than 20,000 feet, is the centerpiece of the park where Princess operates two wilderness lodges. Tours may continue by Midnight Sun Express to **Fairbanks** for gold-mine tours, a paddlewheel excursion, visits to an Athabascan Indian village, and a flight to **Fort Yukon** above the Arctic Circle.

The **Kenai Peninsula** extension provides stays at the wilderness lodge and sportfishing trips, rafting through the Kenai Canyon, naturalist hikes, horseback riding, and a wildlife cruise. Additional tours penetrate into the more remote regions of Alaska into the Yukon Territory.

Address/Phone: Princess Cruises, 24305 Town Center Drive, Santa Clarita, CA 91355; (800) PRINCESS or (661) 753–0000; brochures: (888) 478–6732; fax: (661) 259–3108; www.princesscruises.com

The Ship: *Sapphire Princess* was built in 2004, has a gross tonnage of 115,875, length of 954 feet, and a draft of 28 feet.

Passengers: 2,670, mostly American, all ages

Dress: Formal and casual nights

Officers/Crew: British and Italian officers, international crew

Cabins: 1,337 cabins of which 1,000 are outside, and 750 have balconies

Fare: $$

What's included: Cruise only

What's not included: Transportation to and from the ship, port charges, drinks, tips, shore excursions, and land extensions

Highlights: Spectacular glacier and mountain scenery, creative optional tour programs, and state-of-the-art megaship cruising with lots to do aboard

Other itineraries: Besides these seven-night cruises operating from June to September between Vancouver and Whittier by the *Sapphire Princess, Diamond Princess, Coral Princess,* and *Island Princess*, Princess Cruises' large fleet covers most of the world.

NORWEGIAN CRUISE LINE'S
Norwegian Star
Freestyle Cruising from Seattle to Alaska

Sailing north to Alaska, the choice of embarkation need not always be Vancouver, and for the last several years, Norwegian Cruise Line has established a U.S. base in Seattle, which for most Americans will be a more convenient port to fly into or to arrive by train. As the *Norwegian Star* is foreign-registered, it must call at a Canadian port, in this case, delightful Victoria, British Columbia, located on the southern tip of Vancouver Island.

The colorfully decorated 91,740-ton *Norwegian Star* is a sistership to the *Norwegian Dawn* sailing year-round out of New York. The pair offers the complete concept of "Freestyle Cruising" where passengers may enjoy a wide choice of dining venues, ten in the case of these two ships, and a broad window of hours to enjoy their meals.

While several restaurants come with no extra charge, others command a moderate surcharge or are priced a la carte. Reservations may be made by telephone, and for the most popular dining spots, it is advisable to phone early. Le Bistro is Mediterranean French; The Soho Room, Pacific Rim where eastern cooking meets western; Ginza, Japanese with a teppanyaki grill room section; Endless Summer, Hawaiian and located overlooking the atrium with musical entertainment; La Trattoria, at dinnertime, informal Italian in a partitioned-off section of the main buffet; Cagney's Steakhouse, prime beef and lamb chops; Aqua, a light, healthy menu; Versailles, the French-inspired, six-course main restaurant; Blue Lagoon, fish and chips, hamburgers, and stir fries; and Market Café, the multi-station buffet, for salads, pizza, and pasta. Of the thirteen bar and lounges, the Bier Garten serves weisswurst and a wide selection of brews; the Red Lion Pub recalls an English watering hole; and the Havana Club has a selection of hand-rolled cigars and cognacs.

For the featured nighttime entertainment, the Stardust Theater spans three decks and seats 1,150 in a steeply tiered main section and side balconies for the flashy Broadway-style shows. Live music and singers, for listening and dancing, are found in several of the lounges and bars.

For peaceful retreats, the library and reading room are perfect getaway locations, especially on a rainy day; or spend time in the Internet Café or lounging in the ample number of deck chairs outside and under cover.

Recreation centers on the two-deck spa, operated by Mandara of Honolulu and located overlooking the stern with additional views to port and starboard. For a charge, there are the full range of treatments and a good-size indoor lap pool. Sports include a jogging track, a golf driving range, paddle tennis, volleyball and basketball courts, horseshoes, and a jet-current exercise pool. Children of all ages are well catered to with their own playroom, movie theater, video arcade, teen area, computer room, outdoor pool, a nursery, and nap room. Alaska, once an older-passenger destination, is now family friendly aboard and ashore.

Standard cabins, while of moderate size, are most attractive with rich cherry accents and decent-size bathrooms. Seventy percent are outside, and two-thirds of these have private balconies. Many have third and fourth berths for families, and several sets interconnect for larger family groups. Twenty cabins in several categories are designed for passengers with disabilities. Two of the largest suites afloat, measuring 5,350 square feet, are a pair of Garden Villas located high up on Deck 14. Both offer three double bedrooms with separate bath facilities and a large dining lounge with grand piano and entertainment center that looks down onto the lido pool and waterslide. A large open and covered patio allows for quiet contemplation and meals out of doors, and there's a private sunning deck one level above. These spectacular accommodations sell out fast, primarily to families and groups of friends.

The Itinerary

Sailing from **Seattle,** the ship heads north among the islands of Puget Sound, flanked by Mount Baker and Mount Rainier to the east and the Olympic Peninsula Range to the west, then into the Strait of Georgia between Vancouver Island and the rugged British Columbian mainland.

After two nights and a full day cruising the highly scenic **Inside Passage,** the first call is **Juneau,** Alaska's landlocked state capital wedged into the side of Mounts Juneau and Roberts. The latter, offering short hiking trails, is accessed from the waterfront via an aerial tramway, but don't bother if the clouds are low because you won't see anything from the top, save for mist. On a rainy day, the Alaska State Museum is a twenty-minute walk from the ship. Its well-mounted exhibits tell the story of Alaska's settlement and abundant wildlife. One excursion heads out to Auke Bay, a twenty-minute ride for guided kayaking and good exercise, much appreciated after two days on the ship. On the day we went, we saw a glimpse of Mendenhall Glacier from sea level, lots of eagles eating along a far shore, and a couple of seals bobbing up in the calm waters.

Sailing to the top end of the Inside Passage, **Skagway** offers the authentic stage set of a gold rush town, the port of debarkation for the Klondike region in the Yukon Territory. The Red Onion Saloon is a lively scene offering period music and barmaids dressed in turn-of-the-century prostitute garb. Upstairs, for a nominal price, you can have a tour by one of the maids, in character, talking about the life of a woman living in a rough gold prospecting town. For something really active, book the 15-mile downhill bike ride along the Klondike Road, outfitted with helmuts, gloves, and rain gear. Snowcapped mountains are all about, and the bonus is a quick trip across the border into the Yukon.

Many passengers book the cruise for **Glacier Bay,** and on a clear day, the towering St. Elias Mountains and glaciers are reflected in a glassy sea. The trip into the bay takes a couple of hours before idling off Margerie and Grand Pacific glaciers to wait for the sound of a sharp crack then quickly locate the collapsing ice. Look carefully and you may spot humpback whales as you leave the bay.

Sailing south, the final Alaskan call is **Ketchikan,** a good place for buying Alaskan souvenirs executed in wood, bone, and various precious metals; plus jewelry and oil paintings, watercolors, and prints at shops on the several streets adjacent to the ship. Head to the edge of town for two totem parks, the nearest reachable on foot and the other on an excursion or by hiring a taxi.

Then it's time to relax for next two nights and a day as the ship retraces its route along the BC coast to call in at **Victoria** on Vancouver Island. You can tour the town and its Inner Harbor on foot, visit the Royal Wax Museum, Pacific Undersea Gardens, Royal British Columbia Museum, and Thunderbird Park with its collection of tall totems, have afternoon tea at the famous Empress Hotel, go whale watching, and take an excursion out to Butchard Gardens. Finally, it's but a quick overnight sail back to Seattle for disembarkation.

Address/Phone: Norwegian Cruise Line, 7665 Corporate Center Drive, Miami, FL 33126; (800) 327–7030 or (305) 436–4000; fax: (305) 436–4126; www.ncl.com

The Ship: *Norwegian Star* was completed in 2001, has a gross tonnage of 91,740, a length of 965 feet, and a draft of 27 feet.

Passengers: 2,244; most Americans of all ages in Alaska, especially during the school holidays

Dress: Informal at all times, unless you wish to dress up for one of the specialty restaurants or the captain's party

Officers/Crew: European officers; international crew

Cabins: 1,122; 787 outside and 509 with balconies

Fare: $$

What's included: Cruise fare only

What's not included: Transportation to and from the ship, port charges, tips, drinks, extra tariff restaurants, shore excursions

Highlights: A colorful ship with a huge variety of dining experiences and the majestic beauty of Alaska

Other itineraries: The *Norwegian Star* spends the balance of the year sailing weekly from Los Angeles to Mexico. The NCL fleet cruises Hawaii, including under the U.S. flag NCL America subsidiary; the Caribbean; South America; the East Coast, including year-round from New York; and Europe.

CELEBRITY CRUISES'

Infinity

Alaska Round-Trip from Vancouver

Beautiful surroundings, intimate recesses, and subtly lit lounges. The *Infinity* is as finely decorated and elegant as a megaship can be, full of burled woods, dark velvets, golden brocades, ornate topiaries, intriguing art, and ample ocean views. The 91,000-ton ship is the second in Celebrity's four-ship *Millennium* class; she's not at all graceful to look at from the outside, but within she pleases and excels.

Dining is an event at tables in the Trellis restaurant, where a grand staircase and a two-story wall of glass facing the ship's wake create a glamorously retro backdrop to sample dishes like broiled king salmon in an orange sauce and roasted pork loin stuffed with sun-dried tomatoes. But for the ultimate dining experience, and an extra charge, sample the superb menu and the service in the SS United States restaurant.

Sophisticated and featuring original etched glass panels from the 1950s Blue Ribbon liner of the same name, one is looked after by a team of the most professional waitstaff I've ever seen at sea. They come to the table to toss salads and drizzle hollandaise sauce on asparagus spears. The maitre'd carved a Long Island duckling, an SS United States specialty dish, right in front of us with theatrical finesse. Afterward, a waiter wheeled over a cart with a most impressive selection of cheeses and crackers. The intimate restaurant experience is nothing short of nirvana, well worth the cover charge and dressing up for an occasion. Make your reservations early.

At the opposite end of the dining scale, for informality at breakfast, lunch, and dinner, the windowed buffet restaurant allows you to eat while Alaska floats by.

For a drink to lighten the mood in the evenings, the Rendezvous lounge attracts a good crowd each night before dinner; sit in the oversize golden bucket seats and have a twirl around the dance floor. Following dinner, take in a Vegas-type show in the three-level Celebrity Theater—perhaps it's a *West Side Story* medley—and then check out the sprawling and airy Constellation observation lounge-cum-nightclub, high on the topmost deck. Theme nights include a '50s sock hop party, and gentleman hosts are on hand to circulate, dance, and chat with single ladies. Sip a cappuccino in the rich Venetian-style Cova Café, and browse the shops for high-end clothing, accessories, souvenirs, and Michel Roux cookware.

The standard inside and outside cabins measure a roomy 170 square feet, and more than 200 of the ship's staterooms in the premium and deluxe category measure 191 square feet with a 41-square-foot balcony. Decorated in shades of terra-cotta and butterscotch, they have a sitting area with a reclining couch, lots of storage space, TV, safe, and a stocked minibar.

In the suite categories, butler service operates twenty-four hours a day, and rooms measure from 251 to 538 square feet, with the largest having separate bedrooms, whirlpool bathtubs, and oversize verandas. At the top, the 1,423-square-foot penthouse suites are among the largest at sea with marble foyers, wood floors, a piano, computer stations, and oceanview bathrooms with full-size hot tubs.

When not ashore, you can spend an hour pounding away tension on a step machine in the large, oceanview gym, another bobbing up and down in the spa's thalassotherapy pool, surf the Web at the Internet center, don headphones in the twenty-four-hour music library, attend a wine-tasting seminar or an art auction, and watch a slide show on Alaska wildlife by a guest lecturer to prepare you for the scenic itinerary.

The Itinerary

Cruising the Inside Passage round-trip from **Vancouver,** the thick green forests of British Columbia and icy-blue mounds of southeast Alaska's glaciers form the spectacular backdrop. This cruise begins with two nights and a day en route to **Ketchikan,** a geared up for the tourist type of town, isolated and with no road access to the outside world. Have a simple meal ashore such as a halibut sandwich, the bright white meat as tender as tofu, at a small cafe on the boardwalk of shops lining Creek Street, a place where fishermen and call girls crossed paths a century ago. Visit one of the two totem parks just outside town, or to get reenergized book one of the ship's shore excursions and paddle a kayak across the Tongass Narrows.

Then it's out to sea and up the Alaskan coast to the **Hubbard Glacier** hanging down from the great St. Elias Range. Listen for the crack and quickly look for calving ice. Returning southward, **Juneau,** the state's capital, is even more hemmed in by the mountain geography. It's a short walk from the dock to the Mount Roberts Tramway for a ride up some 2,000 feet above the city for spectacular views of the snowy Chilkat mountain range and the arteries of the Inside Passage. Afterwards, have a look into the Red Dog Saloon, and if not overwhelmed by other boat people, sashay in for a pint and the music. For the more active, there are kayak trips and hikes to the Mendenhall Glacier, and when the weather is poor, explore the Alaska State Museum for its natural history exhibits, Indian cultural artifacts, and pioneering history.

After a short overnight sail, tender into **Sitka,** the former capital of Russian America until the territory was purchased by the United States. Within walking distance, St. Michael's Russian Orthodox Cathedral, rebuilt after a 1966 fire, represents a relic from the past. In a park setting at the edge of town, walk among the best totem collection in all of Alaska and hear and observe the legends they tell.

Finally, it's a relaxing two nights and a day south between the British Columbia coast and Vancouver Island for disembarkation at the mainland city of Vancouver. Add to the Alaska and Pacific Northwest experience with a Canadian Rockies extension, and while this cruise is round-trip from Vancouver, Celebrity offers other itineraries that sail one-way for the inclusion of a Celebrity Alaskan land tour.

Address/Phone: Celebrity Cruises, 1050 Caribbean Way, Miami, FL 33132; (305) 539–6000 or (800) 327–6700; fax: (800) 722–5329; www.celebritycruises.com

The Ship: *Infinity,* completed in 1991, is 91,000 gross tons, has a length of 965 feet, and a draft of 26 feet.

Passengers: 1,950, mostly Americans, forty-five and up, including all ages during school holidays

Dress: Formal, informal, and casual

Officers/Crew: Officers are Greek and the crew international

Cabins: 975 cabins, of which 780 are outside and 590 have balconies

Fare: $$$

What's included: Cruise fare only

What's not included: Airfare, port charges, extra tariff restaurant, drinks, excursions, tips

Highlights: Classy ship; restaurant ambience and the special evening in the SS United States restaurant

Other itineraries: Besides this seven-night itinerary that operates weekly between June and September, Celebrity offers other Alaskan itineraries, land tours, and cruises to and from Hawaii, Mexico, Central America, the Caribbean, South America, Bermuda, and Europe.

RADISSON SEVEN SEAS CRUISES'
Seven Seas Mariner
Inside Passage from Vancouver to Alaska

The newest Radisson Seven Seas ships represent the line's future, offering all-suite accommodations and worldwide itineraries. The 50,000-gross-ton *Seven Seas Mariner,* completed at Chantiers de l'Atlantique in France, became the world's first all-balcony ship; the 2003-built *Seven Seas Voyager* became the second; and the earlier 1999-built, 28,550-ton *Seven Seas Navigator* is not far behind with 90 percent private verandas. Balconies are an ideal way to enjoy the Inside Passage scenery, now just a step from the bedroom.

Although most passengers are well-heeled, well-traveled Americans, the line also attracts other nationalities, mostly Europeans. The top officers are French, and the staff is European and Filipino.

The *Mariner's* roominess has pluses and minuses, and the latter becomes evident in the public lounges and bars, where except for the cocktail hour and meals, the ship often seems rather quiet. After dinner, the show lounge is a draw, but otherwise, many passengers retire to their suites.

The Observation Lounge, located two decks above the bridge, offers comfy rust- and tan-colored seating to enjoy hot hors

d'oeuvres and soothing piano music before dinner, while taking in the grand 180-degree view. From a perch along the horseshoe-shaped bar, the space takes on a magical quality at night. The semicircular Horizon Lounge, facing aft on one of the lowest passenger decks, is the handsome setting for a served afternoon tea with music and light after-dinner entertainment. Additional covered outdoor seating is little used and makes a quiet daytime reading spot. Nearby, the Connoisseur Club is a sophisticated tan-leather-chair and electric-fireplace setting for smoking Cuban and Dominican cigars and sipping liqueurs and wines.

The liveliest venue is the Mariner Lounge, drawing a crowd before dining in the adjacent Compass Rose or Latitudes restaurants. The curvy art deco design is highlighted by deep blue chair fabrics and glass tabletops, embedded with a translucent star pattern and framed by raised wooden rims.

Stars Nightclub cum disco, decorated with black-and-white celebrity photos of Fred Astaire, Ingrid Bergman, and Katharine Hepburn, is an oddly designed space with a spiral staircase in its midst that links to the midsize casino above. The semicircular two-level Constellation Lounge, with continuous brushed blue cotton banquette seating and joined by a symmetrical pair of two stage-flanking staircases, presents full shows and cabaret acts under a starlit ceiling of changing colors. A terrific Welsh comedian was the highlight on my cruise.

It's the choice of dining venues that gives the *Mariner* its most distinctive quality. Two restaurants are open seating with no reservations, and two take reservations for specific tables, and there is never a cover charge. Complimentary wines are served with dinner in all four restaurants. The large Compass Rose is the main dining room, most attractive and spacious with a recessed arched ceiling and faux light-wood columns topped with banded stainless steel capitals. The daily changing menu may offer homemade crab cakes as an appetizer, cream of asparagus soup, two salad selections, a pasta dish, and main courses such as sauteed jumbo prawns and Black Angus beef. The choices also include well-being, vegetarian, and a Menu Degustation, a sampler of dishes appropriate to the cruising region. For dinner, a portion of La Veranda, also open seating, is a Mediterranean bistro with a tapas, mezze, or antipasti buffet, then a served soup of the day, salad, pasta, main course, and dessert trolley.

Le Cordon Bleu of Paris offers Signatures, a reserved-table restaurant. With a much wider choice of entrees and main courses, it is worth revisiting several times on a long cruise. Marinated fillet of red snapper and roast breast of quail with turnips in a morel sauce are two examples from the list of six choices. One appetizing dessert included warm chocolate tart with cinnamon ice cream.

Latitudes serves an "Indochine" menu with such choices as Cambodian watu salad, steamed halibut with gingered vegetables, and spiced rack of lamb in peanut jus. The setting is Oriental with black lacquer chairs, large side windows with slatted venetian blinds, and walls decorated with wooden masks and headdresses.

For breakfast and lunch, Compass Rose offers table service and La Veranda a buffet with sheltered outdoor seating aft at wooden tables and chairs set under an awning. An outdoor grill is sited here. The latter's buffet stations are far too cramped and limited in selection compared to the company's other ships.

The open-shelf library offers a generous selection of hardbacks, reference books, and videos with tables to spread out an atlas and comfortable seating for reading newspapers and magazines. Club.com is the very plainly decorated Internet center with fourteen terminals plus three more in the adjacent library.

Deck space centers around the lido pool, three whirlpools, slatted wooden tables and chairs, a ten-stool outdoor bar, and a mezzanine above and forward and deck space aft. Outdoor sports include paddle tennis, shuffleboard, and golf nets.

The all-suite, all-veranda accommodations measure from 301 square feet to 1,580 square feet with veranda included. Paneling is light-wood surfaces, and the fabric colors are gold, orange rust, and a light green. The deluxe suites are the most numerous and have slightly partitioned and curtained bedroom and lounge, walk-in closets, and marble baths with tubs and showers. Forty-seven suites now have new shower stalls with rain showers and tile seating, in place of bathtubs.

The next up, the penthouse suites, somewhat misnamed, are larger at 449 square feet but not all are located on a higher deck as the designation might warrant. They feature a roomy partitioned lounge with L-shape couch, two lounge chairs, and a glass-top table. The 73-square-foot teak deck balcony has rather ordinary white plastic chairs and a low table. Accommodations increase in spaciousness in the higher categories, and these offer butler service. Some suites will take a third person, and the two-bedroom master suites accommodate up to five.

All accommodations have TV/DVD player, bathrobes, hair dryers, personal safes, telephones, in-suite bar set up upon embarkation, and complimentary replenished bottled water, soft drinks, and beer. Expanded tabletops make in-room meals a pleasure, and a full meal may be ordered from the Compass Rose restaurant or twenty-four hours a day from an in-suite menu. Suite meals are a very popular feature, especially at the end of a busy day ashore. People who like an enticing choice of top restaurants, roomy veranda suite accommodations, and a large element of privacy will love this ship.

The Itinerary

The Alaska cruises embark in **Vancouver** for the northbound itinerary and Seward for the southbound trips. The voyage north follows the Inside Passage between Vancouver Island and the British Columbia coast, with two nights and a day en route to a side trip into **Misty Fjords National Park,** a narrow steep-side waterway that the largest ships do not penetrate. Later that same day, the first port call at **Ketchikan** offers the standard totem park and town tour or a nature hike through a coastal rain forest, perhaps including a light drizzle. At **Juneau,** there are many choices over water such as an ocean kayak trip, a twelve-person traditional Native American canoe ride into Mendenhall Lake, and some gentle white-water rafting near the glacier. Nosing into **Tracy Arm,** there is an excellent chance to see sea lions and a possibility of whales cavorting near the mouth.

At the north end of the natural Lynn Canal, the **Skagway** tours offer a bike ride to **Dyea,** now a partial ghost town but once boasting 10,000 inhabitants, and a trip on the **White Pass and Yukon Route** rail line to the top of the pass and back. At the edge of the Pacific Ocean, **Sitka,** once the Russian American capital, reveals its colorful past on a town center walking tour or more energetically on a bicycle ride along a winding path between mountains and sea. The totem collection here is much finer than at Ketchikan.

Northward into the Gulf of Alaska, the *Mariner* sails up to **Hubbard Glacier,** located in the shadow of the Wrangell–St. Elias mountain range. Listen for the crack of calving ice, then be quick with your camera. Later in the morning, the ship crosses the Gulf to dock at **Whittier,** where there are land extensions to **Denali National Park, Anchorage,** and **Fairbanks.**

Address/Phone: Radisson Seven Seas Cruises, 600 Corporate Drive, Suite 410, Fort Lauderdale, FL 33334; (954) 776–6123 or (800) 285–1835; brochures: (800) 477–7500; fax: (954) 772–3763; www.rssc.com

The Ship: *Seven Seas Mariner* was completed in 2001, has a gross tonnage of 50,000, a length of 709 feet, and a draft of 21 feet.

Passengers: 700, mostly Americans, some Europeans, forty-five and up

Dress: Formal, informal, and casual nights

Officers/Crew: French and European officers, European stewardesses, and international crew

Cabins: 350, all outside suites with balconies, with twins that convert to king-size beds

Fare: $$$$

What's included: Cruise fare, gratuities, wines with dinner, soft drinks and juices, stocked minibar

What's not included: Port charges, airfare, alcoholic drinks

Highlights: Unusually spacious ship, top European service

Other itineraries: In addition to these seven-day cruises northbound from Vancouver and southbound from Whittier that operate between late May and early September, the Radisson Seven Seas fleet covers the world.

ROYAL CARIBBEAN'S
Vision of the Seas
A Pacific Coastal Voyage

West Coasters are fortunate to have numerous chances to sample many different cruise ships en route northward for the Alaska season in the spring and south again in the fall. As most of the ships begin or end these coastal cruises in Canada, it is possible to join or leave one in a U.S. port such as San Diego, Los Angeles, Long Beach, or San Francisco.

Royal Caribbean International, one of the world's largest cruise companies, operates a score of ships on both coasts of North America, in Europe, and elsewhere. The 78,491-ton *Vision of the Seas*, completed in France in 1998, sails from Los Angeles via San Francisco and Victoria to Vancouver, British Columbia, every spring. Her repositioning voyage gives one an opportunity to sample a short cruise on a ship normally sailing longer itineraries while visiting two attractive way ports. Eleven decks high, *Vision of the Seas* uses huge expanses of glass for great ocean views from all decks and public rooms. The interior decor consists of marble, granite, and decorative wood veneer paneling, and distinctive works of art.

Upon embarking on Main Deck 4, one is awestruck by the gigantic hanging sculpture in the Centrum, a stainless steel bird diving in flight. Located amidships and seven decks high, the Centrum forms the ship's nerve center and orientation focus. Glass windows open to the sea to port and starboard from all decks, and attractively tiered balconies provide views into the interior well and public spaces leading off. Sweeping stairways connect the main rooms on Promenade Deck 5 and Mariner Deck 6, and glass elevators rise up to views of the main pool on Sun Deck 9 and the Sun Walk on Compass Deck 10.

At the base of the Centrum, a grand piano or band provides pre-dinner melodies for those enjoying the Champagne Bar or just hanging out. Going aft from Centrum, the two-deck-high Aquarius Dining Room is flanked by large glass windows, and one may enter on upper level Deck 5 and make a grand entrance by walking down the sweeping stairway. The lower level windows are huge and round, and the buff curtains and white slender columns lend lightness to the grand space. Fixed seating dinner is served at 6:00 P.M. and 8:30 P.M., while breakfast and lunch are open seating.

Forward on Decks 5 and 6, the two-deck-high Masquerade Theater affords good sightlines from all angles including the two side balconies. Shows are performed twice, such as Broadway musicals by the Royal Caribbean Singers and Dancers or routines from Los Diablos Gauchos from Argentina, and the Love and Marriage game show or similar. The fiber-optic lighted Casino Royal is adjacent to the theater's lower level.

For another entertainment venue, the Some Enchanted Evening Lounge hosts a Country and Western Hoe Down, Rock 'n' Roll Dance Party, comedy acts, or Majority Rules game show. For soothing piano music, RCI's trademark Schooner Bar offers a kitschy nautically themed lounge with sailing ship ropes and riggings.

Take the Centrum elevator from any deck up to the multilevel, all glass-enclosed Viking Crown Lounge on Deck 11, the ship's highest passenger-accessible point. During the day, you get 360-degree ocean vistas as well as some solitude for a good read. At night the lower level turns into a disco, while the DJ looks down from above choosing the rhythm going to suit the mood. The tiered Windjammer Café, forward on Sun Deck 9, provides a vantage point over the bow and to both sides. Casual dining includes breakfast, lunch, afternoon tea, and dinner for those who do not wish to dress up.

The Main Pool is located in the center of Sun Deck 9 with decorative canvas sun canopies covering the two adjacent whirlpools at both sides. Ample deck chairs are available both in the sun and in the shade. The Solarium Pool on the same deck offers weather protection under a sliding glass "Crystal Canopy" for both outdoor and indoor use. Again deck chairs are plentiful. A poolside snack bar provides refreshments, pizza, hot dogs, and burgers most of the day and well into the wee hours.

All RCI ships are now equipped with a 30-foot-high rock-climbing wall, here located just aft of the funnel on Compass Deck 10. As passengers using the Sun Walk and Jogging Track pass by, the climbers have a ready-made audience.

Cabins are pretty typical with inexpensive inside cabins, and outside cabins with and without balconies. A pleasant surprise is the twenty-four-hour room service menu that includes a hot breakfast. Most ships, except in the high-grade cabins, only offer continental-style breakfasts.

The Itinerary

Sailing from **Los Angeles,** the ship spends two nights and a day en route north to **San Francisco,** entering the City by the Bay via a passage between headlands and under the sweeping Golden Gate Bridge. Sliding by Sausalito, the ship docks conveniently at Pier 35 next to Fisherman's Wharf and close to many attractions.

Historic streetcars stop across the street from the pier for rides to the Ferry Building and Market Street and the famous cable cars are but a short walk. Climb aboard one and head up the steep streets for spectacular views from the Top of the Mark or Fairmount Hotel. Take the streetcar for shopping at Union Square's department stores and upscale shops or to the new Asian Art Museum at the Civic Center.

The ship offers organized tours including San Francisco city sightseeing, Sausalito and Muir Woods for the gigantic redwoods, Alcatraz Island and Sausalito, and to Fisherman's Wharf Wax Museum.

Sailing out to sea, the *Vision of the Seas* turns northward to follow the Pacific Coast en route to **Victoria, British Columbia,** a two-night sail. The Vancouver Island city trades on being the most English place in Canada. High Tea at the famous Empress Hotel is just a start. Enjoy the spectacular Inner Harbor flanked by the English Gothic Parliament Buildings, Royal Wax Museum, Pacific Undersea Gardens, Royal British Columbia Museum, and Thunderbird Park with its collection of tall totems.

For the foot weary, tour the city aboard a horse-drawn carriage or take a bus out to the justly famous Butchard Gardens and Butterfly Gardens or up to the Mount Tolmie lookout. For the thirsty, there's the Victoria Ale Trail & Pub Tour; or go whale watching or take a seaplane flight over the city and the surrounding islands and straits.

Departing Victoria, it's but a short overnight sail to **Vancouver,** entering the harbor between high-rent West Vancouver and heavily forested Stanley Park, then under the slim Lion's Gate Bridge to the terminal adjacent to the city center. As you disembark, the next lot of passengers will be looking forward to the season's first cruise North to Alaska.

Address/Phone: Royal Caribbean International, 1050 Caribbean Way, Miami, FL 33132; (800) 327–6700 or (305) 539–6000; fax: (305) 374–7354; www.royalcaribbean.com

The Ship: *Vision of the Seas* was built in 1998, has a gross tonnage of 78,491, a length of 915 feet, and a draft of 25 feet.

Passengers: 2,000 double occupancy, mostly Americans, some Canadians, and ages fifty and up

Dress: Formal, jacket and tie, casual, and country and western

Officers/Crew: International

Cabins: 1,000 of generally moderate size, with 593 outside, 407 inside, and 229 with balconies

Fare: $$

What's included: Cruise fare only

What's not included: Transportation to and from the ship, governmental fees, tips, drinks, and shore excursions

Highlights: Top of Crown Lounge with spectacular views and the rock-climbing wall, and the seldom-visited cruise port of Victoria

Other itineraries: The *Vision of the Seas* sails to the Mexican Riviera from Los Angeles and Alaska from Vancouver, Canada, while the huge Royal Caribbean fleet covers most of the world.

CRUISE WEST'S
Spirit of '98
Small-Ship Cruising Alaska's Inside Passage

Following my first big-ship Alaska cruise a few years back, I came home very happy, and then I returned to sail aboard Cruise West's wee *Spirit of '98*. It was an altogether different experience. I communed with nature—the stupendous landscape, variable weather, birds of all sorts, wildlife galore in the water and on shore, and sweet scents and pungent smells (those Steller sea lions!)—in an almost spiritual way.

Unlike many small coastal ships, the ninety-six-passenger *Spirit of '98* has considerable character. She exhibits the graceful profile of an early twentieth-century American steamer with a rounded superstructure, upward sheer to the decks, straight stem, and a tall black stack embossed with Cruise West's white bear logo. The *Spirit of '98* began life on the East Coast in the mid-1980s as the *Pilgrim Belle,* and I made one of her very first trips in Long Island Sound, and then I followed her under different owners to the Chesapeake Bay and along the St. Lawrence River and Seaway. Now based in the Pacific Northwest, the *Spirit of '98* looks as if she might have headed north to the Klondike Goldfields in 1898, but the happier reality has her taking modern-day explorers in search of wildlife, scenery, and a good time.

The *Spirit of '98*'s plush interiors are Victorian and Edwardian with pressed-tin ceilings, square mirrored columns, over-stuffed furniture, an elaborate dark wood bar, and mirror-backed dining room buffet. Heads turn when she passes or approaches a dock, and her passengers soon develop a deep affection for their conveyance and the young, all-American crew.

Meals take place in the big-windowed, open-sitting dining room at large round tables and cozy banquettes. A buffet breakfast displayed in the lounge draws early risers and light eaters, and an on-deck barbecue features spare ribs, fresh coho salmon, sausage, and burgers. Dinner menus offer just one soup, two salads, fresh hot breads, a choice of six main courses, and a featured dessert plus sherbets. For the cocktail hour set, the pre-dinner hot hors d'oeuvres serve as appetizers. Cooking is straightforward American style and uniformly very good, better and more varied than expected, with memorable entrees such as Dungeness crab, grilled halibut, and prime rib.

Cabins are all outside and small but not cramped, the majority opening onto one of two covered promenades. The announcement of a humpback whale sighting means just a quick step out the door. TVs, unusual for most small ships, have VCRs for screening freely selected videos. Cabins windows drop open, a big plus, allowing the sound of the sea to lull one to sleep, and it is not an exaggeration to report that I slept better here than at home.

Enrichment includes Native American oral traditions, costumes, and dancing; talks by Cruise West expedition leaders and National Park Service personnel; much socializing and bonding; and the great state of Alaska.

The Itinerary

As the 192-foot *Spirit of '98* sails from **Seattle**'s Pier 69, she makes an early evening tour of the port city's active recreational and commercial waterfront.

On the next morning the first call is at **Friday Harbor** in the San Juan Islands for a visit to the Whale Museum before heading north on a relaxed schedule that allows the captain to dawdle and diverge from the set course when there was good reason.

The first such opportunity arises on the second day when we encounter a large pod of Pacific white-sided dolphins that our interpreters estimate to number one hundred. Once in their midst, those standing one deck above the waterline look directly down as they play in our bow wave, and a few yards away others roll on their sides and even breach. On Day Three, the *Spirit of '98* slips into Green Inlet, and ringing "dead slow," the little ship silently eases up to within a few hundred yards of four brown bears, a sow and three cubs, grazing on the sedge grass and pawing at rocks encrusted with succulent caches of mussels.

Shore trips are offered at Ketchikan, Skagway, and Haines, many similar to those offered by the big ships, but there were differences. On the big ships with 1,500–2,500, passengers have more choices, and they get preferential time slots for the helicopter and float plane trips. Apart from these two examples, Cruise West contracts its own excursions, and with less than one hundred passengers, the groups are smaller when spread over three to five tours.

At **Ketchikan,** we walk independently out to the Totem Heritage Center, then stroll past the shops along Creek Street to an excellent first- and secondhand bookstore with lots of titles reflecting Alaska and the Pacific Northwest.

Petersburg, founded as a Norwegian fishing village, provides a look at a present-day town that does not see any big ships calling, just the comings and goings of the Alaska Marine Highway ferries. Much like several Alaska Panhandle ports, there is no road out of town.

After a swing into iceberg-choked Frederick Sound, the *Spirit of '98* passes into Tracy Arm where we pass through rafts of floating ice to within 400 yards of **South Sawyer Glacier,** remaining for an hour to ogle the massive formations and varied shades of greens and blues. On the way out, we nose up to a waterfall, and those standing at the bow got showered in spray.

En route to Peril Strait we see several humpback whales then follow the narrow twisting channel to **Sitka,** once the capital of Russian Alaska with St. Michael's Church an existing link to the past. Just outside the town, one of the best collections of original totems resides in a wooded park.

The most anticipated event comes on the final day when we enter **Glacier Bay** at 6:30 A.M., not to exit until 8:30 P.M. While waiting for the big ships to leave, our captain takes us close to tufted puffins' and pigeon guillemots' rookeries on North and South Marble Islands.

In Tidal Inlet, we have black and brown bear sightings in four different directions, a bull moose on the beach, a rare wolverine

peering at us from the brush, and a humpback whale feeding close into shore. In South Sandy Cove, we watch mountain goats cavort and yet manage to maintain footing on a seemingly 90-degree slope. At the waterline, a pack of Steller sea lions, mostly males, gives off guttural grunts and an odor that sends one reeling aft in search of fresh air.

Moving up through the bergie bits to Margerie and Grand Pacific glaciers, we stand off watching the calving ice, and when one sizeable bluish white tower collapses, the captain aims the ship's bow into the oncoming swells. That evening in Icy Strait, there is not a cloud in the sky, a light ashore, or another vessel in sight. A full moon rises in the east, and the sun sets over the St. Elias Range in the west. As we slowly drift, the sea first reflects patches of pinkish purple then takes on a golden hue, and the calm waters ripple from diving ducks and a lone humpback whale. Dozens of sharp snowcapped peaks envelop us in a complete circle; and without charts, one wonders which route Captain George Vancouver in 1795 might have chosen to seek the open ocean. No one wants to leave the decks, even at midnight.

At **Skagway,** several White Pass and Yukon trains back down to the piers, and *Spirit of '98* passengers occupy their own private railway coach for the climb paralleling the arduous trail the prospectors followed in 1898. A few years later, the adventurers traveled far more comfortably over this very rail line. The narrow-gauge train whistles out through town then twists and turns up to the summit for long-range views back down to Skagway and west to the distant St. Elias Range. Once I made the complete rail trip to Whitehorse, capital of Canada's Yukon Territory, but the service is now truncated to Lake Bennett and onward travel is by motor coach.

Back in Skagway, the National Park Service runs a free town tour with the interpreter relating stories of hardship, the Canadian government's requirement that prospectors carry a year's supply of provisions before being permitted to cross the border, the terrible toll of 8,000 horses dying along the trail, rampant lawlessness, and greed.

By contrast, the adjacent port of **Haines** is a sleepy little place, not much more than a transfer point between the Alaska Marine Highway ferries and the road north to Anchorage and Fairbanks. Some passengers went birding in the "Valley of the Eagles" aboard a white-water raft, while I took a walking tour of Fort Seward, a former early twentieth-century U.S. Army base. Its line of fine wooden hillside houses looks across a village green to the Lynn Canal, the main channel leading from Skagway south to **Juneau** for disembarkation.

It may be some time before I return to Alaska, but when I do it will be aboard a small ship, and I'll save the big guys for itineraries where nature and wildlife are not so intense. But there is a premium price to pay for choosing small, seeing the forty-ninth state with less than one hundred fellow travelers, having an intimate close-up experience, and sailing with interpreters who are always available for those want to tap their funds of knowledge.

Address/Phone: Cruise West, 2301 Fifth Avenue, Suite 401, Seattle, WA 98121; (800) 203–8306 or (206) 441–8687; fax: (206) 441–4757; www.cruisewest.com

The Ship: *Spirit of '98* was built in 1984 as the *Pilgrim Belle* and later traded as the *Colonial Explorer* and *Victorian Empress,* and has a length of 192 feet and a shallow draft.

Passengers: 96 passengers, mostly Americans and Canadians in their forties and up

Dress: Casual, morning, noon, and night

Officers/Crew: American

Cabins: 49, all outside with windows, some opening onto the side deck and one large owner's two-room suite

Fare: $$$

What's included: Cruise fares, port charges, and some excursions

What's not included: Airfare, optional shore excursions, drinks, and tips

Highlights: Glorious mountains, fjords, and glaciers seen close up; intimate atmosphere on a very special ship

Other itineraries: In addition to this ten-night cruise between Seattle and Juneau, which operates in May, June, and September, Cruise West operates many additional variations along the Inside Passage, in South Central Alaska, the Bering Sea, plus overland extensions, and cruises along the Columbia and Snake Rivers, in California Wine Country, the Sea of Cortez, and Central America. All Cruise West ships fly the U.S. flag except the *Spirit of Oceanus* (Bahamas) and the *Pacific Explorer* (Honduras).

GLACIER BAY CRUISELINE'S

Wilderness Adventurer

The Marvels of Alaska Close Up

The unofficial rule in Alaska is the smaller the vessel, the better the experience, and it is hard to get much smaller than Glacier Bay's *Wilderness Adventurer* and its fleet of twenty-three kayaks. Offering a no-frills but energetic Alaskan experience, the *Wilderness Adventurer* gives passengers a close-up view of the Inside Passage and its varied wildlife on land, sea, and in the air.

Dwarfed in comparison to the megaships that cruise Alaska, the unpretentious *Wilderness Adventurer* seems almost more boat than ship and offers a relaxed and casual atmosphere. In keeping with the company's aim to offer a spirited and adventurous cruise, Glacier Bay boasts that their ships are really "sports utility vessels" focusing on the destination rather than shipboard luxuries.

Passengers range in age from teenagers to those in their seventies, but everyone shares an intense enthusiasm for seeing the forty-ninth state. Most haven't cruised before, but following the line's advance information they come well prepared and fitted with the proper gear such as layers of non-cotton clothing, waterproof jackets and rain pants, and boots or shoes that can get wet and dirty. Adventure-minded, no one complains if it rains when out on a hike, and even in less-than-ideal conditions, a group will be huddled on deck excitedly calling out, "Look, another tufted puffin!"

Life on board takes on an informal, living room ambiance, and the evening agenda has the staff of naturalists talking about what creatures live in the intertidal zone or passengers playfully acting out the distinguishing behavior of a particular bird. A close and friendly shipboard environment soon takes hold during meals and ashore.

Cabins are virtually all outside and very snug, averaging about 95 square feet. None have locking doors, and bathrooms are merely toilets with a showerhead conveniently affixed above. Public rooms are minimal in both decor and space, consisting of a forward homey lounge with the small bar flowing into the dining area on a lower deck. Outside there is also a wraparound deck and a partly covered top observation deck.

Meals are served buffet style for breakfast, family style for lunch, and waiter-served at dinner. The food is simple but good, and the afternoon cookies are especially satisfying after a day on the trail. There are three dinner entrees from which to choose, including a fresh seafood choice, and you make your selection at lunch. The young, all American crew, doubling as waiters and cabin stewards, is enthusiastic and friendly and often linger for a chat in the dining room after dinner. Dress is casual, with passengers taking rain gear and binoculars to dinner in case a naturalist spots a whale.

The Itinerary

Sailing round-trip from **Juneau,** the week-long cruise has a flexible itinerary designed to stay far off the beaten track. We saw other ships mostly in passing but otherwise felt removed from mass tourism and civilization.

The week takes on a distinct summer camp feeling, with a wake up call at 7:00 A.M. and activities beginning at 8:00 A.M. Most days offer combinations of one-hour or longer three-hour hikes and kayaking trips, allowing passengers to choose how active they wish to be. Most hikes follow paths over easy terrain, but a few involve steep climbs over less-than-ideal paths that can be muddy, rocky, and full of roots. Three naturalists offer interpretation on shore and in the kayaks. The tone is often earthy, with some hikes focusing on medicinal uses for plants or poetry readings in the forest to give a sense of place.

The first morning might be at anchor off **Admiralty Island** for kayaking or hiking before cruising to another impossibly beautiful spot in the afternoon. On shoreside hikes, the naturalists point out fresh bear tracks and help us spot birds. During the course of the week, we added golden eagles, horned and tufted puffins, several types of loons, cormorants, and black-legged kittiwakes to the growing list. We did not encounter bears while hiking, but the naturalists bring along bear spray just in case and periodically shout "Here, bear!" to ensure we don't startle any that might be nearby.

In both Tracy Arm and Glacier Bay, the ship gets only a few hundred feet away from a massive glacier, allowing everyone the opportunity to closely study the captivating shapes and patterns as well as the intense color that glows from within. At times, the towering mountains either side completely dwarf the *Wilderness Adventurer*.

A highlight of the cruise is the twenty-four hours spent in **Glacier Bay National Park**. Arriving in the evening at the ranger station, there is time for a self-guided hike before sailing further into the bay. In the morning passengers open their blinds to reveal a mile-long blue wall that is Margerie Glacier looming over the ship, and during breakfast we eat in the glacier's shadow.

The entire day is spent exploring the park's coast and its abundant wildlife. We drifted less than 300 feet off shore for about an hour, watching a black bear and its cub feeding before the cub spotted us

and rose on its legs to intimidate us before thinking better and scampering up a tree. We had mountain goat and brown bear sightings, followed two moose swimming across a bay, and drew close to a large sea lion colony lounging on the rocks and frolicking in the water.

Perhaps the best moment came when we heard a deep guttural sound and realized it was a whale breathing no more than 10 feet in front of the bow. We quickly came to a stop and for a half hour became surrounded by more whales. Sightings of humpbacks and orcas became so plentiful that they hardly drew a glance by the end of the day.

On the final morning the *Wilderness Adventurer* returns its passengers to the comparative bustle of Juneau, Alaska's landlocked capital, amidst both civilization and the big ships that provide an entirely different way to cruise the forty-ninth state.

Address/Phone: Glacier Bay Cruiseline, 2101 Fourth Avenue, Suite 2200, Seattle, WA 98121; (800) 451–5952 or (206) 623–7110; www.glacierbaycruiseline.com or www.glacierbaytours.com

The Ship: The *Wilderness Adventurer* was originally built in 1983 as the *Caribbean Prince*, and has a gross tonnage of 89 tons, a length of 156 feet, and a draft of 6.5 feet.

Passengers: 69, of which most are American, often with a small number from Australia, New Zealand, and Canada; age forty and up

Dress: There is no dress code; instead it's jeans and rain jackets

Officers/Crew: American

Cabins: 32, with a few offering a third berth

Fare: $$$

What's included: Cruise fare, port charges, and shore excursions

What's not included: Transportation to and from the ship, tips, and drinks

Highlights: The daily kayak and hiking expeditions; seeing the Inside Passage away from the larger ships and tourist trade; the friendly, fun, and casual shipboard atmosphere

Other itineraries: The *Wilderness Adventurer* also sails new and unique cruises in Prince William Sound and, during the spring and fall, along the Columbia River. The Glacier Bay fleet also includes the similarly small ships *Wilderness Discoverer, Wilderness Explorer,* and *Executive Explorer,* and together they cruise South Central and Southeast Alaska and the Pacific Northwest.

ALASKA MARINE HIGHWAY'S
Columbia, Malaspina, Matanuska, Taku, and *Kennicott*
The Inside Passage: On Your Own

The Alaska Marine Highway, with its present fleet of nine blue-and-white ferries, was established in 1963 to serve Alaskan Panhandle communities, including the state capital of Juneau, that have no road access to the outside world. Three principal services are of interest for cruise passengers: They begin at Bellingham, Washington, just north of Seattle; at Prince Rupert, British Columbia; and at Juneau, the state capital. You may make one-way or round-trip voyages on all of them.

The *Columbia, Malaspina, Matanuska, Taku,* and *Kennicott,* all named after Alaskan glaciers, share many of the same offerings such as a forward observation lounge, a cocktail bar, and hot and cold meal cafeteria-style dining with big-window viewing. The food, pay-as-you-go, is good American fare, and entrees include Alaskan salmon and halibut, chicken teriyaki, and New York strip steaks. The *Columbia* also has a dining room. The top-deck, heated solarium gives protection and warmth and has seating facing aft. The ship provides films, informal on-deck talks, and an easy social atmosphere in which to meet Alaska residents, other cruisers, backpackers, motorists, and commercial drivers.

The cabins, sold as a unit, are plainly furnished and comprise two-, three-, and four-berth insides and outsides incorporating private showers and with configurations and capacities unique to each vessel. Cabins book up fast for the summer months, and the ships carry deck passengers who find space to sleep in the lounges and the solarium. If making stopovers, some of the connecting daylight passages do not require a cabin. As the ferries serve a basic transportation function, all carry cars, recreational vehicles, and trucks that are driven on and off during port calls. These occur at all hours of the day and night, but stops are short in duration, from one to four hours, so elaborate excursions require a stopover. The scenery en route is never-ending beauty, and some passengers find it satisfying to simply make a round-trip.

The Itineraries
Bellingham to Skagway: Taken as a continuous round-trip voyage, the weekly trip (twice weekly on Tuesday and Friday in summer)

departs **Bellingham, Washington,** located north of Seattle, on a Friday evening aboard the 500-passenger *Matanuska,* the *Malaspina,* or the 625-passenger *Columbia.* The initial two nights and a day are spent cruising north along the British Columbia coast. Vancouver Island, off to port, provides protection from the Pacific swells for much of the way. The scenery is mountainous, forested, and deeply incised with bays and narrow arms of the sea penetrating far inland. The narrow passage through the fast-flowing, and once dangerous, **Seymour Narrows** is particularly dramatic. Most commercial traffic travels on barges and ferries, and in summer you also encounter some of the two dozen cruise ships that ply the **Inside Passage.**

The ferry's first call is at **Ketchikan,** Alaska. As this is a purposeful ship, it remains long enough to load and unload passengers, vehicles, and cargo, giving through passengers time for a quick visit to the town center. **Wrangell** and **Petersburg** come later that same day, and only Marine Highway vessels and small cruise ships treat passengers to the **Wrangell Narrows** passage, where seventy channel markings require several hours of constant course changes. **Juneau's Auke Bay** terminal is reached on Monday morning, and persons wishing to see something of the capital, excellent state museum, and Mendenhall glacier should disembark for a day or two, then continue northward on the daily summer ship to Haines (5.5 hours) and Skagway (6.5 hours). Passengers remaining aboard are rewarded with a beautiful daylight sail up the Lynn Canal, flanked by high mountain peaks and an occasional glacier, to call at **Haines,** where many vehicles leave for the trip through the Yukon Territory to Alaska over the Haines and Alaska highways. An hour later the ship docks at **Skagway,** the most northerly Inside Passage port,

remaining three hours before returning south. Consider leaving the vessel here to explore the restored gold rush entry point for prospectors bound overland to the Klondike from 1898 onward. A road runs inland to Whitehorse, Yukon Territory's capital, and the **White Pass and Yukon Route** operates excursion trains alongside the old Chilkat Trail, which the railroad replaced, to the top of the White Pass and back.

The southbound Marine Highway ferry will leave Skagway early Monday evening, call briefly at Haines, sail overnight to Juneau, then negotiate the twisting Peril Strait route (too narrow for the big cruise ships) to **Sitka.** The island town was Russian Alaska's capital until the United States took possession in 1867. Sights are St. Michael's Russian Orthodox Cathedral and a rain-forest walk through the Sitka National Historical Park to see the great collection of tall totems and an early nineteenth-century fort. The ship retraces the route south, calling on Wednesday at Petersburg, Wrangell, and Ketchikan, then spends two nights and a day cruising through Queen Charlotte Sound and Strait of Georgia for an early Friday morning arrival back at Bellingham, Washington.

Prince Rupert to Juneau: Ferry service sails north to Alaskan Panhandle ports from **Prince Rupert,** two to six times a week, increasing from one- to the three-ship maximum strength in summer. If you're not driving, there are two creative ways to reach Prince Rupert, one by rail and one by sea. From Jasper Via Rail's domeliner the *Skeena* provides a two-day scenic mountain, lake, and valley ride west to Prince Rupert for the Alaska ferry north. From Vancouver and Victoria on Vancouver Island, bus connections to Port Hardy, near the top of the island, connect to the BC Ferries' *Queen of the North* for a highly scenic ferry cruise to Prince Rupert.

Some Marine Highway ferries departing Prince Rupert call at **Ketchikan,** pass through the Wrangell Narrows, then stop at **Wrangell** and **Petersburg,** turning around at Juneau for a twenty-seven-hour one-way transit. Sailings to Juneau take two nights and a day if the route diverts via Sitka. Once a week this latter route is extended to **Haines** and **Sitka** aboard the seagoing *Kennicott.* All ships return to Prince Rupert via the same set of ports, so it is relatively easy to transfer between ships, but remember, cabin space for the overnight portions is at a premium in the summer months.

Prince Rupert to Juneau, Valdez, and Whittier: In 1998 Alaska Marine Highway took delivery of its seagoing ferry *Kennicott,* a deep draft vessel, whereas the rest of the Inside Passage fleet have flat bottoms and shallow drafts. The *Kennicott* is designed to handle the rough waters sometimes encountered when crossing the Gulf of Alaska. For the first time in about a half century, it is now possible to sail twice a month from the Lower 48 and Inside Passage ports to South Central Alaska with onward road and rail connections to Anchorage, Denali National Park, and Fairbanks, avoiding the long Alaska Highway route.

While the *Kennicott* leaves from Prince Rupert for the direct sailing, persons coming from Bellingham can transfer to it at **Ketchikan** or **Juneau.** The *Kennicott* then sails via **Yakutat** and **Tatitlek** to **Valdez,** in Prince William Sound, a three-day passage from **Prince Rupert** and on to **Whittier.** For the return trip the *Kennicott* sails from Whittier and Valdez to Juneau, Ketchikan, and Prince Rupert, the full elapsed time taking three nights and three days.

Address/Phone: Alaska Marine Highway, 6858 Glacier Avenue (P.O. Box 6858), Juneau, AK 99801; (907) 465–3941/42 or (800) 642–0066; fax: (907) 277–4829; www.ferryalaska.com, or www.north-to-alaska.com for Alaska and British Columbia information.

The Ships: *Taku,* built in 1963, length 352 feet; *Matanuska* and *Malaspina,* built in 1963, then enlarged, length 408 feet; *Columbia,* built in 1974, length 418 feet; *Kennicott,* built in 1998, length 382 feet. The first four have shallow drafts.

Passengers: Total capacity including berths and deck: *Taku* 450, *Matanuska* and *Malaspina* 500, *Columbia* 625, *Kennicott* 748; all ages and mostly North Americans

Dress: Casual at all times

Officers/Crew: Alaskan

Cabins: Number of berths: *Taku* 106, *Matanuska* 247, *Malaspina* 272, *Columbia* 294, *Kennicott* 320, all in two- to four-berth cabins sold as units

Fare: $–$$

What's included: Fare, port charges, and cabin (if purchased)

What's not included: Transportation to and from ports, meals, drinks, excursions

Highlights: Great scenery; social life aboard ferries; ease of stopovers, variety of routes

Other itineraries: Alaska Marine Highway also operates several smaller ferries, without cabins, to a half dozen other ports in the Alaska Panhandle. Ferries with and without cabins operate between South Central and Southwest Alaska. The 68-passenger Tustumena (two- and four-berth cabins) makes monthly, six-day round-trips from Kodiak Island to the Aleutian Islands, a seagoing adventure with potentially some of the roughest sea conditions in the world.

BC FERRIES'

Queen of the North and *Queen of Prince Rupert*

The Canadian Inside Passage and Queen Charlotte Islands

BC Ferries, a British Columbia provincial company, operates a forty-vessel fleet providing the missing links in the BC highway system. The routes are complex, so a good map will help when planning itineraries around the two featured ships with cabin accommodations.

The *Queen of the North,* reflecting her Scandinavian origins, is newer, larger, and sleeker than the simpler but no less comfortable Canadian-built *Queen of Prince Rupert.* In the main summer season, the *Queen of the North,* refitted in 2001, holds down the scenic daylight run between Port Hardy at the northern tip of Vancouver Island and Prince Rupert, while the *Queen of Prince Rupert* sails between Prince Rupert and Skidegate on Queen Charlotte Island. Both ships have a lounge, a licensed bar, and cafeteria, and the *Queen of the North* has, in addition, an elaborate prix-fixe buffet for breakfast, lunch, and dinner. These meals may be prepaid at the time of booking, resulting in savings and convenience when making the two-day round-trip. The deck space is well designed for viewing, and both ships have video arcades for children. On the *Queen of the North*'s daylight sailings, entertainment includes films, live music, and informal talks by naturalists and creative artists.

Simple double and quad cabins have lower berths that become sofas during the day, and the uppers fold away. All inside and outside cabins have washbasins and toilets, and those above the vehicle deck have showers, too. The least expensive cabins below the car deck will be claustrophobic for some. On the *Queen of the North*'s

fifteen-hour daylight sailings late May through September, cabins may be booked for the day, or if making a round-trip, they may be occupied that turnaround night. If you are joining at either port early in the morning, you must stay ashore the night before sailing. In the off-season the Port Hardy–Prince Rupert route changes to a longer eighteen-to-twenty-two-hour overnight run, making one to three intermediate calls en route. The *Queen of Prince Rupert may* be substituted when the other ship is undergoing drydocking.

The Itineraries

Port Hardy to Prince Rupert: Port Hardy is an obscure little place that really only exists for the ferry. To connect to the sailings without a car, there is regular bus service from Victoria with pickup stops along the way, which takes most of the day, and another equally long ride from Vancouver using the ferry to Nanaimo to reach Vancouver Island. A creative way is to take Vancouver Island's railway, which operates 1950s diesel-powered railcars from Victoria to Courtney, about halfway to Port Hardy, then switch to the bus. Motels in Port Hardy look close to the ferry landing across the harbor, but a transfer is required.

In summer the *Queen of the North* leaves at 7:30 A.M. every other day for the 275-mile, fifteen-hour, nonstop passage. The first portion crosses a 50-mile stretch of open water called Queen Charlotte Sound, then enters Fitz-Hugh Sound to remain in protected waters for most of the balance of the day. The scenery is fjord land with mysterious arms that head inland, some traversed by a secondary BC Ferry service in summer. In the off-season the *Queen of the North* or *Queen of Prince Rupert* makes a longer overnight run with a few calls at towns without any road access such as McLoughlin Bay, Shearwater, Ocean Falls, and Klemtu. The coastal range will have snowcapped peaks during the early part of summer, and the deck temperatures may vary from being quite warm to chilly. En route you should see bald eagles, and you can expect to see some killer whales (orcas), porpoises, and seals. Many keen eyes will help you spot the wildlife.

Arrival at **Prince Rupert** is 10:30 P.M. for most summer sailings, and except late in the season, there should still be light in the sky. The landing is shared with the *Queen of Prince Rupert* and adjacent to the Alaska Marine Highway, but same-day connections are rare. Prince Rupert's motel district is about 1.5 miles away, and some motels overlook the harbor.

Sleep on board if you are returning the next day to Port Hardy, or, as an alternative, take Via Rail's domeliner the *Skeena* to Prince George, spend the night, and continue on the *Skeena* eastward to Jasper.

Prince Rupert and Skidegate to Queen Charlotte Islands: On this shorter route, sailings are usually during the day to the Queen Charlotte Islands, a six-and-a-half-hour run, with return to Prince Rupert overnight. Turnaround time is five and a half hours (Monday sailing from Prince Rupert is mostly overnight; Monday and Tuesday sailings from **Skidegate** are day).

The mystical **Queen Charlotte Islands** are largely undeveloped, with wonderful misty forests, a rugged landscape, and the strong culture and artwork of the coastal Haida people. For more than a superficial visit, some sort of personal transportation is required, as there are no bus services.

Address/Phone: BC Ferries, 1112 Fort Street, Victoria, BC V8V 4V2; (250) 386–3431; fax: (250) 388–7754; www.bcferries.bc.ca or www.bcferries.com

The Ships: *Queen of the North,* built in 1969 as the *Stena Danica* and rebuilt for BC Ferries in the 1980s, has a gross tonnage of 8,889 and a length of 410 feet. *Queen of Prince Rupert* was built in 1966 and has a gross tonnage of 5,864 and a length of 332 feet.

Passengers: *Queen of the North* 750 (210 berths); *Queen of Prince Rupert* 458 (90 berths); all ages and some non–North American passengers

Dress: Casual

Officers/Crew: Canadian

Cabins: Both ships have two- and four-berth outside and inside cabins with showers, and some are below vehicle deck with washbasin and toilet only. *Queen of the North* offers a reserved seat lounge for day or cheap night travel.

Fare: $

What's included: Cruise fare, port charges, and if booked, cabin and a meal plan (*Queen of the North* only)

What's not included: Transport to and from piers, drinks, meals not purchased in advance

Highlights: Some of the world's most beautiful scenery; lots of creative itineraries

Other itineraries: In addition to these two short getaways, which operate year-round with varying schedules, short ferry routes exist throughout coastal British Columbia, some incorporating through intercity buses between Vancouver-Victoria and Vancouver-Nanaimo.

AMERICAN CANADIAN CARIBBEAN LINE'S

Grande Caribe

Erie Canal, St. Lawrence Seaway, and Saguenay River

The *Grande Caribe* is the creation of Luther Blount, a Yankee shipbuilder and shipowner who has been launching small cruise vessels since 1966, and at 185 feet it is ACCL's longest vessel ever. The one hundred passengers are mainly well-traveled American retirees ready to do without luxuries but not without camaraderie, which they share in rather tight quarters with a score of young American crew members.

The lounge, which also serves as theater and lecture hall, is forward on the upper of two accommodation decks. The dining room, one deck below, doubles as a card room and reading area. The American fare is fresh, well prepared, and served family style at one open sitting. Lunch is soup, salad, pasta, or sandwiches. Alcohol is not sold, but the ship has storage for passengers' own stock and provides setups gratis. The Sun Deck extends nearly the ship's full length and has a protected viewing area. The pilothouse collapses approaching low bridges, and the patented bow ramp lowers for dry landings.

The fifty cabins—forty-one are outside with windows (some slide open) and portholes—have twin or double beds, and a few reduced-rate units have triple berths. Each cabin has air vents, limited hanging and shelf space, and minuscule bathrooms with handheld showers. ACCL has a loyal clientele, thanks to the owner's innovative itineraries and moderate fares.

The Itinerary

The complete twelve-day Erie Canal to Saguenay cruise described here is altered in the fall to Erie Canal to Quebec City only (also twelve days), as sailing farther downriver is also north and nippy. Both fall foliage and the onset of snow come early to the lower St. Lawrence Valley.

Embarking at **Warren, Rhode Island,** the *Grande Caribe* sails overnight, arriving in **New York** about dawn and passing down the East River within 2 blocks of my apartment; then, with a loop by the Statue of Liberty, it turns up the **Hudson River,** stopping at **West Point** for the military academy and **Kingston** for the Hudson River Maritime Museum. At **Troy** the pilothouse is lowered for "low bridge on the Erie Canal." At **Waterford** the ship climbs 150 feet in a set of five locks to enter the canal proper, making stops and tying up at night, allowing the young American crew some freedom and passengers a chance to explore the delights of a small canal town. By breakfast the ship may already be under way, and from the open top deck, you can commune with the locals ashore, who are watching the unusual sight of a passenger vessel gliding by their front yards.

Turning into the **Oswego Canal,** the vast expanse of **Lake Ontario** is ahead, and soon one is threading among the beautiful **Thousand Islands.** Stops are **Clayton's** Antique Boat Museum and splendid **Upper Canada Village,** with houses, churches, and public and farm buildings spanning one hundred years of Canadian architecture and small-town life. The tiny *Grande Caribe* shares the **St. Lawrence Seaway** with huge lake carriers and locks through to **Montreal** for a stop and a bow landing at Bay of Eternity in the dramatic **Saguenay Fjord** where at the mouth, there are possible sightings of beluga whales, seals, and seabirds. From here the ship sails upriver to disembark at **Quebec City.** Passengers return to Rhode Island by bus in one day, and others come up to join the ship at Quebec.

Address/Phone: American Canadian Caribbean Line, 461 Water Street, P.O. Box 368, Warren, RI 02885; (401) 247–0955 or (800) 556–7450; fax: (401) 247–2350; www.acclsmallships.com

The Ship: *Grande Caribe* was built in the company's shipyard in 1997, has a tonnage of 99, a length of 183 feet, and a shallow draft of 6.5 feet.

Passengers: 100; age fifty-five and up and mostly Americans

Dress: Casual at all times

Officers/Crew: American

Cabins: 50 cabins, quite small; 9 inside; smoking on outside decks only

Fare: $$

What's included: Cruise and port charges, soft drinks, setups for BYOB, and bus transportation between Quebec City and Warren, R.I.

What's not included: Airfare, shore excursions (very reasonably priced), tips

Highlights: The company's most popular route; social experience for passengers

Other itineraries: In addition to this twelve-day inland-waterways cruise, which operates June to October, ACCL offers many summer options in the Chesapeake Bay, New England, eastern Canada, Great Lakes, Mid-America, Intracoastal Waterway, and winter cruises in Belize, the Caribbean, and the Bahamas.

MID-LAKES NAVIGATION'S
Emita II
Cruising the Canals of New York State

Mid-Lakes Navigation, run by five sons and one daughter of the company's founder, Peter Wiles Sr., has its home base in Skaneateles, New York. In three decades this small operation has brought due recognition to the state's treasured recreational waterways.

At first sight at the dock in Troy, just north of Albany, the 65-foot *Emita II*, a former Maine coastal passenger ferry, appears not much larger than a cruise-ship launch. The boat's top viewing deck, half protected by a canopy, is attractively furnished with deck chairs and cushioned wooden benches. Mahogany trim accents the pilothouse, and

stairs lead down to the forward open deck and interior cabin. The dining room is aft, arranged with long, custom-built wooden tables, banquettes, and chairs. Oriental-patterned scatter rugs, a red deck, and orange life preservers in the overhead racks give the room and the forward library section both color and warmth.

All meals are taken aboard, and nights are spent ashore in nearby hotels and motels. Breakfast and lunch are buffet style, and dinner is served by waiters. One night features an outdoor summer supper, and entrees run to roast beef and Virginia baked ham; lunch is soup, salads, and sandwiches.

The Itineraries

While the Erie Canal from Albany (Troy) west to Syracuse and Buffalo is by far the best-known waterway, the company's forty-passenger packet boat, *Emita II,* also navigates the **Champlain Canal** from Albany (Troy) to Whitehall, from early June to mid-October. On the three-day Champlain Canal cruise, boarding begins in the morning at **Troy,** and Captain Dan Wiles sets the tone for the come-what-may trip with a short talk before departure.

Within minutes the boat comes to the first of a dozen locks that divide the Hudson River and the Champlain Canal into a series of controlled pools. The *Emita II* plows ahead at a leisurely pace of 8 miles per hour between wooded shores and rolling farmlands, where cows and children come down to the water's edge for a look. Powered yachts gather to share the transit through the toll-free locks. At Fort Edward the boat ties up for the night, and passengers spend two nights at a motor inn in **Glens Falls,** where the captain gives a slide-illustrated talk on canal history and current preservation efforts. On the second day the *Emita II* continues north along the pretty Champlain Canal to **Whitehall,** the turnaround point. The town's Skenesborough Museum recalls the city's past as the birthplace of the U.S. Navy and Marine Corps and as a once-important canal and rail center.

Besides the Champlain Canal trip, the *Emita II* makes three-day **Erie Canal** cruises from Albany (Troy) to Syracuse along the Mohawk River. The highlights are the **Waterford Flight** of five locks, which lift the boat 150 feet, old factory towns such as **Amsterdam** and **Little Falls,** and the 22-mile Oneida Lake crossing. From **Syracuse** to Lockport, near **Buffalo,** the *Emita II* passes through **Montezuma Wildlife Refuge** for possible sightings of bald eagles and Canada geese, restored canal towns such as **Fairport** and **Pittsford,** and the original canal's small locks and stone-arched aqueducts. These last structures were built by Frederick Law Olmsted of Central Park fame. In places the bridges are so low that the crew has to remove the boat's pilothouse, and passengers have to crouch. On this stretch the boat docks at a canal park for the first night, and the hotel is just steps away. Both Erie Canal trips are one-way, with each night ashore in a different hotel and bus return to the port of embarkation.

Address/Phone: Mid-Lakes Navigation Company, Box 61, 11 Jordan Street, Skaneateles, NY 13152; (315) 685–8500 or (800) 545–4318; fax: (315) 685–7566; www.midlakesnav.com

The Ship: *Emita II* was built in 1953 and then modified for day cruising. She has a gross tonnage of 65, a length of 65 feet, and a shallow draft.

Passengers: 40; mostly age fifty and up and many repeaters and whole-boat charters

Dress: Casual at all times

Officers/Crew: American

Cabins: Stay ashore in hotels/motels

Fare: $$

What's included: Cruise fare, port charges, all meals on boat, hotel stays, and transfers

What's not included: Transportation to and from port of embarkation, drinks, tips

Highlights: Cruising historic canals while passing through rural and industrial landscapes

Other itineraries: In addition to the *Emita II*'s three above itineraries, operating between June and mid-October, the boat makes Syracuse-Waterloo two-day cruises.

AMERICAN CRUISE LINES'
American Eagle
Coastal Ship among the New England Islands

Cruise ships don't come much less popu-lated than forty-nine passengers, a full-ship figure for the *American Eagle.* Completed in April 2000, she is a product of the owner's own Chesapeake shipyard in Salisbury, Maryland.

There are five cabin categories, all out-side, and the second grade up, the AAs, measure 192 square feet, larger than what is found on the small-fry ship competition. The six AAV cabins spread out to 249 square feet including verandas, and seven more are dedicated single cabins priced at about a 50 percent premium over the AA category. The cane-style couches are com-fortable for an afternoon's read and watch-ing satellite TV, and the windows slide open to allow salt air to gain supremacy over the processed kind.

Four decks may not sound like much ship, but the public spaces are especially roomy. The forward-facing Nantucket Lounge seats all passengers, and amid-ships, a shipwide foyer offers additional comfy couch seating. A library, occupying a cabin-size space, offers TV, VCR, and books. The decor is a bit plain with utilitarian-looking walls and ceilings, but the carpets and fabrics help to dress things up.

The three-sided, glass-enclosed dining room operates on an open seating plan at large round tables. The ship does not have a liquor license, but there is a complimen-tary bar instead at the very popular cocktail hour and carafes of chardonnay and bur-gundy on the table at dinner. Sumptuous pre-dinner hors d'oeuvres may be jumbo shrimp, beef sate in peanut sauce, or melted Brie on French bread.

Set dinner menus, with a choice of two entrees, include delicious grilled artichoke hearts, hearts of palm in balsamic vinegar, Cornish game hen with all wild rice, grilled catfish, sliced breast of duck, boiled live lobster, and desserts such as pecan peanut butter pie and whipped chocolate mousse in a pastry shell. Lunch is much lighter fare, such as crab cakes and chicken Cae-sar salad with garlic croutons.

The fourth or Sports Deck is both cov-ered and open to the sky with deck chairs for everyone plus tables and chairs and a putting green. Additional covered deck space faces aft, and the open deck forward of the lounge is excellent for viewing ahead.

That's the ship, plain and simple, and delightfully *sans* casino, health spa, shops, staff pitching expensive drinks, fake-friendly celebratory dining room events, and the like. Cruising can be different, and this style adds up to a most pleasant vaca-tion far removed from the milling throngs and multiple entertainment choices aboard the big hulls. All three ships undertake the itinerary below.

The Itinerary

New England Island trips begin either on the waterfront in Providence, Rhode Island, or at the City Pier in **New London, Con-necticut,** a busy Thames River scene shared with ferries to Block Island, Orient Point on Long Island, and Fishers Island. Frequent Amtrak trains operating between Washington, New York, and Boston stop at Providence and New London, where the lat-ter's dock is within walking distance of the ship and the former a short cab ride. For this itinerary we will leave from Providence, and depending on the departure the sequence of ports may change.

Leaving Providence, the *American Eagle* sails down Narragansett Bay into open waters for a short stretch. Drawing only 6 feet, the ship can roll for an hour or so when there is a swell en route to **New Bedford.** Once a major whaling port, the active harbor still hosts a large fishing fleet. In summer, a trolley bus makes stops at the outstanding whaling museum, a historic whaling captain's house, and Seamen's Bethel (Chapel) or you can accomplish the same on foot without much strain.

Then it's onto **Nantucket Island** where the town is a treasure trove of eighteenth- and nineteenth-century architecture, and as the whaling industry declined, very little was built during the Victorian period to upset the rich architectural balance. One could easily spend the entire day in town walking the cobblestone Main Street and turning left or right into the residential lanes. An efficient local bus network allows independent touring to most parts of the island, and one recommended destination is Sconset (Siasconset), an 8-mile ride east across the island. The tiny community has changed very little for many decades, and you'll see some of the smallest saltbox houses imaginable and have a glorious view of the open Atlantic. Buses also run from Nantucket Town to the Jetties Beach for Sound swimming and to Surfside for the ocean.

Sail back across Nantucket Sound to Vineyard Haven on **Martha's Vineyard.** If not joining the ship's tour, take the island bus (day pass available) the short distance to **Oak Bluffs,** and once past the commercial clutter, you will find a beautiful village green rimmed by substantial Victorian houses. Hidden just one street behind is an utterly charming gingerbread Victorian

Methodist summer community with lanes of tiny gaily painted wooden houses and an impressive residential circle facing the campground green.

Reboard the bus near the ferry landing for a brief ride to upscale **Edgartown,** in many respects similar in architecture to the town of Nantucket, with its main street leading down to the harbor, in part created by Chappaquiddick Island across the narrow inlet. The bus returns directly to Vineyard Haven.

Sail via the Elizabeth Islands into Narragansett Bay and pass under the Mount Hope Bridge for a visit to the USS *Massachusetts,* a battleship tied up at **Fall River.** The next call, **Newport,** is easily walkable for its Thames Street shops and adjacent eighteenth- and nineteenth-century historic district. Tour on an excursion or independently the so-called summer cottages lined up along Bellevue Avenue and Ocean Drive such as the Vanderbilt's Breakers or the equally impressive Marble House. A cliff walk of several miles runs between the mansions and the sea and makes a great hike and picnic outing.

Then it's a couple hours' sail out to New Harbor, **Block Island.** Entering the protected anchorage the ship threads among several hundred private yachts to reach the town wharf for an overnight stay. A minivan tour includes a look at Old Harbor, a feast of high Victorian architecture, and the majestic Southeast Lighthouse set atop 100-foot cliffs overlooking the Atlantic. Then return up Narragansett Bay to Providence for disembarkation.

The *American Eagle,* its slightly newer sister *American Glory,* and larger *American Spirit* provide a low-key, uncrowded social cruising experience from New England to the Deep South and Florida via the Intracoastal Waterway.

Address/Phone: American Cruise Lines, 741 Boston Post Road, Suite 200, Guilford, CT 06437; (800) 814–6880; fax: (860) 345–4266; www.americancruiselines.com

The Ship: *American Eagle,* built in 2000, has a length of 165 feet and a shallow draft.

Passengers: 49, mostly Americans fifty and up

Dress: Casual

Officers/Crew: American

Cabins: 28 cabins, all outside with picture windows, 6 with balconies, and 7 are singles

Fare: $$$$

What's included: Cruise fare, open bar before dinner, and wine with dinner

What's not included: Airfare, port charges, tips

Highlights: Small-ship atmosphere with roomy cabins, excellent food

Other itineraries: Besides this seven-day New England Islands itinerary, which operates between June and the end of September, this ship, sister *American Glory,* and the 92-passenger *American Spirit* offer cruises from the coast of Maine to the west coast of Florida.

CLIPPER CRUISE LINE'S
Nantucket Clipper
New York, the Hudson Valley, and Chesapeake Bay

Clipper Cruise Line, based in St. Louis, got started in 1983, and its *Nantucket Clipper,* completed in 1984, is one of two similar shallow-draft cruisers. A young American crew gives friendly, professional service to mostly middle-age Americans from the West Coast and Sun Belt. In no time the ship takes on the atmosphere of an informal seagoing club.

The single lounge, decorated with bold colors and maple trim, faces forward with views ahead and to both sides. Ample seating makes this the social setting as well as the venue for local entertainers and enrichment programs about history and nature. The bar is to one side and the small library collection to the other. The dining room serves passengers and staff at one open sitting, with good table service and a few buffets. Chefs trained at the Culinary Institute of America use fresh ingredients to prepare an American menu that runs to excellent fish, grilled shrimp, veal, lots of different salads, and freshly baked desserts. The Clipper Chipper cookies are an afternoon staple. Hot and cold hors d'oeuvres are served before dinner in the lounge.

Cabins are all outside doubles with twin beds, radios, adequate stowage, and compact bathrooms with showers. Some passengers prefer a cabin that opens to a side deck, whereas others like the traditional door to a central corridor. A few lower-priced cabins have portholes instead of windows, and noise from the engines is minimal, though noticeable, in the cabins located aft. Deck space includes a narrow wraparound promenade, a partly covered Sun Deck, and an observation deck at the bow. The ship has no swimming pool, fitness facilities, or casino. Instead, the *Nantucket Clipper* excels in providing an intimate, social, American-style vehicle to view coastal waters and islands.

The Itinerary

The *Nantucket Clipper* undertakes a variety of seven-, ten-, and fourteen-day cruises along the Eastern Seaboard, and the ports will vary from cruise to cruise, so here are the highlights beginning in New York for a ten-day cruise that sails up the Hudson and south to the Chesapeake Bay. The ship's shallow draft permits close-in cruising, and while most of this cruise is on inland waterways, during the open sea stretch along the New Jersey coast, the unstabilized ship can roll.

Embarkation is the Chelsea Piers, a busy recreational waterfront sports complex located on **Manhattan**'s Lower West Side. After a brief sail into the Upper Bay proudly dominated by Lady Liberty, the ship turns north past the skyline and up the majestic **Hudson** paralleling the Palisades. The Hudson is navigable as well as tidal all the way past Albany to Troy, some 150 miles north of the city. In fall the autumn colors are outstanding, and stately homes with views straight out of the Hudson River School of painting face the river.

The stop at **Kingston,** more than halfway to Albany, gives access to Franklin D. Roosevelt's family home at **Hyde Park** with Eleanor Roosevelt's cottage retreat at Val Kill just a few miles away. Returning south, a stop is made at **West Point** for a visit to the U.S. Military Academy. The river here cuts through the Hudson Highlands, and the depth increases to more than 300 feet at the point where the Bear Mountain Bridge crosses.

Passing New York City, the *Nantucket Clipper* sails under the Verrazano-Narrows Bridge and out into the Atlantic for the voyage south along the New Jersey coast, then into the Delaware and through the **Chesapeake and Delaware Canal** into Chesapeake Bay, known for its abundant bird life, especially ducks and Canada geese, and of course, oysters, steamer clams, and the blue crab. Some cruises visit **Baltimore**'s Inner Harbor, and all stop at **Annapolis,** boasting the oldest state capitol building, with a chance to tour the **U.S. Naval Academy.** On the Chesapeake's Eastern Shore, **St. Michaels** has a wonderful maritime museum featuring the specialized craft that "fished" for the bay's renowned shellfish and an example of a screw-pile (built on stilts) lighthouse.

Sailing into one of the world's largest natural harbors, Hampton Roads, the ship docks in **Norfolk** adjacent to its waterfront marketplace and city center. A ferry crosses the Elizabeth River to historic Portsmouth for a residential walking tour. The final leg is a sail northward through the bay to Old Town **Alexandria, Virginia,** near **Washington,** where the ship is your conveniently docked hotel for one last day and night.

From here the ship will embark a new lot of passengers for ports in the Deep South along the Intracoastal Waterway.

Address/Phone: Clipper Cruise Line, 11969 Westline Industrial Drive, St. Louis, MO 63146; reservations: (800) 325–0010; brochures: (800) 282–7245; fax: (314) 655–6670; www.clippercruise.com

The Ship: *Nantucket Clipper,* built in 1984, has a tonnage of 95, a length of 207 feet, and a shallow draft of 8 feet.

Passengers: 100; mostly Americans fifty-five and up

Dress: Casual, with a jacket for the captain's reception

Officers/Crew: American

Cabins: 50 small doubles; all outside, most with windows, half opening onto a side deck

Fare: $$$

What's included: Cruise and port charges

What's not included: Airfare, shore excursions, drinks, tips

Highlights: Inshore, river, and island cruising, and an easy social life aboard

Other itineraries: In addition to these East-ern Seaboard cruises, which operate in the spring and fall, the *Nantucket Clipper* sails the coast of Maine via the Maritime Provinces into the St. Lawrence River and the Great Lakes and along the Intracoastal Waterway to the Caribbean. The slightly larger *Yorktown Clipper* offers cruises between Panama, Baja California, the California Wine Country, and Alaska's Inside Passage. The expedition-style *Clipper Adventurer* and *Clipper Odyssey* cover much of the world.

AMERICAN CRUISE LINES'
American Glory
Exploring the Chesapeake Bay

With every new class of cruise ship getting ever larger, it is indeed refreshing to learn of one line that believes "smaller is better." Based in Connecticut, American Cruise Lines operates a tiny fleet of two forty-nine-passenger ships and a third taking ninety-two passengers, all built in the company's Chesapeake Shipbuilding yard.

While among the smallest in the coastal ship business, the trio easily qualifies as the most spacious and comfortable and offers top-of-the-line food and service, for a stiff price, on mostly one-week itineraries spanning the East Coast between Maine and Florida.

Embarking passengers are welcomed with printed tags with names and hometowns, and socializing comes easily with a gathering before dinner in the Nantucket Lounge and open seating at meals. Single travelers need never to feel alone on this vessel.

The *American Glory*'s twenty-seven cabins, located on three of the four decks, average more than 200 square feet. All are outside with doors that open to an interior corridor, and fourteen have private balconies, a narrow terrace furnished with chairs and a small table. Amenities include a desk, a couple of chairs, a chest with deep drawers, curtained closet, satellite TV, and large-view windows that slide open. Roomy bathrooms have good counter space and large stall showers.

The *American Glory* has three lounges, unlike most boats this size with just one, offering a choice of camaraderie or a quiet spot to read or play cards. The forward observation Nantucket Lounge, furnished with cane-style chairs and sofas, provides the social center and lecture venue with seating for everyone. At 5:30 P.M. every evening, the line hosts an hour of complimentary cocktails, beer, wine, and hors d'oeuvres served by the hotel manager and an assistant. The captain or first mate appears most nights. Creative hors d'oeuvres include jumbo shrimp, bacon-wrapped scallops, pâté de foie gras, cheeses and crackers, baby lamb Wellington, fresh vegetables and dips, soft-shell crabs, and oysters freshly shucked on the Observation Deck.

The dining room, located on Main Deck aft, offers big-window, three-exposure views from eight round tables of six and seven places. All meals are wait-served. The dining and cabin staff, young American men and women of college age, attends a training course before coming aboard for a contract lasting several months. Because many need only take a semester off, the hiring pool for finding those with the right attitude and personal skills is huge, and an easy relationship develops between crew and passengers.

The ACL chefs are generally trained at the Culinary Institute of America at Hyde Park, New York, and the cuisine geared to cruising region is among the best I have ever sampled on any ship. For breakfast, served from 7:30 to 9:00 A.M., the two or three specials may be a crab omelet, eggs Benedict, a quiche, and pancakes or waffles with a strawberry or blueberry glaze. A small buffet lays out cereals, fresh fruit, and freshly baked muffins.

Served at 12:30 P.M., lunch is a light meal, as preferred by the passengers, and includes an appetizer such as cold gazpacho or a garden salad, then turkey on a croissant, ham and cheese on a kaiser roll, chicken Caesar salad, or Maryland crab cakes.

At 6:30 P.M. dinner, the entrees may be tender roast beef, rack of lamb, veal chop, fresh swordfish, fresh salmon with a béarnaise sauce, and such desserts as three-chocolate praline, strawberry shortcake, and freshly made cashew or chocolate ice cream. Complimentary bottles of good quality California red and white wines are served at dinner. For a nice touch, instead of

announcements, the hotel manager comes around to each table at mealtimes to remind us of the program details and times, and to answer questions.

The Library Lounge one deck above, with an inviting etched glass wall facing the stairway, has shelves of reference books, hard backs, and soft covers. Aft of the Nantucket Lounge, the Midships Lounge is a third spot to roost.

The Observation Deck, with a small covered section, runs from the stern to just above the pilothouse and is furnished with deck chairs, armchairs, and wrought-iron chairs set around oval tables. A sheltered area at the stern one deck below provides seating and a view aft.

The Itinerary

The one-week Chesapeake Bay cruise embarks at **Baltimore** with many passengers arriving a day or two early to stay near the busy Inner Harbor. The cruise features a port a day, and in most instances, the boat stays tied up at night, usually sailing in the wee hours to arrive at the next destination in the morning.

The route into the Chesapeake passes container ship berths, coal piers, military and hospital vessels, and Fort McHenry where Francis Scott Key wrote "The Star-Spangled Banner." Passing under the Key Bridge, the boat soon turns south to sail under the twin spans of the Chesapeake Bay Bridge connecting Maryland's Eastern and Western Shores.

After sailing overnight, by morning the boat is heading up the York River for a day trip to the historic battlefields and colonial homes of **Yorktown** and the world's premier living history museum at **Colonial Williamsburg.**

Very early the next morning, it's a northward sail to **Solomons Island** and the Calvert Marine Museum, then at lunchtime across the Chesapeake to **Tangier Island,** an isolated fishing and blue crabbing center with considerable charm.

The Eastern Shore call at **Cambridge** offers a walking tour into the mostly nineteenth-century historic residential neighborhood or a drive out to Blackwater National Wildlife Refuge to spot bald eagle and osprey, while **Oxford,** just to the north, is anchored by the historic Robert Morris Inn, an attractive waterfront residential district, and an active boat building and repair yard. The Oxford-Bellevue Ferry landing where the boat ties up is the oldest waterborne operation of its kind in North America.

At **St. Michaels**, the *American Glory* docks alongside the Chesapeake Bay Maritime Museum opposite an unusual restored wooden lighthouse that sits on iron pilings. The well-designed exhibits interpret the bay's history, the commercial shellfish industry, small craft such as bugeyes and skipjacks peculiar to these waters, waterfowl migration, and former steamboat routes. The town has developed into a burgeoning shopping and restaurant mecca, and several bed-and-breakfast–type inns cater to the weekend trade.

Crossing the bay, **Annapolis** includes a short bus trip to see the state capital's capitol, the historic center, harbor marinas, and immediate surrounding neighborhoods and then provides a drop off for a tour of the Naval Academy's attractive grounds, commencing with a short introductory film. Then in the afternoon, the *American Glory* sails back to Baltimore, docking adjacent to the Inner Harbor attractions for the night, with disembarkation the next morning after breakfast.

Address/Phone: American Cruise Lines, 741 Boston Post Road, Suite 200, Guilford, CT 06437; (800) 814–6880 or (203) 453–6800; www.americancruiselines.com

The Ship: *American Glory,* built in 2002, has a length of 170 feet and a shallow draft

Passengers: 49, mostly American fifty and up

Dress: Casual at all times

Officers/Crew: American

Cabins: 27, all oceanview and picture windows slide open, 14 with balconies, and 5 are singles. 3 cabins, including one single, have wheelchair access

Fare: $$$$

What's included: Cruise fare, port charges, open bar before dinner, and wine with dinner

What's not included: Transportation to and from the ship, shore excursions (inexpensive), tips (suggested amounts are high)

Highlights: Small-ship atmosphere with roomy cabins, excellent food

Other itineraries: Besides this seven-day Chesapeake Bay itinerary, which operates in June and October, near sistership *American Eagle* and the newer and larger 92-passenger *American Spirit* offer Eastern Seaboard cruises between Maine and Florida. Itineraries cruise the New England Islands, the coast of Maine, the Hudson River during fall foliage, the Intracoastal Waterway between the Mid-Atlantic region and the Antebellum South; and into the St. Johns River and across Florida to the Gulf of Mexico via Lake Okeechobee.

AMERICAN CANADIAN
CARIBBEAN LINE'S

Grande Mariner

East Coast Inside Passage: New England to Florida

The *Grande Mariner* is the latest ship from Luther Blount's Rhode Island shipyard, and very similar to the earlier *Grande Caribe.* One hundred passengers, mainly well-traveled American retirees, are accommodated aboard, enjoying inland-waters cruising and one another's company rather than looking for the luxuries of a deep-sea cruise ship.

The lounge, located forward on the upper of two main accommodation decks, also serves as theater and lecture hall. One deck below, the dining room doubles as a card room and reading area after meals. The galley window opens into the dining room, where American fare is fresh, well prepared, and served family style at one open sitting. Lunch is usually soup, salad, pasta, or make-your-own sandwich. No alcohol is sold, so passengers bring their own stock and the ship provides storage and setups gratis. The long Sun Deck has a protected viewing area, and the patented bow ramp lowers for dry beach landings. The fifty cabins, of which forty-four are outside with windows (some slide open) and portholes, have twin or double beds. Several cabins aft on the Sun Deck open out onto the deck; otherwise, they have access from a central corridor. Cabins have air-conditioning, limited stowage, and minuscule bathrooms with handheld showers. As on all three ACCL vessels, there is a stair lift between decks, and smoking is permitted only on the open decks.

The Itinerary

Although this coastal cruise may begin in either Florida or **Rhode Island,** the narrative here will start in the Yankee North at the company headquarters and shipyard. Embarking the tiny ship, the course aims south into Long Island Sound, passing **New York**'s skyscrapers at dawn, then out through the Narrows along the New Jersey coast for the only stretch of open ocean. Not far beyond Victorian Cape May, the *Grande Mariner* slices through the Delmarva Peninsula via the **Chesapeake and Delaware Canal** into the widening bay.

There are stops at **Baltimore**'s **Inner Harbor,** Norfolk's busy waterfront, and the U.S. naval base at **Newport News.** The waterway opens wide through **Abermarle** and **Pamlico Sounds,** then narrows again south of Cape Hatteras, where happily the ship remains inside the breakers away from the graveyard of the Atlantic. When you stop at **Beaufort, North Carolina,** and **Beaufort, South Carolina,** you quickly learn, but may not remember, that they are pronounced quite differently (*bow-* and *bew-*fort, respectively). **Georgetown, South Carolina,** was once the largest port in the South, but today there's little sign of that, while **Charleston** and **Savannah** certainly impress as you approach and explore ashore.

The waterway is rural again in Georgia, with a stop at **St. Simon's Island;** then crossing into Florida, **St. Augustine** qualifies as America's oldest permanent European settlement. The ship is almost part of a convoy of yachts heading south for the winter, and there are many drawbridges that open for the waterborne traffic. The **Intracoastal Waterway** is especially busy along the Florida coast, with the cruise ending at **Titusville** on the Indian River near the Kennedy Space Center, following two weeks of gradual climate change. Welcome to sunny Florida.

Address/Phone: American Canadian Caribbean Line, P.O. Box 368, Warren, RI 02885; (401) 247–0955 or (800) 556–7450; fax: (401) 247–2350; www .acclsmallships.com

The Ship: *Grande Mariner* was built in the company's shipyard in 1998, has a tonnage of 99, a length of 183 feet, and a shallow draft of just 6.5 feet.

Passengers: 100; age is fifty-five and up and mostly Americans

Dress: Casual at all times

Officers/Crew: American

Cabins: 50 cabins, all quite small with 6 inside

Fare: $$

What's included: Cruise and port charges, soft drinks, and setups for BYOB

What's not included: Airfare, shore excursions (very reasonably priced), tips

Highlights: An intracoastal route spanning the length of the East Coast offering a great variety of stops; a low-key social experience among like-minded passengers

Other itineraries: In addition to this fifteen-day inland waterways cruise, operating several times in spring and fall, ACCL offers summer options in the Chesapeake Bay, New England, eastern Canada, Erie Canal, St. Lawrence Seaway, Great Lakes, and Mid-America, as well as winter cruises in Belize, the Caribbean, and the Bahamas.

DELTA QUEEN STEAMBOAT'S
Delta Queen
Upper Mississippi River: St. Louis to St. Paul

Delta Queen Steamboat Company dates back more than one hundred years to the Greene Line of Steamers. The steamboat *Delta Queen,* first built in Scotland then completed in California in 1926, was first designed for overnight service between San Francisco and Sacramento, running opposite her mate, *Delta King,* now a hotel and restaurant on the Sacramento waterfront. She is a quintessential piece of Americana, evident the moment one treads her wooden decks and eyes the white-painted wood superstructure. The *DQ* may not be the opulent wedding cake like her big sister *American Queen,* but she is the real thing.

The lower of two forward lounges, graced with fluted columns and potted plants, is suitable for reading, playing cards, and having tea. The wooden grand staircase with shiny brass steps rises to the Victorian-style Texas Lounge with a bar, daytime games, a singer-pianist, and a popcorn machine. Dinner is served at two sittings. Service is casual and friendly and the food thoroughly American, featuring some Cajun-style soups and stuffed catfish among the usual meat, fish, and shellfish entrees. Portions are relatively small, yet sensible for diners who sample all five courses, and preparation ranges from good to excellent. The desserts, such as Mississippi mud and pecan pie, are almost sinful.

Evening entertainment is popular, and following dinner, the lower-level dining room becomes a well-attended, old-fashioned music hall featuring ragtime, Dixieland, jazz, and blues. The engine room, where passengers are most welcome, is a spotless, eye-popping feast of brass fittings, multiple dials, and heaving machinery, and I love to go down to watch the slowly undulating Pitman arms turn the thrashing red wooden sternwheel.

Most of the eighty-seven staterooms are plain, with pipe rack closets for hanging clothes, and functional baths. Many cabins open to covered or open decks with chairs on either side of the door. The better rooms feature stained-glass windows and are off the Betty Blake Lounge, a portrait and memorabilia gallery dotted with overstuffed chairs. The old-fashioned steam calliope over the bright red paddle wheel signals the steamboat's arrival at town landings, and the hearty toots to the shoreside warm even the most cynical hearts. People love to watch her pass, as she provides a glimpse of a bygone America. Some passengers are fiercely loyal to the *DQ* and would not consider sailing the other two "new boats."

The Itinerary

As the setting sun framed the **St. Louis** Gateway Arch one mid-August evening on my St. Paul–bound cruise, the *Delta Queen* eased away from the landing and headed upriver. In the week ahead we would sail 659 meandering miles and negotiate twenty-six locks en route to the headwaters of navigation. The average of 100 miles a day may take as many minutes in a car, but speed and distance become irrelevant after a full day on the river. Most travelers quickly find a favorite spot on deck for taking in the slowly passing scenery. Forested banks,

marshy coves, and high bluffs are the main characteristics of the **Upper Mississippi.** The approach to each town becomes a major event, and the *Delta Queen*'s throaty whistle and cheerful tunes from the century-old calliope announce the steamboat's arrival and draw people down to the river.

The Mississippi is a vibrant commercial waterway, and long strings of barges, pushed by towboats, move huge loads of grain, coal, scrap iron, and fuel. During locking operations people ashore share news, weather, and scenic highlights with passengers lining the rails. The passengers in turn answer questions about traveling aboard the *Delta Queen.* Daytime activities include kite flying and river lore and natural history talks at the bow and guided walks ashore.

Fall foliage is a highlight of a cruise along the Upper Mississippi from late September to the end of October.

Hannibal opens the world of Mark Twain: Huckleberry Finn, Tom Sawyer, Becky Thatcher, and Injun Joe, characters penned by Samuel Langhorne Clemens. A complex of museums, located within a few blocks of each other, contains the house that Clemens lived in from 1844 to 1853, Becky Thatcher's House (a real Laura Hawkins lived there), an early drug store, as well as a collection of Norman Rockwell paintings depicting Mark Twain stories. One can visit the cave that Tom Sawyer and Becky Thatcher explored, an intricate labyrinth of passages used by Indians, fur trappers, Jesse James, and slaves traveling the Underground Railroad. Mark Twain wrote in *The Adventures of Tom Sawyer,* "It is said that one might wander days and nights through its intricate tangle of rifts and chasms and never find the end of the cave."

Leave a little time to walk up to Lovers' Leap, a 300-foot-high park overlooking the Mississippi for great views of Hannibal, the steamboat, and the wide sluggish river. One of the tours includes the site, but one can also walk up independently from the landing.

Dubuque, Iowa, named after French fur trapper Julien Dubuque who settled here in the 1780, is best known for the Lead Rush and the area's mining history. The Mesquakie Indians had mined lead for years before Europeans arrived, and because of lead's value for making lead shot, its use in paints and as window frames, Dubuque managed to negotiate control of the lead mines. When he died in 1810, the Indians took back their claims until the U.S. Government moved in and began to grant licenses to mine lead in 1822, and by 1829 there were 4,000 claims. The Lead Rush was on, and the Midwest had its own version of the Wild West.

Riches before the Civil War produced a substantial river town and many mansions. The steamboat tour visits the Mathias Ham House, built by a prosperous lead miner in the 1850s on the site of a log cabin he once lived in. A similar type double log cabin, originally built in 1833 and the oldest building in the state, is on view to illustrate Ham's ascendancy from rags to riches. A film illustrates the history of the Lead Rush.

Dubuque boasts fifty-seven churches, the number reflecting the religions of the many nationalities drawn here the including St. Luke's Methodist Church, featuring some one hundred Tiffany stained-glass windows. The local Museum of Art occupies the old jail, an unusual Egyptian Revival–style building.

At **LaCrosse, Wisconsin,** three rivers converge, the site being a favorite for Sioux Indian games, including lacrosse played on the high bluffs. From atop the highest, some 600 feet above the Mississippi, one can see into three states—Minnesota, Wisconsin, and Iowa.

The City Brewery tour describes beer-making process. It was established here in 1858 as a family business and was once run by Johanna Heileman, one of the country's first female corporation presidents. The excursion includes a German beer hall, an 1870 home built by successful German immigrants (now the company headquarters), and a warehouse that can store an unbelievable forty million cans. Continuing the German heritage, the city celebrates Oktoberfest for a week each year.

The next two landings, Winona and Red Wing, are on the Minnesota side opposite Wisconsin, and they appear on alternating itineraries. This section is a very pretty region of bluffs, many once Indian settlements and now scenic overlooks. Between Wabasha and Red Wing the boat will cross the 3-mile-wide and 25-mile-long Lake Pepin, a natural body of water formed by a sandbar built up from the swifter Chippewa River waters entering the more sluggish Mississippi. Waterskiing got its start here in the 1922. Today Pepin is a very popular boating and sailing lake and wildlife refuge. Eagles and tundra swans are seen in the hundreds during spring and fall migration seasons. The vast expanse can become quite choppy and dangerous to small boats when the wind is strong.

Winona is named after the daughter of a Sioux Chief, and the town grew with the lumber industry, later a grain market center, and now high-tech plastics provide the mainstay industry. The actress Winona Ryder was born here in October 1979 as Winona Laura Horowitz. Polish immigrants working in the lumber and milling industries built the St. Stanislaus Kostka Catholic Church with its European-style dome and beautiful stained-glass windows. From 575 feet up at Garvin Heights, a scenic park, the view extends 20 to 30 miles up and downriver.

Red Wing's origin comes from a Sioux Chief named Red Wing, who wore red-dyed swan wings in his headdress. First an Indian settlement, the present town, settled by Scandinavians and Swiss in the 1840s, became a major exporter of wheat and later headquarters for the Red Wing Shoe Company. The former Red Wing pottery factory that housed the Union Stoneware Company is now a downtown shopping mall. Some of the original salt-glaze pottery is on display at the Goodhue County Historical Society. Main Street restoration is giving the center a rebirth anchored by buildings such as the elegant St. James Hotel (1875) and the active T. B. Sheldon Auditorium Theater (1904), where during the day a multimedia show covers early Red Wing history.

St. Paul, Minnesota, is the beginning or end of an Upper Mississippi cruise, and the more southerly of the Twin Cities, the other being Minneapolis. St. Paul retains a compact center city where most of the great civic architecture is located. If you decide to spend an extra night here, you will find lots to do within walking distance of a downtown location.

The Minnesota State Capitol Building (1905), executed in Beaux Arts style by architect Cass Gilbert of New York's Woolworth Building fame, gives free tours at the end of each weekday. Visit the House, Senate, and Supreme Court chambers to view the stenciled ceilings, murals, and sculpture. In the basement, in true German style—Germans once making up the city's largest immigrant population—there's a restored Rathskeller Café with delicately painted ceilings depicting mottoes from Minnesota's mid-nineteenth-century days.

The Minnesota Museum of American Art, housed in the Landmark Center downtown, exhibits works by noted sculptors Louise Nevelson and Paul Manship. Mural paintings depict everyday scenes of Midwestern life by Thomas Hart Benton, among others who helped interpret pioneering life

and the coming of European sophistication to the region.

The top city attraction for visitors is the James J. Hill House, an elaborate Richardsonian Romanesque mansion built in 1891 for the Great Northern Railway baron and representing the height of the Gilded Age. When finished at a cost of nearly one million dollars, it was Minnesota's largest mansion, 36,000 square feet of living space for Hill, his family, and the servants. The house's carved oak and mahogany interior, which Hill oversaw personally, contains no less than thirteen bathrooms and twenty-two fireplaces. Hill amassed a huge fortune in railroads, ocean shipping, mining, milling, banking and finance, and agriculture, and lived here with his wife until his death in 1916.

Address/Phone: Delta Queen Steamboat Company, Robin Street Wharf, 1380 Port of New Orleans Place, New Orleans, LA 70130-1890; (800) 543–1949; fax: (504) 585–0630; www.deltaqueen.com

The Ship: *Delta Queen* was completed in 1926 for the Sacramento River trade and has been cruising the Midwestern rivers since 1948. The gross tonnage is 3,360, the length 285 feet, and the draft shallow.

Passengers: 174; age range fifty-five and up; mostly Americans

Dress: Jacket and tie optional for special evenings

Officers/Crew: American

Cabins: 87 cabins, all outside and most opening onto the open side deck; 19 have upper and lower berths, with the rest offering twin or queen-size beds

Fare: $$$

What's included: Cruise fare and port charges

What's not included: Transportation to and from the steamboat, shore excursions, drinks, tips

Highlights: Lazy river cruising aboard a floating National Historic Landmark

Other itineraries: In addition to this cruise aboard the *Delta Queen,* which operates in the summer and fall, the three steamboats together offer a huge range of itineraries on Midwest rivers, embarking in many different port cities and with cruises themed to big bands, great American performers, the Civil War, Kentucky Derby, fall foliage, old-fashioned holidays, and many more. See *American Queen* and *Mississippi Queen.*

DELTA QUEEN STEAMBOAT'S
American Queen
The Antebellum South

Delta Queen Steamboat Company traces its origins back to 1890, the oldest U.S. flag cruise line, and today, with its fleet of three steamboats, the company celebrates Americana in music, food, small-town life, big cities, plantation homes, history, and steamboat lore.

I would take the *American Queen* anywhere as long as I could also enjoy the steamboat's remarkable ambience and interiors. Mounting the Grand Staircase for the first time and entering the Cabin Deck Lobby, I was dazzled by a stunning suite of rooms that could easily be the stately home of a nineteenth-century steel magnate or robber baron. Mahogany, silver, stained glass, etched glass, brass, marble, lace, leather, iron, plaster molding, tin ceilings, patterned wallpaper, thick carpets, oil paintings, chandeliers, stuffed animals, and a plethora of knickknacks outfit two Victorian parlors and a richly decorated club lounge.

The Grand Saloon aboard the *American Queen* turns an evening of entertainment into a major event for the staging of American musicals, jazz concerts, Dixieland, and big-band sounds. Designed after a small-town opera house, the theater has upholstered armchairs in curved theater boxes and deep cushioned lounge chairs on the lower level. Two massive globes ringed by gas-style lamps hang from a plaster ceiling of twinkling stars.

The J. M. White Dining Room recalls the main cabin lounge aboard the late nineteenth-century namesake steamboat with a pair of soaring two-deck-high sections decorated with white filigree woodwork, colorful tapestries, and two huge, gilded antique mirrors. The food runs to American, Southern, and Cajun, with consistently satisfying prime ribs, roast duck, fried oysters, catfish stuffed with crab and wild rice, ravioli stuffed with shrimp, seafood gumbo, garlic and leek soup, Mississippi mud pie, and praline and pecan cheesecake.

On Cabin Deck above, the centrally positioned Mark Twain Gallery is a dark-paneled room that sparkles with display cases containing museum-quality collections of nineteenth-century maps, cameras, early radios, and showboat handbills and posters. River-related sheet music invites anyone to pluck the antique Steinway upright piano keys. In one corner a Victorian birdcage is home to a pair of chirpy tiger finches; and from an oversize armchair, there is a sneaky view down into the dining room.

To the right of the entrance foyer's Reed & Barton watercooler, the Gentlemen's Card Room welcomes both sexes to enjoy a game at cherry-wood tables encircled by a standing stuffed black bear, a working upright typewriter, a stereoscopic peep show, an iron fireplace, and Tiffany lamps ordered from an original nineteenth-century catalog. The Ladies' Parlor welcomes anyone to lounge on the swooning couch before a fireplace, its wooden mantle cluttered with black-and-white ancestral photographs and flanking vases. Floor lamps with linen shades, silver tea sets, a rosewood pump organ, and a floral wallpaper all add to the lovely room—a cozy spot for a read and for gazing out at the river through French doors or through a pretty curtained bay window.

The Front Porch of America, on Texas Deck, is aptly named for its sweeping views over the bow and furnishings of white wicker chairs and painted rockers. One deck above, the Chart Room is a hangout for the "riverlorian," who helps people get their bearings using flip charts and who spins tales every morning at eight.

Seven categories of cabins are beautifully decorated in elaborate Victorian style with patterned wallpaper and carpets, richly colored bedspreads, and wooden cabinets. Most cabins have cushioned wicker chairs and footstools and French doors that hook open to connect with the open deck. Twin beds are recessed into shallow arched niches, and bathrooms are tiled in black and white.

The *American Queen* is so much larger than her nineteenth-century predecessors that to slide under the numerous bridges on the Ohio and Upper Mississippi Rivers,

the 109-foot-high twin feathered-topped stacks fold forward into cradles and the pilothouse cupola and rooster weather vane come off. Steam whistles are traditionally handed down from one boat to the next, and the *American Queen*'s comes from the steamboat *Jason,* which accepted it from the *City of Memphis,* a boat that Mark Twain piloted. *Note:* As a result of hurricane Katrina, this suspended itinerary resumes in March 2006.

The Itinerary

The Lower Mississippi from New Orleans north to Natchez and Vicksburg is the quintessential stretch of Old Man River featuring what most travelers expect the South to represent, such as elegant plantation homes, Civil War battlefields, a dash of Cajun heritage, and steamboating. All three stern-wheelers cruise here and for this classic antebellum itinerary, we'll have a look at the *American Queen.* Her most frequent cruises from New Orleans had been three- and four-day trips, but this steamboat is too good to waste for anything less than a full week. The itinerary has many variations, but nearly all include the following calls once the steamboat gets beyond the industrial belt near **New Orleans.**

The landing for the Delta Queen steamboats is convenient to New Orleans' downtown for those who arrive early and want to see some of the Crescent City before sailing, so named because of its location at an arcing bend in the river. It's a good twenty-five-minute hike to the foot of Canal Street, but it is much shorter to the end of the 2-mile-long Riverfront Trolley Line that operates between the convention center and the French Quarter and Jackson Square.

Sailing from New Orleans, the heavily commercial waterway extends for some hours, but most departures are at night so it's mostly bright lights and pungent smells that one experiences. Container and bulk shipping gives way to the oil and chemical industries, and by morning the boat will be paddling through rural, mostly flat southern Louisiana.

The river, however, remains an impressive commercial artery used by the world's most impressive tows. As many as thirty to forty barges may be strapped together to form a solid flotilla that can equal the carrying capacity of 1,800 to 2,400 tractor trailers. Typical loads may be grain, salt, lime, coal, rocks, and petroleum products, and because of a tow's enormous size and lack of maneuverability when sailing with the current, a downriver load always has the right of way.

The Lower Mississippi has been tampered with much more than the rest of the river system to improve navigation and flood control. While there are no locks on the lower river, there are long stretches of levees, embankments built to straighten out the river and to prevent periods of high water from spilling off into the adjoining farmlands and flooding fields and towns as so often happened in the past. Some levees are high enough to block the view inland, except from the highest decks, and in other places the long-range vistas remain.

St. Francisville, built on high ground away from the floods that destroyed the first settlement, is best seen on foot for its attractive range of residential styles: antebellum, French colonial, Victorian, neoclassical, and dog trot, a house divided by a breezeway.

On upriver, **Natchez** has by far the largest collection of antebellum homes, numbering more than 200, and several house tours take in two or three of different styles. One, the largest octagon house in the United States, remains unfinished, but it comes with an amazing tale of a mother bringing up the children in the basement after her husband was killed in the Civil War.

Then **Vicksburg,** the site of a great battle during the War Between the States, offers a military park tour, the Gray and Blue Naval Museum, and a Civil War–era gunboat that was dredged up from the muddy Mississippi. The first Coca-Cola was bottled here to be sent out into the country.

If it's spring, fog may rise from the river in the early evening, and the steamboat will make for the nearest stout tree to tie up for the night or until the visibility improves. The *American Queen* conveniently deposits passengers at levee landings, and on the other side, there are a pair of classic antebellum homes to visit. **Houmas House** and **Oak Alley** both feature excellent costumed guides, good interior furnishings, and attractive gardens through which to stroll. They both acted as settings for Bette Davis's horror film *Hush, Hush Sweet Charlotte,* while Oak Alley also served Tom Cruise in *Interview with the Vampire.* Following a visit to the latter, I walked several miles along the levee and wandered back through tiny church communities set among cane fields.

Baton Rouge, the state capital, invariably leads the guides to reciting colorful accounts of Louisiana's Governor Huey P. Long, none of which required any embellishing. The highlight here is Rural Life Museum, a collection of historic buildings that would have been out the back door of the plantation house, such as slave quarters, animal barn, a small store, one-room schoolhouse, overseer's house, and church. Another tour serves as an introduction to Cajun dancing, music, language, customs, and food.

While the Lower Mississippi itself is largely commercial in its most southerly reaches and not especially scenic, this stretch provides an excellent glimpse into the antebellum and Civil War South.

Address/Phone: Delta Queen Steamboat Company, Robin Street Wharf, 1380 Port of New Orleans Place, New Orleans, LA 70130-1890; (800) 543–1949; fax: (504) 585–0630; www.deltaqueen.com

The Ship: *American Queen* was completed in 1995 and has a gross tonnage of 3,707, a length of 418 feet, and a shallow draft.

Passengers: 436; age fifty-five and up, mostly Americans

Dress: Jacket with tie optional at special dinners

Officers/Crew: American

Cabins: 222 cabins, 168 outside; some opening onto the side deck as well as an inside corridor; some with verandas and some with bay windows

Fare: $$$

What's included: Cruise fare and port charges

What's not included: Airfare, shore excursions, drinks, tips

Highlights: Outstanding re-creation of floating American Victoriana, terrific music

Other itineraries: In addition to this cruise aboard the *American Queen,* she also cruises from several additional Ohio and Mississippi River ports, including Pittsburgh, Cincinnati, and St. Louis. The three steamboats together offer a wide range of itineraries on Midwestern rivers, embarking in many different port cities and with cruises themed to big bands, great American performers, the Civil War, fall foliage, old-fashioned holidays, and many more. See the *Delta Queen* and *Mississippi Queen.*

DELTA QUEEN STEAMBOAT'S
Mississippi Queen
Cruising the Ohio River

Delta Queen Steamboat Company is the largest operator of inland river cruises in North America, and its stern-wheelers are American icons. The 414-passenger *Mississippi Queen,* built in 1976, is the second-largest stern-wheeler ever constructed after fleetmate *American Queen.* She seems more like a cruise ship than does the historic *Delta Queen.* This floating re-creation of nineteenth-century Americana has Victorian wall and fabric decor and furniture design alongside modern comfort and safety features.

The Paddlewheel Lounge rises two decks and overlooks the huge churning red wheel, and the Calliope Bar above also faces astern. The calliope is designed to impress

the local town folks that a riverboat is coming, and the passengers take delight in feeling a tinge of importance at arriving in such a magnificent conveyance. The Grand Saloon, forward on the Observation Deck, serves well as the stylish brass-and-glass venue for a celebration of American music in the form of jazz groups, big bands, riverboat shows, Broadway revues, and cabarets. Port and starboard galleries house a card room-cum-lounge and a bar.

Dinner is at two sittings, and the best tables are by the large windows. The very good food is accented with regional flavors, particularly Cajun and Southern ones. Try the stuffed catfish, chilled blackened sirloin of beef, and crawfish en croute for something different.

All 208 cabins have Victorian-style bedspreads and curtains, phones, two-channel radios, and thermostats. Half of the cabins have private verandas, and seventy-three are inside, with the lowest priced having upper and lower berths. Two of the largest face forward and flank the pilot house, and two more face aft over the wheel. Sixteen suites on Promenade Deck and two on Cabin Deck have sitting areas, twin or king beds, baths, and balconies.

The Itinerary

Some river aficionados consider the Ohio to be the most scenic and varied Midwestern waterway because of its twisting nature below Pittsburgh, the high bluffs, and attractive agricultural landscapes. Add to that the small river towns, rust belt cities' active and abandoned industries, a wide variety of graceful bridges, the occasional cross-river ferries, and the impressive arrivals and departures at Pittsburgh and Cincinnati. Most cruises do not cover the entire Ohio River in one go, but include substantial portions such as between Cincinnati and Pittsburgh, or Cincinnati and Louisville to St. Louis or Memphis. Most towns where the steamboats call put out a warm welcome, showing visitors how the river affected their respective roles in the Midwest's cultural, manufacturing, and transportation development.

Pittsburgh, hemmed in by hills and sited where the confluence of the Allegheny and Monongahela Rivers form the Ohio, occupies the spot where steamboating originated in 1811. Embarkation takes place not far from the Golden Triangle, and once out of sight of the modern skyline, the Ohio becomes a feast of smokestack industry, towns that prospered because of the river location, soaring cliffs, and peaceful rural landscapes.

Geography is everything to Pittsburgh's growth. First the site was an Iroquois camp, then strategic forts—Fort Duquesne (French) and Fort Pitt (British)—built where the Monongahela and Allegheny join. After the British took control in November 1758 following the French and Indian War, the permanent fort grew into a settlement and the most prominent landing for traders and settlers heading west via the Ohio water highway. The steamboat trade mushroomed, and then railroads arrived from all directions to form a major transportation hub, the Pennsylvania, Baltimore and Ohio, and Pittsburgh and Lake Erie railroads being the chief carriers.

Nearby Pennsylvania coal mining built the steel industry, and Pittsburgh became an industrial powerhouse, and because of its river valley setting, one of the smoggiest cities in America. All that has changed, and architecturally rich downtown Pittsburgh, known as the Golden Triangle, is clean and clear, and with a compact center, it is easy to navigate on foot. The steamboats lie along the Monongahela side of the Golden Triangle between Fort Point and the Smithfield Street Bridge.

Leaving Pittsburgh, the boat passes Fort Point, PNC Park and Heinz Field, and soon leaves the city behind to enter an increasingly rural stretch of river for the overnight trip to the first stop. The first lock and dam come within 6 miles, and several more follow during the night. The 172 miles to Marietta are one of the loveliest rural stretches of river in the country.

Marietta, the oldest town in Ohio, is a quintessential riverfront community that still exudes its historical importance, and steamboats dock adjacent to a lovely city park. The city, founded in 1787 by the land speculators Ohio Company and Associates, is named after Queen Marie Antoinette, as a tribute to France for the country's help during the American Revolution.

Because of its prime location along the Ohio River, the town grew as a trading center for the Northwest Territory. Banks opened, and agricultural produce from the rich surrounding land came to the city to be shipped elsewhere. Shipbuilding took hold, and the city prospered.

While there are excursions out to the area's attractions, it is also worth spending an independent day on foot. For a terrific photograph of your ship, walk south to the bridge spanning the Ohio and climb the steps to the footpath. By walking halfway to Kentucky, you can have the steamboat set against the city park, its gazebo, the imposing brick Lafayette Hotel, and an attractive row of Victorian houses.

The Ohio River Museum, minutes on foot from the landing, displays steamboat history in models, photographs, and an excellent film. Visit the *W. P. Snyder, Jr.,* the last steam-powered stern-wheel towboat, and explore the crew's living quarters including the cabins, dining saloon, galley, and bath facilities.

Out-of-town excursions include the Lee Middleton Original Dolls factory, America's largest doll making operation, where artisans are molding, hand-painting, and assembling high-quality models. The second stop, the Children's Toy and Doll Museum at Harmar Village, exhibits a collection of dollhouses, dolls, teddy bears, antique metal banks, and games that once entertained and educated generations of children.

The next stretch of the Ohio is marked by wooded bluffs and the river makes lots of twists and turns often blocking out any sign of habitation. Then around the next bend a Victorian river town will appear and the boat signals a greeting with a burst of tunes from the calliope.

Maysville, Kentucky, is one such place. Once a manufacturing city incorporated in 1796 and rising to importance by the 1830s, Maysville fired bricks and made wrought iron fences and gates and ornamental street furnishings such as clocks, lamp posts, benches, and signs. Daniel Boone once ran a tavern in town. The town's prosperity is revealed in a twenty-four-block, 160-building historic district that is on the National Register featuring brick streets and Romanesque, Georgian, and Victorian styles, all walkable from the steamboat landing.

The graceful suspension bridge (1931) spanning the Ohio was the prototype for San Francisco's Golden Gate Bridge and leads to **Ripley, Ohio,** once an important stop on the Underground Railroad and one that served as the setting for Eliza's escape in Harriet Beecher Stowe's *Uncle Tom's Cabin.* The primary visit on the steamboat excursion is to the Ohio Tobacco Museum displaying the farming procedures, tools and equipment, and the role the river played in shipping tobacco to market. The museum, housed in an 1850 Federal/Georgian–style home, is located next to the tobacco warehouses. However, with more tobacco growers selling directly to the manufacturers, the tobacco auctions have declined by 50 percent in the last few years. Tourism is rising in importance to take its place.

No river city provides a more exciting steamboat arrival than **Cincinnati** with the city and its smaller opposites, Newport and Covington, Kentucky, all fronting directly on the Ohio. The river traffic is intense with through barge traffic threading carefully among a flotilla of excursion vessels, dinner boats, and private craft. Consider staying over in a downtown location before or after a cruise.

The city celebrates Tall Stacks, a gathering of steamboats, every few years. It is a huge civic affair that includes open-house boat tours, excursions, and a waterborne parade along the Ohio. The last Tall Stacks took place in the fall of 2003, and the next one is tentatively scheduled for 2007.

The steamboats drop their stages at the Public Landing opposite the Great American Ballpark, home for the Cincinnati Reds and the stadium for the Cincinnati Bengals. The location is between the Roebling Suspension Bridge, once the world's longest suspension bridge and the 1868 prototype for the Brooklyn Bridge, and the Taylor Southgate Bridge carrying U.S. Highway 27.

Just up from the landing, about a ten-minute walk, downtown Cincinnati, anchored by Fountain Square, is the heart of the city. The combination of offices, hotels, and restaurants generates a lot of pedestrian traffic vitality. Make for the 1931 art deco Carew Tower for the view from the forty-eighth story, and be sure to look inside the Hilton Cincinnati Netherland Plaza, a National Historic Landmark. The French-style art deco building features a beautiful main lobby and a Palm Court restaurant executed in a most colorful Egyptian art deco style. Other than having a meal here, the best view is from the mezzanine.

Bus Route #1 leaves from Fifth and Walnut (Fountain Square) and passes the 1888 Richardson Romanesque City Hall en route to the magnificent art deco Cincinnati Union Terminal, built in 1933, and its broad boulevard approach. While Amtrak intercity trains still call here, most of the building houses the Cincinnati Museum Center. In the central Rotunda, a mural covers the dome, and the *Tom Greene,* one of the Greene Line steamboats (predecessor company to Delta Queen) is up there among the city's icons.

Mount Adams, a short taxi ride up to one of Cincinnati's seven hills, combines a trendy residential neighborhood; restaurants, including an atmospheric bistro in a former Rookwood Pottery kiln; leafy Eden Park where the Cincinnati Art Museum is located; and a wonderful Ohio River overlook.

Be sure to try the homegrown Skyline Chili, Cincinnati-style, at one of several restaurant locations. The spicy chili is served simply, such as over a Coney dog or three-, four-, or five-ways; that is, spaghetti with chili topping then one or more combinations of shredded cheddar cheese, diced onions, and red beans.

Address/Phone: Delta Queen Steamboat Company, Robin Street Wharf, 1380 Port of New Orleans Place, New Orleans, LA 70130-1890; (800) 543–1949; fax: (504) 585–0630; www.deltaqueen.com

The Ship: *Mississippi Queen* was completed in 1976 and has a gross tonnage of 3,360, a length of 382 feet, and a shallow draft.

Passengers: 414; age fifty-five and up; mostly Americans

Dress: Jacket and tie optional for special evenings

Officers/Crew: American

Cabins: 208 in a variety of configurations, including 104 with verandas

Fare: $$$

What's included: Cruise fare and port charges

What's not included: Airfare, shore excursions, drinks, tips

Highlights: Musical entertainment aboard and the antebellum South ashore

Other itineraries: In addition to this Ohio River cruise varying between four and five days, the three steamboats offer a variety of river itineraries and embarkation cities such as New Orleans, Memphis, Chattanooga, St. Louis, Louisville, Cincinnati, Pittsburgh, and St. Paul. Theme cruises feature Dixieland music, the Old South, the annual "Great Steamboat Race," and a Kentucky Derby cruise, when she docks in Louisville. See the *American Queen* and the *Delta Queen.*

RIVERBARGE EXCURSION LINES'

River Explorer

Louisiana Bayou Cajun and Creole Cruising

RiverBarge Excursion Lines is the creation of Eddie Conrad, a New Orleans towboat and barge owner. Building on his commercial experience, he constructed two three-deck hotel barges—one (*DeSoto*) for the cabin accommodations and the other (*LaSalle*) housing the public spaces—lashed them together, and had them propelled by a towboat (*Miss Nari*). The complete rig is a sight to behold, having an ocean-liner length of 730 feet and a width of 54 feet, fitting snugly into the locks of the Intracoastal Waterway.

The interior design is spacious, modern in decor, and features huge view windows. My favorite spot is the Guest Pilot House, an observation lounge facing forward, where there are lots of charts and maps to study and communications between river pilots to listen to. The *River Explorer*'s navigating pilot is one deck above, and he welcomes visitors when the barge is tied up.

The Lobby, aft of the Guest Pilot House, provides lounge and banquette seating, twenty-four-hour coffee, and a jumbo cookie jar. Pretty etched glass panels, which depict highway bridges crossing rivers, decorate the seat backs, and a giant steering wheel has been adapted as a centerpiece. The shop for regional and River-Barge souvenirs is called the Louisiana Purchase, and the Governor Chavez is a midships lounge for borrowing books and videos and for playing board games and cards at three large octagonal tables. The Sprague, a bi-level room with mezzanine, provides the setting for local musicians, storytelling, and bingo during the day and after dinner.

All meals, apart from outdoor barbecues, are served in The Galley, a huge, light-filled space on the lowest passenger deck. Breakfast is buffet, with a cook to prepare omelets. Lunch (called dinner here) is also a buffet, with hot and cold selections, occasionally geared to the region, such as catfish and shrimp dishes on the southern excursions. Dinner (called supper) is wait-served and features an appetizer, a soup, a salad, a choice of two entrees, and freshly baked cakes and pies for dessert. Preparation is good to excellent, and the food reflects what most American passengers like when eating out at a proper restaurant. The helpful and upbeat staff serves coffee, tea, drinks, and wine.

Cabins, named after states and arranged in order of their entry into the Union, are larger than average, all with the same layout; those on the higher of the two decks have narrow verandas. Beds are twins or queens with wooden headboards and good individual reading lights. Cabins have windows that slide open, phone, TV/VCR, fridge, a coffeemaker, desk, two chairs, and decent hanging and drawer space for what is a very casual cruise. Bathrooms have full tubs and showers.

Outdoor space, both covered and open, stretches for 500 feet along nearly the complete length of the top deck, with bar service, hot and cold hors d'oeuvres before dinner, and a popcorn machine. There is a jogging/walking track, whirlpool tub, and shuffleboard.

The Itinerary

Most cruises last between six and eight days and travel the Mississippi, Missouri,

Ohio, Cumberland, and Tennessee Rivers and the Intracoastal Waterway, running parallel to the Gulf of Mexico. My eight-night cruise, themed to Cajuns and Creoles, embarked in **New Orleans** and explored remote bayou country and the lower regions of the mighty Mississippi.

The first night docked at New Orleans allowed an afternoon and evening in the French Quarter. Two hours after setting off downriver, the barge passed through the Algiers Lock into the **Intracoastal Waterway** that runs west and southwest across Louisiana and Texas to the Mexican border. The shipping channel, slicing through swamps and marshlands, was completed in 1949.

Following an overnight anchorage well out of sight of human habitation, we transferred to small launches for an exploratory trip into a cypress swamp to spot alligators, nutrias (a kind of rodent), great blue herons, great white egrets, cormorants, and even water moccasins. Then after a night docked at **Morgan City,** a full-day excursion went deep into **Cajun country,** settled by French-speaking Acadians.

The visits included the Joseph Jefferson House, built in 1870; the state's oldest rice company; the historic village of St. Martinville of the poem "Evangeline" fame; and Vermilionville, a collection of original and reconstructed Acadian buildings that represent how the Cajuns lived, worked, worshiped, and played. A very good seafood dinner took place at a lively Cajun dance hall.

Cruising north parallel to the Atchafalaya River, we enjoyed a barbecue lunch out on deck, which included Cajun spiced crayfish. By the afternoon of the fourth day, we left the bayous and entered the **Mississippi River** to tie up at **Baton Rouge,** the Louisiana state capital.

Most everything in Baton Rouge was within walking distance: the old state capitol building; the art deco capitol building; the USS *Kidd,* an authentically restored World War II destroyer; and two gambling boats. En route down the Mississippi, a final call at **Laura Plantation,** built in 1805, showed how a Creole family and their slaves lived.

Tying up at New Orleans in the afternoon of the final full day, we were allowed additional time to enjoy the city before disembarking the next morning. *Note*: Hurricane Katrina will have lingering effects on New Orleans through 2006.

Address/Phone: RiverBarge Excursion Lines, 201 Opelousas Avenue, New Orleans, LA 70114; (888) GO–BARGE or (888) 462–2743, ext. 1; fax: (504) 365–0000; www.riverbarge.com

The Ship: *River Explorer* was built in 1998 and has a gross tonnage of 8,864, a length, including both barges, of 590 feet, plus a 140-foot towboat, and a shallow draft.

Passengers: 198; Americans, fifty-five and up

Dress: Casual at all times

Officers/Crew: American

Cabins: 99; all similar in size; one deck with verandas and one deck without

Fare: $$

What's included: Cruise, port charges, shore excursions, tips

What's not included: Transportation to and from the barge, drinks

Highlights: Seeing America close up from its waterways, aboard a roomy floating home

Other itineraries: In addition to this eight-day Cajuns and Creoles cruise, there are four- to ten-day cruises of the Mississippi, Missouri, Ohio, Cumberland, and Tennessee Rivers and the Intracoastal Waterway along the Gulf Coast to the Mexican border.

CLIPPER CRUISE LINE'S

Yorktown Clipper

Cruising California's Wine Country

Clipper Cruise Line of St. Louis, in business since 1983, attracts a fairly homogeneous crowd of mostly well-traveled folks to its U.S. flag coastal ships *Nantucket Clipper* and *Yorktown Clipper* and its more newly acquired expeditions ships *Clipper Adventurer* and *Clipper Odyssey,* carrying between 102 and 138 passengers.

Aboard the *Yorktown Clipper,* the wraparound forward observation lounge provides a cozy, clubby experience before meals and during informal talks. The big-windowed dining room operates with one open sitting at tables of four to eight. The chefs, trained at the Culinary Institute of America in Hyde Park, New York, prepare excellent domestic fare using high-quality ingredients. There's an easy relationship between the passengers and the young American dining and cabin staff. Dinner's first course is served during cocktail hour, and the hot and cold appetizers include jumbo shrimp, steamed mussels, smoked salmon, and stuffed mushroom caps. In the restaurant the menu offers a soup, two kinds of salads, and a choice of four entrees, such as shrimp scampi, roast duckling, linguine with clam sauce, a pasta, and a vegetable pie, ending with a freshly prepared dessert, cheesecake, or a variety of ice creams. Wines are moderately priced. As an alternative, the observation lounge serves a continental breakfast and a light soup, sandwich, and salad lunch. Entertainment may be a jazz group one evening, a film on another, and talks by the naturalist and chef, but aboard it's mostly socializing among likeminded passengers.

The sixty-nine compact cabins, all outside, typically have parallel twin beds (some L-shaped beds) set before two picture windows, and thirty-eight open onto the promenade for access to the passing scene. There's a desk-cum-vanity, a chair, a half dozen small drawers, two closets, and a tiny bathroom with shower. Outside, fourteen times around the teak promenade equals a mile, and the sun deck above is partly covered and has a bar, but no swimming pool or whirlpool.

The Itinerary

Every spring and autumn, small U.S. flag coastal cruisers sail into San Francisco Bay for three- to five-day exploratory trips along northern California's waterways. The Bay Area easily qualifies as one of the world's greatest natural harbors, its shores fringed by national parklands and some of America's most prized residential communities. At the bay's eastern end, the Sacramento River Delta leads to the Napa and Sonoma Valleys, the country's leading wine growing region.

While a driving holiday is a fine way to explore redwood and vineyard country, a cruise program includes behind-the-scenes visits, expert presentations ashore and on board, and the delights of San Francisco Bay that can be viewed only from the water. While cruising under graceful bridges and past scenic islands, you enjoy the casual style of a large private yacht.

Clipper Cruise Line's 138-passenger *Yorktown Clipper* draws mostly American passengers in their forties to seventies who have an interest in wines, like to sample them at meals, and want to see something of California.

The primary focus is the wine country, and the several estates visited vary from cruise to cruise. The architectural style may be modern California-ranch, Spanish colonial or Spanish mission, wooden Victorian, or a European-imported chateau design. Many vineyards trace their ancestries back to France, Italy, Germany, and Switzerland, and the initial wave of migrants found the soil and climate highly suitable for the European varietals.

The success of the wine industry saved tens of thousands of acres of agricultural land from housing estate land development and preserved the rural landscape. In 1976 California wines grabbed world attention when at a Paris competition Stag's Leap Winery topped Mouton Rothschild, and the region has been well regarded ever since.

Clipper Cruise Line bases its ship at Redwood City at the southern end of San Francisco Bay and not far from San Francisco's Airport.

San Francisco, the City by the Bay, is a must-see from the water. Its parallel streets run from the shore steeply up Knob, Russian, and Telegraph Hills with North Beach, Marina, and the Financial District sandwiched in between. The harbor entrance flanked by dramatic natural headlands is spanned by the graceful Golden Gate Bridge, its towers often poking through a tongue of mist sweeping in from the colder Pacific.

The captain usually takes his ship under the span, and when the ocean swells begin to gently rock the ship, he makes a 180-degree turn to then hug the **Sausalito** waterfront, the town extending for several miles along the Marin County foreshore. The community ranges from a ramshackle houseboat lifestyle to some of the most expensive waterfront property in America, and a walk from the pier reveals it all, including the popular boutique and art gallery district.

An organized excursion visits the U.S. Army Corps of Engineers, caretakers of the inland waterways, where a 1.5-acre, three-dimensional hydraulic Bay Model lays out the Bay's intricate water control system. The ship's route to the Napa Valley is clearly visible as are the San Joaquin River leading inland to Stockton and the Sacramento River to its namesake, California's state capital.

From Sausalito, coaches drive north into the **Muir Woods National Monument** for a stroll among the California redwoods, the world's tallest trees, set in a canyon beneath Mount Tamalpais. A pedestrian tunnel has been carved through one trunk of amazing girth.

Sailing from Sausalito, the ship passes upscale Tiburon and skirts Alcatraz, now a national historic park and once a notorious island prison, and from here many tried to escape but few made it through the same turbulent waters you are traversing.

Nearby Angel Island, even more impressive in height and size and once the Ellis Island of the West, now provides recreational facilities for picnic and hikes. The ship then turns north past Berkeley and under the Richmond–San Rafael Bridge into a widening San Pablo Bay. Some cruises will sail through the narrow Carquinez Strait into the Sacramento Delta, an expansive area of marshlands and natural and man-made waterways. An early morning is likely to give rise to tule fog, a heavy mist that rises from the swampy bullrushes, then burns off in the morning sun.

In Suisun Bay, the laid-up U.S. Reserve Fleet includes handsome pre-containerized cargo liners, steam tankers, and twin-funnel troopships anchored in military precision. The ready reserve fleet is the official status but it is unlikely these ships will again see active service, and in the meantime they exhibit an album of American naval architecture at its finest.

The ship may dock at **Vallejo** at the mouth of the Napa River or continue up it for several hours to land closer to the wine growing region of **Napa** and **Sonoma.** From here coaches take passengers on full-day trips then return to the ship in the late afternoon.

The valleys run north by northwest between a ridge of low mountains rising not much more than 2,500 feet. The region is a major tourist area, more so in the autumn during the harvest season and to a lesser extent in the green spring.

While many of the vineyard names may be familiar and others unfamiliar—such as Domaine Carneros, Silverado, and Niebaum-Coppola—the chardonnays, merlots, pinot noirs, and zinfandels they produce will be. Wine tastings and those served at meals will include both table and premium quality varieties, including sparkling wines using the champagne method. The chateau at Domaine Carneros is one of the most beautiful in America, while the Silverado Vineyard, located in the Stag's Leap region, overlooks the famous Silverado Trail, and the 1883-built Niebaum-Coppola winery is now owned by filmmaker Francis Ford Coppola.

In Napa Town, there's a visit to newly established (2001) Copia: The American Center for Wine, Food & the Arts, a cultural museum dedicated to the American contribution to wine with food.

Following the wine country visits, passengers enjoy a last gala meal, prepared by chefs trained at the Culinary Institute of America's west coast campus at Greystone, formerly the Christian Brothers' Winery. Some cruises include cooking demonstrations and a lunch at the school where the waiters are cooks in training, experiencing what it is like serving the customer.

At the end of the cruise, the arrival back in San Francisco coincides with dawn breaking over one of the world's most beautiful cities. Be sure to be on deck for this special treat. At this point, you may be glad that you planned to stay on for a few days rather than rushing off to the airport.

Address/Phone: Clipper Cruise Line, 11969 Westline Industrial Drive, St. Louis, MO 63146; reservations: (800) 325–0010; brochures: (800) 282–7245; fax: (314) 655–6670; www.clippercruise.com

The Ship: *Yorktown Clipper,* built in 1988, has a gross tonnage of 97 tons, a special U.S. coastal measurement, a length of 257 feet, and a draft of 8 feet.

Passengers: 138; age forty-five and up, nearly all Americans

Dress: Casual at all times, perhaps a jacket at the captain's welcome party

Officers/Crew: American

Cabins: 69; all outside, most with picture windows, none with verandas, but more than half with opening onto a side deck

Fare: $$$

What's included: Cruise only, port charges, shore excursions, wine tastings, and wines aboard ship at lunch and dinner

What's not included: Transportation to and from the ship, tips, alcohol not served at meals

Highlights: Destination-oriented itineraries; relaxed social atmosphere; great meals

Other itineraries: In addition to the above six-day California rivers cruise, offered in the fall, the *Yorktown Clipper* and *Nantucket Clipper,* between them, cruise to Alaska, British Columbia, Sea of Cortez (Mexico), Panama Canal, Caribbean, Orinoco River, East Coast via the Intracoastal Waterway, Chesapeake Bay, Hudson River, New England, Eastern Canada, and Great Lakes. Expedition ships *Clipper Adventurer* and *Clipper Odyssey* take in much of the world: Arctic, Antarctica, Amazon, northern Europe, the Mediterranean, the Far East, Southeast Asia, and Australasia.

LINDBLAD EXPEDITIONS'
Sea Lion and *Sea Bird*
Columbia and Snake Rivers in the Wake of Lewis and Clark

Lindblad Expeditions, the brainchild of Sven-Olof Lindblad, whose father, Lars-Eric, pioneered expedition-style cruising, offers some of the most creative itineraries afloat, employs wonderful naturalists and historians, and attracts well-heeled passengers keen on seeing the world and sharing the experiences.

The sixty-eight-passenger *Sea Lion* and fleetmate *Sea Bird* are not very fancy, but then luxurious accommodations and lounging by the pool are not why most people book. The 152-foot-long ships, really boats, have just four decks, and apart from a half dozen lower-deck cabins with a tiny porthole high in the cabin, rooms are outside doubles with large windows, parallel or angled twins or queen-size beds. All have tiny private bathrooms. Bridge and Upper Deck rooms open onto a covered side promenade, and those on Main Deck open into a central corridor linking the forward observation lounge and bar to the dining saloon. In the spirit of honesty that prevails onboard, there are no cabin keys, and on my cruise no one seemed to worry. Open seating prevails at all meals, and dinner may offer grilled salmon and roast duckling. Breakfast features freshly baked muffins and croissants and special hot dishes, and lunch consists of very good soups and tasty, overstuffed sandwiches. Wines include reds and whites from vineyards overlooking the river.

The Itinerary
The 450-mile inland water route begins wet and well-watered just in from the Pacific Ocean breakers; passes between forested slopes, apple orchards, and vineyards; cuts through wildlife refuges and increasingly semiarid deep gorges; and negotiates eight commercial locks. The upriver expedition is no sedentary deck-chair cruise. Instead, the inflatable Zodiac rafts, with professional naturalists at the helm, take passengers ashore for visits to scenic sites and salmon fish ladders, and on hikes and exploratory trips along small streams.

The Pacific Northwest's Columbia and Snake Rivers are the country's second-largest system, after the Mississippi and Missouri, in terms of length and area drained. Two hundred years ago, at the beginning of the nineteenth century, Meriwether Lewis and William Clark descended the Columbia and Snake in canoes as part of their legendary Western expedition.

The diminutive *Sea Lion* embarks at **Portland,** and at dinnertime the little ship eases away from her berth for a short cruise under the city's many bridges, up the Willamette River, and then out to the **Columbia River** for an upstream overnight sail.

By morning, the Columbia has completely altered its character. The well-watered landscape gives way to semiarid steppes, gracefully tapered buttes, and diminishing signs of habitation. From the deck, the expedition staff points out great blue herons bobbing on the water, marsh hawks in trees, three soaring bald eagles, a white pelican with a 9-foot wing span, and several mule deer on the shore. A series of locks lifts the ship into another world of colorful canyons leading to the

Snake River, its entrance flanked by the world's largest basaltic lava flow. The **Bonneville Dam,** a massive hydroelectric project completed during the Great Depression, was built with a fish ladder allowing migrating steelhead trout and chinook, sockeye, and coho salmon to travel upriver to spawn and then die. This and other dams encountered are controversial subjects today, and some groups would like them all removed, returning the river to a more natural state.

Arriving at Clarkston, located at the confluence of the Snake and Clearwater Rivers on the border with Idaho, there's a choice of excursions. Either follow the Clearwater to visit several campsites that Lewis and Clark used during their trek to the Pacific, or take a high-speed jetboat into Idaho's **Hells Canyon,** the deepest gorge in North America. The sluggish Snake River becomes increasingly turbulent on the way upstream, making it difficult to imagine the turn-of-the-twentieth-century stern-wheelers climbing through the white-water rapids, even with the aid of cables. The nimble jetboat noses up to 3,000-year-old Native American petroglypghs painted on the flat rocks, and we spot mountain bighorn sheep hundreds of feet up the cliff face.

Returning downstream, the *Sea Lion* passes into the mouth of the **Palouse River** to go in search of deer, beaver, and birds. Take to the kayaks or Zodiacs for a leisurely paddle up to Palouse Falls, and then the ship's crew prepares an outdoor barbecue of salmon and steaks during the passage down the Snake River. The midstream islands are set against a backdrop of orange and red rock cliffs, and the ground cover exhibits the colors of yellow rabbit brush, pink and gray buckwheat, blue astor, and loose brown tumbleweed.

For many the scenic highlight comes during the swift passage through the narrow

Columbia River Gorge, flanked by steep forested cliffs and 620-foot-high, pencil-thin Multnomah Falls visible on the south side. A stop is made at the Columbia Gorge Discovery Center with exhibits on the area's history and geology. One film reveals how the gorge was formed by violent volcanic upheavals and raging floods. Another film shows the building of the Columbia River Scenic Highway that leads to Multnomah Falls. The displays include a working model of a stationary steam engine, steamboat models, black-and-white photos showing industries along the river, ordinary people at work on boats, log jams, and Indians fishing. An exhibit on the Lewis and Clark Expedition illustrates how Lewis divided his equipment needs into seven distinct categories: arms and accoutrements, camp equipment and provisions, clothing, medicines, mathematical instruments, transportation, and Indian presents, the last named items brought to meetings with the Indians for procurement of guides, food, and horses.

After sailing overnight at dawn, in the half-light of a near full moon, I watched the Pacific breakers pounding hard on the Columbia Bar, a sand spit that stretches part way across the river's misty mouth. In the course of time, over 200 major ships and many more small craft had come to grief on the bar. You can feel the gentle Pacific swells and share in the excitement that Lewis and Clark must have experienced at the end of their lengthy westward trek.

The ship ties up at **Astoria,** once a fur trading post established by John Jacob Astor and now a hillside lumber port dotted with Victorian houses. The pier is adjacent to the Columbia Bar lightship *Columbia,* Coast Guard cutter *Steadfast,* and the Columbia River Maritime Museum. Don't miss the twenty-minute walk up Coxcomb Hill to 125-foot Astoria Column that dominates the landscape from its lofty position. Built in 1926, colorful circular story murals surrounding the base show the city's settlement, and 164 spiral steps lead up to a wonderful view of the river meeting the Pacific breakers, and like a layered Chinese painting, the folds of Cascade Range, woodland, and farms. An excursion drives out to Fort Clatsop where the replication reveals the primitive living conditions that Lewis and Clark faced during the very wet winter of 1805–1806. Costumed park rangers demonstrate the making of fire with flint and steel, and they relate tales of how miserable the men were, especially as their clothes never completely dried out. If the day is damp, you are likely to get the picture, but if sparkling, it is much harder to imagine their misery in so beautiful a setting.

On the last evening, cruise upstream from the Columbia's mouth to **Portland,** and consider staying the night, perhaps best before the cruise. Known as the "City of Roses," Portland has developed into a popular destination, for its thriving late nineteenth- and early twentieth-century city center, anchored by Pioneer Courthouse Square, which is laid with 64,000 bricks inscribed with names of those who helped rebuild the plaza; the Willamette waterfront; and the Rose Test and Japanese Gardens. On Saturday and Sunday, the so-called Saturday Market is a huge draw for its open-air handicraft, clothing, and jewelry stalls.

Address/Phone: Lindblad Expeditions, 96 Morton Street, New York, NY 10014; (212) 765–7740 or (800) 397–3348; fax: (212) 265–3370; www.expeditions.com

The Ship: *Sea Lion* (and *Sea Bird*) were built in 1981 and have a gross tonnage of 99.7, a special U.S. Coast Guard measurement, a length of 152 feet, and a draft of 8 feet.

Passengers: 68; ages fifty and up, almost exclusively Americans

Dress: Casual at all times

Officers/Crew: American

Cabins: 34 tiny outside cabins, 30 opening onto the promenade and 4 on the lower deck with a portlight high in the room

Fare: $$$

What's included: All shore excursions, entrance fees, tips to guides ashore, port charges

What's not included: Airfares, alcoholic beverages, tips to crew

Other itineraries: In addition to the above seven-night Columbia and Snake itinerary, offered in May, September, and October, the *Sea Lion* and *Sea Bird* cruise up to Alaska and south to the Sea of Cortez and Baja California. The *Polaris* and the *Islander* are based in the Galápagos Islands, and the deep-sea expedition ship *National Geographic Endeavour,* the former *Caledonian Star,* sails to Antarctica, South America, and Europe.

AMERICAN WEST STEAMBOAT COMPANY'S

Queen of the West

Stern-wheeler Cruise up the Columbia and Snake

The American West Steamboat Company began trading in the Pacific Northwest in 1995, operating a diesel-driven stern-wheeler along three rivers that served as regular trading routes since the middle of the nineteenth century. Although considerably smaller than the Delta Queen Steamboat Company's three stern-wheelers, the ships' ambience and purpose are similar, a destination-oriented cruise with a strong onboard musical program designed for older Americans.

The 163-passenger *Queen of the West* and her new consort, the 235-passenger *Empress of the North,* ply the Columbia, Snake, and Willamette Rivers on seven-night voyages, some longer, nearly year-round, offering the most sailings of any operator. The itinerary and the shore programs differ from some seasonal cruise operators, and the boats are dedicated to this part of the world with the decor appropriately and attractively reflecting Indian and pioneering traditions of the Pacific Northwest.

Externally, the 230-foot *Queen of the West* has a simplified profile of a stern-wheel steamboat while the interiors echo a turn-of-the-twentieth-century style using modern materials. Good reproduction furnishings provide seating in the lounges and cabins, and elaborate metal moldings replicate tin and plaster-style ceilings. A splendid collection of full-color prints of Pacific Northwest Native Americans and early pioneers share corridor and stateroom walls with large framed black-and-white photographs of last century's western river steamboats.

The two principal public rooms, the Columbia Showroom and the Paddlewheel Lounge, are set up for watching the entertainment, a resident trio and pianist and engaging singing groups and guest bands that board for the evening. One night features big-band dance music, another a barber shop quartet, and a third country and western. In addition, a historian gives talks from the deck.

The attractive chandeliered dining room seats all passengers at one open sitting, and half the tables are positioned next to windows. The food is consistently good American fare. Dinner begins with a salad, then includes soup and a choice of three entrees such as grilled salmon, lobster tail, a New York–cut steak, or half a roast duck, and freshly baked cakes and pies or a fruit plate. All breads and pastries are baked on board, and lunch offers a salad, sandwich, or hot entree such as pasta or lasagna. Light continental breakfast, hot dog lunches, and a twenty-four-hour beverage and popcorn service are available in the covered top deck Calliope Bar and Grill. Two decks have a wraparound promenade, and all four passenger decks are linked by a well-used elevator located amidships.

The seventy-three outside cabins, twenty-three with private verandas, are especially large for a vessel of this size. Full-height wooden armoires provide ample storage, and bedside tables have adequate drawer space. All cabins have large-view windows and TVs with a half-dozen cable channels, and a good selection of more recent films are available for use with the VCRs. Queen-size and twin beds are available, and all accommodations have showers.

The Itinerary

The Pacific Northwest's **Columbia** and **Snake Rivers** are America's second-largest system, after the Mississippi and Missouri, in terms of length and area drained. At the beginning of the nineteenth century, Meriwether Lewis and William Clark descended the Columbia and Snake as part of their legendary Western expedition. This cruise retraces a portion of their history-making route, and there are two additional variations to the itinerary described here.

The *Queen of the West* paddles away from its landing to first cruise the Willamette, passing through downtown Portland, continuing upstream a bit farther, then turning back to join the Columbia. By the next morning the boat enters the beautiful **Columbia River Gorge** and locks through a couple of impressive dams. The Bonneville Dam's lock and its 105-foot vertical lift is 20 feet greater than the Panama Canal's three Gatun Locks combined.

At The Dalles, visit the Columbia Gorge Discovery Center, providing palatable background to the geological origins of the region, Native American history, the Oregon Trail, and the now-controversial damming of the Columbia River. At **Bonneville Dam** see the turbine operations and the salmon fish ladder, and then drive parallel to the river to 620-foot-high **Multnomah Falls.** At the grain port of Umatilla, the route inland follows the Oregon Trail and pays a visit to **Pendleton**'s Rodeo Grounds to watch cowboy roundup activities, and also stops at a Native American Center for a dance program, oral history, and exhibits.

The landscape changes to semiarid steppes, gracefully tapered buttes, and diminishing signs of habitation bordering the Snake River en route upriver to **Clarkston, Washington.** An excursion is first made to Nez Perce National Historic Park in Indian Territory, and then by jetboat into **Hells Canyon,** the deepest gorge in North America, where there's a good chance to see wildlife and ancient petroglyphs.

Cruising downriver with different stretches seen during daylight hours, a stop is made at **Maryhill,** a mansion turned European and Native American art museum located high on a cliff, and another stop for tasting the great wines of Oregon, Washington, and Idaho, some of which appear on the steamboat's wine list.

Passing through the Columbia River Gorge and landing at Longview, Washington, an excursion drives through the devastated countryside to a viewpoint overlooking the still-active volcano **Mount St. Helens,** its peak lowered by 1,300 feet in a matter of minutes during a cataclysmic volcanic explosion in May 1980.

The *Queen of the West* ties up at **Astoria,** established as a fur trading post at the mouth of the Columbia River by John Jacob Astor, and today it's a lumber port dotted with seventy-one Victorian buildings listed on the National Register. The landing is adjacent to the Columbia River Maritime Museum, a well-laid-out repository of ship models, historic photographs, paintings, and steamboat relics. The excursion includes reconstructed **Fort Clatsop,** where Lewis and Clark spent a miserable wet winter in 1805–1806, and an hour's stop at the popular wood-shingled resort of **Cannon Beach** fronting on the Pacific Ocean.

On the last afternoon, the boat sails overnight up the Columbia to the Portland landing for disembarkation. Consider staying a night before or after the cruise to visit the "City of Roses," its well-tended parks and gardens, and thriving nineteenth- and early twentieth-century downtown.

Address/Phone: American West Steamboat Company, 2101 Fourth Avenue, Suite 1150, Seattle, WA 98121; (800) 434–1232 or (206) 621–0913; fax: (206) 340–0975; www.americanweststeam boat.com

The Ship: *Queen of the West* was built in 1995 and is 230 feet in length with a shallow draft.

Passengers: 163 double occupancy, mostly Americans fifty-five and up

Dress: Casual

Officers/Crew: All American

Cabins: 73, all outside with some large suites and 23 with verandas

Fare: $$$

What's included: Cruise and shore excursions

What's not included: Transportation to and from the ship, port charges, drinks, and tips

Highlights: A great variety of scenery and activities, enjoyed aboard a gallery of Pacific Northwest history

Other itineraries: Besides these seven-day Columbus–Snake cruises, which operate between mid-February and late December, the 2003-built *Empress of the North* makes eleven-day one-way Inside Passage cruises between Seattle and Juneau from late May to early September.

HAPAG-LLOYD'S
C. Columbus
Cruising the Great Lakes

Offering late summer into early autumn cruises, the 420-passenger *C. Columbus* (commonly known as *Columbus*) attracts a mixture of German-speaking and English-speaking passengers, the latter growing in numbers but still much in the minority. Language is no problem as the Austrian, German, and Filipino crew speaks good English, and the menus, daily programs, lectures, entertainment, and shore excursions are all bilingual. However, on some sightseeing trips during my ten-night September cruise from Toronto to Chicago, I found the local Canadian or American guides so enthusiastic about speaking German that the English version got short shrift, and on board, the German lecturer was better informed than the Scottish-American one.

The ship's atmosphere is traditional and genteel. The nationalities mix well, and at breakfast and lunch in the lido buffet one might elect to share a table with English-speaking Europeans and join them on coach trips and site visits.

The German-built, 14,903-ton *Columbus* was completed in 1997 for Hapag-Lloyd, a long-standing firm that also operates the highly rated *Europa* and expedition ships *Hanseatic* and *Bremen*. The 205 cabins are of average size, and 158 are outside with large picture windows, roomy en suite facilities, bathrobes, hair dryer, TV, telephone, private safe, and stocked mini-bar with typical charges.

The main lounge seats all passengers for the nightly cabaret entertainment, dancing to a five-piece Ukrainian band,

and informal talks. The restaurant, operating with a single sitting at assigned tables, offers a very well-prepared international menu with lots of local fruit and vegetables, fresh fish when available, and a nightly German specialty such as wild pheasant, venison, and duck. The lido buffet's multiple island stations reduces queuing, and daily changing selections cater to European, English, and North Americans tastes. One festive on-deck midday picnic featured an Oktoberfest menu with complimentary steins of German beer. Many passengers then dozed off for the afternoon.

A cozy wine bar, quiet side gallery seating, observation lounge with comfortable cushioned rattan chairs, card room, library, shop, gymnasium, sauna, outdoor pool, and ample deck space on several levels round out the facilities. No one I spoke to remotely missed a casino or Broadway-style entertainment.

The Itinerary

Cruising the Great Lakes had been fashionable from the mid-nineteenth century until the mid-1960s. Giant side-wheel paddle steamers linked Toronto, Buffalo, Cleveland, Detroit, and Chicago with Georgian Bay resorts, Michigan's Upper Peninsula, Isle Royale's natural wilderness, and serene, auto-free Mackinac Island.

One by one, the early twentieth-century steamboats were retired, and the seasonal trade died away, leaving only very small ships carrying fewer than one hundred passengers. Over thirty years passed before the first seagoing cruise ship, Hapag-Lloyd's 420-passenger *C. Columbus,* ventured into the lakes. Built to the lock requirements of the Welland Canal, the ship's overhanging bridge wings swivel inward to clear the chamber walls.

The first Europeans to come this way were Spanish, French, and English explorers; then fur traders, prospectors, missionaries, and farmers followed. Camaraderie and conflict developed with the Native Americans, resulting in European domination and the Indians largely relegated to reservations. Their ancestors and cultural traditions live on today and are shared with visitors.

Poets and writers, captivated by the region's natural beauty, wrote of the majesty of Niagara Falls, the lovely wooded islands of Georgian Bay, steep cliffs fringing Lake Superior, and sand dunes piled up along the shores of Lake Michigan.

Abundant natural resources generated waterborne trade in coal and iron ore, lumber and grain, carried by giant 1,000-foot lake ships whose handsome split-island design exists nowhere else in the world. A gracefully rounded pilothouse up forward is separated by hundreds of feet of cargo space from the aft superstructure, machinery, and often tall stack.

To provide continuous navigation from westernmost Lake Superior eastward to Montreal and Quebec, the Soo Locks tamed the St. Mary's River flowing into Lake Huron, the Welland Canal bypassed Niagara Falls to link Lakes Erie and Ontario, and the St. Lawrence Seaway provided safe passage through the river's white rapids.

Prior to embarking the *Columbus* in **Toronto,** many passengers first take a side trip to **Niagara Falls.** Then under way, the all-day transit of the **Welland Canal** sees the ship being lifted 320 feet from Lake Ontario to Lake Erie, nearly four times greater than that of the Panama Canal. On the upward passage, giant ore and grain carriers fill the multiple locks high above, and we pass under lift-bridges and exchange greetings with visitors watching from land-side observation platforms.

Exiting into Lake Erie in the late afternoon, the *Columbus* sails overnight arriving at sunrise to follow the Detroit River to tie up at Windsor on the Canadian side. Most take the day trip to the **Henry Ford Museum** and **Greenfield Village** just west of Detroit.

The fabulous indoor collections feature scores of antique and classic automobiles, including the presidential limousine in which John F. Kennedy was shot, auto advertising posters, videos of early car and caravan travel, railway locomotives, aircraft, farm equipment, and kitchen appliances. Outside, Greenfield Village re-creates an American town bordering on a village green with examples of residential houses spanning three centuries, an operating steam railway and locomotive turntable, open touring cars and buggies to ride, and a paddleboat to cruise the small lake.

Later that same day, we sail into Lake Huron to enter island-studded Georgian Bay and anchor off **Midland**, a small Ontario port town, to witness a demonstration of aboriginal Canadian culture and traditions in an enclosed Huron Village.

Docking on the Canadian side of **Sault Ste. Marie,** separate sets of Canadian and American locks tame the St. Mary's River rapids flowing from Lake Superior into Lake Huron. During the call, most passengers elect to ride the scenic route of the Algoma Central Railway to a picnic site and hiking trails deep in beautiful Agawa Canyon, where autumn leaves were just beginning to show their colors.

Cruising westward across Lake Superior, the *Columbus* docks at **Thunder Bay,** a huge grain port where Canada's prairie province wheat harvest transfers from rail to laker. Ashore, the main attractions include Old Fort William, a former British fur trading post and fortification, and the unusual rock formations deep in Ouimet Canyon.

At the southwestern corner of Lake Superior, **Duluth**'s Depot Museum, housed in a chateau-style, late nineteenth-century stone station, offers a major rail collection that includes a railway post office, one of the world's largest steam locomotives, that North American curiosity the caboose, colorful china and tableware from the once mighty Union Pacific, Great Northern, Santa Fe, Burlington, and New York Central, and a dramatic video showing a huge snowplow operating at speed to clear the tracks then derailing in a spectacular pileup. The railway station serves a scenic lakeshore tourist line, while the city's landscaped waterfront has a 3-mile-long promenade, a beautiful rose garden, and maritime displays including tugboats and a traditional steam-powered laker.

Leaving Duluth, it's a full day on the lake before retracing the route along the St. Mary's River and through Soo Locks into Lakes Huron and Michigan.

Going ashore at **Mackinac Island,** walk the narrow streets of a white wooden nineteenth-century town where automobiles have been banned since before 1900. One can circumnavigate the entire island on a footpath in about two hours. The village nestles beneath the mighty turreted Grand Hotel, the world's largest summer resort, featuring a colonnaded front porch 660 feet in length; a handsome, light-filled restaurant; intimate parlors scattered on several floors; traditional wood-paneled accommodations, including five suites decorated to the style of five living presidential first ladies; terraced lawns for bocce ball and croquet; tennis courts; two golf courses; and cascading flower gardens.

On the final afternoon, the *Columbus* sails under the soaring Mackinac Bridge linking the state of Michigan with its Upper Peninsula, then cruises south overnight to **Chicago.** Awake to the rising sun reflecting off a majestic skyline that easily matches Manhattan's, with classic early skyscrapers set against a backdrop of soaring newer glass and steel office towers and hotels.

The *Columbus* ties up at the Navy Pier, a combination Mecca, Coney Island, Crystal

Palace, stained-glass museum, and festival marketplace, stretching a half mile out into the lake. It's an exciting place to disembark and an option to stay an extra day or two in Chicago and sign up for one the Architectural Foundation's superb tours.

Address/Phone: For Great Lakes Cruises contact the Great Lakes Cruise Company, 3270 Washtenaw Avenue, Ann Arbor, MI 48104; (888) 891–0203; fax: (734) 677–1428; www.greatlakescruising.com. The ship's parent company Hapag-Lloyd has an English-language Web site with more information on all their ships: www.hl-cruises.com

The Ship: The *C. Columbus* was built in 1997 and has a gross tonnage of 14,903, a length of 473 feet, and a draft of 17 feet.

Passengers: 420, forty-five and up, mostly German-speaking, with Americans and Canadians coming aboard for the bilingual Great Lakes' cruises

Dress: Casual, and two nights jacket and tie

Officers/Crew: German officers, and German/Austrian/Swiss and Filipino crew

Cabins: 205, average size, with 158 outside; just two with balconies

Fare: $$

What's included: Cruise fare, port charges

What's not included: Transportation to and from the ship, shore excursions, drinks, tips

Highlights: A friendly, well-run ship; the only deep-sea ship currently offering Great Lakes cruises

Other itineraries: The *C. Columbus* caters to German-speaking passengers for the remainder of the year, while the highly rated 408-passenger *Europa* offers selected bilingual trips on its worldwide itineraries, and the expedition ships 184-passenger *Hanseatic* and 164-passenger *Bremen* cater to U.S. special-interest groups and individual bookings.

ST. LAWRENCE CRUISE LINES'
Canadian Empress
Steamboating the St. Lawrence River

St. Lawrence Cruise Lines is a family operation based in Kingston, Ontario, that started in 1981 with the sixty-six-passenger *Canadian Empress*. Externally, the ship is odd-looking, whereas her interiors faithfully re-create the warm atmosphere of a turn-of-the-twentieth-century Canadian steamboat. The Grand Saloon on Rideau Deck is a fine period combination dining room and lounge, from its pressed white tin ceiling to the red, orange, and yellow Axminster carpet.

Meals aboard may be one sitting or two, depending on the shore program.

Main dishes at lunch and dinner include fresh fillet of perch, tender roast pork, and succulent roast beef. The soups are uniformly good, but the salads rather nondescript, and desserts are simple cakes, pastry, and puddings. The young waitresses, in keeping with the period decor, wear attractive long, formal, dark-blue skirts and white blouses at night and blue-and-white sailor suits during the day. Entertainment features a band for dancing and sing-along, followed by a shore-side campfire weenie roast.

The thirty-two cabins are priced in four different categories, but twenty-eight are virtually identical, differing only in location. Most have parallel twin beds (four offer double beds) with the pillow-end set beneath the windows that open. The rooms are small, but during the day there is ample floor space, with one bed raised and the other becoming a sofa. Rosewood trim, red curtains and bedspreads, white walls, and white tin ceiling lend a pleasant air. All the cabins, apart from the four most expensive, have a pipe rack and hooks rather than a closet, and a curtain, rather than a separate stall, shields the shower from the toilet.

Observation decks placed fore and aft provide sheltered open-air viewing. The Sun Deck, running nearly the full length of the ship, offers yellow-and-white canvas director's chairs and yellow chaise longues, a relaxing setting to watch a game on the giant checkerboard, the pieces maneuvered with the help of hooked poles, plus shuffleboard and kite flying.

The Itinerary

The *Canadian Empress* sails from **Quebec City,** with its ramparts, city walls, and Old World charm, for a rural stretch of the St. Lawrence punctuated with village churches. Montreal's Market Basin is conveniently situated for visiting **Old Montreal,** and soon after sailing, the ship enters the **St. Lawrence Seaway**'s first set of seven locks that create a series of controlled channels and pools. In minutes the *Empress* rises from the gloomy depths of a dank chamber on a flood of gravity-flow water to reveal the broad countryside beyond. Shortly after completing the transit through St. Catherine's Lock, the *Canadian Empress* ties up, still within sight of the city lights atop Mont-Royal. Great Lakes iron ore and grain carriers slide silently by during the night, gently rocking the little ship.

Upper Canada Village, highlight of the trips ashore, is a composite of houses, public and farm buildings, and churches spanning more than a hundred years of Canadian architecture. This working community came about in 1961, to save something important from each of the eight towns that would soon be submerged by St. Lawrence Seaway construction. In the circa-1800 Ross-Baffin House, women explain how to make colorful quilts for the village beds and how to hook rugs for the floors. The Greek Revival Chrysler Hall offers a beautiful slide presentation. Next door the bakery ovens produce fresh loaves of bread that will soon appear on *Canadian Empress* tables at lunchtime.

Fort Wellington served as a British garrison during the War of 1812 and later as a Royal Canadian Rifle Regiment to protect shipping. On the U.S. side the Frederic Remington Art Museum displays the master of Western American art's paintings, watercolors, and bronzes depicting heroic and savage scenes of cowboys, soldiers, and Indians. The Antique Boat Museum houses the largest collection of inland water recreational boats in the world.

On the final day the *Canadian Empress* cruises among the fairyland of the rocky and wooded **Thousand Islands,** on which stand an enormous variety of simple and elaborate, shingled, clapboard, and stone summer houses. The American Narrows once attracted Helena Rubenstein, Mary Pickford, Irving Berlin, and John Jacob Astor. The granddaddy of all, **Boldt Castle**—a huge eclectic, medieval-style fortress—was never finished with 120 rooms, formal gardens, and outbuildings. A final tour includes the Thousand Islands Skydeck for a panoramic view from 350 feet. The cruise ends approaching **Kingston,** its well-proportioned skyline punctuated by the attractive limestone buildings of the Royal Military College, Old Port Henry, and City Hall.

Address/Phone: St. Lawrence Cruise Lines, 253 Ontario Street, Kingston, Ontario, Canada K7L 2Z4; (613) 549–8091 or (800) 267–7868; fax: (613) 549–8410; www.StLawrenceCruiseLines.com

The Ship: *Canadian Empress,* built in 1981, has a displacement tonnage of 321, a length of 108 feet, and a shallow draft of 4.9 feet.

Passengers: 66; age fifty-five and up, divided between Americans and Canadians

Dress: Casual; jacket and maybe a tie one night

Officers/Crew: Canadian

Cabins: 32; tiny but all outside with windows, a few forward with portholes

Fares: $$

What's included: Cruise, shore excursions

What's not included: Airfare and, if required, rail fare to embarkation port, drinks, tips

Highlights: Varied scenery, the Seaway, Upper Canada Village, friendly ambience on ship

Other itineraries: In addition to this six-night cruise from Quebec to Kingston, the ship also offers five-night cruises between Kingston and Ottawa and a three-night Thousand Islands cruise. The season runs from early May to the end of October.

ONTARIO WATERWAY CRUISES'
Kawartha Voyageur
Exploring the Trent-Severn Waterway

In 1982 a farming family named Ackert went into the cruising business by offering overnight trips here and along the 125-mile Rideau Canal, the latter connecting Kingston and Ottawa, Canada's former and present capital. Between mid-May and mid-October, the forty-five-passenger *Kawartha Voyageur* offers three different five- and six-night itineraries.

At first sight docked at a downtown Peterborough marina, the trim blue-and-white vessel resembles an overgrown houseboat. As you step aboard, the main deck corridor leads to twenty-three outside cabins, minute by deep-sea cruise ship standards. Twenty-one doubles are fitted with twin beds, open shelves, pipe racks for hanging clothes, a curtained-off sink and toilet, and a large screened window that opens. Commodious showers with dressing rooms are located at the end of the passageway. Two additional

cabins cater to the handicapped and single traveler. On the deck above, a cheerful observation lounge occupies the forward end with a one-sitting dining room amidships and a tiny library alcove off to the side. Aft is the galley and crew quarters for the captain, first mate, and an all-female crew. An open deck above runs the full length, and additional covered decks are located fore and aft on the main deck.

The family butcher provides the dinner meats, such as baked ham with candied yams, chicken breasts in melted Swiss cheese with brown and wild rice, and farm sausages with sauerkraut. The bran muffins, banana bread, lemon meringue pie, and English trifle are all baked on board. Though there is no choice of menu, most passengers eat this kind of food at home, so the only "no thank you" would be for seconds. On average the mostly retired passengers are equally divided between Canadians and Americans who come to enjoy a slow-paced, scenic cruise with other genial folks. Many return to complete all three itineraries—Peterborough–Big Chute, Peterborough–Kingston, and Kingston–Ottawa.

The Itinerary

Embarking at **Peterborough, Ontario,** then not an hour into the cruise, the *Kawartha Voyageur* encounters a massive concrete structure and slides into an open chamber, and as the gates close behind, several small boats settle into a second parallel tub 65 feet above. Without getting too complicated, an extra foot of water in the upper chamber causes it to descend while raising its opposite, and soon passengers standing at the stern are peering over a precipice to the channel far below.

Captain Marc Ackert, along with his brother John, constitute the second generation to own and operate the boat, while their wives, Robin and Joy, do the supplying and run the home office in **Orillia,** the largest town we visited. During the day intrepid Captain Marc Ackert takes us ashore to the nineteenth-century home of Stephen Leacock, Canada's Mark Twain, warns us to sit down when we are about to pass under a low bridge, points out an osprey nest, offers freshly baked cookies to lock masters to speed our way through twenty-two locks, and entertains us at the keyboard one night after dinner. He lets us loose on small canal towns to shop or search for historical curiosities and tells us when we might go for a walk between closely spaced locks. We tie up at night, usually adjacent to a quiet park, and get under way after breakfast, threading along wooded waterways dotted with summer camps and through areas devoid of human habitation. Then without warning, the boat comes to a vast expanse of water, makes the crossing of Lake Simcoe, and enters yet another twisting channel.

On the final morning we dock adjacent to the **Big Chute Marine Railway,** an ingenious mechanism for lifting boats around a Severn River waterfall. Boats slide into a submerged transfer platform, and once they're tied down, the structure rises on rails out of the water, crosses a highway protected by gates and flashing lights, and then descends to settle back into the river below. What takes five days to cover by water is but two and a half hours by bus, returning passengers to their cars or to connecting transportation.

Address/Phone: Ontario Waterway Cruises, Box 6, Orillia, Ontario, L3V 6H9 Canada; reservations: (800) 561–5767; inquiries: (705) 327–5767; fax: (705) 327–5304; www.ontariowaterwaycruises.com

The Ship: *Kawartha Voyageur* was built in 1983, enlarged in 1995, and has a length of 120 feet and a shallow draft.

Passengers: 45; mostly fifty-five and up, split between Americans and Canadians

Dress: Casual at all times

Officers/Crew: Canadian

Cabins: 23; 21 tiny twins, 1 handicapped-equipped, and 1 single

Fare: $$

What's included: Cruise, tips, port charges, excursions, and bus back to the starting point

What's not included: Transportation to and from the ship, drinks

Highlights: Scenic waterway cruising

Other itineraries: Besides this five-night cruise between Peterborough and Big Chute, operating between mid-May and mid-October in both directions, the *Kawartha Voyageur* makes five-night cruises between Kingston and Ottawa and Kingston and Peterborough.

What's included: Transatlantic fare only

What's not included: Airfare, port charges, tips

Highlights: Crossing aboard the world's largest and best-known ship

Other itineraries: Besides these regular transatlantic crossings between New York and Southampton, England, the *Queen Mary 2* cruises from New York, Fort Lauderdale, and Southampton. The *Queen Elizabeth 2* now cruises mainly from Southampton and makes the annual world cruise.

OCEANIA CRUISES'
Insignia
Blissful Days at Sea Bound for the Mediterranean

Oceania Cruises got its start with a single ship, the 684-passenger *Regatta* in December 2003, and has since added the virtually identical *Insignia* and *Nautica* to the fleet. The trio once formed part of the eight-ship Renaissance Cruises, built between 1998 and 2001, until that company folded and the ships dispersed.

While the layout remains much the same, Oceania Cruises has upgraded many aspects of food service, décor, and amenities to provide an extremely good value for money whether choosing a sea journey such as this one or a more port-intense Mediterranean cruise.

The interior design is English country house hotel via the Bombay Company, so the overall quality of materials varies, but the effect is both homey and comfortable.

The casino's adjacent bar lounge typifies the period atmosphere with dark wood paneling, rich Oriental carpets and heavy draperies, cushy sofas and chairs, decorative sconces, and a marble fireplace. It's just the place to gather for a drink before or after dinner. High up, the Horizon Lounge, another favorite spot, is light-filled and with stunning wraparound views. A white-glove afternoon tea takes place every afternoon at sea.

When first entering the library, one might immediately wish for a damp day to be able to squirrel away with a good book seated in a high-back chair facing the fireplace beneath a raised ceiling featuring a painted tropical bird setting. The open shelves contain an excellent selection of both fiction and nonfiction, and an honor system prevails. Additional places to roost are the card room, a computer room with ample stations, spa, and the main show lounge for cabaret, orchestral concerts, and jazz and blues.

There is a choice of four restaurants and a wide window of dining hours, and consistent preparation and presentation is evident throughout. The Grand Dining Room seats fully half the ship at one time, and it does get noisy under the low ceiling sections when full. You generally sit with other passengers unless you arrive with your own party. This way, you meet other passengers, and if available, you can request a table alone. The tables to the sides and at the stern are certainly preferable those to the middle. The international menu changes daily.

Two specialty restaurants, both seating less than one hundred, are located high up and aft on Deck 10, and while reservations are required, there is no extra charge. Toscana is Italian with a set menu and a daily chef's special. Roast garlic veal tenderloin with wild mushrooms and gnocchi in a creamy pesto sauce are favorites. The Polo Grill offers a set steak and seafood card featuring prime ribs, filet mignon, rack of lamb, broiled lobster tail, and surf and turf.

For informality at the end of the day, the aft-facing Terrace Café one deck down becomes a Spanish tapas restaurant with dining inside or out under the night sky. Breakfast and lunch take place here and in the main restaurant. During the day, Waves, at poolside, dishes up grilled dishes, salads, and sandwiches.

Service throughout the ship is excellent, and most of the staff is European, and many are from the Renaissance days, so they know the ship and the type of passengers they are serving. Most are semiretired or retired Americans along with other good English-speakers. Since there are absolutely no facilities for children, few will ever be present. Smoking is strictly confined to a miniscule area on deck.

The promenade decks, truncated at both ends by public rooms, provide a peaceful place to read, look at the sea, and ultimately nap. A dozen cushioned wooden deck chairs each side see few passersby. Elsewhere, there is no dearth of chairs, out around the lido pool and under cover, nor is there any need to save spots.

The cabins, nearly all outside and two-thirds with partly partitioned dividers, are of a moderate size with room for a small sitting area with a two-seat sofa and chair. All the bed linens, down pillows, and duvets are of top quality. Bathrooms, however, are adequate for one person at a time, with a small shower. There is plenty of storage and adequate hanging space, but the beds are not high enough to stow most large suitcases beneath. Amenities include

twenty-four-hour room service, TV, movie selections, safe, cotton robes, hair dryer, and 110/120 volt outlets.

The Itinerary

Insignia and *Regatta* both make positioning voyages between the New World and Europe every spring and fall, and in the spring the western departure might be Miami or Barbados. Eight blissful sea days follow en route to Funchal, Madeira, and on through the Strait of Gibraltar into the Mediterranean to Barcelona or Genoa for disembarkation or continuation onto the first full cruise.

Such a crossing offers the ultimate in creative use of your free time—to read books you never had time for; join an art or a computer class; attend a lecture series, daily classical concerts, culinary demonstrations, or wine tastings; or just wind down and commune with the sea.

Address/Phone: Oceania Cruises, 8300 N.W. 33rd Street, Suite 308, Miami, FL 33122; (800) 531–5619 or (305) 514–2300; fax: (305) 514–2222; www.oceaniacruises.com

The Ship: *Insignia*, built in 1998 as *R1*, has a gross tonnage of 30,200, a length of 594 feet, and a draft of 19.5 feet. Sisters are *Nautica* and *Regatta*.

Passengers: 684; mostly Americans, some British, fifty and up

Dress: Casual, country-club style

Officers/Crew: European officers and mostly European crew

Cabins: 342 cabins, all but 25 outside, and 232 with balconies

Fare: $$$

What's included: Cruise only, port charges

What's not included: Airfare, governmental fees, drinks, tips, shore excursions

Highlights: Beautifully run ships, excellent service, consistently good food enjoyed in a country-club–style atmosphere

Other itineraries: Besides this transatlantic positioning cruise, the three-ship fleet cruises in Europe, Caribbean, South America, and in South, Southeast, and East Asia.

RADISSON SEVEN SEAS CRUISES'
Seven Seas Navigator
Transatlantic between Florida and the Mediterranean

The 33,000-ton *Seven Seas Navigator,* carrying just 490 passengers, is ultraspacious and an ideal size for a luxurious cruise, yet small enough to be intimate and large enough to offer plenty of places to roost. Furthermore, with one-and-a-half crew members for every guest, service is a high point, and so is the food in two open-seating restaurants. This ship will provide a most luxurious way to travel transatlantic between Florida and Mediterranean ports at lower than usual Radisson fares.

The attractive decor is a marriage of classic and modern design, autumn hues, and deep blues, with contemporary wooden furniture, chairs upholstered in soft leather, draperies of silk brocade, walls covered in suede, dark-wood paneling, lighter burled veneer, and the use of decorative stainless steel. The ship's hull was originally built to become a Russian spy ship, but when bought, it was integrated into a passenger design and, with three additional decks added, developed a somewhat ungainly and top-heavy profile.

Most public rooms are found on Decks 6 and 7, just aft of the three-story atrium and main elevator bank. A well-stocked library and computer center with e-mail access is adjacent to a card room. Across the way, the cozy Navigator Lounge, paneled in mahogany and cherry wood, is a popular place for pre-dinner cocktails. Next door is the Connoisseur Club cigar lounge, a masculine wood-paneled room with umber leather chairs. Down the hall is the roomier Stars Lounge, with a long, black-granite curved bar and clusters of oversize ocean-blue armchairs, where a live duo sings pop numbers nightly for listening and dancing. The two-story Seven Seas show lounge features sizable Vegas-style song and dance reviews.

High up and aft on Deck 12, Galileo's lounge, surrounded by windows on three sides, takes on a soft golden glow in the evening and becomes the venue for a pianist. On a balmy, starlit night, the doors open to the deck, creating a most romantic scene for dancing. By day, Galileo's sees use for continental breakfast, afternoon tea, and seminars. Another deck up, forward-facing Vista observation lounge is a great viewing spot, and one can step directly out to an open space over the bridge.

The spa vendor Judith Jackson provides seventeen first-rate treatments, including a relaxing twenty-minute hair and scalp oil massage and a one-hour four-hand massage, performed by a staff of five in six rooms. A pair of hot tubs share the midships pool area with a mezzanine of deck chairs above, and some afternoons a five-piece band plays oldies near the pool bar.

Elaborate and elegant meals in both the formal Compass Rose dining room and the more casual Portofino Grill restaurant are served by a mostly European staff. In both venues, red and white house wines are complimentary at dinner. Meals in the Compass Rose are served in a single open seating and start with appetizers like oven-roasted pheasant salad or avocado fritters in a spicy sauce, with main entrees including enticing zucchini-wrapped chicken breast stuffed with olives and tomatoes or herb-crusted roast leg of lamb.

The Portofino Grill serves a buffet-style breakfast and lunch and a sit-down, reservations-only dinner in an intimate setting with tables for two or four curtained off from the self-service section. In the evenings the grill is transformed into a cozy, dimly lit Northern Italian restaurant with antipasti choices of marinated salmon rings or bresaola carpaccio with Parmesan cheese and mushrooms. The pasta course may feature a jumbo prawn risotto, and main courses include a grilled lobster or osso buco.

Elegant suites are cloaked in shades of deep gold, beige, and burnt-orange with caramel-toned wood furniture. Nearly 90 percent have private balconies, the highest for any ship until the 100-percent-suite *Seven Seas Mariner* arrived in 2001 followed by the *Seven Seas Voyager* in 2003. The standard suites are a roomy 301 square feet, plus a 55-square-foot balcony; and the eighteen top suites range from 448 square feet to 1,067 square feet, not including balconies. In addition to palatial marble-covered bathrooms,

every abode has a wide walk-in closet, a tall built-in dresser, safe, terry robes, a TV/DVD player, and minibar stocked with two complimentary bottles of wine or spirits. Twenty-four-hour room service includes a full-course dinner served in the sitting area or out on the private balcony facing the sea.

The Itinerary

Many ships divide their time between winter in the Caribbean and summer in Europe, and twice a year they offer transatlantic positioning voyages between the two regions, usually at lower than normal rates. The *Seven Seas Navigator* sails from Florida to cross the Atlantic to the Mediterranean in the spring and returns in the fall. During the week at sea her intimate size provides, depending on your preference, either a quiet time or a very social experience, and the voyage can be extended another week to or from Moroccan, Spanish, and French ports.

The *Navigator* embarks in **Fort Lauderdale** and makes a direct eight-night crossing to Funchal on the Portuguese island of Madeira. For lovers of the sea, a rhythm of life develops that is uninterrupted by ports of call. You can be as social as you wish or become a hermit in your suite ticking off a list of books that you always wanted to read. Deck game competitions and constitutional walks in the bracing sea air will work up an appetite and keep the pounds off. Join other passengers you meet about the ship at meals in one of the restaurants, take a romantic table for two, or order dinner to be served in your suite. It's your choice and no one else's.

After a week at sea, the lovely island of **Madeira** rises out of the Atlantic, and the ship berths in the very attractive harbor at **Funchal.** The town center is a short walk around the perimeter, and a cable car will take you to the mountaintop for a splendid view down to the port and your berthed ship. In the afternoon, treat yourself to tea at Reid's, one the world's most venerable hotels that has drawn the smart set since the beginning of the twentieth century. The view from the terrace is splendid, and the terraced gardens make for a nice stroll. Reservations should be made in advance.

While some passengers short on time will leave the *Navigator* here, many stay on for the Mediterranean extension. A typical route, with annual variations, would call at **Casablanca** for a day trip to Rabat or Marrakech, then Spanish ports such as **Malaga** for Granada, its Alhambra, and the Costa del Sol; **Barcelona** with its Gothic Quarter, Gaudi architecture, and cafe life; the city of **Palma de Mallorca** in the Balearic Islands; then on to **Monte Carlo** for disembarkation.

The *Navigator* spends the summer in Europe, and the one-week Mediterranean itineraries sail between Monte Carlo, Italian, and Croatian ports and Venice; Venice, Croatian ports, the Greek islands, and Piraeus (Athens); and Piraeus (Athens), the Greek islands, the Turkish coast, and Istanbul.

Address/Phone: Radisson Seven Seas Cruises, 600 Corporate Drive, Suite 410, Ft. Lauderdale, FL 33334; (954) 776–6123 or (800) 285–1835; brochures: (800) 477–7500; fax: (954) 772–3763; www.rssc.com

The Ship: Seven Seas Navigator was completed in 1999, has a gross tonnage of 33,000, a length of 560 feet, and a draft of 21 feet.

Passengers: 490, mostly Americans forty-five and up

Dress: Formal, informal, and casual nights

Officers/Crew: European officers and a largely European crew

Cabins: 245, all outside, and 196 with balconies

Fare: $$$$

What's included: Cruise fare, gratuities, wines with dinner, soft drinks and juices, stocked minibar

What's not included: Port charges, airfare, alcoholic drinks, shore excursions

Highlights: Spacious ship with nearly all balconies, top European service

Other itineraries: In addition to this transatlantic cruise, which operates in the spring and fall, the *Seven Seas Navigator* also undertakes Mediterranean and Caribbean cruises, and the *Seven Seas Mariner, Seven Seas Voyager,* and *Paul Gauguin* together cover most of the world.

STAR CLIPPERS'

Royal Clipper

Mediterranean to the Caribbean under Sail

As you approach by tender, five tall bare poles rise above everything else in the harbor, then the full length of a shapely steel hull appears, stretching from a rounded overhang at the stern forward to the angular raked bow. A thick black stripe runs the full length, and black gun-port squares below give the ship an extra sense of importance. If one did not have a passenger ticket in hand, this ship might pass for a man-of-war, or at least a commercial cargo carrier.

The 228-passenger *Royal Clipper*'s purposeful appearance contrasts sharply with its 168-passenger running mates, *Star Flyer* and *Star Clipper,* both resembling large, white-hull racing yachts. The *Royal Clipper* is a full-rigged ship, with square sails on all five masts, while the earlier four-masters are barkentine rigged. At 439 feet, the *Royal Clipper* is 79 feet longer and qualifies as the longest and largest sailing vessel ever built, besting the Russian training ship *Sedov* in length and the German Flying P Line *Preussen* (1902–10) in overall size at 5,000 gross tons. She carries 56,000 square feet of Dacron sail, compared to 36,000 for the *Star Clipper* and *Star Flyer.* The twenty-member deck crew uses electric winches to angle the twenty-six square sails, and electric motors to furl and unfurl the square sails stored in the yardarms and the eleven staysails, four jibs, and one gaff-rigged spanker.

On the Main Deck, an upward sloping observation lounge has a view of the forward deck and sees use for meetings, informal talks, and Internet connections. The main lounge, located amidships, is as comfortable as they come, with banquette, soft couch, and chair seating, a sit-up bar, and a central well that looks down into the dining room two decks below. Through the aft doors, the covered Tropical Bar recalls the earlier pair, as does the paneled Edwardian library with its electric fireplace, though on a much larger scale.

The handsome paneled dining room with brass wall lamps, reached via a freestanding staircase from the lounge, has a large upper level surrounding a central well with some tables and the buffet. Tables are rectangular, round, and banquette style. An omelet chef cooks to order at breakfast, and a carvery features roast beef, ham, and pork at lunch. Seating is open for all meals, and the lunch buffets are the biggest hit. The menu for the first day at sea includes jumbo shrimp, foie gras, artichoke hearts, herring, potato salad, lots of salad fixings, hot and cold salmon, meatballs, and sliced roast beef. The dining room is set low enough so that in any kind of sea, the water splashes washing machine–style over the portholes. For an actual underwater view, Captain Nemos, the gym, spa, tiled Turkish bath, and beauty salon, has lounge seating to the side where one can look for the creatures of the sea.

The deluxe suites are reached by walking along a central mahogany-paneled companionway, with a thick sloping mast penetrating the corridor at the forward end. The luxurious cabins, mahogany-paneled with rosewood framing and molding, contrast with an off-white ceiling and the upper portion of two walls. Pale gold-framed mirrors enlarge the space, and brass-framed windows bring in light to bathe the far corner sitting alcove. Brass wall lamps and sailing ship prints give the feel of a ship's cabin, upward sloping at that, not a hotel-style room on a hull.

A heavy wooden door leads to a private furnished teak veranda with shrouds passing upward from the ship's side. The huge marble bathroom comes with a Jacuzzi bath, which, like the TV and minibar, happily hidden from view, nods to an upscale cruise ship. There are fourteen of these 255-square-foot deluxe one-room suites, plus two even larger 320-square-foot owner's suites located at the stern and two 175-square-foot deluxe cabins that open onto the afterdeck. The most numerous standard cabins (eighty-eight) in categories 2 to 5 are 148 square feet and vary mostly by location. They have marble bathrooms with showers, TVs, satellite telephones, radio channels, private safes, and hair dryers. Six inside cabins round out the accommodations.

The real show is up on the Sun Deck. The full length of the Burma teak deck is cluttered with electric winches, halyards, belaying pins, lines, shackles, ventilators, lifeboats, and deck chairs arranged around three swimming pools. The center pool, 24 feet in length, has a glass bottom that drops into the piano lounge and serves as a skylight to the dining room three decks below.

A hydraulic platform stages the water sport activities, and the ship offers banana boats, waterskiing, diving, snorkeling, and swimming from the 16-foot inflatable raft. An interior stairway gives access to the marina. Two sixty-passenger tenders, resembling military landing craft, take passengers for beach landings. Two 150-passenger fiberglass tenders ferry passengers between the anchored ship and pier.

The Itinerary

On the westbound ocean crossing, the *Royal Clipper* embarks in **Civitavecchia** (Rome) and makes calls in Spain, varying with every sailing, such as **Palma de Mallorca** and **Malaga,** then **Casablanca** in Morocco, and **Las Palmas** and **Tenerife** in the Canaries. The last landfall signals the start of why people really come, the eleven unbroken days at sea, under sail to Barbados.

In optimum wind conditions, the ship can attain 20 knots, but the schedule calls for half that. When there is no wind, the twin Caterpillar, 2,500-horsepower diesel engines can propel the ship at up to 14 knots. The exhaust leaves from the very top of the hollow mizzen and spanker masts, the highest being 197 feet above the waterline. However, the captains, being sailing ship enthusiasts, use the engines sparingly.

While passengers do not handle the sails as on the windjammers, they enjoy being part of the navigation by collecting on a raised platform with the helmsmen and one of the duty officers above the bridge and chart room. A lot of conversations ensue, and relationships develop over the periods of many days at sea. Crew members give lessons in sailing and rope tying. Passengers, wearing safety belts, may climb the steel masts to a crow's nest 60 feet above the deck, and they may also crawl out on the netting that cascades from the bow sprit. Suspended over the sea, they can watch the bow wave below and the masts swaying against the clouds and sky.

Every day at 10:00 A.M., the captain conducts story time, relating tales of the sea, defining nautical terms, and announcing special events. When the conditions are right, passengers can embark in one of the tenders to watch from a distance the ship proceeding under full sail. From a small boat at water level, the view of the *Royal Clipper* bearing down on you, fully dressed with all forty-two sails catching the wind and sun, is beyond words.

For those who have not crossed the Atlantic by sea, there is variation on the crossing-the-line ceremony, in which passengers and crew are initiated by King Neptune, his mermaid queen, and the ship's doctor.

Address/Phone: Star Clippers, 4101 Salzebo Street, Coral Gables, FL 33146; (305) 442–0550 or (800) 442–0551; brochures: (800) 442–0556; fax: (305) 442–1611; www.starclippers.com

The Ship: *Royal Clipper* was built in 2000. It has a gross tonnage of 5,000, a length of 439 feet, and a draft of 18.5 feet.

Passengers: 228, all ages, Americans and European; English is the lingua franca

Dress: Casual at all times

Officers/Crew: European captain and officers; international crew

Cabins: 114; all but 6 outside, 14 with verandas

Fare: $$

What's included: Cruise only

What's not included: Airfare, port charges, tips, drinks

Highlights: The ultimate in a sailing ship experience; social bonding aboard

Other itineraries: Besides these two annual transatlantic crossings, which take place in the spring and fall and usually last about three weeks end to end, Star Clippers offers sailing ship cruises aboard the *Royal Clipper* and *Star Clipper* in the Caribbean, with all three ships in the Eastern or Western Mediterranean. In the fall the *Star Flyer* sails through Suez to cruise Malaysia and Thailand, returning via the Indian Ocean in April.

CP SHIPS'
Canmar Fleet
Freighter Travel Crossing for Europhiles

The romantic notion of freighter travel is alive and well, and the world can be your oyster on voyages lasting from seven days up to four months. Life on a cargo ship can be solitary or social—your call—but it's all about enjoying the sea, being a member of a close-knit community, and watching freight handling in ports of call.

Cabin accommodations vary from plain to plush but are always comfortable, and fares are pegged at about $90 to $140 per day, less than for most cruise ships. But more to the point, your freighter travel budget will not be punctured by the lure of shipboard gambling, spa treatments, shop-

ping, and extra tariff restaurants. With just a handful of fellow passengers, you take your chances, and the average freighter traveler is up there in age, with seventy to seventy-five typically the upper age limit because most freighters carry no doctor.

Flexibility is most important when considering cargo ship travel because it's the stacks of containers that provide the profits; hence a ship may leave earlier than scheduled or later. The container ships of CP Ships are usually not more than a day or two off schedule, and they generally hold to the itinerary. Be prepared for some rolling and pitching as the ships plow through all sorts of weather without the aid of stabilizers. Meals reflect the officers' nationality, so you will have lots of authentically spicy curries as Indians man the bridge, and preparation varies according to an individual chef's skill. The officers will speak good English, and mealtimes are shared, though passengers sit at separate tables except at deck barbecues when the weather permits.

The large comfortable lounges have TV, VCR, and music center, and you have access to a pantry for hot drinks, fruit, juices, and snacks. Wine, beer, and spirits are available at duty-free prices. Entertainment and activities include videos and tapes, board and card games, table tennis, small gym, walking the decks, and enjoying a good book in a deck chair located out of the wind. Most ships have an open bridge policy, and once you choose your favorite officer on watch, you may find yourself spending hours shooting the breeze and learning about container shipping, navigation, computers, radar, sea rescue, lifeboats, and the complex customs and cultures of India.

CP Ships operates four ships that hold down two routes to England and the Continent. The Canmar Pride and Canmar Honour carry four passengers in one roomy twin and two single cabins, while the Canmar Spirit and Canmar Venture take three in one double and one single. All are equipped with a small refrigerator and a shower bath. Forward-facing windows may have views blocked by containers, depending on how they are stacked.

This company is chosen to introduce freighter travel because voyages are relatively short with frequent departures, and the ships offer high standards as they are company-owned, not chartered, by Canadian Pacific. With England and the Continent as destinations, you may wish to stay over and sail or fly back. Sailings are offered year-round, but the crossing will be largely an indoor experience in winter. The other passengers, only four or five total, will be the luck of the draw, so singles may wish to travel with a friend.

The Itinerary

Both transatlantic routes sail from **Montreal** down the **St. Lawrence River** in protected waters for two days before reaching the open ocean. En route, the ships pass under several bridges, slide by the towering Citadel at Quebec City, then parallel the Ile d'Orleans, where at the far end the river begins to widen into what the Quebecois call *la mer* (the sea). The St. Lawrence narrows again as it flows into the open Atlantic, with one track to the north and the other to the south of Newfoundland.

One container service takes seven days to reach Thamesport, well down river from **London,** then crosses the Channel to dock at **Antwerp, Belgium** (nine days), and then to **Le Havre, France** (ten days), from where it's westbound direct to Montreal. The second route operates first to Antwerp (eight days) and on to **Hamburg** (nine days), where there is the bonus of a four-hour sail up the Elbe to the container berths. After unloading and reloading, the ship makes a return Atlantic crossing. Generally, the round-trips take eighteen days, but the useful nature of these services permits one-way passages in both directions from all ports except Le Havre. Port time ranges from about three to six hours, and in larger ports, the new sprawling container terminals may be well away from the city center. Passengers may elect to stay aboard during the cargo working or take an excursion by taxi.

Booking freighters requires considerable thought and planning to make sure it is the right choice, so be sure to consult an expert.

Address/Phone: The Cruise People Ltd.,
1252 Lawrence Avenue East, Suite 210, Don
Mills, Ontario M3A 1C3 Canada; (416)
444–2410 or (800) 268–6523; fax: (416)
447–2628; www.thecruisepeople.ca. CP
Ships Web site for information only: www.cp
ships.com, then click on Passenger Services.

The Ships: *Canmar Pride* and *Canmar Honour* were built in 1998, have a gross tonnage of 39,174, and can carry 2,800
20-foot containers; *Canmar Spirit* and *Canmar Venture* were built in 2003 and carry
4,100 20-foot containers.

Passengers: *Canmar Pride* and *Canmar Honour:* 4 passengers; *Canmar Spirit* and
Canmar Venture: 3 passengers. Age limit is
seventy-five; seventy in the winter months.

Dress: Casual at all times

Officers/Crew: Largely Indian officers and
crew

Cabins: *Canmar Pride* and *Canmar Honour:*
one twin, two singles; *Canmar Spirit* and
Canmar Venture: one double, one single

Fare: $$ one-way; $ round-trip

What's included: Ship fare, port charges

What's not included: Airfare, drinks, tips

Highlights: Being at sea and sharing the
experience aboard a working ship

Other itineraries: For other freighter-passenger itineraries contact The Cruise
People or TravLtips, P.O. Box 580188,
Flushing, NY 11358; (800) 872-8584;
fax: (718) 224–3247; e-mail: info@
travltips.com; www.travltips.com. This
agency publishes a bimonthly publication
listing options, plus special positioning
type cruises, and has illustrated articles
written by past passengers.

THE BAHAMAS AND
CARIBBEAN ISLANDS

DISNEY CRUISE LINE'S
Disney Wonder
Bahamas Cruising for All Ages

Disney debuted its eagerly anticipated *Disney Magic* in 1998, and since then, the *Disney Magic* and *Disney Wonder* have settled down quite comfortably into a routine that pleases families, honeymooners, and Disney fans of all ages. While Disney's insistence on the ships being "just so" caused them to be delayed and over budget, the company also ended up with lavishly decorated ships with real pizzazz and style.

Inspired by classic ocean liner design, the 1999-built *Disney Wonder* looks very smart with her black hull, long bow, and twin funnels proudly adorned with Mickey's ears. Exploring further, you will find fanciful Disney touches everywhere, including an elaborate scrollwork of Steamboat Mickey on the bow, a larger-than-life Donald Duck hanging over the stern, painting the hull, and a bronze statue of Ariel from *The Little Mermaid* gracing the three-story atrium. However, these flourishes are fun and whimsical and do not overwhelm those with only a passing interest in cartoons.

In fact, much of the art nouveau decor is so stylish that it is hard to remember you are on a family-oriented cruise ship. Staircase railings are festooned with elaborate scrollwork, and the Promenade Lounge, with its wood veneer paneling, soothing dark colors, and chic furniture, is a delightful, elegant retreat from either the Caribbean sun or overactive kids.

In order to attract both families and those without kids, the ship has an "Adults Only" section with three types of entertainment. The Cadillac Lounge, a burgundy-colored piano bar with the fins of a 1958 DeVille on either end of the bar, is an atmospheric spot for pre-dinner cocktails, while Wavebands, a large nightclub decorated with vintage radios and records, becomes popular late at night. Barrel of Laughs is a popular dueling pianos club you won't find on any other cruise line.

Of the three pools on board, the most attractive one, nestled between the forward funnel and the mast, is off limits to kids. As part of Disney's fanaticism for family entertainment, there is no casino on board. Surprisingly, the segregation of kids and adults works well and is rigidly enforced.

Of course, kids have plenty of room to frolic, with activities broken into six age groups including a dedicated nursery. A large computer and science lab entertains the eight- to twelve-year-olds, while a mock pirate ship is the scene for games of make-believe with the younger set. Teens find a new hangout all to themselves, filled with video screens for movies, a teen disco, Internet center, and lounge chairs. With more than fifty youth counselors on some sailings, activities can be really creative, including kids-only shore excursions, animation classes, ship-wide treasure hunts, late-night supervised games on deck, and making commercials on board. Two pools are also open to families, including one with Mickey's gloved hand supporting a slide. A movie theater shows Disney films throughout the day, while the Walt Disney Theatre performs well-received Broadway-style Disney favorites after dinner. Parents get beepers when they check into the nursery or kids' programs to be able to keep in touch with the counselors.

Cabins are large and designed for families, with some even accommodating five people. A unique feature is the one and a half bathrooms in every cabin (except categories 11 and 12).

Another Disney innovation is rotation dining, whereby you, your tablemates, and your waiters rotate each night through three dining rooms. One night you are in elegant Triton's, the next night you are transported to a tropical jungle in Parrot's Cay. Younger kids will probably like Animator's Palette the best (the walls, ceiling, and even the waiters' uniforms start off in only black and white but gradually change color through the meal). Food is standard cruise ship fare throughout, although the adults-only alternative restaurant, Palo, is well worth the moderate charge for both its stunning Italian design and far superior food.

The Itinerary

Most passengers take the cruise as part of a combined Disney resort package, and Disney has made the transition between ship and shore as seamless as possible. Not only does a fleet of custom Disney buses transport you from your hotel to the spectacular art deco cruise terminal in **Port Canaveral,** but the same key you used for your hotel will work in your cabin on board as well. After a late afternoon sailing, you arrive the next morning in **Nassau** for shopping at the **Straw Market,** gambling, or a visit to the Atlantis resort. The ship stays until 1:30 A.M., and in the evening there is a party on deck that culminates with streamers and confetti. At **Castaway Cay,** Disney's private island, the ship actually docks. This is the only cruise line private island where anchoring offshore is not necessary. Certain areas of the island are sectioned off for kids or adults only. After a beach barbecue and last dip in the protected lagoon, it is time to head back to the ship and set sail for Port Canaveral.

Address/Phone: Disney Cruise Line, P.O. Box 10210, Lake Buena Vista, FL 32830; (800) 951–3532; fax: (407) 566–3541; www.disneycruise.com

The Ship: *Disney Wonder* was built in 1999 and has a gross tonnage of 83,000, a length of 964 feet, and a draft of 25 feet.

Passengers: 1,750; many more if all third, fourth, and fifth berths are occupied; mostly American families with kids and couples in their thirties to fifties who love the Disney concept

Dress: Jackets for men are expected in Triton's and Palo; collared shirts are fine in other restaurants. No shorts, jeans, or T-shirts in any restaurants.

Officers/Crew: International

Cabins: 875; 720 outside, 388 with verandas. Most cabins have one and a half baths and a sitting area with a convertible couch to sleep up to five.

Fare: $$$

What's included: Cruise fare

What's not included: Airfare, governmental fees and taxes, tips, drinks, and shore excursions; water sports, bicycles, and strollers on Castaway Cay

Highlights: Fantastic children's facilities and an attractive, creative, and fun ship for families; superb private island

Other itineraries: *Disney Wonder* does both a three- and four-night itinerary, with four-night voyages including a full day at sea. The *Disney Magic* does a seven-night itinerary calling at St. Maarten, St. Thomas, St. John, and Castaway Cay, with alternate trips to the Western Caribbean ports of Key West, Grand Cayman, Cozumel, and Castaway Cay.

IMPERIAL MAJESTY CRUISES'

Regal Empress

North America's Last Classic Cruise Ship

The past few years have witnessed nearly every remaining ship with an ocean liner background going off to South Asian ship breakers, leaving just one lone classic vessel departing from a North American port. She is the *Regal Empress* sailing year-round on moderately priced, two-night cruises from Fort Lauderdale to Nassau and return.

Appealing to both classic ship traditionalists and budget travelers, and with many repeaters who live locally, she represents both a good value and a glimpse back to another era of sleek ocean liner profiles and with wood-paneled public rooms to match.

Built on the Clyde in Scotland in 1953 as Greek Line's 23,800-ton flagship *Olympia*, she first traded between northern Europe and New York then a couple of years later moved to the Mediterranean for transatlantic service to New York. During this period she carried just 138 in first class and up to 1,169 in tourist. After air travel forced her to switch to leisure cruises, the fuel crisis then resulted in her being laid up for nearly six years. Rebuilt for a new role as the Caribbean cruise ship *Caribe I* beginning in 1981, she subsequently did a ten-year stint for Regal Cruises as the *Regal Empress*. In winter she traded from Florida's west coast and in summer mostly from New York. Over the years, she has had her thirsty steam turbines replaced with more efficient diesel engines, had her funnel redesigned, and some public rooms and passenger amenities added, yet she retains some wonderful paneled and etched glass interior spaces.

The *Regal Empress* rates being termed a comfortable ship accommodating a maximum of 1,068 passengers. Because the ship was built for the Atlantic run, she has a glass-enclosed promenade deck and cozy lounges for spending the day, oblivious to the weather outside.

The best parts of the ship include her intimate library, executed in an Edwardian style with heavy, dark wood paneling and glass-fronted bookcases. It is fun to explore a real time capsule of a room in great detail with old writing desks used before the days of instant e-mail communication and with Greek Line crowns carved in the paneling.

For drinks, the Commodore Club, a small bar forward of the nightclub, features two sunken side wells that seat six. From these private nooks, you look out through tall windows onto the boat deck or up to the bar scene in the center of the room.

The forward main foyer and the staircase have well-maintained varnished paneling that simply does not exist on modern ships today. Wall lighting is gracefully curved nickel-plated sconces.

The ship's Caribbean Dining Room—adorned with a lighter maple wood paneling and etched mirrored panels—while in the traditional location low down in the hull, is both pleasant and airy. An original mural of New York City, the ship's original embarkation port in the 1950s, graces one end of the room. Food, served in five courses, is of a quality that certainly exceeds the price, and service is helpful and efficient. Seating, assigned at embarkation, is at 6:00 P.M. and 8:30 P.M.

For breakfast and lunch during the day in Nassau, it's open seating, and La Trattoria, a lido buffet, serves an embarkation buffet, breakfast on the second day, and a midnight Latin Fiesta buffet.

The other non-original public spaces include the Mermaid Bar with its glass ceiling located aft of the Commodore Club and featuring a pianist and karaoke; a low-ceiling Grand Lounge for the two after-dinner, Las Vegas–style shows; a casino with slot machines and blackjack tables; the Mirage Disco; Card Room; Internet Café and coffee bar; and a children's playroom.

Outside and aft, a wooden horseshoe-shaped, sit-up bar faces onto the open deck and pool and is the location for fifties and sixties music by the ship's trio and a steel band.

Cabins come in an intriguing variety of shapes and sizes, and so choosing your specific cabin can be fun. While the nicer accommodations are attractive and spacious, many of the budget cabins are fairly small, arranged with upper and lower bunks and lacking the old-school charm found in other cabins. Every cabin has a TV and a safe.

The most interesting forward-facing cabins were carved out of the original tourist-class card room, with playing card depictions still in place on the paneled walls. Sun Deck cabins have some remaining paneling and furniture from back when they were designated first class, and eight cabins with good-size verandas are found forward on Promenade Deck.

The Itinerary
The *Regal Empress* sails every other afternoon from **Port Everglades** (Fort Lauderdale), and she is the sole remaining cruise ship needing tug assistance to maneuver from the berth and for docking. Powerful bow thrusters on modern ships have pretty much eliminated the need for tugboats except in windy conditions. She seems small next to the megaships, but she receives the traditional bells-and-whistles farewell from the condominium residents who see the ships off every afternoon making their way along the channel and out to sea. Lingering light keeps many on deck until the ship is well away from land. As the overnight passage is short, the ship does not need to make much speed to arrive in **Nassau, the Bahamas,** the following morning about 9:00 A.M.

For the independent minded, shopping and some of the sights are within walking distance, such as Rawson Square and Bay Street for stores, the pink Parliament Buildings (built 1815), the Queen's Staircase cut into the limestone cliffs in 1793 and leading up to Fort Fincastle (also 1793), and the 126-foot water tower for a great view of Nassau and its harbor. Ship's shore excursions offer trips to Paradise Island, other beaches, snorkeling, and a tour of the city. Some ship aficionados may wish to return after a short time ashore to enjoy a quiet day by the pool or reading in deck chair under the life boats. Then about 5:30 P.M. the *Regal Empress* whistles her way out to sea for the overnight run back to Port Everglades.

For anybody interested in experiencing the atmosphere of a former workaday ocean liner, don't wait too long. The price is right, and she won't be around forever.

Address/Phone: Imperial Majesty Cruises, 2950 Gateway Drive, Pompano Beach, FL 33069; (800) 394–3865 or (954) 956–9505; fax: (954) 971–6678; www .imperialmajesty.com

The Ship: Built in 1953 as the *Olympia*, then renamed *Caribe I*, the *Regal Empress*

has a tonnage of 21,909, a length of 612 feet, and a draft of 28 feet.

Passengers: 905 double occupancy, mostly Americans of all ages

Dress: Casual, with a jacket for the cocktail party (second) night

Officers/Crew: International

Cabins: 457, of which 227 are inside and some quite small; 8 veranda cabins

Fare: $

What's included: Cruise fare only

What's not included: Transportation to and from the ship, port taxes, drinks, shore excursions

Highlights: The last remaining classic cruise ship regularly sailing from North America

Other itineraries: None

CUNARD LINE'S
Queen Mary 2
The World's Greatest Ocean Liner from New York to the Caribbean

The ultimate transatlantic liner spends about half her year off the North Atlantic run, making cruises from New York and Florida to New England and Canada, the Caribbean, and South America and from Southampton, England, to European ports. Her high speed and sheer size give her advantages by offering additional ports, a more ambitious itinerary, and a smoother ride. The *QM2* is simply the largest, longest, tallest, and most expensive passenger ship ever built.

Cunard designed the *Queen Mary 2* to wow and impress at first sight at the pier or sailing past the New York skyline. Inside, the *Mary* borrows from the classic ocean liners of the past, with dramatic public rooms on a grand scale. A traditional Winter Garden is the turn-of-the-twentieth-century setting for the ritual of afternoon tea, and the domed Queen's Lounge is dedicated to ballroom dancing, with the largest dance floor at sea. Her main dining room soars three stories with a double staircase for that grand arrival.

During the day, lectures and classes will cover topics ranging from maritime history to U.S.–Russian relations, some given by celebrity authors, entertainment stars, and politicians. A traditional teak promenade deck, wrapping completely around the ship, is designed for communing with the restless sea and is wide enough for walkers and for those who like to wrap up in a steamer rug and spend the afternoon in a wooden deck chair.

For others who want a modern, up-to-the-minute ship, the Canyon Ranch Spa qualifies as the largest and most indulgent spa facility at sea, with a staff numbering more than fifty. An adequate show lounge puts on extravagant productions, and the theater, used for lectures and films, doubles as the first seagoing planetarium when the ceiling opens to reveal a starlit sky.

Additional public rooms, scattered all over the ship and some tucked away up high, include the Commodore Lounge, a quiet piano bar that serves as an observation room, a forward-facing library and cafe, and an English pub, just a few of a grand total of fourteen bars and clubs.

Ten different restaurants cater to all tastes and pockets. As with the *QE2,* your cabin category will determine in which restaurant you eat. The vast majority of passengers will dine at one of two seatings in the Britannia Restaurant, while those occupying larger cabins dine in the more intimate Princess and Queens Grills. A Todd English restaurant, designed by the Boston restaurauteur, serves a Mediterranean menu on a poolside terrace overlooking the stern, and the buffet offers four styles of food at night by reservation.

Cabins for 2,620 passengers are some of the largest standard cabins on any ship, and 73 percent feature balconies. To safeguard against possible North Atlantic wave damage, three decks of balconies are recessed into the steel hull. For those with money to splurge, grand suites range from duplex apartments overlooking the stern to a suite of rooms stretching across the front of the ship a few decks below the bridge.

The Itinerary

Queen Mary 2's cruise itineraries from New York and Fort Lauderdale vary from short introductory trips to cruises to New England, Canada, and the Caribbean. This fourteen-day cruise from New York to the deep Caribbean combines good sea time to become acquainted with the delights of a true ocean liner and no less than seven ports in rapid succession.

Sail past **Manhattan**'s unparalleled skyline and the Statue of Liberty and with just feet to spare, slide beneath the Verrazano-Narrows Bridge. The Sandy Hook pilot leaves in the Ambrose Channel, and the liner gathers speed for a three-night and two-day run into increasing warmer climes while passengers settle in aboard their remarkable conveyance.

The first landing is **San Juan** where Old San Juan's narrow streets rise up from the cruise ship piers. The district exhibits some 400 Spanish colonial buildings dating from the sixteenth and seventeenth centuries

and used as residences, hotels, restaurants, cafes, and shops. At the top on a plain overlooking the sea, walk to El Morro, a Spanish-built fortress constructed between the sixteenth and eighteenth centuries, and take the National Park Service tour. One of the best shore excursions visits El Yunque Rainforest where on a short hike you will hear the sounds of tree frogs and walk among luxuriant semitropical orchids, huge ferns, and palms, and from an observation tower, look down on a pretty waterfall.

After an overnight sail, call at **Philipsburg,** on the Dutch side of the island known as **St. Maarten,** where one finds no border formalities for a visit to French **St. Martin.** If Philipsburg is all about shopping and casinos, **Marigot** is for yachting, the artistic, and beach lovers. Sailing overnight to Fort de France, **Martinique,** the flavor is definitely Caribbean French, immediately apparent from the smartly dressed women seen in the city's streets. The leafy city itself is worth a half day, enjoying the cafe life; the New Orleans–style wrought-iron balconies; the belle epoque–style Schoelcher Library, dismantled at the 1899 Paris Exposition and moved here; and the late nineteenth-century St. Louis Cathedral.

The island is hilly with deep valleys, lush rain forests, and above all volcanic, the last feature providing the greatest moment in its history. On one day in 1902, **Mt. Pelée** blew its top, and St. Pierre, the capital, lost 30,000 inhabitants in a matter of minutes. One ship excursion visits the ruins, the one-room museum, and includes a ride through the rain forest and visits to a botanical garden and a butterfly farm.

Barbados is as far south as the Caribbean goes, and the island is set up to please everyone. Most everything worth visiting is well beyond Bridgetown where the ship ties up. You can get around by agreeing on a price and hiring a taxi, using the island's decent public buses and privately owned minibuses, or renting a car. Driving is on the left, and the signposting is only fair, so have a map in hand so as not to miss the boat at the end of the day.

The west coast beaches are best, while the Atlantic side is pounded by the surf and not suitable for swimming. The south coast beaches are the closest, and windsurfing is popular. Tourist destinations are Harrison's Cave for a view of the underground world, Francia Plantation house for an interior inspection, Gun Hill Signal Station for a sweeping island view, and all about rum at the Mount Gay rum site.

The *Queen Mary 2* docks at Basseterre on the former British island of **St. Kitts**. The best tour, by ship's excursion or in a taxi with an agreed-to price, includes Brimstone Hill, a well-preserved late seventeenth-century fortress that has been called "The Gibraltar of the West Indies." From the top of the hill, on a clear day you can see most of St. Kitts and six neighboring islands. Another popular stop is Romney Gardens, located in a ruined sugar estate and exhibiting orchids, poinsettias, and giant ferns. The island is also well known for scuba diving and snorkeling among the coral and reef fish.

Grenada is the Caribbean spice island, with extremely fertile soil for growing cocoa, cloves, cinnamon, ginger, mace, and nutmeg and colorful flowering bushes like bougainvillea and oleander. The island's capital, St. George's, is worth a wander to enjoy the Georgian colonial buildings and old fortifications. Outside town, there are hikes into an extinct volcano with its bright blue lake, to Seven Sisters Waterfall for a cool pool swim, and up to late eighteenth-century Fort Frederick, with construction started by the French and completed by the British.

Then it's a last call at **St. Thomas** where the active can take bike tours for what are mostly downhill rides and usually include a swim at the end, kayak through mangroves, and take a nature walk at St. Peter Greathouse Estate and Gardens. Shoppers can do just that to their hearts' content, and beachgoers have many choices, all reachable by taxi with an agreement in advance for a return pickup.

Following seven ports in as many days, most will look forward to returning to the ship and taking up life at sea on the three-night and two-day run back to New York.

Address/Phone: Cunard Line, 24303 Town Center Drive, Suite 200, Valencia, CA 91355; (800) 7–CUNARD; www.cunard.com

The Ship: *Queen Mary 2,* completed in 2003, has a gross tonnage of 148,528, a length of 1,132 feet, and a draft of 33 feet.

Passengers: 2,620, Americans, British, Europeans, and other nationalities; all ages especially during the school holidays

Dress: Formal, informal, and casual nights

Officers/Crew: British officers, international crew, British and American social staff

Cabins: 1,310 cabins, 1,017 outside, 879 with verandas, 12 with atrium view

Fare: $$$

What's included: Cruise fare only

What's not included: Airfare, port charges, excursions, tips

Highlights: Cruising aboard the world's largest and best-known ocean liner

Other itineraries: Besides this fourteen-day Caribbean cruise from New York, operated with variations, the *Queen Mary 2* makes regular transatlantic crossings between New York and Southampton, England, and Hamburg, Germany, on occasion; and cruises from Southampton and Fort Lauderdale. The *Queen Elizabeth 2* cruises from Southampton and makes an annual world cruise.

PRINCESS CRUISES'
Caribbean Princess
Eastern Caribbean Megaship Cruising

With the debut of the 113,000-ton *Caribbean Princess* in April 2004, the Grand-class comes in a new enlarged size, with an added deck of cabins increasing the capacity by 500 passengers to 3,100 on a double-occupancy basis. To handle the larger numbers, an additional informal restaurant, an extended main dining room, and a concierge reservation service for all passengers help ease the demand at mealtimes.

The ship holds down a typical popular port itinerary, including St. Thomas, St. Maarten, and the private island Princess Cays, and with three full sea days, shipboard life, for some, may exceed the importance of the destinations.

Overall, the decor found in the foyers, corridors, and on the stairs is unifying throughout with jazzy patterns that mirror the colors of the Caribbean and the undersea coral reefs. I like the stairway art, with paired and triple sets of prints, photographs, and shipping posters.

Within the ship, the public rooms pretty much mirror the *Grand* and *Golden Princess* with one major exception. The after Vista Lounge, the secondary theater-style show room, has been replaced by the Café Fusion, a nightclub-style space used for cabaret acts, take-off TV game shows, horseracing, bingo, ballroom dancing, and the Captain's Circle (repeaters) party.

The primary entertainment lounge, the Princess Theater, is more high-tech than most of Broadway's houses and is able to handle multiple backdrops for several major nighttime production shows. A full kitchen is wheeled out when the executive chef and the maitre d'hotel (both Italians) put on a hilarious cooking performance yet still manage to complete a four-course dinner. They received a much-deserved standing ovation on my cruise. The Explorer's Lounge and its powerful Afro-Egyptian decor, mostly obscured by wall-to-wall art auction paintings during the day, come alive with music and cabaret at night as designed.

The ship offers many intimate and some quiet retreats for a drink or read during the day, such as the maritime-themed Wheelhouse Bar, and Skywalkers, the pod hanging high above the stern. For people watching while bending an elbow, the best venues are the Lobby Bar on Deck 5 and Crooners Martini Bar on Deck 7. Churchill's, tucked under the Princess Theater, is a clubby sports bar with the screens acting as a visual backdrop when the events are not very important.

The library has an excellent and well-organized selection of some 1,200 hardbacks and books on tape to listen to while seated in a comfy easy chair. Other amenities include an average-size card room; an Asian-style spa and fitness center with its own pool and sun deck; an Internet center with twenty-five computer stations and, by cruise ship standards, moderate rates by the minute; a major casino with 260 slots; and a nest of shops on two levels along the atrium's perimeter. The Hearts and Minds Wedding Chapel saw use for renewing vows on my cruise.

The children's facilities include spaces for different age groups, and the use of two pools with adult supervision. The children and teenagers seemed to have a good time and were very well behaved.

A most-welcome concierge reservation service, available to all, helps deal with the additional passenger demand for dining, spa treatments, the reserved-seat outdoor movies, and the ScholarShip@Sea enrichment program. The activities include photography, ceramics, dancing, wine tasting, and computer classes.

The Island Dining Room has traditional first and second sittings, which certainly work best for families and groups who want to eat together, as otherwise preferred times are not always available. The Palm and Coral dining rooms have open seating.

On the first night leaving Fort Lauderdale, an informal dinner in the twenty-four-hour Horizon Court is billed as a Chilled Seafood Extravaganza. The Café Caribe, new to this ship, has themed nightly buffets with table settings and tablecloths, including a German-style Oktoberfest meal with suckling pig, various wursts, and German beer, and a spicy Creole Cookery.

For extra-tariff dining, Trattoria Sabatini delivers an almost endless if delicious onslaught of eight antipasti, pizza, zuppa, pasta, secondi piatti (main course), and tiramisu, not to mention bread sticks dipped in pure olive oil. In the Sterling Steakhouse, one is presented with six cuts of beef such as filet mignon, New York strip, rib eye, and a 22-ounce porterhouse. The open kitchen prepares everything from scratch, and the setting is intimate and uncrowded.

Of the 1,557 cabins 880 have private balconies, the lower ones tiered outward so those above can look down on others below. At the higher elevations, this is not the case. All cabins have twin beds that can be made into queen-size, multifunction telephones, refrigerators, safes, hair dryers, and remote-control TV with CNN, TNT, CNBC, Discovery Channel, movies, special-interest lectures, and interviews. Minisuites and up have tub baths, robes, two TVs, and a separate sitting area with a sofa bed.

The Itinerary

The *Princess Patter* arrives in the evening for a quick review before bed. Then at breakfast, it is time to get serious about managing the day.

Beginning with the most active events of the day, a round robin of paddle tennis takes place high up and forward on Deck 17, and later in the day it's table tennis. To cool down, the spa pool is equipped with a swim-against-the-current machine and a flanking Jacuzzi. The most tranquil pool is the Sun Terrace all the way aft beneath Skywalkers, the disco and lounge housed in an overhead horizontal pod. For a Coney Island on the Fourth of July atmosphere, the Neptune Pool is the most vibrant scene with water games and a band to generate the energy, while the Calypso Pool is overlooked by a huge movie screen with films and concerts during the day and Movies under the Stars at Night.

Other activities are aerobics classes, shipboard-style horseracing, playing a notable course on the golf simulator, bridge instruction, and enjoying formal afternoon tea on this British-registered ship.

Following three night and two full sea days, the ship docks at **St. Thomas,** where there are beach and shopping excursions, the historic buildings in Charlotte Amalie to visit, and an excursion aboard the well-operated Atlantis submarine, diving to about 90 feet to observe the coral reefs and undersea life. At **St. Maarten,** a two-flag tour takes in both the Dutch and French sides, and another visits local artists. Hire a taxi to go to the beach, the casino, or for a major shopping spree in Philipsburg. Then after a sea day, **Princess Cays** offers an active or a passive day of private island life. A barbecue, beach walking, swimming, and lying in a hammock are free; for a fee, go snorkeling, Jet Skiing, or take a fast banana boat ride. It's all in a day's play aboard the *Caribbean Princess.*

Address/Phone: Princess Cruises, 24305 Town Center Drive, Santa Clarita, CA 91355; (800) PRINCESS or (661) 753–0000; fax: (661) 259–3108; www.princess.com

The Ship: *Caribbean Princess* was completed in 2004 and has a gross tonnage of 112,894, a length of 951 feet, and a 26-foot draft.

Passengers: 3,100, mostly Americans and some British, of all ages

Dress: Two formal nights and the rest casual

Officers/Crew: Italian/international officers and international crew

Cabins: 1,557 average size of which 1,105 are outside, and 880 have balconies

Fare: $$

What's included: Cruise fare only

What's not included: Transportation to and from the ship, governmental fees, shore excursions, drinks, lots of onboard extras

Highlights: Big-ship amenities, plenty to do aboard during three sea days

Other itineraries: In addition to this seven-day Eastern Caribbean itinerary, the *Caribbean Princess* alternatively adds a Western Caribbean loop in the late spring, summer, and early fall. Princess Cruises' large fleet offers worldwide itineraries.

CARNIVAL CRUISE LINES'
Carnival Victory
Eastern and Western Caribbean Megaship Cruising

Carnival Cruise Lines took a giant step in size with the building of the highly popular Carnival Destiny-class, and the third ship in this series, the *Carnival Victory,* boasts more than 500 veranda cabins and is extraordinarily popular. When the upper berths are filled, this ship's capacity climbs to 3,400, and when you add 1,000 crew members, you have 4,400 souls living on something less than 1,000 feet long. But they occupy a dozen passenger decks, more for the crew, and the ship is wide, in fact, too beamy to pass through the Panama Canal.

Four glass elevators soar through the ship's nine-deck atrium, which is more tasteful and less glitzy than the one aboard her predecessors. The three-deck Caribbean lounge can seat 1,500 for extravagant Las Vegas–style shows performed on a revolving stage and backed by an orchestra that rises

out of the pit on a hydraulic lift. One club has a two-tiered dance floor surrounded by walls of video monitors, and the sports bar brings in the games on huge TV screens. The casino counts two dozen gaming tables and more than 300 slot machines, and for an intimate retreat, slip into the revolving piano bar.

The two bi-level dining rooms, the first for Carnival, have trios serenading during dinner, but the rooms are crowded, and the waiters work hard to keep up with the demand. The Mediterranean Buffet, designed as an international food court on two levels, seats more than 1,250 and serves everything the heart desires, including wok-prepared Chinese food, cooked-to-order pasta, and grilled hot dogs and hamburgers, and has a twenty-four-hour pizzeria.

Four outdoor pools, including one exclusively for children, a three-deck 214-foot spiral waterslide, and seven whirlpools draw hundreds to the open decks, which can get crowded on the days at sea. The Lido Deck pool has the protection of a retractable dome and the novelty of a swim-up bar. The huge Nautica Spa features two more whirlpools, a large gym, aerobics, and massage, loofah, sauna, and steam rooms. Children are well looked after at Camp Carnival, a two-deck suite of play areas and activities.

The 1,379 cabins are among the most spacious and sophisticated in the Carnival fleet, with TVs that call up a selection of films for a charge, coffee tables, good closet space, hair dryers, and big showers. The ship has family cabins that sleep five and lots more that are interconnecting; more than half the outside cabins have balconies. No ship in the fleet is more popular than the *Carnival Victory*.

The Itinerary

Two alternating itineraries operate year-round and include two or three full days at sea. The ship's eastern Caribbean swing leaves **Miami,** spends a day at sea, and calls at **San Juan** for a flamenco-rumba show or city-sights tour, but you can easily do **Old San Juan** on your own, as it begins at the end of the pier. Sailing the short distance to **St. Maarten,** choose from a minibus tour of this Dutch-French island, snorkeling at an offshore island, 100 percent duty-free shopping, or on your own in a rental car. **St. Thomas** offers a party raft cruise with underwater viewing, snorkeling, and swimming, a trip up to Paradise Point for an island view, and shopping on a tour or on your own. The last two days are at sea, cruising slowly back to Miami.

On the ship's western Caribbean circuit, a full day is spent at sea before docking at **Cozumel,** where a ferry link to **Playa del Carmen** provides access to snorkeling, scuba diving, horseback riding around a ranch, and a trip down the coast to the walled Mayan city of **Tulum.** A second sea day is

spent sailing eastward for a day onto **Grand Cayman.** The shore program includes several tours to Stingray City, to which are added an island tour, a catamaran cruise, and scuba diving. It's an overnight sail to Jamaica, where the most popular tours in **Ocho Rios** are to Dunn's River Falls to scurry 600 feet up the slippery rocks, in the shape of a giant staircase; a peaceful, 3-mile river-tubing ride; and horseback riding along the beach and into the shallow waters. Then enjoy the ship for two final nights and a full day at sea, returning to Miami.

Address/Phone: Carnival Cruise Lines, 3655 NW 87th Avenue, Miami, FL 33178; (305) 599–2600 or (800) 327–9501; fax: (305) 406–4740; www.carnival.com

The Ship: *Carnival Victory* was built in 2000 and has a gross tonnage of 102,000, a length of 893 feet, and a draft of 27 feet.

Passengers: 2,758; mostly Americans in their twenties to sixties

Dress: Suits or tuxes for two formal nights; slacks and collared shirts for casual nights

Officers/Crew: Italian officers; international crew

Cabins: 1,379; 853 outside and 508 with private verandas

Fare: $$

What's included: Cruise only

What's not included: Airfare, governmental fees and taxes, shore excursions and water sports, drinks, tips

Highlights: Nonstop activities, entertainment, pool slide

Other itineraries: In addition to the *Carnival Victory*'s seven-day Caribbean cruises, Carnival has many other itineraries in the Caribbean, Bahamas, Mexican coast, Alaska, New England, Canada, and Bermuda.

DISNEY CRUISE LINE'S
Disney Magic
A Full Week in the Caribbean

The *Disney Magic* was the Walt Disney Company's first foray into cruising, and naturally, it's a vehicle to tout Disney-style innovations in dining, entertainment, kids' facilities, and cabin design, which set the ship apart from its closest peers. In many ways the experience is more Disney than cruise—no casino or library—but first-timers and Disney fanatics, adults and children, will just have a ball. The seven-day cruises allow much more time to enjoy the ship and its activity schedule, while the sea time is punctuated by typical Caribbean ports. The shorter three- and four-day cruises aboard the *Disney Wonder* are more likely to be combined with a land-based Walt Disney World Resort package.

Disney Cruise Line got its cruising start in 1998 with the *Disney Magic* and took delivery of the *Disney Wonder* in 1999. Arriving at the pier, you will immediately notice Mickey's big-eared head on the pair of giant red funnels and fanciful golden curlicues on the pointy blue-black bow. But overall, the ship is engaging and elegant, and the Disney-isms are subtly sprinkled throughout the *Magic*'s mellow, art-deco–inspired interior. Framed story sketches from famous 1930s and '40s Disney animated movies blend tastefully against the caramel-colored wood paneling in the stairways and corridors.

One innovation, setting the *Magic* apart from the big-ship crowd, are three restaurants among which passengers and servers rotate over the course of the cruise. It's the ocean liner, 1930s-era Lumiere's one night, the tropical Parrot Cay another, and finally the signature Animator's Palate

restaurant. This bustling, high-tech eatery starts out completely black and white, and then gradually becomes awash in reds, blues, and greens as the walls, ceiling, and even the servers' uniforms take on color. The food, however, is average cruise fare, tasty but nothing special—French onion soup, escargots, fish, steaks, pasta. For dessert, kids get scoops of ice cream served on a palate-shaped plate, and they can pretend to paint using chocolate and strawberry squeeze bottles.

The Topsider Café serves a buffet-style breakfast and lunch spread, and other options for noshing poolside include Pinocchio's Pizzeria, Pluto's Dog House for hamburgers, hot dogs, and fries, and Scoops ice-cream bar. There's twenty-four-hour room service from a limited menu, but no midnight buffet. For adults only, make early reservations for the romantic, away-from-the-fray Palo, a 138-seat, whimsically decorated Italian restaurant. It's well worth the small extra charge.

The *Magic*'s fresh, family-oriented entertainment is a standout. In the nostalgic Walt Disney Theater, actors disappear into trapdoors, fly across the stage, and go through endless exciting costume changes. After-dinner performances include a sweet musical medley of Disney classics, taking the audience from *Peter Pan* and *The Lion King* to *Voyage of the Ghost Ship* and the *Golden Mickeys*.

Kids have as many as fifty dedicated counselors to supervise five age groups in two huge spaces. The Oceaneer Club, for ages three to seven, is a Captain Hook–themed playroom, where kids climb and crawl on a giant pirate-ship's bow and get dressed up from a trunkfull of costumes. For ages eight to twelve, the far-out Oceaneer Lab harbors all kinds of great activities, such as using microscopes, working on computers, and doing arts and crafts. And for teens (thirteen to seventeen), The Stack, a two-room complex, well isolated from adults, offers video screens for films, a disco, Internet Café, and a place just to hang out. Kids can eat dinner with counselors in the Topsiders Café; and if Mom and Dad want more time alone, Flounder's Reef Nursery takes kids, for a fee, from three months to three years between 6:00 P.M. and midnight and for a few hours during the day, dependent on the ship's schedule.

For gym enthusiasts, the fitness center is on the small side, although a pair of virtual-reality step machines is great fun, and the outdoor decks offer basketball and paddle tennis, a decent-size spa, and three pools (one for kids, one for adults, and one for all ages). The rules about who may use which are usually well enforced.

An adults-only entertainment enclave called Beat Street has three lounges: Sessions, an elegant piano bar; Offbeat, a 1970s-style whimsical comedy club; and Rockin' Bar D, a country-and-western-style disco, plus movies and enrichment lectures. The sophisticated Promenade Lounge has a live jazz band.

The majority of the *Magic*'s cabins are thoughtfully equipped with two bathrooms—a sink and toilet in one, and a shower/tub combo and a sink in the other. Cabin size is a plus, too, with all of the 875 standard cabins having a sitting area with a sofa bed to sleep families of three. Some include a pull-down wall-bunk for a fourth, and nearly half have private verandas. Family suites sleep five. All come with hair dryers, safes, shower and short tub, mini-refrigerator, TV, and phone.

The Itinerary

Alternating year-round seven-day cruises sail on a Saturday from **Port Canaveral.** The Eastern Caribbean loop spends the first two days at sea en route to St. Maarten for the day, then St. Thomas and St. John, a day at sea, and finally Castaway Cay.

At **St. Maarten,** the *Magic* docks at **Philipsburg** on the Dutch side, and apart from shopping near to where you leave the ship, the island boasts eight casinos, popular for those who miss one on the ship. There's horseback riding on a beach, biking and hiking tours in the hills and on the shore, and golf outings. A day later at **St. Thomas,** you can choose from a scuba diving trip, a bike tour, more golf, or head across to **St. John** to kayak, parasail, or windsurf.

After a day at sea Disney ships dock at **Castaway Cay,** the company's private island, allowing for a free flow between ship and shore during the day. The property has a section for adults a bit removed from the main area of activities, plus a section for teenage sports, and then of course specific areas set aside for children's activities and for the entire family to play. The barbecue dishes out hamburgers, hot dogs, fries, and corn on the cob with tables under shelter. The crescent beach faces a protected lagoon for boating activities and swimming. You might rent a Sunfish and tack out to photograph your ship at rest.

The Western Caribbean circuit has only two days at sea, calling first at **Key West,** then a sea day, **Grand Cayman, Cozumel,** a sea day, **Castaway Cay,** and a return to Port Canaveral.

Adults traveling without children might wish to book outside the peak kids' summer and holiday seasons. For Disney fanatics and families not afraid of crowds, the *Magic* offers the classic Disney brand of wholesome fun in an elegant, seafaring setting.

Address/Phone: Disney Cruise Line, P.O. Box 10210, Lake Buena Vista, FL 32830; (800) 951–3532; fax: (407) 566–3541; www.disneycruise.com

The Ship: *Disney Magic* was built in 1998, has a gross tonnage of 83,000, a length of 964 feet, and a draft of 25 feet.

Passengers: 1,750 double occupancy or 3,325 if all third, fourth, and fifth berths are occupied. Mostly American families with kids and couples in their thirties to fifties who love the Disney concept

Dress: Jackets for men are expected in Palo and Lumiere's restaurants; collared shirts are fine in other restaurants. No shorts, jeans, or T-shirts in any restaurant.

Officers/Crew: International

Cabins: 875, most with 1½ bathrooms and sitting area with convertible couch (and sometimes bunk) to comfortably sleep three or four; 625 outside and 378 with balconies

Fare: $$$

What's included: Cruise fare only

What's not included: Airfare, governmental fees and taxes, soft drinks, shore excursions, and water sports, bicycles, and strollers on Disney's private island, Castaway Cay

Highlights: Rotation-style dining in three restaurants; large family-friendly cabins with 1½ bathrooms; large play space and scope of children's programs; separate facilities for adults traveling without children; wonderful private island

Other itineraries: Besides these alternating one-week year-round Caribbean cruises, the *Disney Wonder* makes three- and four-day cruises to the Bahamas, and passengers often combine a cruise with a Walt Disney World Resort package, which offers a seamless transfer between land and sea.

ROYAL CARIBBEAN'S
Radiance of the Seas
A Western Caribbean Loop

The *Radiance of the Seas* class, numbering four ships, represents a new direction for Royal Caribbean with much more attention being paid to a shippy look and the sense of sailing on a ship, from the more maritime-oriented decor, dark-wood paneling and deep-sea blues, to the walls of glass that let you see the sea while dining, imbibing, and conversing. The Centrum features a portside wall of glass soaring from Decks 5 through 10 and four sets of glass-enclosed elevators. Yes, there are still the Royal Caribbean trademark miniature golf and rock-climbing wall, now installed on all the ships.

Most of the public rooms—Crown & Anchor Lounge, Champagne Bar, Singapore Sling's piano bar, Windjammer Café, Sky Bar, and the topmost trademark Viking Crown Lounge—are sheathed in glass, great for viewing port arrivals.

Public spaces are fun to inhabit. One, the Colony Club, an interconnecting suite of five spaces, has a rich look with Oriental-patterned carpets, inlaid wood flooring, intimate seating arrangements, and subdued lighting. Another is Singapore Sling's piano bar, spanning the stern with great views over the wake through full-height windows. For an amazing scene, don't miss having a cocktail here on a moonlit night. Keeping the Asian theme but with a twist, the colonial-styled Bombay Billiard Club provides a patterned wood floor and redwood paneling setting for two high-tech pool tables cradled in gimbals and kept even by motorized gyroscopes to overcome any ship movement.

On the *Radiance,* the Solarium is a dose of Africa with stone elephants, a waterfall, watercolor scenes, and thatch umbrellas, while on the *Brilliance,* it's an East Indian–themed Solarium with Indian elephants, bronze statues, and a ceramic-tiled peacock. Aboard the *Radiance,* the Aurora Theater has an Arctic theme decor with deep ocean greens and blues, and on the *Brilliance* it's gold, purple, and reds. For a direct association with the ship's Alaska cruise program, passengers can look up from the pool to see a 12-foot-high cedar totem pole carved by Native Alaskan artist Nathan Jackson.

More generally associated with Royal Caribbean are such places as the Casino Royale, with more than 200 slot machines and several score of gaming tables, a baseball-themed sports bar offering interactive games, the nautically decorated Schooner Bar, an always open Internet center, and the line's signature room, the Viking Crown Lounge, here a quiet retreat and a disco with rotating bar. Even the public bathrooms—bright, airy marbled spaces with mirrors shaped like portholes—will turn heads.

The two dining rooms are two stories high with an impressive double staircase joining the two levels and a cascading waterfall. More maritime inspiration is designed into the Windjammer Café with navy blue carpeting and fabrics, rich wood veneers, and scattered ship models. The number of food counters, eleven in all, spreads out the lines and reduces crowding, and food may be enjoyed indoors or out. Even more informal, the naturally lighted Seaview Café serves the usual fast foods during lunch and dinner hours at tables with rattan chairs.

For watching steaks being cooked in an open kitchen, the ninety-seat Chops Grill offers seats in high-backed booths and a great sea view. Next door, the larger 130-seat Portofino features an Italian menu, and both restaurants provide a sense of occasion that comes with an extra charge.

The ships have three pools, a Sports Deck that serves basketball, volleyball, and paddle-tennis court players, a 9-hole miniature golf course and golf simulators, jogging track, and a rock-climbing wall fixed to the funnel, now a feature on all RCI ships. For children, RCI's Adventure Ocean program offers four supervised age groups play stations with video games, a computer lab, splash pools, and a waterslide.

Historically, Royal Caribbean cabins have been on the small size, while more space has been allocated to public rooms, but on the *Radiance* class, they are respectable, some even more so, in size. Cabin decor has changed from Miami Beach pastels to rich navy blues and copper. All cabins have small fridges; cozy sitting areas; ample drawer and closet space; interactive televisions that tap into booking shore excursions, keep tabs on onboard spending, and check up on the ups and downs of the stock market; desks-cum-vanities with a pullout shelf for personal laptop computers; and typically small RCI showers.

Suites receive butler service and have access to the Concierge Club for tour and travel information or the latest newspaper.

All Royal Caribbean ships are big and

bustling, but this new *Radiance* class offers a higher standard of just about everything that makes a cruise vacation a happy experience at a moderate price level.

The Itinerary

The *Radiance of the Seas* is based in Miami during the winter months and makes two alternating Caribbean cruises, an eastern loop and a western loop. The latter described here calls at Labadee, Ocho Rios, Grand Cayman, and Cozumel and offers two full days at sea.

Sailing out through **Miami**'s Government Cut, the ship turns south to follow the coast and Florida Keys with two nights and a day to get to know the ship before arriving at Royal Caribbean's isolated private resort, **Labadee,** located on the north coast of Hispanola, an island shared by Haiti and the Dominican Republic. Take a tender for a day at one of the five beaches taking part in some of the organized games such as volleyball, water balloon tosses, and limbo contests, or just relax in a hammock. Parasailing and kayaking are available, and for the kids an Aqua Park offers inflatable slides, water seesaws, and floating trampolines.

Then it's an overnight sail to **Ocho Rios,** Jamaica's busiest cruise port, for river tubing down through a lush forest, a jeep safari, or horseback riding along the beach and into the surf. Taxis are available at the pier, and prices are fixed. Then another overnight cruise brings the ship to **Grand Cayman** for a day on beautiful Seven Mile Beach, kayaking along the coast, cycling through villages, or visiting Stingray City, where you swim with these gentle sea creatures. You can scratch their soft undersides, but stay away from the tail. Grand Cayman is a tax haven, and shoppers will like the duty-free prices for jewelry, watches, china, crystal, and perfumes. When you come across large motor yachts in the Caribbean or elsewhere you may see "George Town, C.I." written on the stern.

The *Radiance* docks at **Cozumel** for the nearby beaches and snorkeling at an underwater national park. Sail across to the Yucatan Peninsula for an excursion down the coast to Tulum, the only Mayan city ruins directly on the shore; or go to Xcaret, an ecological park, for swimming in a lagoon. The site also has an aviary, an aquarium, a botanical garden, cultural shows, and many places to eat. Hire a taxi to visit the popular resort of Cancun with its huge variety of shops, restaurants, and places to swim.

Then the cruise winds down with two nights and a day en route to disembarkation at Miami. On alternate weeks, the *Radiance of the Seas* makes an Eastern Caribbean cruise to call at **CocoCay,** another private resort in the Bahamas; **St. Thomas;** and the Dutch side of **St. Maarten.** This itinerary includes three full sea days.

Address/Phone: Royal Caribbean International, 1050 Caribbean Way, Miami, FL 33132; (305) 539–6000; brochures: (800) 327–6700; fax: (305) 374–7354; www.royalcaribbean.com

The Ship: *Radiance of the Seas* was completed in 2001, has a gross tonnage of 90,090, a length of 962 feet, and a draft of 27 feet.

Passengers: 2,100; mostly Americans with some Europeans and lots of families during the school holidays

Dress: Formal and casual nights

Officers/Crew: International officers and crew

Cabins: 1,050, with 813 outside and 577 with verandas

Fare: $$

What's included: Cruise fare only

What's not included: Airfare, port charges and fees, tips, drinks, shore excursions

Highlights: A stunningly decorated ship lacking none of the megaship amenities

Other itineraries: Besides this one-week cruise to the Western Caribbean, operating between November and April, the *Radiance of the Seas* makes an eastern loop, sails through the Panama Canal in the late spring to spend the summer cruising Alaska's Inside Passage, and returns south via a Pacific Ocean cruise to Hawaii. The huge RCI fleet covers most of North and South America and Europe.

CELEBRITY CRUISES'
Galaxy
Stylish and Affordable Caribbean Cruising to the Panama Canal

Celebrity Cruises began as an upscale brand for Chandris Lines, and soon the lower level Fantasy Cruises was phased out. In 1997 Royal Caribbean International bought Celebrity Cruises, but thus far the line is being operated as a separate brand.

The *Galaxy* is spacious and comfortable and exhibits a kind of glamorous, vaguely art deco style associated with classic ocean liners. The decor casts a chic and sophisticated mood, with lots of warm wood tones as well as rich, tactile textures and fabrics in deep primaries, from faux zebra-skin to soft leathers. The ship attracts a wide range of ages and backgrounds.

Celebrity might be best known for its cuisine, which is indeed better than average. Dinners are served in high style in the ship's gorgeous two-deck main dining room, with a wall of glass facing astern to the ship's wakes and, if you're lucky, a moonlit night. The menu is likely to feature something along the lines of pan-fried salmon with parsleyed potatoes, Pad Thai (noodles and veggies in a peanut sauce), tournedos Rossini with foie gras and Madeira sauce, or prime rib with horseradish and baked potato.

Breakfast, lunch, and dinner (by reservation only) are served in the buffet-style lido restaurant. For snacking there's also ice cream, high tea, and pizza available, and pizza can be delivered in a cardboard box to your cabin. In place of traditional midnight buffets, the ship offers "Gourmet Bites," hors d'oeuvres served by waiters in the public lounges between midnight and 1:00 A.M. Waiters are poised and professional, and sommeliers circulate in the dining room and in the lido restaurant.

Activities during days at sea may include enrichment lectures on topics such as personal investing, body language, or handwriting analysis; wine tastings; bingo; art auctions; arts and crafts; spa and salon demonstrations; and dancing lessons. If you prefer solitude, some semblance of peace and quiet can be had on the far corners of the Sky Deck and on the aft Penthouse Deck. Inside there are many hideaways, including Michael's Club, the card room, or the edges of Rendez-Vous Square.

The ship has a well-stocked playroom, called the Fun Factory, and an attached outside deck area with wading pool. During summer and holidays supervised activities are offered all day long for four age groups between three and seventeen. The Aqua-Spas are among the best facilities at sea. The focal point is a 115,000-gallon thalasso-therapy pool, huge hot tubs with warm jets of water. Although managed by Steiner, as on most other ships, there are more exotic treatments offered on this ship such as mud packs, herbal steam baths, and water-based treatments. In the good-sized, windowed gym, landscapes unfold on the color monitors of the ship's high-tech, virtual-reality stationary bikes. There are also aerobic classes in a separate room, an outdoor jogging track, a golf simulator, and a sports deck with basketball, paddle-tennis, and volleyball courts. There are three swimming pools; one is covered by an all-weather retractable roof.

In addition to the Broadway-style musicals performed on two stages, there are live dance bands and pianists performing in other lounges, as well as innovative entertainment like a strolling a cappella group and a strolling magician, who perform in various lounges and public areas.

With its crushed-velvet couches and leather wingback chairs, Michael's Club is a quiet, sophisticated spot for cigars, cordials, and conversation. The disco within the top-deck observation lounge is open until about 3:00 A.M. The cozy, dimly lit nightclub is the spot for cabaret, dancing, and karaoke. First-run movies are screened in the theater, and the ship has a spacious, sultry casino.

Pleasing cabin decor is based on monochromatic themes of muted bluish-purple, green, or red and light-colored furniture. Although inside cabins are about par for the industry standard, outside cabins are larger than usual, and four categories of suites are particularly spacious. Suite passengers are privy to a tuxedo-clad personal butler who serves afternoon tea and complimentary hors d'oeuvres from 6:00 to 8:00 P.M., handles laundry and shoe shining, and will serve you a full five-course dinner in your cabin. Cabin TVs are wired with an interactive system, from which you can order room service from on-screen menus, select the evening's wine, play casino-style games, or browse in "virtual" shops.

The Itinerary

Galveston, located in South Texas on the shores of the Gulf of Mexico, is a relatively new cruise port and is accessible by air into Houston, just an hour to the north. The city, largely rebuilt after the devastating 1900 hurricane and tidal surges, offers a subtropical early twentieth-century atmosphere in its historic residential district and the tourist-oriented commercial center. It is well worth spending a night at one of the waterfront hotels and enjoy the port's excellent seafood restaurants.

The cruise lasts either eleven or twelve nights with the only difference being Montego Bay added to the longer one. They both offer a good balance between a wide variety of port experiences and five full days at sea to enjoy the ship.

Sailing from Galveston's cruise terminal, it's a two-night and one-day sail south to the island of **Cozumel** on Mexico's Yucatan Peninsula. Water activities include spending the day at the beach, an Atlantis submarine dive to the coral reefs, and a catamaran sail. While on land, visit the Mayan coastal ruins at Tulum or the well-established mainland resort at Cancun.

Further south on the peninsula, **Costa Maya,** a relatively recent port of call, offers a choice of several less-visited Mayan ruins, all-terrain-vehicle trips along the coast and into the rain forest, and visits to present-day Mayan villages and the beach.

After two nights and a day at sea, the *Galaxy* is positioned to enter the **Panama Canal** via a series of three locks lifting the ship 85 feet to the level of the Gatun Lake.

Then while the ship is docked at **Cristobal,** you can go freshwater bass fishing (catch and release) in Gatun Lake, visit an Embera Indian village, ride the Isthmian Railroad that parallels the canal to Panama City on the Pacific Ocean, or visit **Panama City** itself by bus.

Sailing overnight almost due west to **Puerto Limon, Costa Rica,** drive inland to **San José,** the country's colonial-style capital, walk through a rain forest, ride a train along the old banana exporting railroad, and take a boat along the Tortuguero Canal to spot wildlife such as tree sloths and birds. Then it's another relaxing day at sea en route to **Grand Cayman.** Here, there's duty-free shopping, and the beaches are among the best in the Caribbean; or to be more active, go snorkeling and swim among stingrays at Stingray City.

Then the final three nights and two days are spent at sea enjoying the ship as it sails north back to disembarkation at Galveston.

Address/Phone: Celebrity Cruises, 1050 Caribbean Way, Miami, FL 33132; (305) 539–6000 or (800) 437–3111; www.celebritycruises.com

The Ships: *Galaxy* was built in 1996, has a gross tonnage of 77,713, a length of 866 feet, and a draft of 25 feet.

Passengers: 1,870; mostly American couples in their late thirties to sixties, some honeymooners and families, too

Dress: Suits or tuxes for the formal nights, jackets for semiformal nights, and slacks and collared shirts for casual nights; no shorts, jeans, or T-shirts in the restaurants

Officers/Crew: Greek officers; international crew

Cabins: 948; 639 outside and 220 with verandas

Fare: $$

What's included: Cruise fare only

What's not included: Airfare, port charges, excursions, water sports, drinks, tips

Highlights: AquaSpas are some of best at sea. Modern art collection is one of most interesting and provocative in the industry.

Other itineraries: In addition to this Caribbean and Panama Canal itinerary, which operates between late November and April, Celebrity ships cruise to Alaska, Mexico, South America, Bermuda, and in Europe.

ROYAL CARIBBEAN'S
Voyager of the Seas
The Western Caribbean's Largest Cruise Ship

Royal Caribbean clearly won the "who can build the biggest and best" competition with its 137,000-ton *Voyager of the Seas,* a full 25 percent larger than the competing *Grand Princess* and *Carnival Destiny* when new. More importantly, however, the company started with a blank slate and came up with a ship that is more than just an oversize sistership—rather, she is a true trendsetter that leaves most passengers dazzled. Like her smaller fleet mate *Sovereign of the Seas,* the *Voyager* may well be remembered as a daring new ship that set a precedent for all ships to follow, and larger ones are coming!

Unlike other megaships, which often try to hide their size through smaller public rooms, the *Voyager* makes no pretensions about being large—she is huge and she wants everyone to know it. From the Royal Promenade to the three-story dining room to the expansive upper deck space, the ship is full of grand sweeping vistas and cavernous spaces, constant reminders of how big she is. Of course, size does have its downsides as well, including less personal service and occasional waits for elevators or disembarkation.

The first thing that passengers notice upon boarding is the fascinating Royal Promenade, a 500-foot, four-story walkway running down the middle of the ship. Cafes and shops line the path, while three decks of "Promenade View" cabins look down onto the scene through large bay windows. The space is constantly brimming with passengers strolling by, stopping to listen to the piano player in the bar, or simply striking up a conversation at a sidewalk cafe. The space works well, and like any town center it takes on different moods throughout the day and into the evening, especially when street performers and buskers are about.

Just aft of the Royal Promenade is the ship's three-story dining room, easily one of the most spectacular rooms to put to sea within the last twenty years. Crowned by a striking chandelier and flanked by window walls on either side, the three levels are linked by a dramatic grand staircase. Unfortunately, the food does not always live up to the decor in the main dining room, and it is hard to get a reservation for a better menu in the smaller alternative Portofino restaurant.

Much attention has been given to the ship's ice-skating rink, which is used for both shows and free skating for passengers. There is also a rock-climbing wall 200 feet above the keel on the after end of the funnel, and it is equally fun just to watch the passengers doing the actual climbing. For the active set, there is also a full-size basketball court, a miniature golf course, an inline skating track, and a large spa. From the elaborate children's facilities to the wedding chapel to the Johnny Rocket's 1950s-style diner, there really is something for everyone.

Traditionalists will delight in the ship's open deck space, including a wraparound promenade deck that actually cantilevers over the side, giving a unique perspective on the steel hull crashing through the seas. Even the bow is open to passengers, and it is fantastic to go all the way forward at night and gaze back at the darkened superstructure and spinning radar antennae.

Cabins are of good size and generally well laid out, and many have balconies with steel partitions on one side, offering true privacy from at least one of your neighbors. In addition to the standard inside and outside cabins, there are many "Promenade View" cabins (which are slightly more expensive than standard inside cabins) that offer bay windows looking down onto the Royal Promenade. For those who can't get enough of city life, these cabins are perfect—although other passengers can see in just as easily as you can see out unless the curtains are drawn.

Listing the additional spaces on board will not do justice to the *Voyager*. She is visually fascinating, and the extensive use of glass permits some interesting people-watching vistas looking either within or out from the ship. This is not your standard cookie-cutter cruise ship, and the creativity shows.

The Itinerary

The *Voyager of the Seas* sails Sundays seasonally (December to May) from **Miami,** hits the larger Western Caribbean ports, and includes two sea days.

The first day is spent at sea, allowing passengers time to get acclimated and to find their way around. On Tuesday, the ship anchors off **Labadee,** which is Royal Caribbean's private "island," although it's actually a private, secluded stretch of the Haitian coastline. Passengers can enjoy the day sunning on the beach or renting a small sailboat. The next day is spent in **Ocho Rios, Jamaica,** where passengers can climb the famous Dunns River Falls or enjoy a guided bamboo raft journey down a tropical river.

Popular **Grand Cayman** offers some upscale shopping in **George Town** in addition to **Stingray City,** where tame stingrays surround swimmers offering them food. **Seven Mile Beach** and renowned diving on "The Wall" will satisfy those who yearn to spend all their time in the water or on the beach.

The last port is the resort island of **Cozumel, Mexico.** For those who are not into the excellent snorkeling and diving opportunities here, there are the Mayan coastal ruins at **Tulum** or a day trip to resorty **Cancun.** With a last day at sea, here's another chance to rediscover the ship all over again. On alternate weeks the port calls are Belize, Costa Maya, Cozumel, and Grand Cayman.

Address/Phone: Royal Caribbean International, 1050 Caribbean Way, Miami, FL 33132; (305) 539–6000 or (800) 327–6700 for brochures; fax: (305) 374–7354; www.royalcaribbean.com

The Ship: *Voyager of the Seas* was built in 1999. It has a gross tonnage of 137,000, a length of 1,020 feet, and a draft of 29 feet.

Passengers: 3,114 double occupancy; mostly Americans of all ages. As many as 3,608 passengers have been on board at once, a peacetime record for any ship.

Dress: Suits or jacket and tie for the formal night and jackets for informal nights

Officers/Crew: International

Cabins: 1,557; 939 outside, 757 with balconies, and 138 "Promenade View" cabins looking onto the Royal Promenade

Fare: $$

What's included: Cruise fare only

What's not included: Airfare, port charges, tips, drinks, shore excursions

Highlights: An exciting, innovative ship with enough options to please everyone.

Other itineraries: In addition to this December-to-May seven-day cruise, the *Voyager* sails to the Eastern Caribbean and in the summer is based in the Mediterranean from Barcelona. The equally huge *Explorer of the Seas, Adventure of the Seas,* and *Serenade of the Seas* sail year-round on other Caribbean itineraries. Royal Caribbean cruises the Mexican Riviera, Alaska, Hawaii, and Europe.

SEA CLOUD CRUISES'
Sea Cloud
Caribbean Island Hopping under Sail in Style

Few ships can match the sense of privilege and excitement standing on the *Sea Cloud*'s teak deck as the crew unfurls the sails 172 feet above the sea. Combining the romance of a tall ship with the camaraderie and meticulous service found on a luxury yacht, the *Sea Cloud* provides a most inspiring sea voyage.

Built in 1931 for American cereal heiress

Marjorie Merriweather Post, the *Sea Cloud* was then the largest private yacht ever built. Ms. Post spent years designing the ship and spared no expense in its fitting out, even going so far as to rent a Brooklyn warehouse where she constructed interior mock-ups.

Sailing as her own beloved yacht until 1955, *Sea Cloud* had a remarkable career entertaining royalty and being dispatched on diplomatic missions for one of Ms. Post's four husbands. During World War II, the ship saw service in the U.S. Coast Guard against German U-boats but not without initial objections by President Roosevelt, who felt she was simply too beautiful to be sacrificed. Eventually sold and forgotten in Panama, she was bought by a group of German investors who returned her to service in 1979 as a cruise ship for sixty-four passengers and sixty crew.

Today, Ms. Post's personal touch and elegant lifestyle continue to be felt onboard as if it was yet her home at sea. Rich mahogany woods and constantly shined brass forms the superstructure while varnished wooden railings and benches line the teak promenade deck. Blue cushions arranged around the stern are the perfect location for sunbathing, chatting, or stargazing. Most days on deck are spent reveling in the joys of being under sail in the company of like-minded passengers.

The intimate library and adjoining dining room may be two of the most beautiful public rooms at sea, with gilded chandeliers, oil paintings, and dark wood paneling. For the formal dinners elegant table settings are navy blue, gold, and white china embossed with the ship's logo; silver napkin rings; candlelight; and fresh flowers.

Delectable lunch buffets are served on the promenade deck, and the ship's long-serving crew carries one's laden trays up one deck to the partially covered Lido. Treats such as freshly made waffles with ice cream or crepes to order are served outside each day at 4:00 P.M., an indulgent temptation not to be missed.

Two nights a week, passengers dress up in suits or jackets and are served off a fixed menu, and on other nights, polo shirts are fine for the outdoor dinner buffet. While the menu is not as extensive as on other ships, the quality is comparable to the very best. Choices such as veal steak with Calvados sauce and potato strudel, or duck breast with kumquat sauce, and leek and rissole potatoes reflect the ship's occasional German clientele. However, menus are adjusted each week according to the nationalities sailing.

If you have the money and inclination, book one of the eight original cabins that resemble suites at Ritz Carlton or Waldorf Astoria rather than anything found at sea. Marjorie's Suite (#1) displays an opulence reminiscent of Versailles: a blue-canopied bed in antique white with gold-leaf ornamentation, Louis Philippe chairs, chandeliers, and plaster ceilings with intricate moldings; while the dark paneling with deep-red furnishings leave no doubt that Cabin #2 was E. F. Hutton's domain.

All eight are unique and lavish, with fireplaces, antique dressers, and bathrooms with Carrara marble and gilded faucets, while some even have two walk-in closets or extra-deep bathtubs. They are so fabulous that one night is designated an "open house" where passengers dress up and freely inspect the cabins while the crew offers champagne and canapés.

The majority of cabins, however, are modern additions located on the upper decks with windows onto the deck space. Those on the top level are elevated above the deck and do give a fairly private view. While furnished attractively and fitted with quality materials, they are significantly smaller than both the original cabins and what you'll find on most ships, especially given *Sea Cloud*'s high fares.

The real beauty, however, is in the traditional rigging, masts, and sails that require a large deck gang to climb aloft. A four-masted barque, the *Sea Cloud* has twenty-nine sails and hundreds of lines that run from the deck to the very top of the mast. Seen without the sails up, the rigging is stark and haunting in its complexity, and with full sails set, it is an evocative call to the past. There is a tremendous joy being onboard with the sails set. *Sea Cloud* is an authentic remnant from another era possessing a mystique and cache that cannot be duplicated.

The Itinerary

Embarking in **Antigua,** a sunset departure provides the first introduction to the *Sea Cloud* life and the quiet yacht harbors that defined the Caribbean before mass tourism. Outside the port the ship takes on a gentle motion that is more like a sailboat than a large ship, and the intricate rigging and masts backlit against the setting sun are hauntingly beautiful.

At 9:00 A.M. the next morning, everyone gathers on deck to hear the captain explain the setting of the sails. Soon, the deck crew scampers effortlessly up the shrouds and out onto the yardarms and one by one, the sails unfurl and start to fill. With the engines shut off, *Sea Cloud* spends the rest of the day under sail before anchoring just before sunset in **Virgin Gorda**'s North Sound.

A complimentary shore excursion the next morning takes everyone for a swim and a walk through the Baths, a naturally formed collection of house-size boulders strewn across the beach. After returning to the ship for lunch, there is time for a quiet afternoon on a mostly deserted beach, water lapping at our feet and the *Sea Cloud* anchored just offshore. With the ship remaining here till morning, after dinner many passengers visit the popular Bitter End Yacht Club.

The next morning with the sails unfurled the ship is underway, and a champagne brunch is served while cruising past the British Virgin Islands. Dropping anchor off **Jost Van Dyke** shortly after noon, *Sea Cloud* shares the long, white beach with visiting sailboats, and passengers visit the Soggy Dollar Bar, so named because yachtsmen swim ashore with their wallets.

Most days follow a similar pattern, with a half day in port, often at the beach, and half onboard under sail. We all find our own deck space, to read or chat about the sails, enjoying a casual Caribbean pace. Entertainment is limited to pre- and post-dinner piano music, and one evening crew members sing salty sea shanties then join passengers at the bar in a tradition that started in the early 1980s.

On British colonial **Anguilla,** you can enjoy an island off the beaten track and its many virtually empty beaches as tourism here centers on upscale resorts. Also try out the ship's windsurfing gear or be towed behind a Zodiac in a variation on the banana boat. An entire next day is spent in posh **St. Barts,** and with the ship anchored till midnight, some go ashore for a French dinner in Gustavia. In Basseterre, **St. Kitts,** a complimentary shore excursion takes everyone to Brimstone Hill, a seventeenth-century fort that has been called "The Gibraltar of the Caribbean."

Setting sail from this lush mountainous island, you have one more chance to experience the joy of *Sea Cloud* under sail before docking the next morning in **Antigua.**

Address/Phone: Sea Cloud Cruises, 32–40 North Dean Street, Englewood, NJ 07631; (888) 732–2568 or (201) 227–9404; fax: (201) 227–9424; www.seacloud.com; Agents are: Elegant Cruises & Tours, Inc., (800) 683–6767; www.elegantcruises.com

The Ship: *Sea Cloud* was originally built at the *Hussar* in 1931, and was rebuilt into a cruise ship in 1979. She has a gross tonnage of 2,532, a length of 360 feet, and a draft of 17 feet.

Passengers: 64 well-heeled Americans, often part of a group; and occasionally Germans

Dress: Casual during the day, with passengers smartening up for dinner and dressing semiformally for two or three nights

Officers/Crew: European captain, international crew

Cabins: 32 with a wide range of choice, all outside with windows or portholes

Fare: $$$$

What's included: Unless part of a group, cruise only; plus shore excursions, wines at dinner

What's not included: Airfare, port charges, drinks, tips

Highlights: Experiencing the opulence of a former private yacht and the magic of a tall ship under sail; the company of like-minded passengers

Other itineraries: In addition to this seven-night cruise in the Caribbean, operating during the winter months, there is a second Caribbean loop, a variety of Mediterranean sailings, and a westbound Atlantic crossing in November. Running mate *Sea Cloud II,* built in 2001, sails to the Caribbean and Northern Europe.

WINDSTAR CRUISES'
Wind Spirit
Motorsailing the Eastern Caribbean

Windstar Cruises, founded in 1986, operates three high-tech motor sail ships, the sails being a highly decorative feature that unfurl with the push of a button on the bridge and give an extra couple of knots when the winds are favorable.

With the distinctive profile of a large yacht and a maritime atmosphere within, the *Wind Spirit* immediately pleases the eye when boarding. The main lounge, located aft, has a sailing ship–style skylight over the dance floor that rises into an attractive centerpiece for the open deck above. It becomes the social venue before and after meals with light entertainment after dinner. An adjacent room offers a two-table casino and slot machines, but this is not a late-night ship. Many passengers enjoy selecting

from several hundred videos or CDs and squirreling away in their cabins.

The wood-paneled dining room offers open-seating flexibility, and dress is always casual, with jackets and ties seen only at the captain's table. Entrees may feature linguine with frutti di mare, crisp duck breast, and grilled filet mignon. In good weather only dinner is served here, while the Veranda provides glass-enclosed protection for breakfast and lunch with sheltered tables out on deck and under parasols. Food is available from a menu or the buffet; at breakfast, a chef prepares omelets and pancakes and, at lunch, a pasta or a superb bouillabaisse. Bread pudding is a daily lunchtime staple.

Dinner takes place under the stars one evening, a romantic outdoor setting with tables arranged around the pool and with dancing on deck between courses. The spread includes jumbo shrimp, mussels, crab, lots of salad fixings, and freshly grilled tuna, lobster tails, steak, lamb chops, and chicken breasts.

The daytime gathering spot is the lido, partly a covered lounge with sit-up bar and partly an open area with a small pool for dipping, a whirlpool, deck chairs, and cushioned mats. The water-sports program is a big draw and includes diving instruction and snorkeling in several ports and complimentary use of sailboats, sailboards, banana boats, and kayaks that are launched from the marina deck. Gym equipment includes aerobic trainers, two treadmills, two bicycles, a rowing machine, weights, and a sauna.

The ship's seventy-four roomy outside cabins on two decks are similar, with beds, either twins or queen-size, set beneath twin portholes. Amenities include flat-screen TVs—with news, features, and three movie channels—and a built-in combination of a CD player, DVD player, minibar, and refrigerator. A dining table folds out for in-cabin dining from a full menu at mealtimes. The bathrooms have teakwood floors and circular, steel-gray shower and toilet stalls.

The Itinerary

The week's itinerary is planned around water sports, beach outings, and slow-paced sightseeing, a terrific combination for a week of unwinding.

At **St. Thomas,** the embarkation port, the harbor may be crowded with huge cruise liners, but once the *Wind Spirit* slips out of the harbor, another world is ahead. **St. John,** also in the U.S. Virgin Islands, is an overnight call where the ship gently swings at anchor. Spend the morning on a scenic island drive to the Virgin Islands National Park and the afternoon at the beach, one of the Caribbean's finest. Anchoring off

Marigot, St. Martin, on the French/Dutch island's less commercial side, the most popular activity features a spirited sailing race aboard an America's Cup 12-meter boat with you acting as crew.

On nearby and upscale **St. Barts,** there's a chance to go horseback riding and snorkeling, and, for a change of venue, check out Gustavia's restaurants lining the small harbor. They all have menus out front, and once you have made a choice, go inside to make a reservation for dinner, as the ship does not sail until late. Tortola and Jost Van Dyke, both in the British Virgin Islands, are serenely peaceful places. Cruising to **Tortola,** take a taxi to Mount Sage National Park for a hike along the Rain Forest Trail or the Mahogany Forest Trail. **Jost Van Dyke** is an ideal destination for a morning on the beach. The ship anchors overnight at **Virgin Gorda,** and from the stern marina, you can go for a sail or take out a kayak. The most popular excursion is to the Baths, an area of massive boulders by the sea, where there are narrow rock cuts and caves to explore.

Address/Phone: Windstar Cruises, 300 Elliott Avenue West, Seattle, WA 98119; (206) 281–3535 or (800) 258–7245; brochures: (800) 626–9900; fax: (206) 286–3229; www.windstarcruises.com

The Ship: *Wind Spirit* was built in 1988 and has a gross tonnage of 5,350, a length of 440 feet, and a draft of 13 feet.

Passengers: 148; mostly American, forty and up

Dress: Casual

Officers/Crew: British officers; Filipino and Indonesian crew

Cabins: 74; all similar, roomy outside with portholes, apart from one owner's suite

Fare: $$$

What's included: Cruise fare and port charges, basic tips

What's not included: Airfare, governmental fees, drinks, shore excursions, extra tips

Highlights: A carefree and casual lifestyle in small Caribbean ports

Other itineraries: In addition to this seven-day Caribbean cruise aboard the *Wind Spirit,* which operates between December and April, the fleet includes sistership, *Wind Star,* and the 14,745-ton, 312-passenger *Wind Surf* (formerly *Club Med I*). Itineraries, mostly seven days, are offered in the Mediterranean and Caribbean, plus longer Signature Voyages, transatlantic crossings, and a renewed program in Costa Rica.

STAR CLIPPERS'
Star Clipper
Caribbean Cruising under Sail

The *Star Clipper* and sistership *Star Flyer* were conceived by Swedish yachting enthusiast Mikael Krafft as near replicas of mid-nineteenth-century fast clipper ships. Built in Ghent, Belgium, in the early 1990s, the pair qualify as two of the largest and tallest sailing ships ever built and, in summer 2000, were joined by the brand-new, five-masted *Royal Clipper.*

In price and accommodations the *Star Clipper* falls between the simpler Windjammer Barefoot fleet and the upscale four Windstar Cruise vessels. At sea the ship is generally under sail from late evening to early or mid-morning the next day. Passengers may help with the lines, but there is no pressure to do so. When the wind dies, the 1,370-horsepower Caterpillar diesel engine kicks in.

The Tropical Bar provides the *Star Clipper*'s social center, located amidships on a sheltered deck under a protective canvas awning. One of the two public rooms is an Edwardian-style library, with a wall of mahogany-fronted bookcases flanking a fireplace and comfy seating for reading and cards on a rainy day. The other, with light wood-paneled walls and recessed seating, serves as a piano lounge, with a pianist seated beneath circular skylights cut into the bottom of the suspended swimming pool.

In good weather the lounge and library see little use during the day, and most passengers gather around the wheelhouse and the two sun-deck swimming pools or at the midships bar. In the morning the captain holds forth at story time, when he recites sailing-ship traditions and rules of navigation and discusses the day's program.

Meals are served to both officers and passengers at one open sitting in a wood- and brass-accented dining room. Breakfast and lunch are buffet style, with a good choice of hot and cold items, while dinner is served by a waiter with the menu offering a fish, meat, and vegetarian entree. The food is of good quality and well prepared but by no means gourmet. Dress is casual but never ragged.

Cabins, nearly all outside and some shaped by the ship's hull, are of moderate size and have a sailing-ship feel, using wood trim, electric lamps mounted in gimbals, and decorative brass counter railings. Amenities include phones and televisions and tiny bathrooms with water-saving push-button showers.

The Itinerary

The Treasure Islands week embarks and disembarks at **St. Maarten,** the Dutch and shopping half of the island shared with St. Martin, the more peaceful French side. The first call is at the upscale resort island of **Anguilla,** then the beaches at **Sandy Cay** and **Soper's Hole** provide opportunities for swimming, snorkeling, and windsurfing. Norman Island, in the British Virgin Islands, the site of Robert Louis Stevenson's *Treasure Island,* is now a private, protected preserve. **Virgin Gorda,** an overnight stay, is noted for its Baths, an area of massive boulders by the sea, with narrow rock cuts and caves to explore.

Jost Van Dyke is an offbeat stop for cruise ships, and the *Star Clipper* is likely to be the largest vessel in the Great Harbour. Wander over to Foxy's, a classic beach bar for locals and the yachting set.

At **St. Kitts** there is an island tour to old plantation sites, great views from Brimstone Hill, golfing, and a chance to shop at **Basseterre.** Off **St. Barts,** always a favorite stop, the little harbor island at Gustavia provides an appropriate setting for the *Star Clipper.* It being the biggest sailing ship to call, you can expect a lot of curious onlookers. There are moderately priced and expensive restaurants within walking distance of the landing, and the shopping here is good and less frenetic than on **St. Maarten,** where the cruise ends.

When the weather permits, a very special treat is offered, a Zodiac ride to observe just how splendid the *Star Clipper* looks slicing majestically through the water, with all sixteen sails catching the wind. From a water-level position ahead of the bow, passengers watch the ship bear down on them; and viewed from the stern, the ship appears to be leaving you behind. The *Star Clipper* is a democratic experience—it's not easy to tell the difference between passengers with money and those who have saved up for this easygoing cruise with visits to small ports.

Address/Phone: Star Clippers, 4101 Salzebo Street, Coral Gables, FL 33146; (305) 442–0550 or reservations: (800) 442–0551; brochures: (800) 442–0556; fax: (305) 442–1611; www.starclippers.com

The Ship: *Star Clipper* was built in 1992 and has a gross tonnage of 2,298, a length of 360 feet, and a draft of 18.5 feet.

Passengers: 168; all ages; some Europeans, but English is the lingua franca

Dress: Casual at all times

Officers/Crew: European officers; international crew

Cabins: 84; 78 outside, most relatively compact; no verandas

Fare: $$

What's included: Cruise only

What's not included: Airfare, port charges, tips, drinks

Highlights: A terrific outdoor sailing experience; small yachting ports; thoroughly relaxed, social atmosphere

Other itineraries: Besides this and an alternative seven-night Leeward Islands' cruise, which operates between November and April, the *Star Clipper* offers Western Mediterranean itineraries and spring and fall transatlantic positioning voyages. The sistership *Star Flyer* operates in the Greek islands and along the Turkish coast from May to October, then travels via the Suez Canal to cruise the coasts of Malaysia and Thailand, returning through the Indian Ocean in April. The five-masted *Royal Clipper,* completed in 2000 and the largest sailing vessel ever built, also cruises the Caribbean, Mediterranean, and Atlantic.

WINDJAMMER BAREFOOT CRUISES'
Legacy
Eastern Caribbean Sailing Fancy-Free

The famous Captain Mike Burke, now retired, founded the company in 1947. He purchased a slew of ships with interesting histories, transformed them into one-of-a-kind sailing vessels, and for years hosted party cruises popular with singles. Burke's children run the company now and, over the past few years, have been making a conscious effort to shake off the vestiges of the old self and create a more mainstream experience. Windjammer has recently hired its first hotel manager to improve the overall quality of the dining and cabin service, has added a kids' program (arts and crafts, snorkeling trips) on the *Legacy* during the summer months, and has plans to build additional new sailing ships.

Launched in 1997, the *Legacy* is the line's biggest and most modern. Built in France in 1959 as a research vessel called the *France II,* the ship was acquired by Windjammer in 1989 and converted into a traditional tall ship. The brightest and most spacious in the fleet, the *Legacy* is a departure from Windjammer's fleet of old-timers. It has comfortable cabins with bunk-style beds and good-sized private bathrooms, a cheerful dining saloon with large, round booths, and a roomy expanse of outdoor deck space. There's space to move around and then some.

Dining is informal family-style and ranges from unmemorable to really tasty. All breads and pastries are homemade, and at dinner, after soup and salad are served, passengers can choose from two main entrees, such as curried shrimp and roast pork with garlic sauce. Unlimited carafes of red and white wine are complimentary. Tasty breakfast, like eggs Benedict as well as the normal fare, and lunch, such as lobster pizza and apple salad, are served buffet style. At Jost Van Dyke the crew lugs ashore a picnic lunch for an afternoon beach party.

The Itinerary

The *Legacy* makes its way to off-the-beaten-track Caribbean ports of call like **Tortola, Virgin Gorda, Jost Van Dyke, Norman Island,** and **St. John** (as well as touristy ones like **St. Thomas**), anchoring offshore a mile or two and shuttling passengers back and forth by tender. Landings may require wading through knee-deep water to get ashore. Several excursions, like island tours and snorkeling, are offered in each port. The ship is usually the biggest vessel in port, and you'll feel like a quiet visitor, not an interloper.

With a palpable pirate-ship feel, the four-masted barquentine (powered by both sails and engines) and its yards of sails, chunky portholes, and generous use of wood lures passengers into a fantasy world of fairytale adventure. Guests are invited to help pull in the sails, crawl into the bow net, which juts out over the water, and sleep out on deck whenever they please (mats are provided). There are few rules and lots of freedom. The *Legacy* delivers an ultrainformal seafaring adventure rich in eccentricities. For example, there are no keys for the cabins (you can only lock cabins from the inside), rum punch is served in paper cups, daily announcements are written in magic marker on a bulletin board, and the purser doubles as the nurse and gift-shop manager.

Corny yet cute rituals make the trip feel like summer camp for adults: for instance, the doubloon system at the bar (a debit card of sorts that is punched with holes each time you buy a drink), the hymn "Amazing Grace" loudly broadcast over the PA system each time the ship's sails are hoisted, and morning "story time," when the captain regales guests with the day's schedule and some funny tall tale he's concocted on the fly.

Besides this morning dose of down-home entertainment, you're on your own until happy hour. Just about every day is spent in port somewhere, and the occasional day at sea might feature a knot-tying demonstration and a bridge tour. The entertainment is the ship itself and the camaraderie among passengers. At 5:00 P.M. every day gallons of complimentary rum swizzles are generously offered with hors d'oeuvres like spicy meatballs, chicken fingers, and cheese and crackers. Guests gather on deck, often still in their sarongs and shorts, mingling in the fresh sea air, with taped music playing in the background. Sometimes an impromptu song or skit takes shape from a couple of fun-loving, down-to-earth guests. After dinner head up to the bar for drinks—you won't spend more than $3.00 a pop—or grab a chaise longue or mat and hit the deck. One or two nights a week a local pop band is brought on board for a few hours of dancing, and there's a weekly barbecue buffet dinner and a costume party. Generally the ship stays late in one or two ports so that passengers can head ashore to one of the island watering holes. From honeymooning couples in their twenties to grandparents in their seventies, Windjammer attracts a broad range of adventurers, who return again and again.

Address/Phone: Windjammer Barefoot Cruises, 1759 Bay Road, Miami Beach, FL 33119; (305) 672–6453 or (800) 327–2601; fax: (305) 674–1219; www.windjammer.com

The Ship: *Legacy* was built in 1959 as the research vessel *France II* and was converted in 1997 to a windjammer. It has a gross tonnage of 1,165, a length of 294 feet, and a draft of 23 feet.

Passengers: 122; all ages and mostly Americans

Dress: Casual at all times

Officers/Crew: American and British officers; West Indian crew

Cabins: 62 cabins, outside with either a window or porthole and relatively compact

Fare: $$

What's included: Cruise only, rum punch at happy hour, and wine at dinner

What's not included: Airfare, port charges, shore excursions, tips, bar drinks

Highlights: Carefree, very casual onboard atmosphere; unstructured; few rules

Other itineraries: In addition to the *Legacy*'s seven-night Caribbean cruises in winter and spring, round-trip from St. Thomas, visiting the British and U.S. Virgin Islands, and from St. Lucia to the Windward Islands, the fleet includes four other windjammers (*Flying Cloud, Mandalay, Polynesia,* and *Yankee Clipper*) plus the passenger supply vessel *Amazing Grace,* which sails year-round in the Bahamas and Caribbean.

LATIN AMERICA

CRUISE WEST'S
Spirit of Endeavour
Small-Ship Adventure Cruising in the Sea of Cortez

Cruise West, an American firm in business since 1973, may be the best known of the Alaska-to-Mexico small-ship operating companies, offering intimate encounters along the West Coast of North America with a casual, folksy atmosphere aboard seven ships. One of the company's most sophisticated vessels is the 102-passenger *Spirit of Endeavour,* once belonging to Clipper Cruise and a near sister to the *Nantucket Clipper.* From its decks, you are able to get ever so close to nature and the sea and all that inhabits therein, and even on occasion practically reach out and touch friendly whales. That's the beauty of exploring by small ship, foraging for adventure in a remote northwest corner of Mexico.

Oak and teak are used throughout this light and airy ship. There's an all-purpose lounge bathed in windows where guests congregate, socialize, and listen to presentations by the expedition leaders on the landscape, geology, and local culture. In keeping with the informal atmosphere, the speakers mingle with passengers to answer questions and share experiences.

The dining room serves up well-prepared American fare and Mexican specialties in one open-seating arrangement. Young crew members earn an A in enthusiasm and a B on the finer points of dining room service, contributing to Cruise West's laid-back, summer-camp feel. Before dinner each evening, there will be an informal talk about the next day's attractions and a question-and-answer session. Videos and books are available for borrowing.

All cabins are outside, most with picture windows for superb views, and Upper Deck cabins open to the side promenade. The TVs are closed circuit for viewing the ship's video collection.

Outside decks are ample fore, aft, and topside for relaxing and viewing. It's commonplace for the captain to speed up, slow down, backtrack, or do whatever it takes to spot the wildlife, such as gray whales, sea lions, and bottle-nose dolphins, that inhabits the Pacific lagoons.

The Itinerary

The *Spirit of Endeavour* sticks mainly to the uninhabited or sparsely populated islands along the **Sea of Cortez's Baja California** coast, anchoring at dinnertime and then often moving in the middle of the night to allow passengers a day of hiking, kayaking, and snorkeling at a new location. It is unusual to see another ship, and if so, it is another small expedition vessel.

Cruise West carries an expedition leader and assistant, both Americans, and a Mexican park ranger. Passengers have access to two-person kayaks, and they may go paddling in groups with a naturalist or on their own within sight of the ship.

The week's cruise begins and ends at **Cabo San Lucas,** a busy place with hotels, condos, restaurants, cafes, and souvenir and craft shops, but once away, it's another world for nearly a full week, mostly nature-oriented but with visits to small towns and a Mexican mission.

Drop anchor off **Isla Espiritu Santo** and go ashore to Bonanza Beach for the day in the *Endeavour*'s inflatable boats to swim, snorkel, and kayak in crystal clear waters that provides a habitat for 900 species of fish. A hike into the desert reveals a tropical world with water-based plants and all manner of bugs living underneath. The terrain, with tangles of cacti, is treated like the Galápagos, and great care is taken not to stray from a recognized path. Two animals found nowhere else are the black-tailed jackrabbit and the antelope squirrel.

Back on the ship, you learn that the Sea of Cortez provides an ideal home for common and bottle-nosed dolphins, and blue, fin, humpback, and minke whales. It is great fun to watch the bottle-nosed dolphins leaping over the bow waves and the wake. Birds are not quite as numerous, but there should be sightings of turkey vultures, brown pelicans, and diving cormorants.

Then during the ship's winter season, the best whale sightings are in the Pacific, so passengers transfer across the Baja peninsula to **Bahia Magdalena** to board eight-person motorized pangas. There is a good chance but no certainty of seeing gray whales and their calves stopping in lagoons during their 6,000-mile annual migration from Alaska's Bering Sea. Sometimes a 40-foot whale might swim right up to the side of the boat and even allow patting. When they dive, the water is so clear, you can see the entire whale and calf swimming below the boat.

Isla San Jose and Isla San Francisco are pristine volcanic islands, and the energetic can climb one of the peaks and gaze down on the kayakers dotted about the mangrove-backed lagoon below. Others can go swimming, snorkeling, and beachcombing.

The **Loreto Mission,** founded at the end of the seventeenth century as the mother church for all other missions as far north as Sonoma, California, hosts a wine and cheese reception accompanied by a singer and guitarist. Loreto also offers a small museum of artifacts from the area's colonial era.

The captain cruises slowly by a seamount called Los Isotes to observe a colony of blue-footed boobies, one of the unusual species also found in the Galápagos. The location is a favorite spot for sea lions, and often there is a chance to swim among the females and their young pups.

Sail on to Isla Partida for a beach visit or a nature walk into the deep canyons, then make an afternoon stop at Ensenada Grande, a sheltered cove fringed by mangroves, where the sandy bottom gradually deepens over some several hundred feet from the beach.

Tying up at **La Paz,** Baja California Sur's capital, the long seafront promenade is lined with souvenir and craft shops, hawkers, a strip of hopping bars, and kids cruising in cars. But there's also Old Baja to explore before attending a private fiesta with Mexican musicians and dancers on the terrace of the Governor's mansion.

Sail overnight, and in the morning pass the spectacular rock formations known as Los Arcos, located at the very southern tip of the Baja Peninsula, before entering the inner harbor at Cabo San Lucas.

Consider extending your stay by booking the four-night extension that includes a train journey deep into the roadless **Copper Canyon,** four times larger and 1,000 feet deeper than the Grand Canyon. Flying to Los Mochis on Mexico's west coast, spend the night at colonial El Fuerte before boarding the **Chihuahua-al-Pacifico** train for the climb to an elevation of 8,000 feet and pass over deep ravines, through eighty tunnels, and a half dozen interconnected canyons and on to Divisadero.

Spending two nights at a hotel on the rim of the Copper Canyon, take a guided hike and visit with the seminomadic Tarahumara Indians, who derive their living from farming and crafts. On the final day, drop out of the Sierra Madre by bus to the gateway town of Creel and onto Chihuahua for a visit to Pancho Villa's house, the cathedral, and one last night.

Address/Phone: Cruise West, 2301 Fifth Avenue, Suite 401, Seattle, WA 98121; (800) 203–8306 or (206) 441–8687; fax: (206) 441–4757; www.cruisewest.com

The Ship: *Spirit of Endeavour* was built in 1983 as the *Newport Clipper* and has a length of 217 feet and a shallow draft.

Passengers: 102 double occupancy; mostly Americans in their forties to seventies, but also families during the school holidays

Dress: Casual morning, noon, and night

Officers/Crew: American

Cabins: 51, all outside, most with windows, and most have twin beds, some at right angles

Fare: $$$

What's included: Cruise fare, port charges, shore excursions

What's not included: Airfare, drinks, tips, some optional shore excursions

Highlights: A fantastic opportunity to get close to nature while also having a warm, comfortable ship to come home to at day's end

Other itineraries: In addition to this seven-day cruise in the Sea of Cortez, which operates between December and April, there are many additional Cruise West expedition-style cruises throughout Alaska, including overland extensions, in the Pacific Northwest, along the Columbia and Snake Rivers, and in California Wine Country. The *Spirit of Oceanus* cruises along the North Pacific Rim and in the South Pacific.

ROYAL CARIBBEAN'S
Vision of the Seas
The Mexican Riviera from Los Angeles

Counting the world's biggest cruise ships, such as the 137,000-ton, 3,100-passenger *Voyager of the Seas* class, Royal Caribbean has a score of ships in its mostly-mega fleet, and more are in the works. The 78,491-ton, 2,000-passenger *Vision of the Seas* is the newest and last member of the line's Vision Class, all built between 1995 and 1998.

The *Vision of the Seas,* like its sisters, is bathed in glass (especially good in Alaska), with glass canopies and windbreaks, skylights, and floor-to-ceiling windows with sweeping views. The focal point is a soaring, seven-story atrium with a huge, dramatic sculpture within and lots of shops around it. Overall, the ship is designed with warm woods and brass, fountains and foliage, crystal, soft leathers, and eye-catching artwork. The *Vision* is easy to navigate, despite its size. Glass elevators take passengers up through the Centrum atrium into the stunning Viking Crown Lounge, the line's signature, glass-sheathed observation-lounge-cum-disco, perched high above the rest of the ship. The Schooner Bar is a casual piano bar with lots of wood and rope, befitting its nautical name, and ditto the Champagne Bar, at the foot of the atrium, where you can listen and dance to a trio while sipping wine or a glass of bubbly. Full musical revues are staged in the two-story show lounge, which has an orchestra pit that can be hydraulically raised and lowered. Likewise, the sprawling casino is dressed in Vegas-style flash and splash and assures gambling folk of an atmosphere conducive to at least having fun trying to beat the odds.

The ship's vast open areas include the Sun Deck's two swimming pools (one covered by a retractable glass roof), six whirlpools, and the Windjammer buffet-style restaurant. Poolside, you'll find loud, live music serenading the party along with silly contests that most passengers seem to just love. The soothing ShipShape spa is truly one of the most attractive around, and adjacent is a spacious solarium with a pool, chaise longues, floor-to-ceiling windows, and a retractable glass ceiling. Surprisingly, the gym is small for the ship's size. Families will like the extensive, supervised kids' activities for four age groups, including a children's playroom, a teen center and disco, and a video arcade.

The large dining room spans two decks that are interconnected with a very grand staircase and flanked with walls of glass nearly 20 feet high. Each has contemporary and tasteful decor, replete with stainless steel, mirrors, dramatic chandeliers, and a massive grand piano for dinnertime serenading. The food is generally tasty enough for a ship of this size, featuring choices like oven-roasted crispy duck served with rhubarb sauce or grilled pork tenderloin on a bed of stewed tomatoes and eggplant. A light and healthy vegetarian dish and pasta are offered at each meal.

Standard cabins are compact, although larger than the cramped cubicles featured aboard the company's older ships. Nearly one-fourth of the cabins have private verandas, and all have TVs (offering some twenty channels of video, four music channels, three for movies, and three with satellite programming), preprogrammed radios, and safes. Bathrooms are small.

The Itinerary

Exploring the **Mexican Riviera** on this floating resort couldn't be more enjoyable. Sailing seven-night cruises round-trip from **Los Angeles** and sometimes **San Diego,** you can savor the spice of Mexico's culture, its dramatic rocky shoreline, and great beaches at a string of Pacific coast ports.

Cruising south, two nights and a day at sea bring the ship within sight of the dramatic rock formations of **Cabo San Lucas** peninsula. During the port call snorkel, take a seat in a glass-bottom boat or semisubmersible to view the reefs and sea life, and spend the day at a beach resort for sunbathing and swimming. While waiting for the tender back to the ship, browse the open-air craft market. Sailing overnight to **Mazatlan,** a city that's worth exploring on foot or a tour for its main square, historic district, huge produce market, and lots of handicrafts and practical clothing for these hot climes for sale. Take a drive inland to picturesque colonial villages and mission churches set among the **Sierra Madre,** go deep-sea fishing for marlin and sailfish, and take in a folkloric show.

Just down the coast beautiful **Puerto Vallarta** is often the favorite call for its setting, winding cobblestone streets, tropical gardens, and now-distant connections to Elizabeth Taylor and Richard Burton and *Night of the Iguana.* Enjoy two full sea days back north to San Diego.

Address/Phone: Royal Caribbean International, 1050 Caribbean Way, Miami, FL 33132; (305) 539–6000 or (800) 327–6700 for brochures; fax: (305) 374–7354; www.royalcaribbean.com

The Ship: *Vision of the Seas* was built in 1998, has a gross tonnage of 78,491, a length of 915 feet, and a draft of 25 feet.

Passengers: 2,000; mostly American, all ages, especially during school holidays

Dress: Suits or tuxes for the formal nights, jackets for informal nights, and slacks and collared shirts for casual nights

Officers/Crew: International

Cabins: 1,000 average size, 593 outside, 25 percent with verandas

Fare: $$

What's included: Cruise only

What's not included: Airfare, governmental fees and taxes, shore excursions, drinks, tips

Highlights: Spa and solarium, overall design, lots of outdoor activities aboard and ashore

Other itineraries: In addition to these seven-night *Vision of the Seas* Mexican Riviera cruises, operating from September to May, the ship cruises Alaska in summer and occasionally the Panama Canal and Hawaii. Other Royal Caribbean ships cruise the Caribbean, New England/Canada, and Europe.

PRINCESS CRUISES'
Sapphire Princess
Megaship Mexican Riviera

Princess Cruises became rapidly famous with the long-running TV show *Love Boat*, and the company is now part of the Carnival Family of World's Leading Cruise Lines. The *Sapphire Princess* sails from Los Angeles, California, every Saturday from October through April to the Mexican Riviera ports of Puerto Vallarta, Mazatlan, and Cabo San Lucas. The *Sapphire Princess* and her sistership, *Diamond Princess*, at 115,875 gross tons, are presently among the largest ships cruising the Pacific.

While the ship is huge, it is easy to navigate, especially from the Grand Plaza, a three-deck-high atrium that serves as the heart. For vertical travel, three elevator banks and stair towers will connect you to all decks, and consider it healthy to have to walk from one end of the ship to the other.

Princess's Personal Choice dining provides traditional fixed seating in the aft International Dining Room or anytime from 6:00 to 10:00 P.M. in one of four restaurants

on Decks 5 and 6 located aft of Grand Plaza. Pacific Moon serves Asian cuisine; Santa Fe, Mexican; Vivaldi, Italian; and Sterling, a variety of prime steaks. Sabatini's Trattoria, for an eight-course eating extravaganza, charges an extra tariff and requires reservations. For informal dining, the Horizon Court is open twenty-four hours a day high up on Lido Deck 14, and counters there and by the pools serve pizza, burgers, and sundaes.

Princess Theater, bi-level and forward on Decks 6 and 7, presents the main production shows, twice on one day with a third performance the following day. There is no need to rush to secure a seat if you can wait for the second night, with the bonus of a critique from fellow passengers.

Explorer's Lounge, with its Middle Eastern and African decor, presents cabaret acts such as magicians and comedians, alternating with popular dancing sessions. Club Fusion serves multipurposes as a nightclub, cabaret room, and the platform for TV Trivia and game shows. For light entertainment and a drink before or after dinner, try the Wheelhouse Bar with a classy British pub atmosphere, a trio, and P&O Princess maritime memorabilia; or Crooners Bar off the Grand Plaza featuring a pianist who encourages requests.

From 11:00 P.M. night owls flock to Skywalkers Night Club, perched high on Deck 18 just aft of the funnel, for a disco hosted by a DJ who manipulates the music, neon, strobes, moving lights, and interactive TVs.

Forward on Sun Deck 15, the Lotus Spa houses the beauty parlor, massage rooms, gymnasium, a lap pool, aerobics classes, and fitness programs. Princess Links is a 9-hole golf putting green on Sports Deck 16 just forward of the funnel. Five swimming pools include the Calypso Pool and Bar enclosed under a glass dome, the outdoor Neptune's Reef, and a children's splash pool, plus eight whirlpools.

One thousand of the 1,337 cabins have ocean views, and 75 percent of these have balconies. All cabins have twin beds that can be made into queen-size, multifunction telephones, refrigerators, safes, hair dryers, and remote-control TV with CNN, TNT, CNBC, Discovery Channel, movies, special-interest lectures, and interviews. Minisuites and up have tub baths, robes, two TVs, and a separate sitting area with a sofa bed.

The Itinerary

Cruising south to **Puerto Vallarta,** there are twenty-one tours to consider during the two seas days—if you have not booked them in advance on the Princess Web site—ranging from city and coastal drives to bicycle trips, horseback rides, golf, wildlife dolphin encounters, sailing adventures, scuba diving, and the beach. If the ship does not dock but instead anchors, tenders operate to Marina Vallarta, about 4 miles from the town center. Taxies are plentiful and a local

bus is also available, and when coming back, take one marked "Marina Vallarta." The town square and its cathedral are charming, and if you are lucky, there may be a Mexican wedding. Old Town is across the river, and locations in *Night of the Iguana,* where Elizabeth Taylor and Richard Burton stayed and filmed, are well marked on tour maps.

Then at **Mazatlan,** a somewhat dirty city of 250,000 people, the *Sapphire Princess* docks, and a golf cart taxi provides the best way to negotiate the narrow streets to the cathedral and town square. The Mercado (market) lies just a few blocks away and offers local produce and tourist handicraft items.

The famous cliff divers perform here, and to get the best view, you have to pay an entrance fee. The hill at harbor entrance is topped by a lighthouse reported to be the second highest in the world. Tours take in the town's highlights and Old Town, the spectacular cathedral on a walking tour, bird watching, golf, and to Deer Island for hiking, kayaking, and a swimming beach.

Nearing **Cabo San Lucas,** be sure to be on deck for spectacular views of natural rock formations at Los Arcos. The *Sapphire Princess* anchors off the town landing. Tours include Los Arcos, natural arches at Land's End, a boat ride and scenic coastal drive, golf, horseback riding, kayaking, sportfishing, sailing, snorkeling, and scuba diving. Hotel Finistera at Land's End affords a great view of the Marina and beaches, and the district has plenty of restaurants, bars, and shops, catering to the condominiums, apartments, and hotels.

Leaving Cabo, it's a northward sail of two nights and a day back to Los Angeles. Beginning in late September 2006 through April 2007, sistership *Diamond Princess* will assume this itinerary.

Address/Phone: Princess Cruises, 24305 Town Center Drive, Santa Clarita, CA 91355; (800) PRINCESS or (661) 753–0000; brochures: (888) 478–6732; fax: (661) 259–3108; www.princesscruises.com

The Ship: *Sapphire Princess* was built in 2004, has a gross tonnage of 115,875, length of 954 feet, and a draft of 28 feet.

Officers/Crew: British and Italian officers, international crew

Passengers: 2,670, mostly American and all ages

Cabins: 1,337 cabins of which 1,000 are outside, and 750 have balconies

Dress: Formal and casual nights

Fare: $$

What's included: Cruise only

What's not included: Transportation to and from the ship, port charges, shore excursions, drinks, and tips

Highlights: Brand-new megaship cruising with lots to do aboard and ashore

Other itineraries: Besides this seven-night cruise to the Mexican Riviera that operates from October through April, the *Sapphire Princess* also cruises the Pacific to and from Australia and Alaska. Princess Cruises' large fleet covers most of the world.

CRUISE WEST'S
Pacific Explorer
Costa Rica's Pacific Coast

Cruise West's *Pacific Explorer* focuses on protecting the natural environment while enabling tourists to visit unusual sites in Costa Rica, Belize, Guatemala, and Panama.

Originally built as a U.S. supply ship, the *Pacific Explorer* was converted into a passenger ship in 1995 and sails exclusively along Costa Rica's Pacific coast and on to Panama. The ship takes up to ninety-nine passengers in a friendly atmosphere on an all-inclusive program of shore excursions. The passengers are likely to include families, couples of all ages, and singles.

The forward observation lounge has comfortable chairs and couches for quiet reading, watching the sights, or browsing the corner library's local reference books and donated paperbacks. Socializing takes place at the Tortuga Bar on Upper Deck, where drinks are complimentary. Entertainment may be local

musicians or dancing under the stars.

Open-sitting meals are served in a pleasant dining room at tables and at banquettes next to large panoramic windows. Continental breakfast is available on deck, but most passengers choose the dining-room buffet for fresh fruit, croissants, pastries, cold cereals, and hot dishes to order such as huevos rancheros or French toast. Lunch is served buffet style on the Upper Deck or on the beach at tables with red-checkered tablecloths. The choices may be cold cuts and salads and entrees such as sea bass, roast turkey, chicken, and pizza. For dinner passengers sign up for one of three flavorful entrees such as tenderloin steak with mushroom sauce, mahimahi with tartar sauce, and fettuccine with tomato sauce.

The attractive cabins are simply furnished with either twin or queen beds, matching night tables, a double closet and storage drawers below, a five-shelved unit, and a demilune table beneath a mirror. Rich Costa Rican woods are used in the furniture highlighted by the maroon red, dark green, and navy blue–striped bedspreads. Cabin windows open to bring in the sounds of the birds and the sea. The bathroom is functional and has a shower. At day's end a briefing session, held in the Toucan Lounge, lays out the upcoming shore activities, which invariably means an early wake-up knock.

The Itinerary

Experienced and highly competent local naturalists lead groups of fourteen to sixteen on hikes rated as easy, medium, and difficult, depending on length and terrain. Shore excursions begin at the swim platform, the launching spot for the Zodiacs and for taking a kayak or banana boat or waterskiing.

The *Pacific Explorer* sails from **Los Seuños,** Herradura Bay, to the Nicoya Peninsula and the privately owned **Curu Wildlife Refuge.** The dry, tropical-forest vegetation allows relatively easy spotting of howler monkeys and native birds such as trogons, blue-tailed manakins, and motmots. On **Isla Tortuga** passengers swim or snorkel from the white sandy beach, or they can try the Canopy Ride, where people "fall" from a platform in the treetops with the aid of a harness attached to a cable-and-pulley system.

In the evening the ship sails south overnight to **Corcovado National Park,** one of the most remote parks in Costa Rica. Located 75 miles north of the Panamanian border, it covers 108,000 acres and is one of the richest, most diverse tropical regions in the world. Although biologists have identified 285 species of birds, 500 species of trees, 139 species of mammals, and 116 of amphibians and reptiles, we were content with spotting howler monkeys, scarlet macaws, morpho butterflies, and pizotes (raccoonlike animals).

Sailing to the large Panamanian Isla de Coiba, snorkel among white-tipped reef sharks, manta rays, and puffer fish. Offshore, **Isla Cano,** an ancient burial site, is excellent for snorkeling. Deep-sea-fishing and scuba diving enthusiasts spent the morning on a chartered boat.

Midweek we anchored in **Golfo Dulce** off **Golfito,** once an important port for the United Fruit Company. We visited two privately owned preserves, the lush rain forests and beautiful gardens at **Cana Blanca,** a peaceful, family-owned resort complete with its own resident scarlet macaw; and **Casa Orquideas,** a landscaped botanical garden.

On the last day we visited **Manuel Antonio National Park** to finally spot the elusive two-toed sloth high on the branches of a ceiba tree, iguanas, whitefaced or capuchin monkeys, and agoutis (native rodents). During a final afternoon swim and snorkel beneath Cathedral Point came the sound of howler monkeys in the distance.

Address/Phone: Cruise West, 2301 Fifth Avenue, Suite 401, Seattle, WA 98121; (800) 203–8306 or (206) 441–8687; fax: (206) 441–4757; www.cruisewest.com

The Ship: *Pacific Explorer* was first built in 1970 and completely rebuilt in 1995 and has a length of 185 feet and a draft of 12.5 feet.

Passengers: 100; average age fifty; families welcome; 95 percent American

Dress: Very casual

Officers/Crew: Costa Rican, American expedition leader

Cabins: 46 double cabins and 4 suites; all with large picture windows

Fare: $$$

What's included: Cruise, port charges, drinks, excursions, water sports, laundry service

What's not included: Airfare, tips

Highlights: Exploring remote areas of Costa Rica's Pacific coast and Panama; seeing lots of wildlife

Other itineraries: In addition to this seven-day cruise, which operates in April, November, and December, plus a slightly altered route in June, July, and August, there are other Central American itineraries in January, February, and March that sail farther south to Panama, including a canal transit. Cruise West also operates cruises from Baja California north to Alaska and around the Pacific Rim.

LINDBLAD EXPEDITIONS'
Sea Voyager
From Costa Rica to the Panama Canal

For anyone with the experience of ocean travel, the immediate impression on first seeing the Sea Voyager is one of astonishment and delight—how tiny this ship is! Advantages are soon apparent. The vessel is compact and cozy and rides low in the water, so that one feels a part of the ocean and not the more usual remote observer aloft. The Sea Voyager is an ideal conveyance to the remote Pacific coastal and island side of Central America.

The passenger cabins are sited on all three decks, and they are outside with windows. Twin beds in some standard cabins convert to a double while in the deluxe category they form a queen-size bed. The Bridge Deck (highest) cabins open onto the side promenade. The lounge is aft on this same deck and opens onto the partly covered sun deck. A small fitness center and a reference library face forward, and the latter opens onto the forward observation deck.

The dining room on Main Deck has large-view windows facing to port and starboard. Varied and delicious meals are served at one open seating, and the Hon-

duran serving staff is friendly and helpful. Breakfast is a buffet in the dining room; lunch is buffet in the dining room or on deck; and dinner is a served meal in the restaurant with a choice of entrees that always includes meat, fish, and vegetarian dishes. The Sea Voyager is a most comfortable conveyance for this creative expedition-style itinerary.

The Itinerary
Each day there is a tempting choice of activities, all involving Zodiacs (stable motorized rubber dinghies), for trips ashore to a secluded beach, to a national park, and to observe birds and wildlife. Apart from the Panama Canal transit, it is rare to even see another ship, as this trip is "far from the maddening crowd." The trip starts with a transfer from San Jose Airport to the Pacific coastal port at **Herradura.**

Lindblad trips include an expedition leader and naturalist staff who take passengers ashore and host briefings in the lounge each evening before dinner. At the end of the cruise, passengers receive a trip diary including a complete list of animals and birds seen.

Landing at **Manuel Antonio National Park,** the naturalists will seek out the very lethargic three-toed tree sloth and spot the difficult-to-see tropical birds blended into the thick vegetation.

An early-morning landing at Osa Peninsula involves a hike through the **Corcovado National Park** with likely sightings of howler, spider, and squirrel monkeys. You can also swim in waterfall pools and ride a horse on the beach. In the **Golfo Dulce,** go kayaking and visit the Casa Orquideas gardens, an unexpected surprise, a veritable botanical garden with a fine collection of plants, shrubs, and trees—and visiting exotic birds—that is in no way artificial but a controlled extension of the natural wild.

Off the coast of Panama the **Isla Coiba** is a relatively new national park with hiking along lush forest trails, snorkeling to see tropical fish, and swimming. The ship's underwater specialist will photograph the fish life and present a film that evening before dinner.

Then **Las Perlas Islands,** sited in the Gulf of Panama, provide a lingering Zodiac visit among hundreds of seabirds—brown pelicans, brown and blue-footed boobies, and the magnificent frigate birds.

The grand finale is the **Panama Canal** transit from the Pacific to the Atlantic, and a very different experience aboard a tiny ship rising and descending in the huge lock chambers. Two sets of locks, then a single set, raise the ship to the level of the **Gatun Lake,** where the vessel anchors for the night and includes a visit by special arrangement to **Barro Colorado Island,** accompanied by scientists from the Smithsonian Tropical Research Institute to look for marmosets, sloths, tapirs, and peccaries.

The *Sea Voyager* then leaves Gatun Lake via the three lock chambers down to the level of the Caribbean and docks at **Colon** for a coach transfer to Panama City for the flight back to the United States.

Address/Phone: Lindblad Expeditions, 96 Morton Street, New York, NY 10014; (212) 765–7740 or (800) 397–3348; fax: (212) 265–3370; www.expeditions.com

The Ship: *Sea Voyager,* built in 1982 as the *America* later becoming the *Temptress Voyager,* has a gross tonnage of 1,195, is 175 feet long, and has a draft of eight feet.

Passengers: 60, mostly Americans, fifty and older

Dress: Casual at all times

Officers/Crew: Honduran officers, crew, and staff; American expedition leader

Cabins: 31 cabins, all outside with sliding windows

Fare: $$$

What's included: Cruise fare, port charges, all shore excursions, transfer between group flights and the ship, tips to local guides/drivers, soft drinks, services of ship's doctor

What's not included: Airfare, tips to ship's crew, alcoholic drinks

Highlights: An expedition cruise to remote Central America and numerous wildlife sightings

Other itineraries: Besides this seven-day expedition cruise from Costa Rica to Panama, operating in both directions between March, April and November, December, the *Sea Voyager* also cruises Baja California and the Sea of Cortez. Other Lindblad ships offer expedition trips in the Galápagos, Baja California and the Sea of Cortez, Columbia–Snake Rivers, Alaska, Antarctica, Canada, Greenland, Iceland, northern Europe, and the Mediterranean.

CRYSTAL CRUISES'

Crystal Symphony

The Panama Canal and Caribbean

Upscale, classy, and much larger than all other high-end cruise ships, the *Crystal Symphony* and running mate *Crystal Serenity* provide lots of space, amenities, and activities for any itinerary. During the late fall and winter months, the *Symphony* undertakes a series of Panama Canal trips that sail between South Florida and the Pacific Coast of Costa Rica.

Crystal Cruises, owned by Japan's NYK Line, offers top European-style service to a largely American clientele who enjoy worldwide cruising and spending multiple days at sea.

The most popular lounge is the Palm Court, a large glass-enclosed wraparound room that serves as the venue for sightseeing in hot southern climes, reading, enjoying formal afternoon tea, and drinks before and after dinner during the hours of waning daylight. On this same Lido Deck, there's an outdoor lap pool, a second indoor-outdoor pool and adjoining Jacuzzis, lots of deck chairs in a wide variety of groupings, a snack and ice-cream bar, and indoor-outdoor buffet. The deck above has one of the largest ocean-view spas at sea with an elaborate fitness center, saunas, steam rooms, aerobics, and body treatments, plus a paddle tennis court, golf driving range, and putting green. The jogging/walking teak deck at the promenade level runs the full length of the superstructure, and you can walk the perimeter of the Sun Deck.

Tiffany Deck 6 houses most of the public rooms radiating off the two-deck-high central atrium, understated compared with the glitzy Caribbean megaships. The forward Galaxy Show Lounge presents large-scale productions that are not a feature of smaller upscale ships. Additional public spaces include a large casino, a proper cinema for screening films and hosting lectures on theme cruises, several boutiques surrounding the atrium, a cozy bar, nightclub, library, and card room.

Dining is a delight, and the two special dinner options by reservation are Prego, a smartly decorated Italian restaurant, and the Jade Garden, Chinese on this ship rather than Japanese as aboard the *Serenity*. The main dining room has two seatings, unusual for a ship of this caliber, but the food is excellent and the wine list, emphasizing California selections, is fairly priced. The Crystal Cove is a popular rendezvous for drinks outside the Crystal Dining Room.

All cabins are outside with well over half having private verandas, and the majority range the full lengths of Decks 7 to 10. Amenities include sitting area, queen or twin beds, desk, TVs and VCR, Internet access, refrigerator, safe, and bathrooms with stall showers and tubs. Room service from an extensive menu is available twenty-four hours, and penthouses have butlers.

The Itinerary

Panama Canal cruises operate one-way between Fort Lauderdale or Miami and Puerto Caldera, Costa Rica, and extensions to and from California occur at the beginning and end of the season.

To access the embarkation port of **Puerto Caldera,** passengers fly to the Costa Rican capital at San José then transfer down to the Pacific Coast. The port has little of interest to recommend. Two nights and a day are spent on a southward trek to the **Panama Canal** entrance, where pilots and a narrator board for the all-day transit.

The *Symphony* will slide beneath the Bridge of the Americas while passing the port of Balboa and the skyline of Panama City to enter the canal proper. The first set of locks at Miraflores has two 100-foot chambers and a popular visitor center and the second, Pedro Miguel, just one chamber. Now the ship has been raised 85 feet, and there are several hours of sailing along a channel cut through the Continental Divide with tropical rain forests either side. In the winter season, you may encounter other cruise ships, and most certainly will meet container ships making long runs between Atlantic Ocean ports and the Pacific Rim countries.

After passing the canal's maintenance base at Gamboa and the mouth of the Chagres River that provides the canal with all its water, the twisting channel leads into Gatun Lake where, at the far end, there may be ships waiting to enter the triple Gatun Locks, stepping down to the Atlantic side at Cristobal-Colon. The pilots disembark, and the *Symphony* increases its speed for the Castries in **St. Lucia.** The port town is a busy place, and the lively market on Saturday morning is worth a diversion as is a climb up to Fort Charlotte for the battlements and the views over the port and the mountainous island.

Excursions here include the unspoilt island's interior with a drive to Soufriere for a short hike in the Diamond Botanical Gardens and views of the dramatic Gros and Petit Pitons, two conical-shaped peaks covered in thick vegetation. There are also trips to the beach, biking tours, and kayaking.

The next day at **Antigua,** the largest of the Leeward Islands, ships usually dock at Heritage Quay from where it's a short walk into the rather sleepy town of St. John's with its colorful wooden houses and cobblestone sidewalks. The principal attraction is Nelson's Dockyard at English Harbour, reached via a pretty 11-mile, cross-island drive. Still a working Georgian-era dockyard, the national park hums with activity as a yachting center focusing on the protected anchorage that acted as a refuge for English privateers and Admiral Nelson, the latter who established his headquarters here in the late eighteenth century. Visit the Dockyard Museum housed in the mid-nineteenth–century Naval Officer's House, walk the park's nature trails, and climb up to Fort Berkeley (1704) for its view. The Admiral's Inn serves a good lunch.

As a contrast, **St. Barts** is thoroughly French West Indian and one of the Caribbean's most upscale resort islands. Gustavia surrounds the small harbor where the tenders land with brand-name boutiques and some excellent French restaurants with menus posted out front. A taxi tour or rental car can cover much of the hilly island in a day to visit the fishing port of Corossol, hotel properties, and some of the score of superb beaches.

After a full day at sea, a stop is made at Grand Turk in the **Turks and Caicos,** still flying the Union Jack, for a last leisurely beach day and some of the best coral reef diving and snorkeling in the world. One-quarter mile offshore, a coral reef wall runs the island's full length with steeply sloping to sharply vertical drop-offs. Returning to the ship, disembarkation is two nights and a day away in Miami.

Address/Phone: Crystal Cruises, 2049 Century Park East, Suite 1400, Los Angeles, CA 90067; (866) 446–6625 or (310) 785–9300; fax: (310) 785-0011; www.crystalcruises.com

The Ship: *Crystal Symphony* was built in 1995, has a gross tonnage of 51,044, a length of 781 feet, and a draft of 25 feet.

Passengers: 940 double occupancy; mostly North Americans, age fifty-five plus

Dress: Fit to kill on formal nights; jackets and ties on informal nights

Officers/Crew: Norwegian and Japanese officers; European and Filipino crew

Cabins: 470 cabins, all outside and more than half with private verandas

Fare: $$$$

What's included: Cruise fare, port charges, bottled water, soft drinks, specialty coffees

What's not included: Airfare, alcoholic drinks, shore excursions, tips

Highlights: Alternative Japanese and Italian restaurants, excellent waiter/bar service, lots of onboard amenities

Other itineraries: In addition to these eleven-day Panama Canal cruises, which operate from November to February, the *Crystal Symphony* and *Crystal Serenity* undertake New England–Canada trips, and cruise in northern Europe, the Mediterranean, and around the world.

PRINCESS CRUISES'
Coral Princess
The Western Caribbean and Panama Canal

French-built *Coral Princess* and her same-year (2003) sister, *Island Princess,* represent advances in cruise ship design over both the *Grand Princess* and *Sun Princess* classes. From the exterior, the pair looks less like slab-sided structures on a hull and veer more toward a sleek cruise liner profile. Twenty percent larger than the *Sun Princess* class, the *Coral Princess* boards just about the same number of passengers, so there's more space for everyone. At more than 91,000 tons, the ship is hardly small, but Princess has been successful in creating a smaller ship feel with the downsized scale and greater number of public rooms. Some shared spaces, such as the Wheelhouse Bar, are wood-paneled, traditional, and clubby, while others are cruise-ship-slick bars.

Most public rooms range over two decks, and one of the largest is the Princess Theater, located forward on one gradually sloping level with very good sightlines. Another entertainment venue is the Explorer's Lounge for cabaret-style revues, game shows, and before-dinner dancing. All the way aft, the innovative Universe Lounge sees lots of varied uses such as cooking demonstrations from an onstage kitchen, computer instruction with fifty computers, straight lectures on finance and photography, and ambitious stage productions on a multilevel stage.

Always a favorite for me on Princess ships is the Wheelhouse Bar, a paneled space with leather couches and chairs set in private recesses and groupings. The maritime theme touts P&O's 175-year history with displays from the company's collection, here a brass bell from the 1950s Orient liner *Oronsay* and a collection of postcards from the recently departed and much loved SS *Canberra*. Classical music is performed by a quartet in the afternoon, and a dancing band plays in the evenings.

A four-deck atrium is rimmed by shops, a big-windowed yet very cozy cigar lounge, a trendy piano bar with solo pianist, and the Internet center with a news ticker. On the next deck down, the large ship's library and card room suffer from being walk-through spaces.

Children's facilities are well thought out with a Fun Zone, Pelican's Playhouse, and an outdoor play area with a pool for kids and parents. Off Limits for teenagers is equipped with computers, music for dancing, or just lounging about. In the same area, adults gravitate to a pottery studio for hands-on lessons in design and hand-painting ceramics.

Princess's Personal Choice concept features two similar restaurants with both fixed-seating dining and dine-when-you-wish. There are two specialty restaurants, with service charges: Sabatini's Trattoria, a traditional-looking Italian eatery with an open kitchen that provides a set menu with dish after dish brought to one's table, plus a choice of entree and the adjacent Bayou Café, with a New Orleans decor and a jazz trio, serving appetizers such as exotic barbecued alligator ribs, fried catfish, seafood gumbo, and chicken-and-chorizo jambalaya.

The Horizon Court buffet, open twenty-four hours, may be the only space that ever gets crowded, but picking one's arrival time can cut down on waiting. Above the main pool a grill serves hot dogs and hamburgers and next to the pool is a pizzeria. Those using the main swimming pool, three large hot tubs, and sunning areas with white plastic chairs are serenaded during the day by a steel-drum duo, while the Lotus Pool, protected by a sliding glass roof, is quieter, with a Balinese theme and handsome wooden deck chairs. Additional chairs line the wraparound promenade deck. Exercise activities take place in the

gym and aerobics room, Lotus Spa; on the basketball cum volleyball court; at the computerized golf simulator; and on a 9-hole miniature golf course.

The cabin accommodations boast 74 percent with tiered private balconies, a very high figure for a popularly priced ship. The balcony size is more generous than the *Sun Princess* class but otherwise even with most of the competition. Most cabins are similar in design with nonflashy decor and vary by location such as high up or low down, forward, amidships, or aft. Standard features are good storage space, TVs broadcasting CNN, CNBC, ESPN, and lots of entertainment channels and films, hair dryers, and safes. Minisuites come with much more space for the sitting area, larger verandas, two TVs, and bathrooms with tub baths and good storage space. Sixteen proper two-room suites have curtain-divided sitting and sleeping areas, walk-in closets, spacious balconies, a wet bar, whirlpool tub baths, and separate showers.

The Itinerary

This ten-day itinerary combines a trip into, but not entirely through, the Panama Canal, popular Western Caribbean ports, and three days at sea to explore the ship. Embarkation and disembarkation are at **Fort Lauderdale.**

Sailing from the South Florida port, you have two nights and a day aboard on a route that rounds the state's southernmost tip and aims west-southwest toward the port of **Ocho Rios** on the island of Jamaica, where the shore trips include horseback riding into the surf, downhill mountain biking, underwater coral reef viewing by semisubmersible, and Dunn's Falls for a 600-foot climb up a slippery rock staircase.

Then it's a two-night sail to the entrance to the **Panama Canal.** The *Coral Princess* is lifted 80 feet through a set of three locks into the **Gatun Lake,** the reservoir for the canal's gravity-flow operation. Anchoring here, passengers have numerous choices of excursions: to an observation point to view the ships passing through the lock system, to an Indian tribe living deep in the rain forest, or a dome car train ride along the Panama Railroad, the world's shortest true transcontinental route, which runs mostly parallel to the canal's 50-mile length.

Exiting the canal, the ship turns north to **Puerto Limon, Costa Rica**'s principal outlet on its Atlantic side. Trips are made inland to the misty cloud forests, home to more than 800 species of birds, including the colorful quetzal, for an aerial tram ride over the treetops of **Brauillo Carillo National Park.** Another trip boards a boat to explore the **Tortuguero Canal** and its tributaries to look for howler monkeys, crocodiles, sloths, and toucans. The narrow-gauge railway, built to carry bananas from inland plantations to the coast, is again open for tourist train travel, providing a two-hour ride through the rain forest and over bridges spanning numerous streams.

Sailing east to **Grand Cayman,** a British colony and a tax haven for the rich, you can rent a bike and travel around this relatively flat island, stopping at Seven Mile Beach for swimming and lunch. Stingray City is perhaps the most popular attraction, where hundreds of people descend on the shallow waters that are home to from thirty to one hundred tame stingrays that, when you don snorkeling gear, you can feed and gently stroke. Another excursion is a ride in a submersible down 100 feet alongside a portion of the 500-foot drop of the Cayman Wall sloping away to a depth of 6,000 feet. Another, very expensive, venture for just two at a time drops 800 feet past the "sponge belt" to view the deeper coral and the giant limestone pinnacles.

The last call at the Mexican island of **Cozumel** gives access to great beaches, horseback riding, snorkeling, shopping, and sportfishing—a catch-and-release outing for dolphins, barracuda, sierra, wahoo, and tuna. The short trip across to the Yucatan Peninsula is the jumping-off landing for the Mayan coastal ruins at **Tulum** and some very fine beaches.

The final two nights and a day are spent returning through the Caribbean to Fort Lauderdale for disembarkation.

Address/Phone: Princess Cruises, 24305 Town Center Drive, Santa Clarita, CA 91355; (661) 753–0000 or (800) 774–6237; fax: (661) 259–3108; www.princesscruises.com

The Ship: *Coral Princess,* completed in 2003, has a gross tonnage of 91,627, a length of 964.5 feet, and a draft of 26 feet.

Passengers: 1,970; mostly Americans; all ages and some families, especially during the school holidays

Dress: Formal and casual

Officers/Crew: British and Italian officers and international crew

Cabins: 987; 879 outside and 727 with verandas

Fare: $$

What's included: Cruise fare and port charges

What's not included: Airfare, shore excursions, tips, drinks

Highlights: Lots of activities and varied itinerary

Other itineraries: Besides these ten-night Panama Canal cruises, which operate between late September and April, the *Coral Princess* and other Princess ships cruise to Alaska, the Caribbean, and Europe—indeed most of the world.

AMAZON TOURS & CRUISES'
Arca and *Rio Amazonas*
Upper Amazon Expedition-Style Cruising

Amazon Tours & Cruises, in business for three decades, is run by an American living in Iquitos, Peru. Although the firm's riverboat fleet numbers a half dozen, only the two largest, making the full six-night cruises to and from Iquitos, Peru, are described here.

The thirty-one-passenger *Arca,* the smaller of the two, is a three-deck riverboat that was most recently upgraded in 2001. Public areas include a non-air-conditioned covered and uncovered top deck. The dining room and lounge are air-conditioned, as are the cedar- and mahogany-paneled cabins, eight with upper and lower berths, two triples with lower berths, and three triples/quadruples with bunk beds; all cabins have private showers.

The *Rio Amazonas,* the largest in the fleet, is a true veteran of the Amazon with a battered white steel hull to prove it. First built in 1896 as a passenger-cargo boat, then rebuilt into a river cruise vessel in 1981, it was last refitted in 1994. The public spaces include an air-conditioned dining room and a small library, a lounge and bar, and a Sun Deck with open and covered seating, hammocks, and a hot tub. The air-conditioned cabins, all outside with showers and baths, have two lower beds; three are triples; and two family cabins hold four.

Both vessels have buffet-style dining. The food includes fresh fish, vegetables, and fruit, but some food is preserved to avoid spoilage in this tropical climate.

The Itineraries
Cruises operate downstream and upstream, with some different landings for each three-night segment between Iquitos and the small Peruvian port of Santa Rosa opposite Leticia (Colombia) and Tabatinga (Brazil). Either or both riverboats may be used. The days are always warm, with rain likely once a day from December through March. Jungle walks are invariably hot and sticky, but when cruising and at night, the temperatures are surprisingly moderate. Air-conditioning during meals and while asleep provides additional relief.

Downstream: Iquitos, located east of the Andes, may qualify as the world's largest city with no road access to the outside world. Navigable rivers provide local transportation. This sprawling city experienced a very brief rubber boom, and there is some evidence of past wealth but not much, so it is a relief to begin the downriver cruise. There are no channel markers, so the pilots simply memorize the river. The water level can change 30 to 40 feet between the dry and rainy seasons, and any buoys would simply be carried away by the high and fast-flowing waters.

The first full day is spent visiting **Indian villages,** isolated communities that depend on the river for transportation, water, and fishing. There is a tour of the stilted compounds and a blowgun demonstration. At the larger town of **Pevas,** built mostly on high ground, there is a chance to visit an artist's house. The landscape paintings draw on the colors of the bromeliads in the forest.

The second full day begins with a rainforest walk to see the giant water lilies and perhaps howler monkeys. While they are easily heard, without a good guide or binoculars they are often hard to spot. Piranha fishing is not as frightening as it may sound, but the setting, a dark backwater pond beneath a thick canopy of tree branches, can be an eerie experience. If the catch, including catfish, is large enough, the cook on board will prepare it for dinner. The afternoon is spent visiting a missionary village, and after sunset, small boats take passengers into a reedy swamp for Amazon caiman spotting, using flashlights to set the eyes aglow.

Passengers on the three-night cruise transfer across the Amazon to **Leticia, Colombia,** for onward flights; a new group boards here, joining those making the round-trip voyage.

Upstream: The boundaries of Brazil, Colombia, and Peru come together at the turnaround location, and the river traffic is busy. The first afternoon may include a rainforest walk or a river tributary exploration.

The first full day provides a fishing trip, using hand lines, deep into the forest canopy for catfish or piranha. In the afternoon there is a visit to a leper colony at **San Pablo** and time to buy wood carvings, dolls, and artwork. After dark the launches follow a tributary, and there will be red-eyed caiman to spot with the aid of flashlights.

The second day revisits **Pevas** and a last chance to trade items for local handicrafts of handmade masks and bark paintings. As the current can be strong, the upriver cruise provides less time ashore. The *Arca* sails to the foothills of the Peruvian Andes upriver from Iquitos.

If you are taking only one segment, it is highly recommended to add a stay at one of the lodges or campsites. Whatever stretch is chosen, the line is a thoroughly experienced Amazonian operator, and its river vessels offer comfortable accommodations and a very good value.

Address/Phone: Amazon Tours & Cruises, 275 Fontainebleau Boulevard, Suite 173, Miami, FL 33172; (305) 227–2266 or (800) 423–2791; fax: (305) 227–1880; www.amazontours.net

The Ships: *Arca* was built in 1980, has a gross tonnage of 95, a length of 99 feet, and a shallow draft. *Rio Amazonas* was first built in 1896, then rebuilt in 1981, and has a gross tonnage of 350, a length of 146 feet, and a shallow draft.

Passengers: *Arca,* 31; *Rio Amazonas,* 46 (maximum capacity); age thirty and up, Americans and Europeans

Dress: Casual

Officers/Crew: Peruvian

Cabins: *Arca,* 13; *Rio Amazonas,* 20; twin beds, upper/lower berths, some with a third upper berth; all air-conditioned, outside, and with shower and toilet

Fare: $$

What's included: Cruise fare, excursions

What's not included: Airfare, governmental charges, drinks, tips

Highlights: Remote and roadless Upper Amazon; exotic bird life, Indian villages

Other itineraries: In addition to these year-round three- and six-night cruises, the company runs four smaller vessels, some for charter, on other parts of the Upper Amazon, its tributaries, and the Rio Negro. Lodge and jungle camp stays can be added.

LINDBLAD EXPEDITIONS'
Polaris
Exploring the Galápagos Islands

No matter how many National Geographic specials you've seen or how many stories you've heard, nothing prepares you for a visit to the Galápagos Islands. From swimming with sea lions to sidestepping hundreds of marine iguanas stretched out in the sun, these unique islands are best visited with a well-established expedition company that can offer access and insight. Among the many options sailing the Galápagos, there is none better than Lindblad Expeditions and the MS *Polaris*.

Founded by Sven-Olof Lindblad, the son of Lars-Eric Lindblad who pioneered expedition-style cruising, Lindblad Expeditions employs the most knowledgeable naturalists and gives them the best tools to create the most organized and educational experience possible. Lindblad's sensitivity to ecological tourism is evident throughout the week and most evident in their establishment of the Galápagos Conservation Fund and the company's adoption of Santiago Island.

After a forty-year career that included decades of worldwide cruising, the eighty-passenger *Polaris* has settled in comfortably to her year-round itinerary. Cozy and charming, the little ship is well maintained and full of nautical character.

With large windows on either side, the lounge seats all passengers and provides the location for numerous daytime lectures and the "Recap," a Lindblad tradition where the day's experiences are discussed and questions answered. Naturalists using three TV screens project images of brine to discuss whales' feeding habits or show different pebbles of sand to discuss erosion.

Local dancers and musicians come aboard on some evenings.

In the intimate library further aft, you can read accounts of past expeditions and grab a soda, beer, coffee, and snacks from the refrigerator and pay on an honor system. Outside, a partially covered deck offers traditional wooden furniture and two hammocks, ideal for snoozing in the shade. On one evening a deck barbecue is served.

Just below, a recently extended deck has space for sun loungers and storage for wet suits and snorkel gear. A small gym with treadmills, stationary bikes, and a Stairmaster is located on the port side. The masseuse works not only in the massage room but sets up a floating spa where passengers receive treatment in a glass-bottom boat while peering at the marine life below.

Forward is the ship's attractive, wood-paneled dining room with large wraparound windows and open seating at tables from two to twelve. Breakfast and lunch are buffets, while dinner is served with an appetizer, a choice of three entrees, and a dessert. Often, the ship's six naturalists dine with passengers, sharing their intense enthusiasm for the islands.

With long-serving chefs, the food, skewed to Ecuadorian dishes, is both flavorful and memorable. Ninety percent of the provisions come from the islands or mainland Ecuador, ensuring fresh fish such as Galápagos steamed wahoo in coconut sauce or Galápagos dorado. A traditional Ecuadorian Sunday lunch consisted of a huge spread of llapingachos (potato patties with cheese and peanut butter sauce), mote pillo (corn cooked in milk and eggs), lechon hornado (suckling pig roasted in beer and mustard), and ceviche mixto (seafood marinated in lemon and tomato juice).

There is a small radio room for e-mails but no Internet access, and the navigation bridge is open to interested passengers twenty-four hours a day. Above the bridge on the observation deck, passengers look for the green flash at sunset, and at night with the ship's lights darkened, a naturalist uses a laser beam to point out more constellations than you've ever seen.

The *Polaris* has a hydrophone that can broadcast underwater sounds throughout the ship if whales are seen. The undersea specialist uses a splash cam and underwater camera to film sharks and sea lions to provide footage at recap time. Families with children are welcome on board year-round, and special kids programs are arranged in the summer and during holidays.

Cabins are typically expedition-ship snug with ample storage space for a casual cruise. Excepting the larger Category 5 cabins, rooms are of similar size with substantially larger windows on Upper Deck. Going ashore in a fleet of Zodiacs, the expedition leader briefs the passengers as to a dry landing at a pier or a wet landing on a beach.

The Itinerary

Because Lindblad passengers are eager to see and learn, within hours of embarkation we were preparing to go ashore on the island of **Santa Cruz**. Riding a Zodiac through quiet lagoons with both mangroves and cactus, we were overwhelmed by our first close-up views of land iguanas, pelicans, and sharks and sea turtles surfacing next to us. Our naturalist urged us not to take photos, guaranteeing that we would soon see more and get even closer.

The next morning we called at **Española**, and the guides were proven right when we

landed among several sea lions and fifty marine iguanas. Lacking fear, the animals stayed put and we had to be careful not to step on them. On our first walk, we saw endemic albatrosses mating and walked through thousands of comical and endearing blue-footed boobies doing a mating dance by lifting one foot, bending their wings and whistling.

In the afternoon we snorkeled with experience dictating whether you did a deep-water snorkel, a more protected snorkel, or looked through the *Polaris*'s glass-bottom boat. Afterwards, we lounged on the beach shared with a hundred contented sea lions. As the islands are a national park, we were escorted at all times by Lindblad's extremely knowledgeable naturalists in groups never exceeding twelve to fifteen.

Several days began early, such as 6:30 A.M. for a Zodiac ride and a wet landing at Post Office Bay, where letters deposited in a barrel are sorted through by visitors who then select ones addressed to near their own home and hand deliver them. We had our first chance to snorkel with sea lions, playfully swimming to within an inch of our masks then darting away. On **Isabela Island,** one of the few inhabited islands, we visited the Tortoise Breeding Center to learn about conservation efforts.

Another early wake-up brought us to Roca Redonda for a circumnavigation of the large rock home to thousands of seabirds. Later dropping anchor in a stark volcanic caldera, we took a Zodiac ride along the steep coast to see a penguin, an iguana, and a sea lion sleeping within 5 feet of one another. Returning to the ship, we saw two Bryde's whales and followed them for over an hour in the Zodiac.

Sailing to **Fernandina Island,** we walked over lava fields while learning about the islands' geology, again sidestepping hundreds of sunning iguanas and two dozen rare flightless cormorants.

One day is spent entirely on **Santa Cruz,** the most populous island, and included a visit to the Charles Darwin Research Center, which has successfully bred giant tortoises and reintroduced them back into the wild. Later, we saw some of them in their natural habitat. One could also scuba dive to see hammerhead sharks, sea lions, sea horses, and large schools of fish.

On **Genovesa,** we encountered countless mating frigate birds with large elastic red pouches fully inflated. Unlike other areas, where birds are often inaccessible and only seen briefly through trees, here the birds are so abundant they are found right next to you on the beach or along the path, proving a far more interesting experience. On the beach, a baby sea lion cavorted and crawled onto some of the young passengers.

On the final full day, we had prebreakfast hike up the lunar landscape of the volcano islet **Bartolome** and later went snorkeling among penguins. On **Santiago Island,** we snorkeled with grazing sea turtles while white-tipped reef sharks cruised close by. Our last hike, we came upon a newborn baby sea lion. Lindblad even kept us entertained with a video on the islands while we awaited the flight to mainland Ecuador.

Address/Phone: Lindblad Expeditions, 96 Morton Street, New York, NY 10014; (800) EXPEDITIONS or (212) 765–7740; www.expeditions.com

The Ship: *Polaris* was originally built in 1960 as the day ferry *Oresund* and rebuilt into the cruise ship *Lindblad Polaris* in 1982, then simply *Polaris* after 1986. She has a gross tonnage of 2,138, a length of 238 feet, and a draft of 14 feet.

Passengers: 80 double occupancy, mostly Americans. Age is generally fifty and up, but Lindblad offers family theme cruises and encourages younger passengers year-round.

Dress: Casual at all times

Officers/Crew: Ecuadorian

Cabins: 41, mostly small, all outside with windows; portholes on A Deck

Fare: $$$$

What's included: Cruise fare and port charges, sodas, shore excursions, national park entrance fees

What's not included: Alcohol, tips to crew and guides, pooled at the end of the trip. A package is available to include airfare from Miami to and from the Galápagos, a one-night hotel stay in Guayaquil, and another night in Quito.

Highlights: The best-presented expedition cruise to this region; the opportunity to witness an abundance of unique species that show no fear of humans; swimming with sea lions

Other itineraries: Lindblad recently added a 49-passenger ship, the 164-foot *Islander*, for year-round service in the Galápagos. This ship is newer with all-window cabins and offers much the same standards as the *Polaris.* The 68-passenger *Sea Lion* and *Sea Bird* cruise the Columbia and Snake Rivers, the British Columbia coast up to Alaska, and in the Sea of Cortez and Baja California, Mexico; and the 60-passenger *Sea Voyager* sails to exotic locations in Central America. The deep-sea 110-passenger expedition ship *National Geographic Endeavour* cruises the world, calling at ports including Antarctica, South America, the Pacific, the Arctic, and Europe.

SEABOURN CRUISE LINE'S
Seabourn Pride
Down South America Way

Seabourn Cruise Line, owned by the Carnival Corporation, operates a similar trio of all-suite ships, the *Seabourn Pride, Seabourn Legend,* and *Seabourn Spirit.* Although a Seabourn cruise is about as sophisticated an experience as one will find at sea, the atmosphere is less stuffy and more friendly and relaxed than in the past.

The principal public spaces revolve around The Club, a trio of glass-partitioned rooms, offering an intimate lounge setting, a cozy bar, and a small casino for blackjack, poker, and roulette. The location is popular before dinner, with hot hors d'oeuvres served and live music; after dinner a small group performs cabaret acts, and a band plays for dancing. The tiered main lounge is used for the captain's parties, films, special-interest lectures, and piano concerts. A quiet spot is the observation lounge for an unimpeded view forward and for checking the ship's position. A tiny library stocks books and videos to take out.

Outside, the attractive lido deck has sun-protected areas for chairs, two heated whirlpools, and a little-used swimming pool awkwardly sited in a shadowy pit. Constitutional walks and jogging take place on the circular deck above.

Dining aboard a Seabourn ship may be as private or as social as one would like, an option that extends to all times of the day. On two formal nights a week, the top officers host tables, and, on informal evenings, there may be invitations from the cruise staff or the enrichment lecturers. The main restaurant meals are uniformly excellent, with memorable dishes being the fresh fish, veal dishes, and beef tenderloin. For an Italian dinner,

with reservations required, the Veranda Café has a set menu that might include antipasto, minestrone, linguine al Don Alfredo, tender osso buco, and tiramisù. On another night it might be Asian or French. Complimentary wines are served at lunch and dinner. The indoor-outdoor Veranda Café never repeats its lunch menu and is equally a lovely spot for breakfast, especially at a table under the awning-covered afterdeck poised over the stern. Once during the cruise, an outdoor barbecue will feature a cold buffet of jumbo shrimp, smoked mussels, smoked salmon, oysters, caviar, and salad fixings galore, while the hot carvery will offer sliced roast beef, duck, and ham. The Market Galley Buffet, a lavish lunch extravaganza, is set up in the ship's serving pantry.

The Seabourn suites offering lots of amenities are most inviting, with blond wood grain outlining the furnishings and cabinetry and natural light pouring through the 5-foot-wide picture window. Thirty-six suites have French balconies in place of the window. The refrigerator is stocked and replenished daily with sodas, beer, and, as ordered prior to the cruise, one complimentary bottle of red and white wine or spirits. The walk-in closet has ample hanging space and a safe, but drawer space is limited and shallow. The bed is queen-size (or two twin-size) with good, focused reading lights, and the lounge has a sofa, two chairs, two stools, and a coffee table that could be raised for in-suite entertaining and dining.

The Itinerary
The northbound direction of the four-week cruise outlined here may in some years

operate in reverse, southbound from Fort Lauderdale. Passengers may elect to take the shorter segments from Rio to Manaus or Manaus to Fort Lauderdale.

Embarking in **Rio de Janeiro,** the sail out past Sugar Loaf is a breathtaking spectacle. Reaching the Atlantic, the *Seabourn Pride* turns northward along the Brazilian coast with leisurely days at sea en route to **Salvador de Bahia.** The high-rises of the new city envelop the old, the latter best visited on a walking tour. The architecture of the 400-year-old colonial upper city reflects the former Portuguese capital's opulence and has been designated a UNESCO World Heritage Site. The next call is **Natal,** a seaport for exporting cotton, coffee, hides, and sugar, located on the extreme east of Brazil's bulge. During World War II, Natal served as the base for the shortest flying route across the Atlantic to West Africa. Farther north, **Forteleza** is known for its lace, beaches, and beach-front fish restaurants.

The waters begin to turn muddy more than 100 miles from the mouth of the **Amazon.** Although the Nile is slightly longer, the Amazon discharges sixty times more freshwater, fully one-third of the world's supply, much of its content laden with silt. The river mouths are a confusing complex of navigable waterways leading inland from the open Atlantic.

Upstream, a stop is made at **Alter do Chao,** where the blue waters of the Rio Tapajos join the Amazon and provide a sandy beach worry-free of piranhas. The Lower Amazon officially ends 1,000 miles upstream at **Manaus,** a deepwater port near to where the waters of the **Rio Negro** merge into the main stream. Once a rubber-boom city that boasts an opera house and a market pavilion built by Gustav Eiffel, the sprawling urban center is by far the largest in the Amazon basin, and the river traffic is intense.

Some passengers will leave the *Pride* here and others will join.

Sailing back down the heavily forested Amazon highway, calls are made at **Parintins,** a town known for its folkloric samba dancing, and **Santarem,** a sizeable city where you should see some gray and pink freshwater dolphins in the vicinity.

Exiting the Amazon, the ship crosses the equator at Macapa, then heads out to **Devil's Island,** where a picnic takes place in honor of the notorious former French penal colony's most famous prisoner, Papillon. Depending on the specific cruise chosen, the Caribbean ports will vary, but one included **Bridgetown** on the island of **Barbados** with its British heritage; **Gustavia** on the upscale French island of **St. Barts;** and American **St. Thomas** for shopping and sightseeing, before a relaxing last stint at sea en route to **Fort Lauderdale** and disembarkation.

Address/Phone: Seabourn Cruise Line, 610 Blue Lagoon Drive, Suite 400, Miami, FL 33126; (305) 463–3000 or (800) 929–9391; fax: (305) 463–3070; www.seabourn.com

The Ship: *Seabourn Pride* was built in 1988 and has a gross tonnage of 9,975, a length of 440 feet, and a draft of 17 feet.

Passengers: 204; mostly Americans in their fifties, some Europeans and South Americans in the mix

Dress: Formal, and casual nights

Officers/Crew: Norwegian officers; mostly European crew, plus some Filipinos

Cabins: 102; all outside suites, the majority identical except for location. Thirty-six French balconies (window-type double doors set before a railing) added to some suites in place of sealed windows.

Fare: $$$$$

What's included: Cruise fare, port charges, wine and drinks, gratuities, one special excursion per cruise

What's not included: Airfare, governmental fees, transfers, shore excursions

Highlights: Exotic ports and a most luxurious ship to come home to at day's end

Other itineraries: In addition to this twenty-eight-day cruise from Rio de Janeiro via the Amazon to Fort Lauderdale operating during the northern winter, the Seabourn trio offers itineraries that cover the globe, including Vietnam.

ORIENT LINES'
Marco Polo
Passages from the East to West Coast of South America

Orient Lines, originally a British-owned company, is now a separate brand for Star Cruises, also owners of Norwegian Cruise Line. The 826-passenger *Marco Polo* was designed for worldwide cruising. First built in 1965 for the Soviet Black Sea Shipping Company as a rugged ice-strengthened transatlantic liner, the ship was completely rebuilt in 1993 as the *Marco Polo,* happily retaining her handsome ocean liner profile.

Public rooms, with an understated decor, and the outdoor swimming pool and lido bar occupy one deck and include the forward Ambassador Lounge, the venue for enrichment lectures on such topics as Indian and European influences and South American politics, plus entertainment. Further aft is the Polo Lounge, a piano bar; the Palm Court, furnished with cane chairs for afternoon tea; Le Bar, a cozy watering hole; a card room; a well-stocked library; and a small casino.

Raffles offers varied high-quality buffet selections for breakfast and lunch and gets magically transformed at night for an Oriental dinner (extra charge for tip and wine). The outdoor grill prepares steaks, sausages, and hamburgers by the pool. On the decks above are the Charleston Club's dance band and disco and the well-equipped Health Club and Beauty Center. The Sky Deck Jacuzzis, overlooking the stern, become a popular gathering spot when the ship is leaving port. Deck space is attractively tiered, and wooden steamer chairs line the wide teak Promenade Deck. The circular Boat Deck above, while narrow, is for serious walkers.

The Seven Seas Restaurant provides two sittings at dinner and a tasty selection of salads and soups such as curried pumpkin and lentil. Entrees include grilled sea shrimp, Alaska salmon with almonds and ginger crust, and seared prime beef with tempura vegetables.

The 425 cabins have mostly twin beds, some convertible to queen-size, with light-wood trim, TVs with VCRs, three-channel radios, phones, good storage, and hair dryers. Large staterooms and suites have tub baths. The cabin dividers are thin and leak noise from the neighbors.

The Itinerary
Argentina to Chile: Happily, there are still frontiers that offer travelers an unusual and

uncrowded cruising experience, and Argentina's **Patagonia** and the **Chilean fjords** are just such places. Together they possess great scenic beauty, unusual wildlife, a thinly scattered population, and limited access. This South American itinerary may operate in the reverse direction and add or subtract ports. The itinerary may also begin in Rio de Janeiro before heading south to Cape Horn.

The selected cruise tour begins with two full days in the stylish European city of **Buenos Aires.** Argentina's capital is a feast of flamboyant Victorian and Beaux Arts buildings. The outdoor cafes and restaurants, handsome limestone apartment buildings, and smart shopping arcades seem even more French than those in Paris. The rich hire dog walkers; smartly dressed ladies lunch with friends; schoolboys wear blue blazers, ties, and white shirts; and no one likes to eat before ten o'clock. In Recoleta, a smart residential neighborhood, Eva Peron is buried in a cemetery of elaborate mausoleums.

The cruise begins in earnest by sailing across the muddy Rio de la Plata to **Montevideo,** Uruguay's capital. The nearby resort of **Punta del Este** attracts jetsetting South Americans.

Sailing into the South Atlantic, the *Marco Polo* calls at **Port Stanley** and **West Point** in the **Falkland Islands,** a British colony with the look of a northern Scottish isle. Sheep raising and fishing are the main occupations, and the islands are home to cute rockhopper penguins and southern elephant seals.

Sailing westward around **Cape Horn,** the land to starboard is **Tierra del Fuego,** shared by Argentina and Chile. At **Ushuaia,** a catamaran cruise into the Beagle Channel visits an island covered with seals. The next call, **Punta Arenas,** is Chile's southernmost city, the center for the sheep farming industry and gateway to **Patagonia.** Climb La Cruz

Hill for great views of the surrounding forests, lakes, sand cliffs, **Strait of Magellan,** and Tierra del Fuego.

Glaciers come down to calve into the sea, and when the channel widens, the *Marco Polo* leaves the sheltered waters and aims westward and northward to the Pacific and the Chilean fjords. There are more than 5,000 islands in the Chilean archipelago, and most channels have had no soundings. Navigation is made even trickier by unexpected mountain downdrafts that strike ships broadside. A call is made at the fishing village **Puerto Chacabuco,** set along a coast of soaring fjords and Andean peaks, then you'll sail north to **Puerto Montt,** located at the northern end of the Chilean fjords in the lake district. **Lake Llanquihue,** the country's largest lake, is overlooked by the conical 8,000-foot **Osorno** volcano, one of more than two thousand in Chile alone.

Cruising back into the Pacific, this leg of the cruise ends at **Valparaiso,** Chile's main port and now the location for the country's parliament. The lower and upper sections of Valparaiso are connected by more than one dozen hundred-year-old elevators or funicular railways, a diversion for those so inclined. Five miles distant is **Vina del Mar,** one of the continent's foremost resorts with an elegant seafront, a presidential summer palace, and a splendid casino, maintaining a strict dress code, set among formal gardens.

Santiago, the capital, is 75 miles inland, a modern city at the foot of the snowcapped **Andes,** with enough attractions to warrant the additional nights tacked onto the cruise. You can travel by a good subway system to visit the cultural center housed in a now-disused railway station, arcaded Plaza de Armas, the 1805 Palacio de la Moneda, now a museum for paintings and sculpture. In the evening the arty Bellavista District is the place for street life, shops selling lapis lazuli, art galleries, theaters, cafes, and restaurants.

Chile via Panama to the Caribbean: Santiago, Chile's sprawling capital, is nestled in the Andes Mountains east of the main seaport of **Valparaiso,** where the *Marco Polo* is waiting to sail. This northbound itinerary is nicely spaced, with a day at sea between most ports. At Coquimbo, Gustav Eiffel (of Eiffel Tower fame) built one of the churches, while nearby **La Serena** is a beach resort with no less than twenty-six churches.

The coastline changes dramatically as the ship reaches **Arica,** Chile's northernmost city, rising among the foothills of the Andes. To the east the **Atacama Desert** qualifies as the driest place on earth, while beyond are the **High Andes.** The archaeological museum displays mummies that are reputed to be older than those in Egypt, and the desert hills have pre-Columbian petroglyphs. There's a terrific city and sea view from the Morro, a fort, and in Arica be sure to visit iron San Marcos Cathedral and the equally splendid custom house.

After cruising up the coast to **Callao,** the commercial port for **Lima,** it's a short drive to Peru's colonial capital quarter. Lima now counts roughly seven million inhabitants, and tours are highly recommended here and at all the ports along the coast. In Lima, the cathedral on the Plaza de Armas has a splendid interior with finely carved seventeenth-century stalls, silver-covered altars, and beautiful wall mosaics. **Miraflores,** a trendy, expensive suburb and Lima's social center, is worth a visit for beaches and the upscale shops built around a handsome park.

Salinas is a popular Ecuadorian beach resort, and to the north are **Machalilla National Park,** a dry tropical forest, and **Isla de la Plata,** home to a colony of blue-footed boobies. There is also a flying excursion inland to Quito, the capital.

Before sailing though the Panama Canal, the ship docks in **Balboa,** the port for **Panama City.** Its San Felipe district is a United Nation's World Heritage Site featuring a mixture of Spanish, French, and early American architecture. A tour visited a village on stilts in the rain forest.

Taking on the pilots early the next morning, the ship begins the **Panama Canal** transit with the 85-foot climb through the two Miraflores Locks and a half hour later moves into the single Pedro Miguel Lock. The ship then begins a peaceful sail amid lovely tropical surroundings to the Gaillard Cut through the Continental Divide and past the canal headquarters at Gamboa and into **Gatun Lake.** At the eastward end, the three-step, 85-foot drop through the Gatun Locks lowers the ship to sea level again. By mid-afternoon the pilots disembark at **Cristobal-Colon** and the ship sails into the Caribbean.

After an overnight sail, **Puerto Limon,** Costa Rica's Caribbean port, is the gateway to the inland cloud forests, home to more than 800 species of birds including the flamboyant quetzal. In 2006, the *Marco Polo* calls at George Town, Cayman Islands, and Montego Bay, Jamaica, before crossing the Atlantic to begin the European season.

Address/Phone: Orient Lines, 7600 Corporate Drive Center, Miami, FL 33126; (305) 436–4000 or (800) 333–7300; fax: (305) 436–4124; www.orientlines.com

The Ship: *Marco Polo* was originally built in 1965 as the Soviet-flag *Alexandr Pushkin,* then completely rebuilt from the hull up in 1993. She has a gross tonnage of 22,080, a length of 578 feet, and a deep draft of 27 feet.

Passengers: 826 double occupancy; age range is fifty and up, mostly English speaking

Dress: Some formal nights, otherwise jacket

and tie, with casual nights in port

Officers/Crew: Scandinavian or British captain; mostly European officers and Filipino crew

Cabins: 425, most average size; 294 are outsides, none with verandas

Fare: $$$

What's included: Cruise, hotel nights, sightseeing, transfers

What's not included: Low airfare add-ons

from U.S. gateways, port charges, shore excursions, tips, drinks

Highlights: Exotic itinerary to some remote coastal locations at an affordable package price. Great ambience on board.

Other itineraries: In addition to these South American cruise tours, which operate from February into April, the *Marco Polo* spends the summer in Northern Europe and the Mediterranean and winter in Antarctica.

SILVERSEA CRUISES'
Silver Wind
Around the Bottom of South America

The newest line in the ultraluxury cruise market, Silversea Cruises made a splash in 1994 when it introduced the brand-new, 296-passenger *Silver Cloud* and *Silver Wind* followed by the 388-passenger *Silver Shadow* and *Silver Whisper*. The ships combine the spaciousness and entertainment options of a larger ship with the best of intimate, yachtlike cruising.

Following a refit in 2003, the *Silver Wind*'s public areas, inside and out, are again stylish and open. Dusty blues, teal greens, and deep burgundies and violet are blended with lots of Italian marble and the odd tile mosaic tabletop. Entertainment is low-key, but there are decent options, considering the small size of the ship. Afternoon tea is served in the windowed Panorama Lounge and evenings a pianist plays there. Broadway-style production numbers with a four-dancer cast are performed in the two-story Venetian show lounge, and most nights a dance band plays oldies or a DJ spins rock 'n' roll in

the intimate, softly lit Bar. Organized activities include trivia contests, port talks, movies, and wine tasting. Mostly people socialize, read in the library, surf in the Computer Center, or roam around the roomy decks.

The outdoor deck space is sweeping, and there's never overcrowding in and around the pool, two hot tubs, and ocean-view gym.

The formal, open-seating dining venue is delicately decorated in pale pink and gold, and elegant candlelit tables are set with heavy crystal glasses, chunky Christofle silverware, and doily-covered silver show plates. Rivaling the best restaurants in New York City or Paris, delectable dishes like grilled tournedos of beef with foie gras and truffles and marinated crab with leek salad and star anise are prepared in conjunction with Le Cordon Bleu Culinary School. Several nights a week, the Terrace Café, where buffet-style breakfast and lunch are served, is transformed into a cozy, reservations-only alternative-dining venue, featuring mostly regional Italian cuisine. Here the ambience is darker and more intimate, and there are a good number of tables for two. The wine bar, Le Champagne, offers intimate dinners for thirty.

All 148 suites have sitting areas, roomy walk-in closets, bathtubs, vanities, TVs and VCRs or DVD players, and stocked minibars. Natural light pours in through the glass veranda doors, casting a warm glow on the creamy-beige fabrics and the abundant golden-brown-colored wood. Swirled peachy-gray marble covers the bathroom from head to toe.

The Itinerary

Embarking in **Valparaiso,** 75 miles from Chile's capital at Santiago, the *Silver Wind* sets sail for **Puerto Montt,** located in the lake district at the northern end of the Chilean fjords. Just to the east, **Lake Llanquihue,** the country's largest lake, is overlooked by the conical, 8,000-foot Osorno volcano.

Sailing south in protected waters, the ship comes to the weathered **Chiloe Island** town of Castro, where unpainted wooden houses perch on stilts. Leaving the *Silver Wind* in the ship's launches, a complimentary excursion enters **Laguna San Rafael,** a saltwater lake connected to the sea by a narrow tidal channel. Cruising amid broken ice, the launch eases toward 25-mile-long San Valentine glacier. The pack ice reveals a wonderful kaleidoscope of colors and shapes.

Two more days are spent cruising the fjords and the **Beagle Channel,** often within sight of glacial remnants of the Ice Age, to **Ushuaia,** Argentina, on Tierra del Fuego, where a catamaran heads out to island rookeries for a close-up view of lounging, smelly sea lions and the protected nests of black-and-white cormorants. After a cruise past **Cape Horn,** the ship returns to protected waters and calls at **Punta Arenas,** Chile, for a two-day stay.

The excursion to **Torres del Paine National Park** is an absolute must, where you will encounter herds of guanaco (an American relative of the camel that resembles the llama), Darwin's flightless rhea, Chilean flamingos, black-necked swans, buff-necked ibis, and the soaring Andean condor, with a 10-foot wingspan. Gauchos with their horses sit by the roadside brewing tea. A footpath leads to a rolling, tufted green-and-yellow alpine meadow that recedes toward a deep chasm, behind which rise jagged granite peaks, each topped with a layer of brown lava. The higher, snow-covered mountains are draped with hanging glaciers.

From Punta Arenas the ship sails along the **Strait of Magellan** and out into the Atlantic Ocean to **Puerto Madryn,** a town settled by Welsh in the mid-nineteenth century. To the south **Punta Tombo** is a refuge for up to one million Magellanic penguins, who swim ashore to lay their eggs in dusty, shallow burrows. The last day is spent negotiating the muddy River Plate while en route to the European-style city of **Buenos Aires,** a civilized and sophisticated cap to the sixteen-day cruise. Plan to stay on to take in this most European of cities.

Address/Phone: Silversea Cruises, 110 East Broward Boulevard, Fort Lauderdale, FL 33301; (954) 522–4477 or (800) 774–9996; fax: (954) 522–4499; www.silversea.com

The Ship: The *Silver Wind* was built in 1995 and has a gross tonnage of 16,800, a length of 514 feet, and a draft of 17 feet.

Passengers: 296; mostly North American couples in their late fifties to seventies

Dress: Formal nights; informal jacket

evenings; jackets and slacks for casual nights

Officers/Crew: Italian officers; European and Filipino crew

Cabins: 148; all outside and all but 38 with verandas

Fare: $$$$$

What's included: Cruise fare, one shore excursion, unlimited wines and liquors, tips, and sometimes airfare

What's not included: Port charges, most excursions and airfare when not part of a package

Highlights: The outstanding beauty of Chile and Argentina; veranda suites, cuisine, service, ship's interiors

Other itineraries: In addition to this sixteen-day *Silver Wind* itinerary between Valparaiso and Buenos Aires, which operates in both directions in December and January, there are South American cruises on other stretches of both coasts. With two new larger ships now in service, *Silver Shadow* and *Silver Whisper,* Silversea truly covers the world in great style, including the Indian Ocean, South Africa, and Australia/New Zealand.

EUROPE

CRYSTAL CRUISES'

Crystal Serenity

Scandinavian Capitals and the Baltic

Crystal Cruises has uniquely positioned itself by operating the largest ships that fall into the top end of the cruise market. Yet the pair *Crystal Symphony* (51,044 tons; 1,100 passengers) and *Crystal Serenity* (68,000 tons; 1,080 passengers) are not megamassive by today's standards.

Crystal's passengers look for food and service on par with the other top lines—Seabourn, Silversea, and Radisson—while also desirous of big-ship choices, amenities, activities, and entertainment. The *Crystal Serenity*, making its first cruise in July 2003, was designed to offer just that within a newer, larger, and roomier version of the previous pair completed back in 1990 and 1995. The *Crystal Harmony* has since joined the parent company NYK as *Asuka II*.

Spaciousness is evident throughout—in the public room corridors, under heightened ceilings, in the oval atrium, and out on the widest open promenade I have ever tread, a veritable teak boulevard with nary a lifeboat to block out the sky.

Strolling into the Palm Court high up on Deck 12, one instantly takes to this expansive blue-gray room with natural light flooding in through 270-degree floor-to-ceiling windows. Six hexagonal skylights provide additional light and sunlit settings for healthy-looking pairs of potted palms. The rattan furnishings arranged atop a fern-pattern carpet in cozy groupings on two levels nicely define the observation room setting, one that offers a fine location for the captain's welcome party, dancing after dark, and for the best served afternoon tea I have experienced at sea.

The 635 crewmembers are 40 percent European, 40 percent Asian, and 20 percent North American; the captain is Norwegian, and the top officers are Scandinavian and Japanese. Crystal Cruises is owned by the Japanese shipping firm NYK.

Most cabin accommodations are large aboard the *Serenity*, with the 286 A and B categories measuring 269 square feet. A new category AA, eighty-two penthouse staterooms with veranda, also 269 square feet, offers butler service plus a complimentary wine and spirit selection upon embarkation. Eighty-five percent of the 548 cabins have private verandas, and no cabin has a lifeboat-obstructed view as they have been stowed below cabin levels.

Evening dining choices include the traditional Crystal Dining Room with two seatings, unique to such a high-end ship, but this did not seem to be a problem as most people like to eat at a specified time anyway, as they do at home. The room is nicely divided by overhead panels and by a railing rimming a raised center section set under a starlit dome. The room buzzes with activity but is never noisy. Memorable selections on my cruise were Alaska crab soup with Brie cheese, ricotta and sun-dried tomato–stuffed chicken breast, sesame-crusted seared ahi tuna steak, and chocolate hazelnut pudding soufflé.

Prego, the Italian specialty restaurant, is entirely different in style on this ship. It is a long room located aft on the starboard side, executed in white and gold with bas-relief urns filled with fruit on the bulkhead pilasters, while creative light boxes show Florentine scenes. Two Italian favorites were pumpkin ravioli flavored with apricot and Gorgonzola-topped filet of Angus beef.

On this ship the Asian restaurant, called the Silk Road, had Nobuyuki "Nobu" Matsuhisa as the consultant for a pan-Asian menu that offered such signature dishes as lobster with truffle yuzu sauce, black cod with miso, and chicken with teriyaki balsamic. The airy port-side setting was executed in lime green and soft blue lighting with Sushi Bar at the entrance, a new offering for Crystal. None of these alternative restaurants carry a surcharge; though, with the exception of the Sushi Bar, reservations are required.

For casual poolside dinners, Tastes has attractive table settings next to the Trident Pool and under the Magrodome. Lunchtime Lido buffets proved very popular and one, Asian themed, had an outstanding selection of hot and cold dishes with the cold, creamed litchi nut soup and the peanut satay especially tasty.

The Galaxy Show Lounge, where every seat has good sightlines, puts on major big-ship productions—shows such as Million Dollar Musicals, Fascinatin' Rhythm, Curtain Call, and Forever Plaid, the last named a barbershop quartet singing and bantering about the 1950s and 1960s. Other entertainment venues are the Stardust Club for cabaret acts and dancing; Pulse, the late-night disco; Hollywood Theater for films and lectures; and a large casino.

For the mind, the innovative Crystal Learning Institute offers more than a dozen sign-up courses such as Yamaha piano instruction, drawing workshops, Spanish lessons, Cleveland Clinic health talks, and tai-chi.

The 8,500-square-foot spa and fitness centers, located high up and aft, are arranged with separate entrances and very good soundproofing, hence the thumping of exercise machines does not intrude upon treatment room serenity or the Lido Café below.

For sports, two paddle tennis courts sit side by side on the Sun Deck 13, and under the supervision of a sports director, they see constant use. Aft down on Tiffany Deck 6, there is a cluster consisting of two golf nets, a putting green, and two Ping-Pong tables in a quiet wind-protected setting with a wake's view.

The staffed library of books and DVDs has three cozy bays for curling up in a comfy chair with footstool, and the Bridge Lounge offers sixteen well-patronized tables and instruction.

For drinks, besides the Palm Court, the Avenue Saloon, a Crystal trademark, features a pianist in a clubby paneled setting, and cigar smokers and after-dinner imbibers reside next door to the even woodier Connoisseur Club. For an open setting, the Crystal Cove off the Atrium, topped with a colored-glass oval dome, has a pianist at times and a Lucite player piano at other times. One deck above, The Bistro has a sit-up bar and table seating for enjoying the all-day snack buffet of cold meats, salads, cheeses, fruit, and desserts. The Atrium's mezzanine is also the setting for two high-end shops selling clothing, jewelry, china, and glass and a Crystal souvenir shop.

For past Crystal passengers, just about everything feels familiar; now there is more of it.

The Itinerary

In the summer, the Crystal Serenity offers a number of Northern European cruises that call at ports in the British Isles, Scandinavian capitals, and Baltic Sea cities. Embarkations and disembarkations are typically at Dover, southeast of London, Copenhagen, and Stockholm.

The eleven-day day cruise described here begins in wonderful **Copenhagen** where a pre-cruise stay allows time to visit the Stroget, Europe's first major pedestrian street, lined with both high-end and touristy shops; Amalienborg Palace, the royal residence for the last 200 years; the tightly packed line of outdoor cafes and restaurants along the Nyhavn, a waterway that feeds into the harbor; and Tivoli, the 150-year-old amusement park, restaurant, and entertainment center in a garden setting that inspired Walt Disney to create his stateside equivalents.

Copenhagen's cruise terminal is about 2 miles from the city center along a waterfront promenade that serves as a favorite ship-watching pastime for the city's residents on a fine summer's day. About two hours after departing Copenhagen, the *Serenity* sails past Hamlet's Castle at Helsingor, then it's overnight to the Oslo Fjord and a scenic 60-mile cruise up to **Oslo,** Norway's capital.

The dock, located beneath Akerhus Castle with its park and museums inside the fortifications, is within walking distance of the city center and the principal shopping district along Karl Johans Gate. Take the ferry over to Norway's maritime heritage centers to view the expedition raft *Kon Tiki*, the polar exploration ship *Fram*, traditional Viking ships, and cruise liner models.

Following a leisurely two-night sail via Denmark's Great Belt, a natural waterway that splits the country into two sections, the *Serenity* docks at **Gdansk** on the Vistula River delta, a port only recently included in cruise ship itineraries. Gdansk, Poland's maritime capital and once a major player in the Hanseatic League, is a remarkable city that combines a rich history with striking natural beauty. Visit the bustling Long Street Market and breathtaking St. Mary's church. Nearby **Gdynia** is a competing port and a much newer city.

An even less visited port is **Riga,** the capital of Latvia, one of the three Baltic States that used to be under Soviet influence. In the Middle Ages it was thought that he who ruled Riga, ruled the Baltic, and it was an important member of the Hanseatic League. For centuries, battles were waged for control of the city by the Poles, Russians, Swedes, and Germans. Riga has a vibrant nightlife and a progressive cultural scene. The city's fine architecture, concentrated on Alberta Street, features splendid buildings of the *Jugendstil* style. Look up toward the rooftops for gables decorated by astonished faces, fascinating masks, and sculptures of animals.

Two nights and a day at sea bring the ship to the old naval fortress at Kronstadt and on to **St. Petersburg** for a generous three-day stay. The ship's shore excursions are the best route here, easing the way through the crowds and hassles at the Hermitage to take in the superb collection of Italian, Flemish, Dutch, and French art and eighteenth- and nineteenth-century czarist opulence. Tours include the Winter Palace, St. Isaac's Cathedral, Peter and Paul Fortress, and often an evening ballet performance. Usually, there is a bit of time to wander the nearby streets and squares to soak up the atmosphere of Peter the Great's Window on Europe. Just over 20 miles from the ship on the southern shore of the Gulf of Finland, Peterhof, the town of palaces, fountains, and parks, was built by Peter the Great to rival Versailles. For over 200 years, Peterhof was used for lavish ceremonies, feasts, and receptions. After the revolution, the picture-perfect setting of parks and gardens were opened to the public and became a favorite place for locals to visit.

The extended stay allows for a trip inland to **Moscow,** Russia's capital, to visit the Kremlin, Red Square, St. Basil's Cathedral, and the KGB Museum and have a ride on the Metro. Some Moscow excursions use air both ways, and one includes an overnight luxury train for the return to St. Petersburg.

After a nighttime passage, the ship gingerly passes through a narrow channel between rocky islands to dock adjacent to the center of **Helsinki.** You can visit the Finnish capital on foot and by tram beginning with the Kauppatoru (Market Square) for its fruits, vegetables, flowers, and handicrafts, and just around the harbor's perimeter, the old market hall selling meat and fish. The popular loop tram, making a figure eight, connects most of the most interesting residential neighborhoods featuring wonderful Finnish art nouveau architecture; the Rock Church, where concerts take place all summer; and Finnish architect Eliel Sarineen's massive stone railway terminal. Adorned with great red-granite figures, trains depart for all of Finland, its lake district, St. Petersburg, and Moscow.

Approaching **Stockholm,** the ship traverses a vast wooded archipelago peppered with summer camps and permanent residences, from where the residents of the latter commute by ferry into the capital city. The *Serenity* will dock within sight of the Royal Palace, the Grand Hotel, and the Wasa Museum, the last-named displaying the sailing ship that sank on her maiden voyage in 1628 and resurrected in 1961. Stockholm, Sweden's capital, sprawls over fourteen islands and is linked by over fifty bridges. It is considered to be one of Europe's best preserved low-rise cities, and having a relatively compact urban center, an independent walking tour is an ideal way to see the sights. You might consider staying on a night or two following the cruise.

Address/Phone: Crystal Cruises, 2049 Century Park East, Suite 1400, Los Angeles, CA 90067; (866) 446–6625 or (310) 785–9300; fax: (310) 785–0011; www.crystalcruises.com

The Ship: *Crystal Serenity* was completed in 2004, has a gross tonnage of 68,870, a length of 820 feet, and a draft of 25 feet.

Passengers: 1,100; mostly Americans, some Europeans and Japanese, ages fifty and up

Dress: A dressy ship; formal nights, jackets and ties on informal nights

Officers/Crew: Norwegian and Japanese officers; European and Asian crew

Cabins: 550 good-size cabins, all outside and 466 with verandas

Fare: $$$$

What's included: Cruise fare and port charges, soft drinks, and specialty coffees

What's not included: Transportation to and from the ship, alcoholic drinks, tips

Highlights: Excellent service, alternative restaurants, big-ship amenities, a terrific itinerary

Other itineraries: *Crystal Serenity* and *Crystal Symphony* (960 passengers) provide worldwide itineraries. *Crystal Harmony* (960 passengers) left the fleet at the end of 2005 to join the parent company as NYK's *Asuka II*.

CUNARD LINE'S

Queen Elizabeth 2

Norway and the North Cape

Cunard Line is virtually synonymous with cruising and transatlantic travel, with ships that have plied the world's oceans since 1840. Today, the company continues to steep itself in its history and British formality, happily keeping the classic era very much alive. In early 2004 a new Cunard liner, the *Queen Mary 2,* entered service, ensuring an almost uninterrupted 175-year continuum of North Atlantic *Queens.* The *QE2* now spends much of the year based in England cruising from Southampton.

As a holdover from the former class system, your cabin grade determines the restaurant in which you will dine. Although the menus are basically the same throughout, there is a noticeable difference in preparation and service, not to mention ambience. The Mauretania restaurant is the largest and offers two traditional seatings. One category above is the single-sitting Caronia, resplendent in mahogany wood trim. The ship's smallest restaurants, the Britannia Grill and Princess Grill, both seat slightly more than one hundred people, and here, ordering off the menu is an added feature.

At the very top of the ship is the Queens Grill, complete with its own private lounge. The three grills provide an unmistakable feeling of exclusivity, and each is reached by a private entrance. In addition, the Lido Restaurant provides three casual meals a day.

Over the years, the *QE2* has undergone many renovations and refits, transforming a product of the late 1960s into a somewhat successful celebration of the mid-1930s. Of particular note is the Chart Room, a wonderful transatlantic setting adorned with the *Queen Mary's* original piano.

There is an amazing variety of spaces on board, from elegant, large rooms to cozy corners in bars. The Queens Room, the ship's ballroom, boasts the biggest dance floor at sea and is the cherished venue for a formal afternoon tea. An elaborate library and book shop are supervised by the only seagoing professional librarians. The spa and gymnasium are deep down in the ship, offering thalossotherapy and a saltwater indoor pool. The 550-seat, two-story theater screens films and hosts lectures by well-known experts on topics ranging from maritime history to America's influence on Russian culture. The two-story Grand Lounge is used for cabaret and play productions, and the Golden Lion Pub supplies beer aficionados with contentment well into the night.

Outside shuffleboard, golf driving, deck tennis, and basketball keep the active happy, while a nursery and teens club provide reassurance for harried parents.

Cabins come in all shapes and sizes, and with the coupling of the restaurant to your cabin grade, this is a most important choice. The minimum-grade cabins, inside with upper and lower berths, are small and not what one expects on a luxury ship, but they allow the less well-heeled to travel, ensuring that the passenger load includes most income levels. Cabins increase in size from there, and most have personality, with odd shapes and quirky designs. Grill category cabins have wood paneling, and the original One Deck rooms are just gorgeous, complete with walk-in closet, satin-lined walls, and oval-shaped windows.

The *QE2* has developed one of the most loyal followings afloat, and past passengers return time and time again. For anyone wishing to experience a trip in the grand style of the past, a cruise on one of the most famous ships in the world is absolutely not to be missed. Be advised, the *Queen* is showing her age.

The Itinerary

The *Queen Elizabeth 2,* now mostly based in Southampton, England, undertakes a variety of nonrepeating cruises to Northern Europe, the Atlantic Islands, and into the Mediterranean. One attractive North Cape cruise featured here cruises the Norwegian coast and its fjords, and makes an overnight call in Amsterdam. Other cruises operate somewhat similar northern itineraries between May and August that may add Spitzbergen and Icelandic ports to the mix.

The North Cape cruise to the Land of the Midnight Sun is the longest-running show at sea, dating back 150 years to the early steamship era. Passengers then as now were mainly British, German, and North American. This cruise begins with a late-afternoon departure from the Queen Elizabeth 2 Terminal in **Southampton** and a two-night and one-day passage to the mouth of the **Sognefjord** and a sail well inland to the tiny town of **Flaam.** The port, located at the head of a narrow fjord, is the terminus for the world's steepest adhesion railway with a spectacular climb up past waterfalls to the town of Myrdal, a junction on the main Oslo-Bergen rail line. Leaving the Sognefjord, the ship sails on north to **Aalesund,** a town destroyed by fire in 1904 and rebuilt into a handsome Norwegian style of art nouveau. The fit can easily make the twenty-minute climb to an observation point overlooking Aalesund and the *QE2* docked below. On north to **Trondheim,** the much older town center features an eleventh-century medieval cathedral and a colorful wooden Hanseatic League–style waterfront. Visit the Bishop's Palace alongside the Nidaros Cathedral, the Musical Museum, and open-air Folk Museum.

Crossing the Arctic Circle, where a ladle of ice-cold water down one's back is the typical initiation, the ship arrives at the **North Cape.** In June on a clear day the sun should remain visible above the horizon for the complete twenty-four-hour cycle, and even on a cloudy night, the sky should be light enough to read and take photographs. The North Cape Center is heavily visited during the midnight sun period, so the best sense of how far north you are may come from the deck of the ship looking up at the North Cape.

After a call at the northernmost fishing port of **Skarsvag,** sail on south for two nights and a day to enter the **Geirangerfjord,** Norway's most famous, passing pencil-thin Seven Sisters and Bridal Veil Falls to disembark passengers at **Hellesylt** for a mountain drive to the famous fjord overlook at Geiranger.

Sailing out into the Norwegian Sea, the ship turns south to visit **Bergen,** Norway's second-largest city and major west coast port. Much of the city is walkable from the ship, and be sure to take in the fish market at the end of the inner harbor; the Bergen Art Museum featuring Norwegian artists plus Braque, Picasso, and Paul Klee; Bryggen with its row of timbered Hanseatic League buildings, once merchant houses and now shops and cafes; and if the weather cooperates, take the Floibanen Funicular up the mountain for a superb view of the city and seascape.

A last call is made at **Stavanger,** with its twelfth-century medieval cathedral and wooden old city representing the past, and the base for the North Sea oil business the present. As a finale, the *QE2* takes two nights and a day to cross the North Sea and then into the English Channel for disembarkation at Southampton.

Address/Phone: Cunard Line, 24303 Town Center Drive, Suite 200, Valencia, CA 91355; (800) 7–CUNARD; www.cunard line.com

The Ship: The *Queen Elizabeth 2* was built in 1969, has a gross tonnage of 70,327 tons, a length of 963 feet, and a deep draft of 32 feet.

Passengers: 1,740; mostly British, some Americans, and Europeans of all ages, especially during the summer vacation months

Dress: Formal, informal, and casual nights

Officers/Crew: British officers and international crew

Cabins: 925 in a wide variety of shapes and sizes; 30 with verandas. Cabin category determines your restaurant. There are more than 100 single cabins available.

Fare: $$ to $$$$$

What's included: Cruise fare only

What's not included: Port charges, airfare, drinks, tips

Highlights: Cruising on a true liner to the magnificence of Norway and the North Cape; social life and a wide variety of activities onboard

Other itineraries: In addition to this summer cruise to Norway, the *QE2* makes other northern European cruises and sails to the Canary Islands and Mediterranean, with the occasional transatlantic cruise to New York, New England, and Canada, and the annual January to April world cruise. Fleetmate *Queen Mary 2* makes crossings between New York and Southampton and cruises from both ports and from Florida.

HOLLAND AMERICA'S
Rotterdam
Northern Europe and Baltic Capitals

The *Rotterdam* carries one of Holland America's most famous names, and one well known for making long voyages and world cruises. The previous *Rotterdam* of 1959 made twenty-nine circumnavigations, so the current one comes with an experienced pedigree including many staff who know how to please passengers for a couple of weeks or more.

Holland America Line began operating ships in 1872 with the first *Rotterdam,* and the 1997-built ship, the sixth bearing this name, represents a larger and faster ship than the successful series that began with the *Statendam* in 1992. While there are some attempts at providing a continuum of features from the *Rotterdam* of 1959, this *Rotterdam VI* is a completely new ship designed for today's market with many more amenities and a faster service speed (25 knots) to allow for more calls and additional time in port.

Like the *Statendam*-class ships, there is an enormous range, size, and style of public rooms, so only the hopeless will become bored by lack of venues. The Crow's Nest on this ship is truly a lounge, not a disco in disguise, with three distinct sections for use as a reading-cum-dozing room during the day, a quiet bar before dinner, and a spot to dance the night away on a lighted, colored, cracked-glass dance floor. Walking aft the door opens onto the vast lido deck, protected in bad weather by a roll-back roof, with a pool, wading pool, and two octagon-shaped whirlpools. A pair of affectionate bronze California sea lions, obviously in love, look on. The covered, outdoor seating provides an extension to the huge, nearly 400-seat air-conditioned Lido Restaurant with duplicate serving stations for most items.

Most of the indoor public spaces are arranged the entire length of Upper Promenade and Promenade decks. Production shows use the 557-seat Queens Lounge, a bi-level theater with a stage that can revolve and lift to create a staircase of four levels. Aft of the balcony level, one enters the three-story atrium dominated by an elaborate replica of a seventeenth-century Flemish clock showing time from cities around the world. To the side, the Ocean Bar is often the social center with a band, dance floor, and sit-up bar.

The Explorer's Lounge has a beautiful marble, floral-patterned dance floor, a bright red piano, and a new painting showing the old Amsterdam waterfront, the setting out place for Dutch explorers. The high quality fabrics here and throughout the ship turn the eye with attractive, bold designs and colors. Also on this deck are the casino; the Explorations Café, a combination coffee bar, Internet Center, and library; and some tacky terra-cotta Xian warriors, plus some lovely eighteenth-century watercolors on Chinese silk, and museum-quality Chinese artifacts. For maritime buffs, the six *Rotterdam*s are featured in outstanding original oil paintings by Bermuda artist Stephen Card, one per landing on the forward staircase.

Promenade Deck features a 165-seat cinema with popcorn machine, and the Pinnacle Restaurant (now a feature of all Holland America ships), an alternative Pacific Northwest restaurant and steakhouse, seating eighty-eight by reservation. The menu makes a distinctive change from the international-style menu found in the spectacular two-level La Fontaine Dining Room, seating 747. It's a giant space with an orchestra balcony, double staircase, and a ceiling featuring stars and glowing Murano colored-glass bits that looks out to sea in three directions. The early and late seatings each have two starting times about one-half hour apart. Small groups and large families can request to dine in the smaller attached Queen's Room and King's Room.

On deck, there are two pools, practice tennis courts, a wide wraparound promenade, and several quiet recesses away from the maddening crowd for deck chair lovers. The spa has a beauty salon, sauna, steam room, massage, and equipment that includes stationary bicycles, rowing machines, trotters, and leg and arm extenders—all with a great view over the almost invisible bow.

Eighty percent of the 660 cabins are outside and include an entire concierge deck with four penthouses (1,126 square feet) and thirty-six veranda suites (565 square feet) with a private concierge reception lounge and writing room tucked in the middle. One hundred twenty-one veranda minisuites occupy all of Verandah Deck, long, relatively narrow rooms with twin or queen beds, sofa, chair, stool and coffee table, vanity-cum-desk, minibar, fridge, and TV/VCR. The standard staterooms occupy three complete lower decks with those on Lower Promenade facing the open deck and some, marked on the plans, have partially obstructed views.

This *Rotterdam*, loaded with artworks, is a cut above the popular and successful *Statendam* class in spaciousness, improved layout, and speed, while steaming into the future alongside her fleet mates.

The Itinerary

While the order of the ports will vary from year to year, this twelve-day Scandinavian and Baltic capitals itinerary is good example of Holland America's summertime offerings in this part of the world. Independent touring ashore is an easy option apart from Warnemunde for the long trek to see Berlin in a day and at St. Petersburg, where without possessing a Russian visa, a ship's shore excursion is required to go ashore.

The ship boards in **Rotterdam** not far from Holland America Line's original Dutch headquarters when the line offered regular transatlantic sailings between Europe and New York. The prominent early twentieth-century building survived the bombing of the port during World War II and is now operating as the Hotel New York, also housing a very popular bar and restaurant on the ground floor.

To reach the North Sea, the *Rotterdam* sails along the New Waterway and out past the Hook of Holland to then sail northeast for two nights and a day to reach **Oslo.** The beauty of Norway's capital is easily three-fold—the scenic approach from the sea along the 62-mile-long Oslo Fjord, center city docking location below Akerhus Castle, and the gentle charm of its parks, waterfront, tree-lined boulevards, and urban architecture.

It is a ten-minute walk to the city center, while the liveliest harbor scene is just beyond the city hall where on warm summer days residents flock to cafes, restaurants, shops, and street entertainment. Boats leave from here for Bygdoy where Norway's maritime heritage is presented at the Maritime Museum, Fram Museum for polar exploration, Thor Heyerdahl's pioneering expeditions in the *Kon Tiki* across the Pacific and aboard the *Ra II* across the Atlantic, the Viking Ships Museum, and Folk Museum, a collection of 150 buildings

from all over the country and a beautiful wooden 1200-era stave church.

Sailing overnight, the ship calls at **Arhus,** Denmark's second city where the city center, much of it a pedestrian district, and the green marble city hall housing the most helpful tourist center are just a few minutes' walk from the pier. The major attractions are Arhus Cathedral, first executed in Romanesque style in 1201 and enlarged over a long period (1450–1520) in Gothic style, an occupation museum in the old Gestapo headquarters, and Aboulevarden where all ages come at late in the day and at night to enjoy the line of restaurants facing the canal. A once rundown section called the Latin Quarter now offers designer shops, art galleries, antiques stores, and cafes.

Just outside the center, Den Gamle By (The Old Town) forms a delightful composition of seventy-five buildings brought from all over Denmark to create a small market town with cobbled streets, an enclosed square, and a pretty stream running through. Inside, visitors see a bygone way of village life, including active gardens and kitchens baking crullers and cakes.

After an overnight passage, the ship calls at **Warnemunde,** a north German port with access, via a very long bus or train ride, to **Berlin,** the country's recently reestablished capital. The fast overview reveals one of Europe's great revived cities, burgeoning with new construction around Potsdam Square, and maintaining its handsome prewar scale along Unter den Linden. The principal cultural and architectural artery starts at the Brandenburg Gate and continues past the Opera House, Humboldt University, and the Berlin Cathedral to several superb art and archeological museums.

To the south of Unter den Linden, you come to the city's smart shopping district surrounding Galeries Lafayette and Gendarmenmarkt, the city's most beautiful square, bounded by a theater, the German Cathedral, and the French Cathedral. Further along stands the Jewish Museum, exhibiting Jewish contributions to German society, the Nazi era, dispersal, and the life of Jews living in Berlin today.

Checkpoint Charlie, once the principal crossing point through the Berlin Wall between the American and Soviet sectors, is invariably a stop, but there is almost nothing left of the wall but poignant reminders that can be seen in the Berlin Wall Museum.

With a day at sea to recover, take a walking tour of or explore **Tallinn,** Estonia's capital, a lively medieval Hanseatic League city speaking a language that has connections to Finnish, hence the huge numbers of Finns who will also be visiting by ship.

The route into **St. Petersburg** passes the old naval fortress at Kronstadt to then dock for two days. Shore excursions are the best way to see the former imperial city, the St. Peter and Paul Fortress, St. Isaacs Cathedral, the Winter Palace and the Hermitage to take in the Italian, Flemish, Dutch, and French art and eighteenth- and nineteenth-century czarist opulence, and perhaps an evening ballet performance. Usually, there is time to wander the nearby streets and squares to soak up the atmosphere of Peter the Great's Window on Europe.

Sailing overnight to **Helsinki,** the ship may dock adjacent to the city center and an outdoor craft and produce market. Finland's capital is a treasure trove of art nouveau architecture and perhaps best visited independently using the Loop Tram. The tracks make a figure eight starting out from near the port to run into residential neighborhoods, to Eliel Sarineen's magnificent 1912-built railway station, and the Rock Church, set in a stone quarry and a site for summer concerts.

Sail into the beautiful Swedish archipelago, islands dotted with weekend retreats, and homes within commuting distance of the capital, to dock at **Stockholm.** Built around a pretty harbor as well as facing a lake, the city has maintained its traditional skyline by sensible zoning and is relatively compact and easily walkable. The most prominent buildings seen from the ship are the palace, the Grand Hotel, and the Wasa Ship Museum.

Then two nights and a day brings the *Rotterdam* to **Copenhagen.** From the cruise terminal a landscaped waterfront promenade leads past the Little Mermaid and the royal palace to Nyhavn's canal-side outdoor restaurants and to the busy Stroget, a pedestrian street with several connecting branches that provides the setting for the capital's best shopping, dining, and entertainment opportunities. If staying over after the cruise, be sure to take in the festive atmosphere in the Tivoli Gardens, Copenhagen's 165-year-old entertainment park with thirty-two restaurants, ballet, and concert venues, and said to be the inspiration for Walt Disney's American-style theme attractions.

Address/Phone: Holland America Line, 300 Elliott Avenue West, Seattle, WA 98119; (800) 426–0327; fax: (206) 281–7110; www.hollandamerica.com.

The Ship: *Rotterdam* was completed in 1997 and has a gross tonnage of 59,652, a length of 778 feet, and a draft of 25 feet.

Passengers: 1,316; mostly Americans sixty and up

Dress: Formal, informal, casual, and theme nights

Officers/Crew: Dutch officers, and Indonesian and Filipino crew

Cabins: 660; 542 outside and 160 with verandas

Fare: $$$

What's included: Cruise only

What's not included: Airfare, port charges, drinks, tips, shore excursions

Highlights: A classy and beautifully decorated new ship, and a wonderful Baltic capitals' itinerary

Other itineraries: Besides Northern European itineraries, Holland America's large fleet cruises the Mediterranean, New England and Canada, the Caribbean, Panama Canal, Hawaii, Alaska, Australia and New Zealand, and around the world.

HEBRIDEAN ISLAND CRUISES'
Hebridean Princess
Scotland's Western Isles

Hebridean Island Cruises, a well-kept secret in North America, got its start in 1989, when a 600-passenger Scottish ferry was transformed into a posh, floating country house for a maximum of fifty mostly British guests. She came under new ownership in 1997, and the public rooms have been completely redecorated, making her even more attractive.

The cozy public rooms evoke the feel of an old-fashioned country inn, nowhere more so than in the forward observation lounge, with its comfy upholstered armchairs and settees and rustic brick-and-timber fireplace. A small bar is off to one side. The library has leather and tartan-upholstered seating. Two other lounges feature afternoon tea and cigar smoking amid wicker furniture. Some evenings are formal, and in warm weather, passengers gather aft on deck for champagne receptions with hot hors d'oeuvres. Top-deck spaces also include comfy, wind-protected chairs for reading. Bicycles are carried for passengers' use.

The restaurant operates like a hotel dining room. Passengers sit with friends or at tables for two, but singles are seated with fellow singles and usually an officer. Presentation and service are top-notch. The menu is typically British, featuring a Sun-

day roast with Yorkshire pudding at lunch, sliced duckling at dinner, black pudding and kippers at breakfast, and fresh strawberries on meringue for dessert. Other dinner choices include Scottish highland game and mushroom pie, sautéed and smoked salmon, and raw oysters. Unfamiliar Scottish delicacies that may startle the palate are haggis, a mixture of calf or lamb hearts, lungs, and liver with onion, suet, and seasonings, and kedgeree, a rice and smoked-fish combination.

The twenty-nine individually designed and furnished cabins, carrying the names of Scottish isles, lochs, sounds, and castles, vary widely, but all show fabric frills above headboards and around windows that open. TVs, refrigerated bars, coffee- and tea makers, irons and ironing boards, trouser presses, hair dryers, dressing tables, and ample stowage are standard throughout. Two cabins on the lowest deck share baths, and there are eleven dedicated inside and outside singles. The ship is not air-conditioned, but this is seldom a problem in these northerly waters. Although the fares are as high as they get, the *Hebridean Princess* is a one-of-a-kind treasure appealing to the well-heeled, many of whom come back year after year.

The Itinerary

A guide accompanies all cruises, and excursions include visits to stately homes, country gardens, fishing villages, and remote, rugged islands. Passengers should come prepared for Scottish mists and uncertain weather, and the ship anchors or ties up at night except on an occasional overnight sail to the outer islands and across the North Sea to Norway's fjords. The *Hebridean Princess* most often boards in **Oban,** a popular Scottish seaside resort about two hours by train northwest of Glasgow. Port descriptions here are meant to be typical examples, as itineraries vary from cruise to cruise. A two-hour sail takes you to **Tobermory Bay** on the **Isle of Mull** for a guided tour of the neat, white-washed town, founded by the British Fisheries Society. Underway, the ship cruises into **Loch Stuart,** overlooked by the rugged and scenic beauty of **Ardnamurchan Peninsula,** where its point is the most westerly mainland in the British Isles, beating out much-better-known Land's End by 20 miles.

The **Sound of Sleat,** separating the mainland from the **Isle of Skye,** leads to the pastel-fronted island capital of **Portree** for a bit of a wander. In **Upper Loch Torridin** the surrounding peaks create a dramatic setting for an overnight anchorage. The village of **Plonkton** offers the unusual sight, in these northerly parts, of an arc of palm trees, and later in the day from the dock at the **Kyle of Lochalsh,** a drive explores **Cuillin Hills** across the sea on Skye.

Cruising past Rum and Eigg, the ship anchors off **Muck** for a beach landing and a walk across the island to have a proper afternoon tea with local residents. A cruise up **Loch Linnhe** may offer a glimpse of Scotland's highest peak, **Ben Nevis,** snow-capped for much of the year. Northwest Scotland's remarkable climate has encouraged the creation of some beautiful gardens, including those at **Torosay Castle,**

which exhibit, depending on the time of one's visit, glorious spring flowers or colorful autumnal leaves. The *Hebridean Princess* spends one more night at anchor, then slips into Oban in the morning.

Address/Phone: Hebridean Island Cruises, Griffin House, Broughton Hall, Skipton, North Yorkshire, BD23 3AN England; (011) 44–1756–704794 or (800) 659–2648 (9:00 A.M.–5:15 P.M. U.K. time); fax: (011) 44–1756–701455; www.hebridean.co.uk

The Ship: *Hebridean Princess* was rebuilt in 1989 from the Scottish ferry *Columba* and has a gross tonnage of 2,115, a length of 235 feet, and a shallow draft of 10 feet.

Passengers: 49; age fifty and up, largely British with perhaps a handful of Americans

Dress: Formal nights, and jacket and tie

Officers/Crew: British

Cabins: 29; wide range of shapes and sizes but all prettily furnished, including eleven singles, and four with balconies

Fare: $$$$$

What's included: Cruise and port charges, excursions, tips, wine at meals, wine by the glass at the bar, beer, soft drinks

What's not included: Airfare

Highlights: Sailing aboard a most genteel, floating, country-house hotel to a beautiful part of the world, weather cooperating

Other itineraries: The *Hebridean Princess* offers many different six- to nine-night Scottish itineraries, plus trips to Norway, Northern Ireland, Ireland, and the Isle of Man from March through November. The 78 passenger, 4,200-ton *Hebridean Spirit* joined the fleet in mid-2001, offering wider-ranging cruises to Norway, the Baltic, the Mediterranean, and through Suez into the Red Sea and Indian Ocean.

NORTHLINK FERRIES'

Hjaltland and *Hrossey*

To the Isles North of Scotland

For well over a century, a fleet of "North Boats" has linked Scotland's Orkney and Shetland Islands with the mainland. The ships are designed to sail in some of the world's roughest seas, but when the weather cooperates, the island scenery is absolutely gorgeous. With frequent schedules, it is quite easy to plan the sea trip and then stop over a couple of days on each island chain. The ship names *Hjaltland* and *Hrossey* (old Norse for Shetland and Orkney) are the only aspects of this service that are not brand-new. Taking over the concession from P&O Scottish Ferries in 2002, Northlink, a joint venture between Scottish west coast ferry operator Caledonian MacBrayne and the Royal Bank of Scotland, had a fleet of fast, 24-knot, high-standard ships built in Finland. To match this investment, the Scottish Executive built new terminals at all the ports.

Every day in the late afternoon, a ship leaves Aberdeen for the 200-mile overnight journey north to Lerwick (Shetland), calling en route on alternate sailings at Kirkwall (Orkney) about midnight. Aberdeen boarding takes place up to two hours before sailing, allowing passengers to settle into their comfortable, tastefully furnished outside two-bed cabins or more economically in an inside four-berth cabin. Private facilities and hair dryers are included in all cabins.

The forward bar, the live entertainment center of the ship, overlooks the bow and is a particularly pleasant spot for a drink before dinner. The small a la carte restaurant (booking essential) offers high-quality ingredients, including lamb, steaks, fish, and scallops, sourced mainly from the islands and carefully prepared and beautifully presented in

elegant surroundings. The fine food is complemented by a fairly extensive wine list, and coffee may be taken after dinner in the adjacent lounge. Other facilities include a large self-service restaurant for dinner and breakfast, a cinema, a children's playroom, and a small shop carrying necessities, souvenirs, and local knitwear. The public spaces throughout are furnished with wood-effect paneling, and outside there are small semi-sheltered areas amidships and a large open deck aft. Although the arrival comes early, at 7:00 A.M., breakfast is served until 9:30 A.M., and final disembarkation is at 10:00 A.M. For a small fee, including breakfast, the ship's staff will unload those traveling with a car and put it on the quayside, allowing a more leisurely disembarkation.

The Itinerary

As these ships operate mostly overnight, sightseeing en route is limited, though lengthened summertime daylight extends viewing hours.

Aberdeen's harbor, packed with oil rig supply vessels and numerous fishing boats, is a tight squeeze for the *Hjaltland* and *Hrossey* on their way out to the North Sea. The ships turn north to parallel the Aberdeenshire coast for about two hours, then in the morning the ship docks at **Lerwick,** the principal town of the hundred-island chain.

The Shetlands are much wilder than Orkney, with crofting (small farm holdings) and fishing the main industries. At anchor may be Russian and Polish fish factory ships known locally as klondykers, which arrive every summer to buy and process herring and mackerel.

If you have not arrived with a car, you can rent one or hire a taxi for the short ride to numerous bed-and-breakfasts or a small hotel. The Lerwick Hotel, located on the south side of town, has good views across the water to the Island of Brassay, but it is quite expensive.

Directly accessible from the pier is a headland walk leading to the ruins of **Clickimin Broch,** a first-century fortified stone tower built in a shallow loch by the Picts. Then in the afternoon, tour the country-side dotted with stacks of freshly cut peat and ruins of old stone crofts. There are sweeping views to both sides out to the North Sea and to the Atlantic Ocean. Stop at **Jarlshoff,** Sir Walter Scott's early-nineteenth-century name for an ancient site that saw 3,000 years of habitation, from the Stone Age to the seventeenth century. In the distance Sumburgh Head, the Shetlands' most southerly point, beckons walkers for a few hours' hike.

The crossing from Lerwick to **Kirkwall** on Orkney takes about six and a half hours, and the terminal, also serving cruise ships, is about 2 to 3 miles by road from the center of town. A taxi transfer is the best option. The arrival, whether from Aberdeen or Ler-wick, is usually just before midnight, but the hotel operators are used to latecomers.

One recommended place to stay is the Orkney Hotel (formerly the Royal Hotel) on Victoria Street, Kirkwall. The rooms are attractive, and the restaurant food is excel-lent with the Scottish breakfasts especially good. The hotel is located about 100 yards from **St. Magnus** cathedral, built in Norman times of weathered red sandstone. The town itself and the stone harbor are interesting places to explore on foot, and local ferries sail from here to the northern islands for additional exploring ashore.

Not far from town, the Italian chapel, crafted from scrap metal by Italian prisoners

of World War II and overlooking the historic naval anchorage at Scapa Flow, is well worth a visit, as is **Maes Howe,** a neolithic burial chamber built before 2700 B.C. Most of the island is gently rolling farmland and grazing fields for cattle and sheep, but the shoreline has sharp edges. Driving is a joy and roads are uncrowded.

Sailings return from Kirkwall overnight to Aberdeen, or alternatively from the Orcadian port of **Stromness** on a ninety-minute crossing to the very northern tip of Scotland at **Scrab-ster.** By road from Kirkwall to Stromness, the journey takes about twenty-five minutes, and buses travel the route and meet the ferries. Orkney's second city is an intriguing rabbit warren of quiet lanes and is another good place to spend the night. The largest hotel is the Stromness, overlooking the harbor, and the local maritime museum at the edge of town crams a lot of history into a small space.

On the very-early-morning ferry departure for the mainland, passengers may board about 10:00 P.M. the night before and occupy a cabin until the morning's arrival at Scrabster. The Scrabster ferry *Hamnavoe* has a self-service restaurant, two large bars, a shop, and small play area. Decor is similar to the larger ships. She measures 8,780 gross tons, is 366 feet long, and carries the old Norse name for safe haven (a name associated with Stromness).

The route passes some of Europe's high-est vertical cliffs and a 450-foot-high pin-nacle of rock known as the **Old Man of Hoy** about twenty-five minutes out of Strom-ness. It serves as the nesting grounds for thousands of noisy gannets, kittiwakes, puffins, razorbills, and oystercatchers.

At the port of Scrabster, a bus operates to the railway station at **Thurso,** the end of the rail line that links the far north of Scotland with **Inverness** and points south. Three trains a day take about three and a half hours over a highly scenic line to reach Inverness.

Address/Phone: Northlink Orkney and Shetland Ferries Limited, Kiln Corner, Ayre Road, Kirkwall, Orkney, Scotland KW15 1QX; (011) 44–1856–885500; fax: (011) 44–1856–879588; www.northlinkferries.co.uk (the site has helpful tourist information)

The Ships: The *Hjaltland* and *Hrossey* were both purpose-built in Finland in 2002, have a gross tonnage of 11,486, a length of 409 feet, and a draft of 17 feet.

Passengers: 600 total occupancy; the majority of passengers are British of all ages

Dress: Casual at all times

Officers/Crew: British

Cabins: 300 berths in 50 outside twins and 50 inside fours, all with private facilities; two recliner lounges

Fare: $ to $$

What's included: Fare, with cabin if purchased, port charges

What's not included: Connecting transportation, meals, drinks

Highlights: High standard on board and beautiful island destinations

SUPERFAST FERRIES'
Superfast IX and *Superfast X*
From Edinburgh, Scotland, Overnight to Bruges, Belgium

There is no more stylish way to travel from Scotland to mainland Europe than by one of the sleek red-hulled ships of Superfast Ferries. With their distinctive winged funnels and gleaming white superstructures, these ships slice through the North Sea at up to 27 knots, providing one of the very best overnight ferry experiences in the region.

Superfast Ferries is a relatively new company, founded in 1993, and two years later took delivery of its first ships for service in the Adriatic Sea. Now, the company operates eight ferries, the oldest built in 2001, on routes in the Adriatic, Baltic, and North Seas.

Superfast IX and *Superfast X* were delivered from their German builder at the beginning of 2002 and first placed into service between Germany and Sweden. Within a few months they were transferred to their current route and have justifiably built up a loyal following.

In the early twenty-first century freight is king in the North Sea ferry trades. However, sitting atop two freight decks packed with trailers is some of the most attractive passenger accommodations to be found in these waters. The public rooms, identical on both ships, are on Deck 7, with the aptly named Colours Lounge (aboard *Superfast IX*) overlooking the bow. Red, green, and blue are not often seen together in one color scheme, but they work well here. This lounge features at table service rather than self-service, rarely found these days on Northern European ferries. A musical duo (usually very good) performs here, and at the after end of the room are the unobtrusive snack bar and the small casino.

Further aft on the starboard side is the card room with both board games and Internet access available. The shops sell a range of souvenirs and local produce such as whisky, smoked salmon, cheeses, and shortbread from Scotland and pâté, chocolate, and biscuits from Belgium.

The Mosquito Bar, aft of the main stairway, while potentially an intimate retreat, is usually smoky and suffers from proximity to the busy side corridors leading to the restaurants.

The Eggs buffet restaurant provides a self-service dinner at a reasonable price, but the better choice would be the Flowers a la carte with superb locally sourced Scottish salmon, Aberdeen Angus steaks, and Belgian mussels. Some specialties on our trip included hare pie, wild boar, pheasant, and venison. Try the astonishingly good chicken mulligatawny soup and the exquisite baked apple with cinnamon sugar and a light whisky cream sauce. Service is exceptionally good. An extensive breakfast buffet is served in the Eggs restaurant.

Situated on Decks 6, 8, and 9, cabins, ranging from an inner four-berth to an outer twin, are tastefully furnished with light woods and attractive fabrics. They are reasonably sized for a short voyage and provide good hanging and storage space. In addition, there are several luxury doubles at the forward end of Deck 8 and on Deck 10, the highest passenger deck. Deck 10 also features the Health Club, with saunas, Jacuzzi, exercise machine, and a massage service. The extensive open Decks 7 and 10 have lots of railing space for viewing the passing scene.

The Itinerary

For most of the year, sailings operate from Scotland and Belgium every day except Sunday, with exception of January to March, when a single ship sails three times weekly. Sunday sailings are added on peak summer dates.

Prior to sailing, consider spending a few days in **Edinburgh** to visit, at the very least, the imposing Edinburgh Castle, set

upon a mighty volcanic rock overlooking the city, the fifteenth-century Palace of Holyrood (now Holyrood House and still used as a royal residence) at the bottom of the Royal Mile, the elegant Georgian-style New Town, and the Scottish specialty shops along Princes Street facing the gardens. Just north of the city at **Leith,** the former Royal Yacht *Britannia* is open to visitors.

To reach the ferry without a car, an express bus (X2) departs at 2:15 P.M. on sailing days from the main bus station, not far from Edinburgh's Waverley railway station. The route passes over the scenic Forth Road Bridge to the ferry port at Rosyth, located adjacent to the Royal Naval base.

The bus arrives as embarkation begins two hours prior to the 5:00 P.M. departure. During *Superfast*'s transit along the Firth of Forth, it is worth being out on deck to see the passage under the road bridge and the massive cantilevered Forth Rail Bridge. Opened by the Prince of Wales in 1890, it carries the main rail line from London and Edinburgh to the north of Scotland. Then about twenty minutes later, some ways off to starboard, it's possible to catch a glimpse the distinctive buff funnel of the former Royal Yacht *Britannia* and, in the far distance, Edinburgh Castle. The Scottish coast remains visible for another four hours as the ship plows south through the North Sea.

Soon there will be little to see until the next morning after breakfast when the ship enters the busy shipping lanes at the eastern end of the English Channel. About 11:30 A.M., after a voyage of some 400 nautical miles, the ship ties up in the container port of Zeebrugge. A shuttle bus runs from the terminal to the railway station in **Bruges,** a perfectly preserved medieval city and capital of Flanders.

Bruges achieved its zenith during the fourteenth century when it was continental Europe's largest wool-producing town and the recognized trading center of the Hanseatic League. A short walk north from the railway station brings you to the historic heart, now a UNESCO World Heritage Site, with the Market Square, the magnificent Belfry, and the Provincial Government Palace. Nearby is Burg Square, with its impressive Gothic city hall, one of the oldest in the Low Countries. For a wander, the city is laced with canals and streets of attractive gabled buildings.

The bars and restaurants are known for hundreds of locally produced beers, outstanding mussel dishes, delicious ice cream, and superb chocolate, the latter produced in small backroom factories, some open to visitors.

Just thirty minutes from Bruges by train is the attractive historic city of **Ghent,** located at the confluence of the Rivers Leie and Scheldt. By the eleventh century, Ghent had achieved considerable prominence as a major port in north Western Europe. The city's history, from the Middle Ages to the French Revolution, comes to life in the Bijloke Museum, housed in a former Cistercian monastery.

Among the many impressive views is one from St. Michael's Bridge with the skyline punctuated by the three towers of St. Nicholas' Church, the Belfry, and St. Bravo's Cathedral.

Address/ Phone: Amphitrion Holidays USA, 1506 21st Street, Suite 100A, Washington, DC 20036; (800) 424–2741 or (202) 872–9878; fax: (202) 872–8210; Superfast has an easy-to-use information and direct-booking site at www.superfast.com

The Ships: *Superfast IX* and *Superfast X* were built in 2002 and have a gross tonnage of 30,825 tons, a length of 664 feet, and a draft of 23 feet.

Passengers: 717; mostly British, Dutch, and German of all ages. English is widely spoken, and onboard announcements are in English, Dutch, French, and German.

Dress: Casual at all times

Officers/Crew: Greek officers and mixed European crew

Cabins: Moderate size ranging from luxury outsides to inner four berths; budget accommodation in airline-style seats

Fare: $ to $$

What's included: Ferry fare and port taxes only

What's not included: Meals, drinks, tips

Highlights: Ships with outstanding passenger accommodations, wonderful food, and excellent service, offering a voyage between two major European centers of history.

Other itineraries: Superfast Ferries sail from the north German port of Rostock to Hanko, Finland, and from the eastern Italian port of Ancona across to Patras in Greece.

NORWEGIAN COASTAL VOYAGE'S
Nordkapp
Norwegian Coastal Voyage

The locals refer to their domestic passenger and cargo service as the *Hurtigruten*—fast route. For more than one hundred years, a fleet of ships owned by several different companies has operated a water highway linking three dozen towns along the rugged Norwegian coast between Bergen in the south and the North Cape and beyond. Norwegian Coastal Voyage markets them all in North America. The ships' role as the primary means of access has diminished, and while many Norwegians still travel this way and expedite their cargo, the *Hurtigruten*'s future lies with local and overseas tourism.

The eleven ships fall into three categories, the newest being the Millennium class ships of 15,000 gross tons with 674 berths, some with balconies. In the next few years, this class will grow to five and replace two of a trio of Mid-Generation ships, built and then enlarged in the 1980s to 4,200 tons with 325 passenger berths. The Contemporary class numbers six 11,300-ton, 490-berth ships built between 1993 and the end of the decade. As this class is the most numerous, one of these, the *Nordkapp*, will be used as the example.

At 11,300 tons, the 1996-built *Nordkapp* can take up to 490 cabin passengers. Most cabins are of a uniform design, with large windows, two lower beds, a vanity, decent storage space, and private facilities. The *Nordkapp* is beautifully decorated in attractive bold colors and with distinctive Norwegian paintings of landscapes, seascapes, and historic steamers, plus lots of glass and mirrors,

creating a most cheerful atmosphere. The large, 110-seat panorama lounge, done in blues and greens, has sweeping views in three directions, and aft a spacious lounge/bar looks out to port and starboard. A second deck of public rooms includes a lounge with musical entertainment offered during the high season, conference rooms, a quiet reading room, a twenty-four-hour cafeteria, a souvenir shop, a children's playroom, and a long gallery lounge leading aft to a big, windowed dining room that seats 240.

The size of the ship and the presence of tour groups often make meeting other passengers more difficult than on the more intimate ships, such as the traditional passenger-cargo ships *Lofoten* (1964) and *Nordstjernen* (1956) that operate only in the off-season, and in the summer make off-route cruises. There is limited outdoor seating on three afterdecks and a wrap-around deck for walking. Cargo is wheeled through doors in the ship's side, and watching the handling is less a pastime than on the older crane-loading ships.

The food is Norwegian, which means, besides standard continental-breakfast items, eggs and bacon (on some mornings), cold meats, cheeses, and a variety of herring. Lunch, also a buffet, is the most elaborate meal, with a choice of several hot and cold entrees such as salmon, halibut, lamb chops, and veal, as well as soup, salads, cheeses, and desserts. Dinner is a set three-course menu, but a certain sameness sets in after a week aboard. Alcohol is heavily taxed. If you like a drink before dinner, bring your own.

The Itinerary

Tourists are attracted to Norway's scenery, which does not disappoint in good weather. The route is a coastal one, and the ships do not penetrate the deepest fjords, except for summertime visits to the Geiranger Fjord, but there are some quite spectacular narrow passages that the big cruise ships cannot negotiate.

The thirty-five ports, called at different hours northbound and southbound, range from small villages and good-size fishing ports to major market centers, most rebuilt after World War II. Time in port ranges from fifteen minutes to several hours, but a quick walk is nearly always possible.

The cities vary considerably in their offerings. **Aalesund,** destroyed by fire in 1904, was rebuilt into a handsome Norwegian style of art nouveau. **Trondheim** has a much older center, a magnificent eleventh-century medieval cathedral, and a wooden waterfront. An excursion is offered both northbound and southbound, including the Museum of Music History on the latter.

Crossing the **Arctic Circle** is marked with a globe set on an island, and the ship celebrates the event with proclamations and an ice-water "ceremony."

The **Lofoten Islands,** a popular subject for maritime artists, rise dramatically out of the sea as the coastal express approaches from **Bodo.** Depending on the weather the ship is likely to sail into the narrow **Troll Fjord** and turn 180 degrees in a very tight basin surrounded by steep cliffs oozing water that become cascading waterfalls in the wetter seasons.

One of my favorite excursions, and there are up to eighteen in the high season, leaves the southbound ship at **Harstad,** stops at a thirteenth-century stone church, continues into interior farming regions, crosses a fjord by ferry, and rejoins the ship at **Sortland. Tromso** is a delightful university city. The Arctic Cathedral, built in a layered A-frame style, possesses Europe's largest glass mosaic.

The landscape becomes more rugged and less populated, and, at **Honningsvåg,** if snow isn't blocking the road (normally open by mid-May), there is an excursion to the **North Cape** that passes reindeer and an encampment of the indigenous Sami people and then culminates in a glorious view northward over the sea.

Rounding the top of Norway, the ship skirts some of Europe's highest sea cliffs, populated with nesting gannets. Again the coastal steamer is exposed to the open sea, so be prepared for hours of pitching before reaching **Kirkenes.** This is where most one-way passengers leave to fly south or come north to join the trip. Round-trippers will stop at the same ports but at different times of the day, so those missed at night come during the day.

Address/Phone: Norwegian Coastal Voyage, Inc., 405 Park Avenue, New York, NY 10022; (800) 323–7436 or (212) 319–1300; brochures: (800) 666–2374; fax: (212) 319–1390; www.norwegian coastalvoyage.us

The Ship: *Nordkapp* was built in 1996 and has a gross tonnage of 11,200 and a length of 414 feet.

Passengers: 490; all ages; mostly forty and up, traveling as individuals or groups (aboard the newer ships); largely Norwegian, German, and British, with some Americans and other Europeans

Dress: Casual

Officers/Crew: Norwegian

Cabins: 217, all outside, plain but decent size

Fare: $$

What's included: Varies, from cruise only, including port charges, to a complete package, airfare, hotel, tips, transfers, and a prepaid shore-excursions package

What's not included: Drinks, and airfares when not part of a package

Highlights: Norway's spectacular coast; cargo handling, especially aboard the older ships; maritime atmosphere; Norwegian art aboard the newer ships

Other itineraries: The coastal voyage may be taken as a twelve-day round-trip, calling at thirty-five ports each way, leaving Bergen almost every night at 10:30 P.M. throughout the year. One-way six- and seven-day sea-air trips are available between Bergen and Kirkenes and can be combined with hotel stays and the highly recommended Bergen-Oslo train ride. The northbound itinerary has better port timings for Aalesund, Trondhiem, Tromso, and the North Cape. The midnight sun is visible in clear weather above the Arctic Circle between mid-May and late July, whereas the Northern Lights are most often seen in winter. The summer months see many deck passengers, but by early September they are mostly gone. The older ships make summertime cruises, and one or two of the Contemporary ships spend the northern winter in Antarctica.

DFDS SEAWAYS'
Crown of Scandinavia
Ferry Cruising between Copenhagen and Oslo

DFDS (Det Forende Dampskibs Selskab— The United Steamship Company), Denmark's largest and oldest passenger shipowner, began sailing the Capital Cities Route in 1866. The company now operates a fleet of seven overnight cruise ferries on routes between Denmark, England, Sweden, Norway, Germany, and Holland. Advertising proudly proclaims DFDS as "Masters of the Northern Seas," and there is no disagreement here.

In recent years this route annually carried about 750,000 passengers, of which Norwegians and Danes accounted for about 75 percent. Many British and American passengers also use this service, and language presents no problems, as English is generally spoken throughout Scandinavia. Sailings are geared to the business traveler and tourist, with daily departures at 5:00 P.M. from terminals close to both city centers and arrivals at 9:00 A.M. next day.

Crown of Scandinavia is the newest passenger ferry in the fleet, the last in a series of four ships built at Split in Croatia for various Scandinavian owners. Delivered in July 1994, she runs alongside the slightly larger *Pearl of Scandinavia,* dating from 1989. Boarding by car or on foot, the passenger arrives at the spacious reception area to be directed to the cabin. *Crown of Scandinavia*'s 662 cabins include, unusual for a ferry, twenty-two with verandas, and a further forty-six larger cabins feature extra facilities and limited room service, designated as Commodore Class. Every cabin has a shower and a toilet.

Dining options cater to all price ranges. The most popular is the Seven Seas restaurant, with its panoramic forward view, serving buffet dinners and traditional Scandinavian smorgasbord. Dinner with wine costs about $65 for two. The window seats at breakfast are quickly taken during the transit up the Oslofjord. My preferred dining option is the elegant, Chinese-style setting of Sailors Corner, with its dark cherry furniture and paneling. Grilled meats, fish, and shellfish are specialties here, and a drink, wine, and coffee are included in the three-course price ($105 for two). Always book a table in either restaurant on embarkation. As an alternative, the Scandia Café provides light meals and snacks.

The well-patronized Admiral Pub, adjacent to the Sailors Corner, is modeled on a dark wood–furnished English bar, a style featured on a number of Scandinavian ferries. The main lounge is the Columbus Club, with three bars, a dance floor, and a nearby casino. Entertainment includes a singing group, bingo, and shipboard horse racing. In the afternoon this lounge provides a good position to view the passing scenery, and outside the extensive sundecks provide more viewing platforms. Other facilities aboard include cinemas, a disco, a Jacuzzi, a sauna, an indoor pool, a children's playroom, and teen activities.

The Itinerary

The ship sails from a new terminal just outside **Copenhagen**'s city center. Shortly after entering the **Öresund**, Middleground Fort is rounded and a course set for **Helsingborg** in Sweden, where the ship arrives at about 6:45 P.M.; this is a brief call to pick up passengers and vehicles for Oslo. Helsingborg is a busy ferry port annually handling more than thirteen million passengers, most traveling to **Helsingor** in Denmark.

Ten minutes after sailing from Helsingborg, the *Crown of Scandinavia* passes to port **Kronborg Castle** at Helsingor, famous as the setting for Hamlet. Soon the ship enters the **Kattegat**, following the Swedish coastline northward for about another hour. During the night the **Skaggerak** is crossed,

and arrival at the mouth of **Oslofjord** is at about 5:00 A.M.

The 60-mile passage to **Oslo** takes about four hours, and at 7:30 the ship enters the narrowest part after passing **Oscarsborg Fortress.** At 9:00 A.M. the *Crown of Scandinavia* docks adjacent to the thirteenth-century **Akershus Castle,** a short walk from the city center. On arrival all passengers (including the round-trippers) must disembark, but returning passengers can leave luggage aboard. The nightly departures permit flexible planning.

Address/Phone: DFDS Seaways, Sea Europe Holidays, Inc., 6801 Lake Worth Road, Suite 107, Lake Worth, FL 33467; (800) 533–3755, ext. 114; fax: (561) 432–2550; www.seaeurope.com; www.europeonsale.com

The Ships: *Crown of Scandinavia* was built in 1994 and has a gross tonnage of 35,498 and a length of 559 feet. *Pearl of Scandinavia* was built in 1989, has a gross tonnage of 40,039, and a length of 584 feet.

Passengers: 2,400 full capacity; mostly Danish and Norwegian, but English spoken

Dress: Casual

Officers/Crew: Mostly Danish, some Filipinos

Cabins: 662, inside and out, with a total of 2,126 beds

Fare: $ to $$

What's included: Cruise only; Commodore class includes breakfast

What's not included: Meals, drinks, tips

Highlights: Lots to do and eat aboard; scenic approaches to and from both capitals

Other itineraries: In addition to this daily overnight ferry cruise between Copenhagen and Oslo, DFDS operates popular overnight sailings between Denmark, Germany, the Netherlands, and England.

SILJA LINE'S
Silja Serenade and *Silja Symphony*
Cruise Ferries in the Baltic

The Silja Line, headquartered in Helsinki, has been trading in ships for larger new ones as often as Americans trade in their cars. Among the world's largest cruise ferries, the *Silja Europa* has a gross tonnage of 59,914 and passenger capacity of 3,013; near sisters *Silja Symphony* and *Silja Serenade* are slightly smaller at 58,400 tons and take up to 2,852.

On the *Serenade* and *Symphony,* Decks 2 to 12 are fitted with cabins, restaurants, cafes, bars, nightclubs, a cinema, lots of shopping, a casino, a children's playroom, a video arcade, saunas, small pools, whirlpools, and several levels for vehicles of all shapes and sizes.

Dining options include no less than three a la carte restaurants: Maxim a la Carte, with a large menu; Casa Bonita for steaks; and Happy Lobster, a fish and seafood eatery. The latter features smoked, slightly salted, grilled and poached fish, mustard herring, Baltic herring, fish roe and shrimp, and if desired, Finlandia vodka. Buffet Serenade and Buffet Symphony (smorgasbord) have an incredible range of food for one set price, with reserved timed entry to avoid queues. Snack bars and cafes for light meals and hot hors d'oeuvres are scattered about the ship.

Most spectacular is the Promenade, a shopping and restaurant arcade running fore and aft for 475 feet, five decks and 60 feet high, decorated with mobiles and topped with skylights. Glass-enclosed bridges run across the horizontal atrium.

Entertainment and drinking venues are Atlantis Palace, a tiered cocktail lounge and nightclub with dance music; a casino for roulette, blackjack, and slots; Stardust, for karaoke and disco, located under the funnel; a British-style pub; and a panorama bar and pastry cafe overlooking the stern. High up, the Sunflower Oasis is the spa with small pools and whirlpools, and low down is a bank of saunas. Siljaland is a play area for children, and the electric bazaar features the latest video games. Seminars and corporate meetings are big business, and the Conference Center can be adapted to large or small gatherings.

Nine hundred eighty-five cabins with 2,980 berths fall into eight categories, the top being Commodore class, set high up and forward; others include standard outsides with windows, insides, promenade-view cabins, and budget accommodations below vehicle decks. Deck 12 is open for viewing in all directions, and the enclosed central portion looks down into the Promenade Arcade. Deck 7 permits a walk under lifeboats completely around the ship.

The onboard atmosphere is that of an urban entertainment center, with everything geared to encouraging passengers to spend money and have a good time doing it. It's one late-night party, but with cabins located on separate decks, passengers wishing to sleep can do so.

The Itinerary
The Silja Line and its arch competitor, the Viking Line (sporting bright-red hulls), offer daily year-round overnight service between Stockholm and Helsinki, and both overnight and daylight sailings between Stockholm and Turku. All sailings call briefly at the scenic **Åland Islands** in order

to maintain the duty-free status aboard the ships. The most popular trip leaves Stockholm at 5:00 P.M., sails overnight to Helsinki, arriving at 9:30 A.M. for a day in the Finnish capital, and then returns overnight to Stockholm.

Departing **Stockholm,** the ship threads for three hours through an amazing wooded archipelago—some islands residences for daily commuters into the city, others summer and weekend camps, and many uninhabited. The outdoor experience is best enjoyed in the late spring and summer, when the lingering daylight stretches almost to midnight. The approach to **Helsinki**'s inner harbor the next morning is among rocky islands.

If making the return sailing, you keep your cabin and spend the day ashore sightseeing the Finnish capital, its waterfront markets, neighborhoods, and individual styles of architecture. If staying longer, consider the daylight, all-island route from **Turku,** Finland's second port, 125 miles and two hours by train from Helsinki. The sophistication and size of these cruise ferries exist almost nowhere else in the world.

Address/Phone: SeaEurope Holidays, Inc., 6801 Lake Worth Road, Suite 107, Lake Worth, FL 33467; (800) 533–3755, ext. 114; fax: (561) 432–2550; www.seaeurope.com; www.silja.com

The Ships: Sisters *Silja Serenade* and *Silja Symphony,* built in 1990 and 1991, have a gross tonnage of 58,400, a length of 656 feet, and a draft of 23 feet.

Passengers: 2,852 maximum capacity; all ages, mostly Swedes and Finns but also Germans, other Europeans, and some Americans (language not a problem)

Dress: Casual

Officers/Crew: Finnish officers; Scandinavian crew

Cabins: 985; modern and simply furnished, outsides and insides

Fare: $ to $$

What's included: Cruise fare only

What's not included: Everything is extra unless part of a package.

Highlights: A floating restaurant, cafe, and nightlife center; island scenery in summer

Other itineraries: Besides the above overnight cruise, SeaEurope, Inc. represents DFDS Seaways and several other northern European ferry operators with Scandinavian and North Sea routes.

SWAN HELLENIC'S

Minerva II

Iberian-Mediterranean Cultural Cruise: British Style

Swan Hellenic, a long-established British firm based in London, has traditionally drawn its clientele from the upper end of the British market, plus a modest percentage of North Americans to its cultural-enrichment cruises in Europe, the Americas, and the Nile Valley.

The 30,277-ton *Minerva II* was built as the *R8* for Renaissance Cruises and is now chartered by P&O Princess Cruises for its subsidiary Swan Hellenic. The newly acquired ship, replacing the much smaller 12,500-ton *Minerva,* made its debut in April 2003. The *Minerva II*'s more elaborate surroundings are meant to woo a slightly younger clientele (age forty and up) and more Americans. Cruising with Swan Hellenic does not come cheaply, but the advertised rates are virtually all-inclusive.

The ship's hotel decor is traditional Britain afloat from stem to stern, and original paintings, prints, antique maps, and passenger-donated photographs line the public room and corridor walls.

In a high-up location on its own, the large library, stocked with about 4,000 volumes, offers travel guides, references, and novels for all destinations, tables for opening an atlas, and lots of comfy chairs. Guest speakers, integral to any Swan Hellenic voyage, include noted historians, archaeologists, diplomats, writers, broadcasters, clergy, and chefs who give forty-five-minute talks in the main lounge. In the evening, the lounge hosts concerts, drama or comedy performances, and local artists.

The Orpheus Room, recalling the name of a long-serving Swan Hellenic ship, serves as a forward observation lounge, while the pre- and post-dinner cocktail set gravitate to the traditional Wheeler Bar, with a nightly pianist in attendance, and the Gallery Bar adjacent to the main restaurant.

Four open-sitting dining venues help break down the barriers between the reserved British and more open American passengers. Besides the large main restaurant, the Swan Restaurant features Mediterranean fare, while next door the Grill is the place for steaks and chops. For informality, the Bridge Cafe offers buffet meals indoors and out on deck.

A sheltered lido deck pool, flanked by a pair of Jacuzzis, jogging track, a couple of shops, beauty salon, fitness center, card room, and Internet room round out the comprehensive facilities.

Cabins are roomy and well equipped, most are outside, and many have private balconies. TVs bring in the lecture program, but attending the talks in person is highly recommended.

The Itinerary

Swan Hellenic cruises offer onboard seminars. Names and short biographies of the historians, archaeologists, anthropologists, geologists, and clergy appear in the brochure. Most hail from British universities. For this Iberian cruise, topics range from historic connections between Britain and Iberia to the wine trade. The program forms an integral part of the cruise experience, and lecturers join passengers at meals and accompany them ashore. The ports of call vary every year but usually include calls at Iberian ports on the Atlantic and Mediterranean coasts. All cruises start or end in England and Italy, paired with a one-way charter flight between the ship and London.

Sailing southward through the Bay of Biscay to **Vigo** or **La Coruna,** northwest Spain, you make the historic pilgrimage to **Santiago de Compostela,** where, at the magnificent Roman Catholic cathedral, Swan arranges for the giant incense burner, requiring eight men on the ropes, to perform its dramatic swings overhead, soaring to the rafters.

The Douro River city of **Oporto** is famous for its port-wine production; narrow, cobbled streets; and outstanding Baroque architecture. The old-fashioned capital city of **Lisbon** spreads over hills above the **Tagus River.** The residential neighborhoods are best enjoyed with a bus-and-tram day pass. Great museums and waterfront monuments demonstrate Portugal's pioneering maritime feats of exploration.

The attractive port of **Cadiz** leads inland to **Seville** for its great Gothic cathedral, Moorish Alcazar Palace, and quiet residential squares. From coastal **Malaga** the excursion visits **Granada**'s Alhambra Palace and magnificent Arab-style formal gardens. At **Barcelona,** you'll have time to enjoy cafes and restaurants lining the medieval streets, a Gothic district, Gaudi's architecture, and the Picasso Museum. Then sail eastward to Italian ports with trips inland to Pisa, Florence, Tuscany, and Rome.

Address/Phone: Swan Hellenic Cruises, 631 Commack Road, Suite 1A, Commack, NY 11725; (877) 219–4239; fax: (631) 858–1279; www.swanhellenic.com

The Ship: *Minerva II* was built in 2001 as the *R8* and has a gross tonnage of 30,277, a length of 594 feet, and a draft of 20 feet.

Passengers: 684; mostly British, fifty and up

Dress: Jacket and tie is expected on evenings at sea in the three main restaurants. Two formal nights

Officers/Crew: British and European officers; Filipino and Ukrainian crew

Cabins: 342, with 317 outside and 242 with balconies

Fare: $$$$

What's included: Cruise and port charges, program of shore excursions for every port, all tips aboard and for guides ashore, flights between London and the ship

What's not included: Airfare between the United States and London, optional shore excursions, drinks

Highlights: Excellent enrichment program, terrific organization aboard and ashore

Other itineraries: In addition to the above cruise between England, the Iberian Peninsula, and Italy, which is offered in the spring and summer, the *Minerva II* makes year-round, nonrepeating four-to-fifteen-day cruises in the Mediterranean, the Black Sea, around Britain, to Scandinavia, and across the Atlantic to South and North America.

SILVERSEA CRUISES'

Silver Whisper

Passage from Northern Europe to the Western Mediterranean

In an era of stressful travel, it is a sheer delight to find a cruise that allows one to enjoy a relaxing life aboard and the sights ashore. Silversea Cruises fills the bill, offering an uncrowded, sophisticated, and culturally rich experience.

The *Silver Whisper*, a 28,282-ton ship, carries up to 388 passengers in all-suite accommodations, the smallest measuring 287 square feet and the largest 1,435 square feet. Fares, while pegged at the upper end of the cruise market, include all gratuities and drinks in the bars and selected wines in the restaurants.

Silversea draws an international passenger list to its four ships, and while on most voyages Americans are in the majority, Europeans, British, and Australians are also present. The officers are Italian, and the crew is European and Filipino.

The ship's layout has the cabin accommodation placed forward and most of the public rooms aft, with the exception of the forward observation lounge and the adjoining spa and fitness center. The larger *Silver Whisper* and *Silver Shadow* have much in common with the smaller *Silver Cloud* and *Silver Wind* in design and amenities, and the company hopes that its high percentage of repeat passengers will move freely among them to choose the itineraries they would most enjoy. Some do prefer the more intimate pair and others like a larger ship, but the fleet shares far more similarities than differences.

Dining is open seating in the main restaurant, and the Terrace Café offers a smaller setting for all meals, plus alternating French, Italian, and Asian specialty menus by reservation but with no extra charge. A newish thirty-seat restaurant called Le Champagne provides an exquisite dining experience in a wine tasting room atmosphere. On the evening we ate there, the menu featured foie gras raviolis in a truffle sauce, tempura fried lobster tail in a Belgian endive salad, spiced beef filet with candied leeks and roasted shallots, and a strange-sounding but eminently tasty dessert of glazed stuffed cherry tomatoes and vanilla ice cream. Adjoining Le Champagne, the Humidor is a clubby roost for after-dinner cigars, vintage ports, and cognacs.

On another evening, we asked a guest to join us for dinner in the suite, and we ordered by phone from the restaurant menu. The meal arrived in separate courses and included complimentary bottles of chardonnay and merlot. The sliding door to the veranda brought in fresh breezes, and as the sky darkened, we were soon looking at a very orange Mars in the southeast sky.

For avid readers, there are lots of cozy places to enjoy a good book, in a wooden deck chair with steamer rug on the covered promenade, sheltered teak decks aft facing over the wake, in the library, or one of several lounges with sweeping sea views.

At night, the Jean Ann Ryan troupe performed creative dance routines, and the ship's band played jazz one evening in the Panorama Lounge. As on many smaller ships, socializing and enrichment lectures rather than big-time productions provide the principal diversions. We had a colorful, well-versed history professor on our cruise, and we attended all his lectures.

We thoroughly enjoyed the cruise's leisurely pace, the lack of hassle going ashore, the varied and unusual set of ports, and the luxurious living that included such a great range of fine dining experiences.

The Itinerary

The *Silver Whisper* often divides summertime between North Europe and the Mediterranean, and two north–south cruises link the regions. This fourteen-day, end-of-summer itinerary begins in the north at Amsterdam and ends in the Mediterranean at Barcelona, with a varied selection of French, Portuguese, and Spanish ports en route.

Arrive **Amsterdam** a day or two before the cruise and walk its concentric streets where gabled houses line the intricate canal system. Buy a day transit pass and ride the trams along the city streets to the Rijks and Van Gogh Museums, the indoor/outdoor maritime museum and its ship collection, flower market, and Anne Frank's house.

Embarking in the *Silver Whisper* you sail past the city center into the North Sea Canal that cuts through the Dutch countryside. Enjoy a sea day en route to **Rouen,** an inland city 50 miles up the Seine or nearly halfway to Paris. Known as "The City of a Hundred Spires," the largest is the French Gothic Notre-Dame Cathedral facing the central square in the heart of the historic quarter. The ship remains docked for two days, so one day could be devoted to **Paris,** an hour-plus train ride to Gare St. Lazare located within walking distance of the Galeries Lafayette and Opera.

Sailing west through the English Channel, the ship next calls at **St. Malo,** where its medieval center, largely rebuilt after World War II, is within the original and walkable city walls. Not far away **Mont St. Michel** seemingly rises out of the sea, especially at high tide, and to the south, walk through the medieval walled city of **Dinan** with its fifteenth-century towers and timbered row houses.

Sailing out into the Atlantic and around the western tip of Brittany, the ship turns south into the sometimes rough, but most often not, Bay of Biscay. Calling in at **La Coruna,** in the Galicia region of northwest Spain, the principal destination is **Santiago de Compostela** and its cathedral. Since the Middle Ages, pilgrims from all parts of Europe have flocked to what is considered Christendom's third most important site after Rome and Jerusalem.

Then south along the Iberian Peninsula, the ship docks at Leixoes, a port at the mouth of the Douro River and 9 miles from **Oporto,** the city that brought the world the sweet fortified port wine. The grapes are grown inland then come down the Douro for processing. Oporto, a UNESCO World Heritage Site, achieved its now somewhat faded grandeur during the Crusades, the era of Portuguese maritime exploration, the gem and gold trade with Brazil, and the port wine links with Britain.

On down the coast, the *Silver Whisper* sails into Tagus River under one of Europe's longest suspension bridges to dock at one of several locations adjacent to **Lisbon.** An earthquake in the mid-eighteenth century and a large fire in 1988 have both destroyed and created a city that features Moorish architecture in the Alfama district below the Castle of St. George, neo-classical in the center, and examples of baroque, art nouveau, and modern architecture. Tram Line #28 provides one of the finest neighborhood rides in all of Europe, winding up and down impossibly narrow streets that a bus could never negotiate. Ride Gustave Eiffel's public elevator between the Baixa (lower town) and Bairro Alto (the upper city).

From Lisbon, sail southeast to **Cadiz,** a city reputed to be Europe's oldest and almost entirely surrounded by water. The overnight call allows for multiple excursions. The city center, with Moorish, baroque, and neo-classical architecture, is a delight. **Seville,** a 90-mile scenic drive inland, was the Moorish Empire capital. One relic of that era is the 270-foot Giralda or Weather Vane Tower, the remaining section of a huge mosque. Next door is the fifteenth- and sixteenth-century cathedral that contains the tombs of Columbus and Spanish monarchs. Thirdly, the fourteenth-century royal palace, modeled after the Alhambra in Granada, has interior courts, apartments, and gardens to visit.

Passing through the Strait of Gibraltar into the Mediterranean, **Malaga,** an attractive Gothic and modern city in its own right, is also the gateway to the resorts of the Costa del Sol, such as Torremolinos and Marbella and to Granada, where the **Alhambra** represents the height of Moorish magnificence, and the great Christian churches, the re-conquest by Spanish rulers.

Following five port days in a row, the two nights and a day at sea provide a relaxing intermission before calling in at **Palma de Mallorca,** the most important of the Balearic Islands. Palma, the city, is some distance around the large bay, and its historic center, with Moorish and Gothic influences and dominated by the great cathedral, is easily walkable. One delightful day excursion by train passes through groves of olive, fig, and almond trees then climbs into the mountains and winds down to the pretty town of Soller. Continue to the port by tram and have lunch.

Finally, an overnight sails brings the ship into **Barcelona,** one of Europe's great cities with its medieval Gothic Quarter, tree-lined boulevards, museums to Picasso and Miró, and Gaudi's unusual architecture, seen in apartment buildings but especially with his unfinished but still progressing Church of the Holy Family. Consider staying on for a few days following the cruise.

Address/Phone: Silversea Cruises, 110 East Broward Boulevard, Fort Lauderdale, FL 33301; (954) 522–4477 or (800) 722–9955; fax: (954) 522–4499; www.silverseacruises.com

The Ship: The *Silver Whisper* was completed in 2001, has a gross tonnage of 28,258, a length of 610 feet, and a draft of 19.6 feet.

Passengers: 388; many Americans, some Europeans, forty-five and up

Dress: Formal, informal, and casual nights

Officers/Crew: Italian officers, and a European and Filipino crew

Cabins: 194 spacious one-room suites, all outside, and 157 with balconies

Fare: $$$$$

What's included: Cruise fare, drinks and wines at lunch and dinner, gratuities, and usually a special shoreside event

What's not included: Airfare, port charges, shore excursions

Highlights: Stylish atmosphere, unusual itineraries

Other itineraries: Besides this *Silver Whisper* warm-weather cruise in Europe, plus many more in the region, Silversea's four-ship fleet, including the *Silver Cloud, Silver Shadow,* and *Silver Wind,* covers virtually the entire world.

VIKING RIVER CRUISES'
Viking Europe and *Viking Spirit*
Cruising the Danube from Budapest to Nuremberg

Viking River Cruises got its start in 1997, and when the company bought KD River Cruises, a venerable German company dating back to 1827, it instantly counted up the largest riverboat fleet in Europe. Ten of Viking's two dozen ships cater exclusively to English-speaking passengers, which sets them apart from Peter Deilmann's vessels, which draw an international clientele. The seven-day cruise described here, operating between Budapest and Nuremberg, is just one of more than a dozen European river itineraries.

The 150-passenger *Viking Europe* and *Viking Spirit* are sleek three-deckers built in 2001 and designed to slip under low bridges, including a hydraulically lowered wheelhouse. On the Upper Deck boarding level, the forward observation lounge affords terrific views of the river and has a bar, music for dancing, and coffee, tea, and snacks in the morning and afternoon. A small library is adjacent and the bi-level lobby serves as a second lounge. The ships are completely nonsmoking within.

The restaurant, located aft, offers open seating and good views to port and starboard. Breakfast and lunch are either buffet or from a menu, while the five-course dinner is served. European regional entrees include braised venison, Viennese schnitzel, and Hungarian goulash while North American–style favorites include roast beef and poached salmon. All soups are made on board.

Seventy-five cabins are arranged on three decks, and the sixty-three deluxe rooms on the two highest decks have large windows that slide open, showers, telephones, TVs, safes, and hair dryers.

Most of the top deck is available for passenger viewing, and portions are sheltered from the sun and rain. A viewing promenade envelops the observation lounge.

The Itinerary

For this seven-day itinerary embarking from **Budapest,** the cruise manager will advise passengers, when it's recommended, to take an organized tour and, when it's convenient, to take independent walks. While cruising in daylight, English commentary picks out the castles, bridges, monuments, and natural sights; most nights are spent tied up. The riverboat stays overnight in Budapest to visit Hungary's capital, its hilltop castle and church complex in Buda, and the busy streets of Pest adjacent to the landing.

The call at **Vienna** allows an afternoon, overnight, and morning to visit the tree-lined Ringstrasse, St. Stephen's Cathedral, and eighteenth-century French-style Schön-brunn Palace, at one time the summer home of the Austrian monarchs, set in a large park with shaped trees and flower beds. From Krems to Melk the boat passes through the narrow and steep **Wachau Valley,** with woods clinging to the slopes on the left and vineyards on the sunny right side. Picturesque villages are **Durnstein** and **Melk,** the latter marked by a yellow baroque abbey sitting high on a rock.

Crossing into **Bavaria, Passau** is located at the junction of three rivers. Here you can take a walking tour and visit Feste Ober-haus, a castle atop a steep hill. **Regensburg**'s city center contains thirteenth- and fourteenth-century houses, a fourteenth-century city hall, and baroque and Gothic churches; Walhalla, the German Hall of Fame built in the nineteenth century, honors German heroes. Visit Weltenburg Abbey and the Danube Gorge's 400-foot cliffs by ferryboat. Near the end of the upstream cruise, the *Viking Europe* or *Viking Spirit* enter the 106-mile **Main-Danube Canal** and the first few of sixteen locks, which raise the riverboat 30 to 50 feet each time. Completed in 1992, the canal connects the Danube's 1,498 navigable miles to the Main River and the Rhine. The cruise ends with a bus transfer to **Nuremberg.**

Address/Phone: Viking River Cruises, 21810 Burbank Boulevard, Woodland Hills, CA 91367; (818) 227–1227 or (877) 668–4546; fax: (818) 227–1237; www.vikingrivercruises.com

The Ships: *Viking Europe* and *Viking Spirit,* built in 2001, have a length of 375 feet and a shallow draft.

Passengers: 150; mostly Americans and British fifty and up

Dress: Two optional dress-up evenings; otherwise casual

Officers/Crew: European

Cabins: 75; all outside, and 63 have windows that slide open

Fare: $$$

What's included: Cruise fare, port charges, local transfers, and shore excursions. Airfares are included in some cruise tours.

What's not included: Airfare, drinks, tips

Highlights: Scenic Danube River cruising and lots to see ashore in towns and cities

Other itineraries: In addition to this seven-day Danube cruise, which operates between April and November, there are five- to seventeen-day cruises along the Rhine, Main, Moselle, the full length of the Danube, Elbe, Seine, Rhone, Soane, and Russian Rivers. Extend your stay with cruise tour packages.

PETER DEILMANN'S
Mozart
Cruising the Danube in Style

This Danube River cruise, like the middle Rhine, is a traditional favorite for first-time river cruisers as the itinerary includes well-known cities such as Vienna and Budapest, romantic small towns, and some delightful rural river scenery. Unlike stretches of the Rhine, the Danube is not paralleled by major highways, and often there is not a road nor railway in sight. The peaceful, strong-flowing river is punctuated by numerous locks and low bridges requiring the pilothouse and wind screens to be lowered.

Boarding the *Mozart* at the Danube River port of Passau, one senses spaciousness throughout the vessel, in the rosewood paneled foyers, public rooms, main restaurant, and in the cabins. In fact, the ninety-six outside cabins (three are inside) are the largest of any European riverboat and measure a uniform and roomy 203 square feet. Upper deck cabins have a large picture window, while one deck below it's two smaller divided panes. The water laps at the side of the boat about a foot below the glass, and from time to time the window gets a wash from the passing river traffic. Two beds can be pushed together to form a generous queen.

The lounge area is furnished with a two-seat couch, coffee table, and desk-cum-vanity. Triple-slatted wood doors open to hanging closets and generous shelf space. The TV broadcasts both CNN and CNBC, and the radio airs music channels. A stocked minibar's contents are available for a moderate charge. The adjoining bath has a circular shower stall, sink surrounded by generous counter surface, a hair dryer, and terry cloth robes. The light, airy room is attractive for enjoying a few hours' read after the sun goes down and it gets too chilly topside for outdoor sightseeing.

The observation lounge provides seating for all passengers and sees use mostly for after-dinner entertainment, which runs from classical concerts and operetta to a pianist and a joyful crew show, put on by a mostly Hungarian staff. Most live in or near Budapest, so they get to see their families once a week, a regular rhythm that results in a very happy atmosphere.

A small lounge cafe hosts afternoon tea with pastries and evening dessert treats. A bar with sit-up stools and window tables runs fore and aft between the main lounge and the central foyer. A paneled library offers deep leather chairs, glass-fronted bookshelves with a small English-language collection, and a large-screen TV.

As one of the most elaborate European river vessels, the *Mozart* boasts a fitness center facing forward though big glass windows and is equipped with an indoor swimming pool, whirlpool, massage and sauna, plus a gift shop and beauty salon.

Less formal and lighter in decor is the main restaurant, where tables seat from two to eight people, many located by the large-view windows. Meals are a sheer delight and feature both a menu and an elaborate buffet for breakfast and lunch. The midday meal is my favorite, and while I may order hot carrot cream soup with oranges or the cold tipsy peach soup, I invariably find the buffet so appetizing that I save menu ordering for dinner. Choices include avocado and shrimp with choice of dressings, roll mops, smoked salmon, several types of salad beans and cole slaw, cabbage, cold lobster tails, artichoke hearts, a pasta station, leg of duck in orange sauce, and roasted fillet of plaice.

Dinner on three occasions offers a sampler menu of eight to nine delicious courses that lists several appetizers, two soups, two salads, two hot entrees, sherbet, two main courses, several desserts, and a selection of cheeses and biscuits. My favorite entrees were roasted piglet with braised cabbage and dumplings and roasted knuckle of veal with jus and sour cream and wine sauerkraut.

Service by two Hungarian waiters and a wine steward is most attentive, friendly, and knowledgeable, especially important when larking off into unfamiliar Middle European cuisine. We dined in true European style, enhancing the travel experience, rather than being offered menus that pander to American tastes. Apart from Americans and British who dine together, fellow passengers are largely German. Going beyond a nodding relationship with table neighbors requires some effort, and initial conversations usually occur more successfully on deck.

The Itinerary

Before setting off, there is time to explore **Passau**, a German town wedged on a narrow peninsula between two rivers with a third emptying into the Danube at the town's pointy end. Happily, few cars roam the angled stone-paved streets, so one can enjoy the pastel-colored architecture and pretty plantings without keeping a constant eye out for traffic.

As you cruise down the **Danube** on a Monday afternoon, Austria's **Wachau Valley** is bathed in a patchwork of sunlight and shadow. To the left, sloping vineyards produce some excellent dry white wines that are sampled aboard, while to the right the land is forested and stands of bushy trees rise from the river during the high-water period. Small towns appear around nearly every bend, tightly clustered around a church or situated beneath a castle poised on a rocky promontory. Standing next to me were a couple of passengers who live near the Danube in Germany, on board to see what their river looks like in Austria and Hungary.

After an overnight sail, the first landing at **Durnstein** in the Wachau Valley provides a forty-five-minute climb to a ruined twelfth-century castle for a rewarding view of the bucolic river valley below. A bus tour is also available here and in most ports, but independent exploring is both easy and rewarding.

Vienna's docking location is some distance from the city center, so many passengers take a coach tour, but for those familiar with urban living, it's a ten-minute walk to the Metro, then a fifteen-minute ride into Stefanplatz to tour the area of the Sacher Hotel and opera house, Gothic city hall, some handsome residential neighborhoods, and very pretty parks.

Sailing on downriver, I found the contrast between orderly and picture-perfect Austria and notably less prosperous Hungary to be most revealing.

Esztergom, once the capital of Hungary and still titular capital of Catholic Church, now exudes a small-town atmosphere with leafy residential squares and a lively street market, overlooked by a huge Renaissance basilica fortress. The riverine scenery then turns rural and wooded, and we pass a medieval wall that connects the river to a fortress high on the hill.

Approaching **Budapest,** the outlying districts are pretty bland, but soon the *Mozart* is sailing right through the heart of the city

past the English-derivative Gothic Parliament Buildings and under a half dozen bridges between **Buda** rising to the right and **Pest** laid out on the left. The overnight landing is located just above the bridge leading over to the Gellert Hotel and Spa.

On the first afternoon, walk the streets that parallel the river and enjoy looking into the stylish stores and up at the handsome art nouveau and art deco architecture. Apart from some shabby facades near the *Mozart*'s landing, the city sparkles and offers a livelier atmosphere than Vienna.

The next morning, a ship's tour visits both the Pest and Buda sides with the latter providing a visit to the thirteenth- to fifteenth-century Gothic-style Matthias or Coronation Church and the adjoining conical bastion towers of the fishermen's market. If there is time, spend an hour at the grand tiled market hall (1897) inspecting the fresh produce on the ground floor and souvenirs, handicrafts, embroidery, and food stalls on the upper level.

At departure, afternoon tea is served up on deck, and the *Mozart* sails upstream through the city center for an overnight cruise to **Bratislava,** the capital of **Slovak Republic.** The heart of the city is a lovely, tranquil pedestrian precinct with squares, churches, theater, opera, cafes, stores, and a large castle looming over all. From the ramparts, look across the Danube to the largest Soviet-inspired housing complex in the world, row after row of monotonously identical white concrete and brick apartment blocks.

Melk, a smallish city, offers a tour to an outstanding eleventh-century mustard-colored Benedictine monastery located high above town, later rebuilt in a high baroque style and now part monastic, part grammar school, part museum. Down in the town center, it is a Saturday morning and several wedding parties are gathered outside the town hall.

The small river town of **Grein,** the last stop, is essentially closed on Saturday afternoon, but one can climb to a castle overlooking the small town square and the river highway leading back to Passau and disembarkation. The *Mozart*'s seven-day cruise through Austria to the Slovak Republic and Hungary has a distinctly international flavor shared with German-speaking passengers cruising not far from home.

Address/Phone: Peter Deilmann Cruises, 1800 Diagonal Road, Suit 170, Alexandria, VA 22314; (703) 549–1741 or (800) 348–8287; fax: (703) 549–7924; www.deilmann-cruises.com

The Ship: *Mozart,* built in 1987, has a length of 396 feet and a draft of 5 feet.

Passengers: 200; age fifty-five and up, mostly Germans and Americans

Dress: Informal is the norm, with jacket and tie the standard dress

Officers/Crew: Hungarian and a few Germans

Cabins: 100, roomy, and 97 are outside with windows; some are sold as singles for a moderate premium

Fare: $$$

What's included: Cruise only

What's not included: Airfare, port charges, excursions, tips, and drinks

Highlights: Views while sailing of beautiful scenery, castles, and villages; easy access for independent touring at most landings; wonderful onboard restaurant

Other itineraries: In addition to the above seven-day Danube, which operates from Passau between late March and early October, the *Mozart* occasionally extends the Danube cruise all the way to the Black Sea. Deilmann's riverboat fleet cruises the Rhine, Moselle, Main, Elbe, Oder, Danube, Rhone, Soane, and the Belgian and Dutch waterways.

VIKING RIVER CRUISES'
Viking Neptune
Lower Danube to the Black Sea

Viking operates two fleets, one solely for English-speaking passengers and the other for mostly Europeans. On the former, passengers hail from the United States and Britain with a scattering from Australia, and such was the breakdown on our cruise. All announcements, menus, programs, and shore excursions are in English only.

We arrived at the Danube landing on the Pest side of Budapest to find the long, white *Viking Neptune* securely tied to a floating pontoon and buffeted by a springtime 8-mile-an-hour current that carried rafts of tree trunks and floating debris thumping along the hull.

Built in Holland in 2001, the *Viking Neptune* has huge windows through which to view the passing scene whether in the restaurant, one of the two lounges, or in the cabins. Two of three cabin decks have windows that slide open. The decor is Scandinavian modern with light and medium wood tones and complementing medium blue and rust fabrics.

The main lounge provides a social setting throughout the day, with a sit-up bar, multi-instrumentalist, and twenty-four-hour coffee and tea. Passengers read here without missing anything passing by outside, enjoy afternoon tea and fresh pastries or a drink before lunch and dinner, gather after dinner for folkloric entertainment or a quiz game, or indulge in a late evening snack. A small library with reference books, hardbacks, and paperbacks forms part of the starboard passage between the reception lobby and the lounge. Two mezzanine wings in the reception lobby provide snug secondary lounge areas, and the cabinets hold the board games and Viking logo clothing for sale.

Aft the big-window restaurant offers open seating for all meals at tables of four, six, and a few with eight. A small semicircular buffet provides a moderate selection of hot and cold breakfast items and lunchtime salads and the featured always tasty cream soup. Menu selections are also available, and dinner is strictly from the menu. The food is a good standard of European preparation but without risky flavors or heavy sauces that might intimidate some palates. Normally, there are two featured entrees and daily staples such as Caesar salad, grilled chicken breast, and grilled steak. On the Danube, specialty items will be Viennese schnitzel, Hungarian goulash, and duck breast with Cassis sauce. The hotel crew hails mostly from countries fringing the Danube, so many visit their families on a regular basis, making for a happy lot.

Cabins are of moderate size (most 154 square feet and some few 120 square feet) and arranged on three levels. Two cabin decks have large windows where one half slides open, while others have fixed glass, and the lowest cabin deck is fitted with much smaller windows. Amenities include showers in the baths, hair dryers, safes, TV with CNN and published program of films, and decent counter, drawer, and closet space. Passengers may wear what they want throughout the cruise with perhaps a slight dressing up at the captain's reception.

Deck space runs nearly the full length of the sun deck with a small canopied section aft of the pilothouse furnished with chairs and tables. When approaching extremely low bridges, the pilothouse can drop into a cavity and the signal masts fold down to the deck. A narrow promenade deck wraps around the forward lounge, and passengers are encouraged to use it for early morning power walks rather than thumping on the sun deck above the cabins.

This Viking riverboat, one of a series of four sisters, offers a most cheerful environment and a comfortable conveyance for spending two weeks aboard.

The Itinerary

The Danube has provided a river route for human migration, invasions, and trade since Celtic, Greek, Roman, Mongol, and Turkish times, in effect serving as a link between the Occident and Orient, Christianity and Islam. The layers of civilization and strife that have occurred along its banks make for an incredibly complex history as we would discover on our two-week cruise. It is highly recommended to read up before you arrive, and at least buy a good tourist guidebook to Eastern Europe and the Balkans.

We enjoyed the better part of two days tied up in **Budapest,** taking the ship's excursion and walking the streets on our own. Once a rich country, Hungary's architecturally diverse capital is a pleasure to explore from Pest's English Gothic–style Parliament Building, the Victorian central market, to the homegrown art nouveau commercial structures. On the Buda side, spiky church steeples and bastions and crenellated battlements punctuate the medieval heights. At night the city is beautifully illuminated from the citadel on high, along the Danube and across the Chain and Elizabeth Bridges.

Casting off, the boat sailed swiftly with the downriver current to unfamiliar places that proved to be intriguing surprises. We stopped at the Hungarian market town of Mohacs for an hour's drive inland past cattle farms and vineyards to **Pecs** (pronounced *Paich*), a UNESCO World Heritage Site surrounded by the longest reconstructed wall in Europe. In the town center, a church cross rose out of a crescent moon recalling that St. Peter's Basilica had been converted to a mosque during the years of Ottoman Empire rule. While again functioning as a church, the interior decoration is unmistakably Islamic.

On a nearby rise, Pecs's 200-year-old cathedral includes eleventh-century sections and sits atop a fifth-century crypt. During our visit, the transept was filled with high school students who since the fall of the Communism may again attend Roman Catholic schools.

To reach **Novi Sad** in Serbia, the boat used to pass through a pontoon bridge that opened only three nights a week, then as of 2006 the new high clearance Liberty Bridge has been completed. From Europe's second largest fortress, we had a sweeping view of the river and farmlands that extended to the horizon. From the main square we followed a curving pedestrian street to the produce and clothing market and to a landscaped wooded park filled with school children at play.

The Danube forms the boundary between Bulgaria and Romania, and landing at Giurgiu, we drove inland to **Bucharest.** Since my last visit over a quarter century ago, Romanian dictator Nicolae Ceausescu had demolished a huge section of the old capital, destroying twenty-six churches and synagogues and housing for 70,000, to build his monstrous marble House of the People, exceeded in size by only the Pentagon. The looming white elephant fronts on a boulevard longer than the Champs Elysees. Our guide pointed out the office balcony where in December 1989 Ceausescu made his last desperate speech before fleeing by helicopter, only to be captured and executed, along with his wife, several days later.

On the way back to the ship, we encountered donkey and horse carts moving goods and villagers along the narrow highway, and in the fields a few farmers tilled the fields using horse-drawn plows. Migrant Roma or Gypsies gathered by the roadside, and the guide pointed out several turreted mansions built and owned by rich Gypsies who curiously choose to live in traditional tents in the back and out of sight.

Our window on the Black Sea arrived at **Constanta**, where besides a strip of tourist hotels primping for the upcoming season, the city exhibits layers of history dating from Greek colonization then Roman, Turkish, and Communist domination. During the interval between Muslim call to prayer, I climbed a minaret for a view down to an uncovered third-century Roman mosaic promenade and out over the sprawling container port to the Black Sea, sparkling blue on this sunny day.

Sailing upriver, we docked at the Bulgarian port of Russe for a ninety-minute drive through lovely rolling farmland devoid of residences, as landowners cluster in villages. The destination was **Veliko Tarnovo,** Bulgaria's twelfth- to fourteenth-century hillside capital approached through a deep gorge. The Ottoman Empire controlled the region until the last quarter of the nineteenth century, and a sizable minority remains Turk, mostly secular descendents of those who stayed on.

After a walk along cobbled streets, we had lunch at nearby **Arbanasi,** originally settled by Greeks and Macedonians and now a mountain retreat for better-off Bulgarians. The village featured an unassuming seventeenth-century Eastern Orthodox

Church, designed not to attract Ottoman wrath, but within richly painted frescos, illustrating more than 3,600 religious images, decorated separate-sex chambers.

Returning over rough country roads to a Danube River coal and lumber port, we cruised through the **Iron Gate,** a dramatic series of gorges where the Transylvanian Alps cross the river. Once-dangerous rapids, where steam locomotives hauled the upriver traffic, have now been tamed by a dam and locks providing safe navigation and hydro-electricity. We shared the deep lock chambers with Ukrainian and Romanian barges laden with iron ore and coal.

From the Bulgarian river city at Vidin, it's an attractively hilly drive inland to visit the Ottoman castle at **Belgradshick** with terrific views of the town and rock formations the several levels of terraces. Leave the boat at Orsova, and head to the Romanian resort spa at **Baile Herculane** where the present nineteenth-century medicinal baths are built next to the early Roman site. Then in **Dakovo** in Croatia, tour a horse farm established in 1506 that breeds those beautiful white horses known as Lipizzaners, and see them perform.

Belgrade, Serbia's capital, seemed uninviting from the river, but once ashore, the city exhibited majesty and importance. From the landing we walked up through the battlements, constructed from the fifteenth century onward and sitting atop a Roman well. Beyond, the city center is strung along by an attractive pedestrian street lined with stylish cafes and prosperous-looking stores. We learned that Belgrade had witnessed 115 major battles, and since Roman rule has been completely destroyed forty-four times, has had forty different names, and served as a capital of five different states. Ruined government buildings from the 1999 bombing raids from Kosovo had been left as a disturbing artifact.

Sailing past farms we had missed during the night on the downriver passage, we stopped twice for lengthy border crossing formalities where the captain and hotel director spent hours ashore and then back aboard entertaining officials before we could proceed.

Disembarking at Budapest we joined buses for a scenic drive, made a stop at the touristy town of **Szentendre,** known for its ceramic art and a museum dedicated to marzipan, and enjoyed a glorious view from on high down to the *Viking Neptune* heading to **Esztergom**. Hungary's former capital is marked by a huge Renaissance-style Roman Catholic Cathedral set high above the river.

Sailing on upriver, we tied up at **Bratislava** opposite a Victorian redbrick school building as the students filed in the door. The easy walk from the ship to the center revealed a complex layout of large and small squares, enclosed courtyards, narrow lanes and wide boulevards, quietly gliding trams, numerous finely sculpted fourteenth- and fifteenth-century churches, and a fortified citadel positioned high over the city.

On the final stretch to **Vienna,** river towns suddenly became tidier and more prosperous. Vienna, a sophisticated city with a glorious past under the Hapsburgs, had once ruled many of the places we visited. But this city had never suffered post–World War II Communist rule that had sent the lower river economies into a downward spiral that they are now attempting to reverse, including entrance into the European community.

The layers of Danube River history are incredibly complex, and it is well advised to study up in advance, otherwise much of what the guides relate will be brand-new and difficult to fathom with little enrichment provided aboard the boat.

Address/Phone: Viking River Cruises, 21810 Burbank Boulevard, Woodland Hills, CA 91367; (818) 227–1227 or (877) 668–4546; fax: (818) 227–1237; www.vikingrivercruises.com

The Ship: *Viking Neptune*, built in 2001, has a length of 375 feet and a shallow draft.

Passengers: 150; mostly Americans and British fifty and up

Dress: Casual, dressing up is optional

Officers/Crew: European

Cabins: 75; all outside, and 63 have windows that slide open

Fare: $$$

What's included: Cruise fare, port charges, local transfers, and shore excursions. Airfares included in some cruise tours.

What's not included: Airfare, drinks, tips

Highlights: Lower Danube River cruising to both popular and less-visited parts of the Balkans

Other itineraries: In addition to this fourteen-day Danube to the Black Sea cruise embarking in Budapest or Vienna, which operates from April and the middle of October, there are additional five- to seventeen-day cruises along other portions of the Danube, Rhine, Main, Moselle, Elbe, Seine, Rhone, Soane, and Russian rivers. Extend your stay with cruise tour packages.

PETER DEILMANN'S
Frederic Chopin and *Katharina von Bora*
The River Elbe from Berlin to Prague

Glancing at a map of Europe, the Continent is laced with canals and waterways, built for commerce and increasingly frequented by creative cruising itineraries that stretch from Amsterdam to the Black Sea and from the south of France deep into Poland. Riverboat vacations mean unpacking just once, then settling in for delightful doses of sightseeing from the top deck and daily excursions ashore to market towns and cathedral cities, riverfront palaces and hilltop castles. Many landings are within walking distance or a short drive to the sights, and separate guides are provided for each group.

Operated by German ship owner Peter Deilmann, the 2002-built, two-deck-high *Frederic Chopin* and 2000-built sistership *Katharina von Bora* were designed to slip under the very low bridges that span Central Europe's waterways. When clearances permit remaining on the Sun Deck, the ship's surgeon keeps a watchful eye, and if the gap narrows to mere inches, it's time to clear off. The railings and chairs collapse to deck level, and in turn, the captain lowers his pilothouse and pops up now and again to keep the boat on the straight and narrow.

The passenger capacity is seventy-nine, split between English-speaking and German-speaking passengers. Most of the latter and the German staff speak good English, and for the majority, it is often a first visit to eastern Germany since unification.

All cabins have the same dimensions (140 square feet), shower baths, and TVs with CNN broadcasts. The preferred upper deck units come with French doors that open inward, while lower deck rooms have large picture windows with the sill barely above river level. A forward observation lounge, decorated in art nouveau style, offers 180-degree viewing, conversational seating, bar, morning bouillon and afternoon coffee, tea, cakes and pastries, a pianist, and occasional evening cabaret.

In the similarly styled restaurant, tables are assigned and located next to large picture windows. Breakfast and lunch provide elaborate menu and buffet selections, and the very long dinner hours run to five courses and up to nine on special occasions. We enjoyed excellent evening meals such as sliced duck with kumquat sauce, sweetbreads on a bed of lentils, and fresh grilled salmon. Cheese selections vary daily, but there are no biscuits, only breads. Wines and beers are fairly priced.

The Itinerary

As this week's cruise on the **Elbe** begins either in Berlin (embarking in nearby Potsdam) or Prague, it would be wise to consider staying a couple of nights in one or both capital cities. All cruises include one night docked on the Vltava River near Prague's Charles Bridge, and some port calls vary depending on the direction of travel, though all include Magdeburg, Wittenburg, Meissen, and Dresden.

Berlin reveals a boomtown atmosphere and the most amazing transformation of neighborhoods from empty lots left over from World War II bombing to thriving office, hotel, residential, cultural, and entertainment complexes. For me, who knew Berlin before the wall and during its construction in August 1961, many sections have become unrecognizable, especially the new corporate and entertainment complex at Potsdamer Platz and the city's most famous avenue, Unter den Linden.

Before boarding at **Potsdam,** visit **Sanssouci,** one of the great palaces and tiered gardens of Europe, and the Tudor-style **Cecilienhof,** a manor house that served as the site for the last World War II conference, involving Truman, Stalin, Churchill, and Attlee, that partitioned Germany.

Joining the River Elbe, the *Frederic Chopin* sails along fast-flowing portions and slack water sections between locks. Some bridges are low enough to make us duck if standing up on the top deck and high enough, in most cases, to pass under while sitting down. The ship's doctor keeps an eye on everyone, happily allowing passengers to remain outside to enjoy the passing scene of tidy farms, small-town life, people fishing and swimming, and the busy river traffic. Barges laden with coal, stone, sand, grain, lumber, and fuels glide past, outfitted with all the comforts of home, including a patch back aft to park the family car.

Madgeburg, largely destroyed in 1945, has monumental Middle Age and baroque buildings set among monotonous rows of Communist-era apartment blocks, while **Wittenberg** most attractively trades on Martin Luther's life and activity during the start of the Protestant Reformation. According to the guide, the town facades, now sparkling with colorful restorations, were mostly gray and dilapidated during the German Democratic Republic days.

The stop at **Meissen** includes the china factory tour to see how the prized porcelain is sculpted and hand-painted, followed by a scenic drive along the Elbe to **Dresden,** perhaps the most amazing twentieth-century example of a city rebuilt after total destruction during one awful night in 1945. The Semper Opera House, **Zwinger Palace,** churches, royal residences, museums, offices, and many apartments have been reconstructed in the original styles, an ongoing fifty-year project that has brought back grandeur to one of Europe's most beautiful cities. Over time, the sandstone has weathered, and someone who knew nothing of the wartime bombing might not realize that the city center is now quite young. At night, from the deck of our ship, the floodlighting provides a wondrous spectacle and a draw to partake of the smart cafe life.

The countryside now becomes hilly in what is known as **Saxon Switzerland,** and a trip to **Pillnitz Palace** shows a delicate eighteenth-century royal retreat with Italian and Oriental influences and an English-style botanical garden. After a short drive along the Elbe, the bus climbs along a twisting drive to **Konigstein,** a castle fortress perched on a promontory overlooking a horseshoe bend in the Elbe, where one can watch the boats approach and tie up alongside the town far below.

On the final leg, the *Frederic Chopin* passes out of Germany and the Elbe into the **Czech Republic** and the **Vltava,** stopping at **Leitmeritz,** a riverside market town, followed by a scenic river transit into the heart of **Prague** to dock near the center and within the shadow of **Prague Castle.** Architecturally, the Czech capital is one of Europe's most spectacular, with displays of Romanesque, Gothic, Renaissance, baroque, rococo, art nouveau, and turn-of-the-twentieth-century Paris, contrasting yet neighborly styles often lined up side by side.

Walk the city's embankments; cross the tower-gated **Charles Bridge,** the city's gathering place all day and into the night; and climb up to the Prague Castle complex. Visit the Old Market Square and its 500-year-old astronomical clock and the Mucha Museum (Alphonse Mucha created the art

nouveau style in poster art and architectural design). At night the city is beautifully floodlit and the top deck of *Frederic Chopin* provides an orchestra seat, one very hard to vacate at the end of the cruise.

Address/Phone: Peter Deilmann Cruises, 1800 Diagonal Road, Suite 170, Alexandria, VA 22324; (703) 549–1741 or (800) 348–8287; fax: (703) 549–7924; www.deilmann-cruises.com

The Ship: *Frederic Chopin,* built in 2002, and *Katharina von Bora,* built in 2000, have a length of 272 feet and a very shallow draft of 3.5 feet.

Passengers: 79; fifty-five and up, mostly split between German and Americans

Dress: Informal is the norm, with jacket and tie the standard dress

Officers/Crew: Czechs and Germans

Cabins: 41 cabins; all outside, with the upper deck units having French doors

Fare: $$$

What's included: Cruise fare only

What's not included: Airfare, port charges, excursions, tips, and drinks

Highlights: Views while sailing of beautiful scenery, castles, and villages; easy access for independent touring at most landings

Other itineraries: In addition to the above seven-day Elbe itinerary, which operates between Berlin and Prague from April to October, the *Frederic Chopin* also operates along the Oder River from Germany into Poland. Deilmann's riverboat fleet cruises the Rhine, Moselle, Main, Elbe, Oder, Danube, Rhone, Soane, and the Belgian and Dutch waterways.

ABERCROMBIE & KENT'S
Litote
Barge Canal Cruising in Burgundy

The fleet that A&K charters was established by a Francophile Englishman in 1966 and now numbers twenty hotel and charter barges and riverboats. *Litote* takes up to twenty passengers and a young French and English crew of eight. The barge has two decks, one with a forward plant-filled sun deck, a salon with bar, and a dining room. There are four cabins aft, and the rest of the accommodations are on the deck below.

A dinner bell summons passengers at 8:00 P.M. from the foredeck and lounge bar to the adjoining oak-paneled dining room, where one chooses places at four candlelit tables. Both lunch and dinner begin with brief descriptions of the white and red wines and the cheese course. On the first evening on my cruise, the appetizer was whiting in a phyllo pastry with sorrel sauce, followed by grilled lamb with thyme, cheese, and a peach tart. On another occasion we started with a mild gazpacho and continued with tender pork cutlets, ending with a rich chocolate mousse. Lunch is a lighter meal that might include sausage in puff pastry, cold roast beef or pasta, and a variety of salads. Breakfast consists of fresh juices, cereals, bread, croissants, and pastries fetched by the deckhand, who, before you rise, peddles off to the nearest village bakery.

Air-conditioned accommodations are four twin and two double-bed cabins on the lower deck, with opening portholes, and two windowed twins and two doubles on the upper deck. There's adequate floor space for two to move about, reasonable drawer and closet stowage, and a tiny bathroom with shower. Insulation from outside noise is excellent.

The Itinerary
The Burgundy itinerary described here is just one example of this type of cruising, and under the A&K umbrella there are numerous variations within this region and elsewhere in France. A&K sells cabins on about two dozen additional hotel and charter barges.

Ten minutes out of **Paris,** the rakish high-speed TGV hits 168 miles an hour, streaking southeast to Dijon, and just over two hours later, the pace drops to the speed of a slow walk aboard the 128-foot hotel barge negotiating the **Burgundy Canal.** Boarding at **Vandenesse-en-Auxois,** the deep-blue hulled *Litote* travels the short distance to the village of **La Repe** to moor before dinner and for the night. In warm weather it's drinks out on the foredeck, while on a chilly night the cozy bar welcomes the newly embarked.

An A&K coach parallels the route and takes passengers on a half-day trip to the **Chateau at Commarin** and the medieval village of **Chateauneuf-en-Auxois.** Moving along the canal to **Pont d'Ouche,** there's time to borrow one of the bicycles for a ride along the smooth towpath or peddle off into the countryside. Noncyclists can walk the towpath and stroll into the village. The canals once handled commercial traffic in coal, locally manufactured tiles, and farm product, but the waterway now sees pleasure boats and barges. Cruising through the **Ouche Valley,** time seems to have stood still on the rolling farmlands and fields, either side populated by the attractive white Charolais cattle.

Visits to châteaux and wineries are planned at the medieval cellars in the village of **Meursault** in the **Cote de Beaune** and two days later at **Beaune** itself. Beaune is Burgundy's wine capital and the site of one of the finest examples of medieval architecture, the Hotel Dieu, built in the fifteenth century as a charity hospital. Here at Beaune, or at one of the other wineries, the crew may take back a case of wine for dinner on board that night.

Dijon is Burgundy's regional capital and an important market town. The excursion takes in the Ducal Palace, the stronghold of the Dukes of Burgundy, and the historic city center with time at the end to wander the open market. On the last day, the visit is to **Clos de Vougeot,** a center for making wine since the twelfth century, where the process is described and antique presses are on display. The final afternoon is spent cruising onto Dijon, where the barge ties up for a farewell dinner and the night. After breakfast, passengers transfer back to Gare de Lyon Paris by TGV. Barging is a terrific way to sample the culinary, potable, historical, and scenic delights of La Belle France and rivers and canals throughout Europe.

Address/Phone: Abercrombie & Kent International, 1520 Kensington Road, Oak Brook, IL 60523; (630) 954–2944 or (800) 554–7016; fax: (630) 954–3324; www.abercrombiekent.com

The Ship: *Litote* was first built in 1982 as a commercial barge and has a gross tonnage of 250, a length of 128 feet, and a shallow draft.

Passengers: 20; all ages, mostly Americans; families welcome

Dress: Casual at all times

Officers/Crew: French and British

Cabins: 10; 4 doubles and 6 twins

Fare: $$$$

What's included: Cruise, port charges, excursions (except ballooning), drinks, and wines

What's not included: Airfare, train fare from Paris to embarkation and return, tips

Highlights: Food, wines, and the lovely Burgundy countryside at a relaxing pace

Other itineraries: Besides this six-night cruise through Burgundy aboard the *Litote,* which operates from April into November, there are many other itineraries along the French waterways, and in Holland, Belgium, Ireland, and England, some with themes such as walking, wine, antiques, châteaux, gardens, golf, and tulip time. ·

P&O CRUISES'
Oriana
England to the Black Sea

The Peninsula and Oriental Steam Navigation Company invented cruising in 1844, and although P&O cruises, separated from its parent in fall 2000, is now part of the mighty Carnival Corporation, it retains its very British style of ocean travel.

The *Canberra* of 1961 had been the last passenger ship built by the company for the British market, and the *Oriana,* delivered in 1995 from the Meyer shipyard in Germany, is easily identifiable as a modern development of that famous ship, with a wide wraparound promenade deck, a large and delightful selection of public rooms, and an elegant profile in an era when ship design is often less focused on the exterior appearance.

The *Oriana* was the first ship to be purpose built by any company for British cruising, and in the ten-plus years since she was introduced has developed a very loyal following. Be aware that this is a British ship, and on a typical cruise sailing from Southampton, England, at least 95 percent of the passengers will be from the United Kingdom. The ship has won awards as the most family-friendly ship cruising from Britain, and the children's staff, with the help of the extensive facilities, has a very good reputation for keeping the younger passengers entertained, leaving the adults to enjoy the ship in relative peace. On longer cruises, such as that described below, the passenger mix is slightly older than on a two-week cruise to the Western Mediterranean, and there will be far fewer families.

The *Oriana* offers some wonderful public spaces. The Crows Nest Bar, with its stunning 6-foot builders' model of the 1920s' P&O liner *Ranpura* and top-of-the-ship location, affords great views forward while enjoying a pre-dinner drink and listening to gentle music. Andersons, six decks lower on Promenade Deck and outfitted in the style of a country club, is the place for after-dinner coffee and a liqueur. Regular classical recitals normally take place in the elegant chandeliered Curzon Room. The main production shows are staged in the Theatre Royal, while the Pacific Lounge is the venue for less glitzy entertainment. Harlequins' hosts dance classes during the day and later becomes the nightclub. Other rooms include Lords Tavern, a bar with a cricket theme, and Crichton's, one of the largest card rooms afloat and the venue for the very well attended and highly competitive quizzes. For some peace and quiet, try the well-stocked Library and Thackeray's, both with furniture from the workshops of Lord Lindley. Numerous original artifacts and reproductions spread around the ship are reminders of the company's long maritime pedigree. P&O still welcomes passengers and does not use the term "guests."

The food is British, well presented, and good, with semi-silver service (plated entree and passed side dishes) in the two main restaurants for both lunch and dinner. The Conservatory on Deck 12 serves buffet breakfasts and lunches, and in the evening green linen tablecloths, special china and glassware, and soft lighting transform this room into Jardins Bistro, an alternative cover charge restaurant.

Al Fresco's, forward on the same deck, is open for light meals twenty-four hours a day. P&O curries are excellent, reflecting the company's links with the Indian subcontinent, and maintained to this day through the employment of superb Indian waiters and mainly Pakistani galley crew. Lunch always features a curry, and at least two Indian theme nights take place in the Conservatory on a long cruise.

On the spacious upper decks there are three pools, one of which is reserved for families. The wonderful tiered afterdecks give a grandstand view over the stern of the ship. Sports facilities include football and cricket nets, a golf range, quoits, deck tennis, and shuffleboard. For the more energetic, a fully equipped gym with its spa complex occupies a prime position above the bridge.

Standard cabins are of average size and tastefully decorated with pastel-colored fabrics and light-wood furniture. All feature convertible twin beds, refrigerator, small safe, TV, and ample storage, with tub baths in the higher grades. The relatively modest number of balcony cabins, twins and suites, are high up on Britannia Deck. Perhaps better value are the outside LA- to LD-grade cabins on the lower decks, but stay away from a four-berth sold as a double as the upper berths, when folded away, still protrude into the cabin space.

The Itinerary

The Black Sea cruise usually sails from **Southampton, England,** in late August or early September, returning eighteen days later after a voyage of 7,000 nautical miles with lots of sea time and visits to six very different ports in five countries.

After a day and a half at sea, take up position on the forward observation deck as the ship approaches **Lisbon,** the Portuguese capital. Soon visible port side are the sixteenth-century Belem Tower (now a UNESCO World Heritage Site) and the Monument to the Discoveries. The ship then passes under the Twenty-fifth April Bridge, modeled on the Golden Gate Bridge and named to commemorate the date of the bloodless overthrow of the dictatorship in

1974. To starboard rises the 359-feet-high statue of Christ the King, erected in 1959.

The *Oriana* may dock near the bridge with a free shuttle bus operating into the heart of the city or walk back along the river to visit the sixteenth-century St. Jeronimo's Monastery, also housing the maritime museum with its excellent collection of ship models. When the ship docks near Black Horse Square, the city center is only a few minutes' walk.

The *Oriana* sails in the early evening and the following morning transits the Strait of Gibraltar, with the mighty Rock visible to port. During three full sea days, it's time to find a favorite spot on deck and to attend a port lecture, cooking demonstration, or dancing or computer class.

Piraeus, the port for **Athens,** has intense ferry traffic and offers scant room for a big liner to maneuver to the dock. For first-timers, Athens and the Acropolis are a must either on the ship's tour or via a bit of a walk around the harbor to the Metro. Both Corinth and Cape Sounion are attractive bus tour alternatives.

In the early hours the ship passes through the **Dardanelles,** that 37-mile-long stretch of water known in ancient times as the Hellespont, and enters the Sea of Marmara. Soon after midday, the imposing skyline of **Istanbul** appears, and once in the Bosphorus, the Blue Mosque, Topkapi Palace, and St. Sophia can be seen to port. East meets West in Istanbul, and with an overnight stay, many interesting sites can be seen independently. Walk towards the Galata Bridge and board a tram to Sultanahmet for the Blue Mosque, St. Sophia, the Grand Bazaar, and the Underground Cistern. Take a ferry to Kadikoy or Uskadar on the Asian side and sit on deck watching the busy Bosphorus ferries going about their business.

Leaving Istanbul at 1:00 P.M., the ship passes Dolmabahce Palace to port and proceeds under two impressive suspension bridges, entering the Black Sea ninety minutes later.

In the Black Sea Ukrainian port of **Yalta,** the attractive town center is a few minutes' walk from the ship and set in the shadow of the Crimean Mountains. Nearby, Levadia Palace, built in 1911 as the summer residence of Czar Nicholas II, served as the site where in 1945 the future of Europe was decided by Churchill, Roosevelt, and Stalin.

Odessa, an overnight sail from Yalta, is the largest Black Sea port and boasts wide avenues and many large buildings. *Oriana* docks by the bottom of the Potemkin Steps, the formal entrance to the city from the sea. A short walk or shuttle bus ride leads to a compact area featuring the Opera House, several churches, and the maritime museum housed in a former gentlemen's club.

The *Oriana* again enters the Bosphorus, passing through the city of Istanbul into the Sea of Marmara. By evening in the Dardanelles, the Gallipoli Peninsula appears to starboard with Turkish, French, and British war memorials backlit by the setting sun. The *Oriana*'s ensign is dipped and her whistle sounded as she draws level with each monument, a very moving few minutes.

After three continuous sea days, the imposing sight of the Mediterranean's largest Gothic cathedral appears, and the ship slips into the harbor of **Palma de Mallorca.** The Bellver Castle, located on a hill overlooking the town, can be accessed by tour or taxi, and the ship's shuttle operates to the Cathedral at the edge of the old town. From Palma it's three final sea days to disembarkation at Southampton.

Address/Phone: P&O Cruises, Richmond House, Terminus Terrace, Southampton SO14 3PN England (011) 44–2380–523419; www.pocruises.com

The Ship: *Oriana* was built in 1995, has a gross tonnage of 69,153, a length of 853 feet, and a draft of 26 feet.

Passengers: 1,828; all ages, and older on longer cruises. At least 95 percent British, with a few Europeans, and others

Dress: A mix of formal, informal, and casual; generally five formal nights on this cruise

Officers/Crew: British officers, mainly Indian hotel staff with some Filipinos; Pakistani deck, galley, and engine crew

Cabins: 914, with a wide range of configurations from four-berth insides to veranda suites; no dedicated singles and supplements range from 20 to 70 percent; 118 cabins with verandas

Fare: $$$

What's included: Cruise fare, port charges, and shuttle buses in cruise ports

What's not included: Transportation to and from Southampton, drinks, shore excursions, and tips

Highlights: A thoroughly British atmosphere on a beautifully appointed, well-run ship, lots of activities on sea days; exceptional itinerary featuring many sea days and far-flung Black Sea ports

Other itineraries: P&O Cruises operates five ships from Southampton (the others are *Arcadia* built 2005 and 83,000 tons; *Artemis* built 1984 as *Royal Princess* and 44,588 tons; *Aurora* built 2000 and 76,152 tons; *Oceana* built 2000 as *Ocean Princess* and 77,499 tons) from April to November on itineraries of four to twenty-two days to the Baltic, Norway, Iceland, the Atlantic Isles and Iberian Peninsula, Eastern and Western Mediterranean, and the Caribbean. In winter three ships offer Grand Voyages of around one hundred days, including at least one World Cruise, while the others cater to British fly-cruisers in the Caribbean.

ROYAL CARIBBEAN'S
Brilliance of the Seas
The Mediterranean Eastward from Barcelona

The *Radiance of the Seas* class, numbering four ships, represents a new direction for Royal Caribbean with much more attention being paid to a shippy look and the sense of sailing on a ship, from the more maritime-oriented decor, dark-wood paneling and deep sea blues, to the walls of glass to let you see the sea while dining, imbibing, and conversing. The Centrum features a port-side glass wall soaring from Decks 5 through 10 and four sets of glass-enclosed elevators. Yes, there is still the Royal Caribbean trademark rock-climbing wall and miniature golf.

Most of the public rooms—Crown & Anchor Lounge, Champagne Bar, Singapore Sling's piano bar, Windjammer Café, Sky Bar, and the trademark Viking Crown Lounge—are sheathed in glass, great for viewing arrivals in the world's ports.

Public spaces are fun to inhabit. One, the Colony Club, an interconnecting suite of five spaces, has a rich look with Oriental-patterned carpets, inlaid wood flooring, inti-mate seating arrangements, and subdued lighting. One room is Singapore Sling's piano bar, spanning the stern with great views over the wake through full-height win-dows. For amazing views, don't miss having a cocktail here on a moonlit night. Keeping the Asian theme but with a twist, the colonial-styled Bombay Billiard Club provides a pat-terned wood floor and redwood paneling setting for two high-tech pool tables cradled in gimbals and kept even by motorized gyro-scopes to overcome any ship movement.

On the *Brilliance,* the Solarium is East Indian–themed with Indian elephants, bronze statues, and a ceramic-tiled peacock, and in the Aurora Theater the colors are gold, purple, and reds. More generally asso-ciated with Royal Caribbean are such places as the Casino Royale, with more than 200 slot machines and several score of gaming tables; a baseball-themed sports bar offer-ing interactive games; the nautically deco-rated Schooner Bar; an always-open Internet center; and the line's signature room, the Viking Crown Lounge, here a quiet retreat and a disco with rotating bar. Even the public bathrooms will turn heads, bright, airy, marbled spaces with mirrors shaped like portholes.

The two dining rooms are two stories high with an impressive double staircase joining the two levels and a cascading waterfall. More maritime inspiration is designed into the Windjammer Café with navy blue carpet-ing and fabrics, rich wood veneers, and scat-tered ship models. The number of food counters, eleven in all, spreads out the lines and reduces crowding, and food may be enjoyed indoors or out. Even more informal, the naturally lighted Seaview Café serves the usual fast foods during lunch and dinner hours at tables with rattan chairs.

For watching steaks being cooked in an open kitchen, the ninety-seat Chops Grill offers seats in high-backed booths and a great sea view. Next door, the larger 130-seat Portofino features an Italian menu, and both restaurants provide a sense of occa-sion that comes with an extra charge.

The ships have three pools, a Sports Deck that serves basketball, volleyball, and paddle-tennis players, a 9-hole miniature golf course and golf simulators, jogging track, and a rock-climbing wall fixed to the funnel, now a feature on all RCI ships. For children, RCI's Adventure Ocean program offers four supervised age groups play stations with video games, a computer lab, splash pools, and a waterslide.

Historically, Royal Caribbean cabins have been on the small size while more space has been allocated to public rooms, but on the *Radiance* class, they are respectable, some even more than respectable, in size. Cabin decor has changed from Miami Beach pastels to rich navy blues and copper.

All cabins have small fridges; cozy sitting areas; ample drawer and closet space; interactive televisions that tap into booking shore excursions, keep tabs on onboard spending, and check up on the ups and downs of the stock market; desks-cum-vanities with a pullout shelf for personal laptop computers; and typically small RCI showers. Suites receive butler service and have access to the Concierge Club for tour and travel information or the latest newspaper.

All Royal Caribbean ships are big and bustling, but this new *Radiance* class offers a higher standard of just about everything that makes a cruise vacation a happy experience at a moderate price level.

The Itinerary

In spring the *Brilliance of the Sea,* with its speedy 25-knot service speed, sails transatlantic to the **Mediterranean** to take up residence at Barcelona for the summer. Alternate sailings head eastward to the Adriatic or to Greece and Turkey, while both itineraries share the ports of Villefranche for Nice; Livorno for Pisa and Florence; Naples for Capri, Pompeii, and the Amalfi Drive; and Civitavecchia for Rome. In this instance we will feature the one that sails into the Adriatic.

Barcelona is much more than an embarkation port, and you would be wise to spend a couple of nights to take in the city's cafe life, medieval streets, the Gothic Quarter, Picasso Museum, and Antonio Gaudi's art nouveau architectural masterpieces.

Then embark in the *Brilliance* and sail to the **French Riviera,** anchoring off **Ville-franche** to visit the elegant casino and palace in the principality of **Monaco,** the classy urban resort of **Nice** with a seafront walk on the Promenade des Anglais, or the pretty medieval hill town of **Eze,** perched above the azure sea.

Sailing overnight along the Italian coast to **Livorno,** excursions head inland to the Leaning Tower of **Pisa** and to **Florence** for the Duomo, Ponte Vecchio spanning the Arno, and the works of Michelangelo. On down the coast, the ship enters the **Bay of Naples** and docks at the city's elegant old maritime station, where, in decades past, millions of Italian immigrants left for new lives in North and South America and Australia.

Mount Vesuvius is clearly visible across the bay, and during the boat ride to the **Isle of Capri** or on the road to the ruins at **Pompeii** and to **Sorrento,** where you join the famous cliffside Amalfi Drive to **Positano,** one of Europe's most charming seaside resorts.

Leaving Naples, you have two nights and a day to enjoy the ship as she passes through the Strait of Messina, under the shadow of still-active Mount Etna, then around Italy's boot and a turn northward into the Adriatic. Enter **Venice** via its lagoon, dock at the edge of the island city, and spend the day getting lost, if only briefly, in the pedestrian streets and alleyways. A day pass will allow you to hop on and off the vaporettos, the Venetian canal buses plying the Grand Canal, heading across to the Lido and stopping at the glass factory island of **Murano.**

It's an overnight sail south through the Adriatic to **Dubrovnik,** the medieval city that survived the nasty Balkan War and is again receiving visitors to explore the streets and enjoy the seaside setting during a walk of the walls, which completely enclose the old town. The next call is at **Corfu,** an island favored by European tourists for its climate, the beaches, and Corfu Town's arcaded cafe life. Linger over a cup of espresso and let the world go by.

Enjoy a full sea day en route to **Civitavecchia,** the port for **Rome,** and the ninety-minute drive into the Eternal City. First-time visitors will want to take a tour to get an overview of the city, and then perhaps concentrate on Vatican City, its art collection, and St. Peter's Cathedral or ancient Rome, represented by the Coliseum, the Forum, Arch of Constantine, and the Palatine Hill.

After the hectic pace of trying to see one of the world's foremost capitals in one day, the *Brilliance* puts to sea again and takes two leisurely nights and a day westward en route to Barcelona and disembarkation.

On alternate weeks, the Eastern Mediterranean ports include the islands of Mykonos and Santorini; Piraeus, the port for Athens; and Kusadasi on the Turkish coast for the outstanding ruins at Ephesus. Shared ports with the first itinerary are Villefranche (Nice), Livorno (Pisa and Florence), Civitavecchia (Rome), and Naples (Capri, Pompeii, Sorrento, and the Amalfi Drive).

Address/Phone: Royal Caribbean International, 1050 Caribbean Way, Miami, FL 33132; (305) 539–6000; brochures: (800) 327–6700; fax: (305) 374–7354; www.royalcaribbean.com

The Ship: *Brilliance of the Seas* was completed in 2002, has a gross tonnage of 90,090, a length of 962 feet, and a draft of 27 feet.

Passengers: 2,100; mostly Americans with some Europeans and lots of families during the school holidays

Dress: Formal and casual nights

Officers/Crew: International officers and crew

Cabins: 1,050; with 813 outside and 577 with verandas

Fare: $$

What's included: Cruise fare only

What's not included: Airfare, governmental fees and taxes, tips, drinks, shore excursions

Highlights: A stunningly decorated ship lacking none of the megaship amenities

Other itineraries: Besides this twelve-night Mediterranean cruise, operating in late spring, summer, and early fall, Royal Caribbean ships cover itineraries in North and South America and Hawaii.

OCEANIA CRUISES'
Nautica
From Barcelona to Athens

Oceania Cruises got its start with a single ship, the 684-passenger *Regatta* in December 2003, and has since added the virtually identical *Insignia* and *Nautica* to the fleet. The trio once formed part of the eight-ship Renaissance Cruises, built between 1998 and 2001, until that company folded and the ships dispersed.

While the layout remains much the same, Oceania Cruises has upgraded many aspects of food service, decor, and amenities to provide an extremely good value for money whether choosing a sea journey such as this one or a more port-intense Mediterranean cruise.

The interior design is English-country-house hotel via the Bombay Company, so the overall quality of materials varies but the effect is both homey and comfortable.

The casino's adjacent bar lounge typifies the period atmosphere with dark wood paneling, rich Oriental carpets and heavy draperies, cushy sofas and chairs, decorative sconces, and a marble fireplace. It's just the place to gather for a drink before or after dinner. High up, the Horizon Lounge, another favorite spot, is light-filled and with stunning wraparound views. A white-glove afternoon tea takes place every afternoon at sea.

When first entering the library, one might immediately wish for a damp day to be able to squirrel away with a good book, seated in a high-back chair facing the fireplace beneath a raised ceiling featuring a painted tropical bird setting. The open shelves contain an excellent selection of both fiction and nonfiction, and an honor system prevails. Additional places to roost are the card room, a computer room with ample stations, spa, and the main show lounge for cabaret, orchestral concerts, and jazz and blues.

There is a choice of four restaurants and a wide window of dining hours, and consistent preparation and presentation is evident throughout. The Grand Dining Room seats fully half the ship at one time, and it does get noisy under the low-ceiling sections when full. You generally sit with other passengers unless you arrive with your own party. This way, you meet other passengers, and if available, you can request a table alone. The tables to the sides and at the stern are certainly preferable those to the middle. The international menu changes daily.

Two specialty restaurants, both seating less than one hundred, are located high up

and aft on Deck 10, and while reservations are required, there is no extra charge. Toscana is Italian with a set menu and a daily chef's special. Roast garlic veal tenderloin with wild mushrooms and gnocchi with a creamy pesto sauce are favorites. The Polo Grill offers a set steak and seafood card featuring prime ribs, filet mignon, rack of lamb, broiled lobster tail, and surf and turf.

For informality at the end of the day, the aft-facing Terrace Café one deck down becomes a Spanish tapas restaurant with dining inside or out under the night sky. Breakfast and lunch take place here and in the main restaurant. During the day, Waves, at poolside, dishes up grilled dishes, salads, and sandwiches.

Service throughout the ship is excellent, and most of the staff is European and many from the Renaissance days, so they know the ship and the type of passengers they are serving. Most are semiretired or retired Americans along with other good English-speakers. Since there are absolutely no facilities for children, few will ever be present. Smoking is strictly confined to a miniscule area on deck.

The promenade decks, truncated at both ends by public rooms, provide a peaceful place to read, look at the sea, and ultimately nap. A dozen cushioned wooden deck chairs each side see few passersby. Elsewhere, there is no dearth of chairs, out around the lido pool and under cover, nor is there any need to save spots.

The cabins, nearly all outside and two-thirds with partly partitioned dividers, are of a moderate size with room for a small sitting area with a two-seat sofa and chair. All the bed linens, down pillows, and duvets are of top quality. Bathrooms, however, are adequate for one person at a time, with a small shower. There is plenty of storage and adequate hanging space, but the beds are not high enough to stow most large suitcases beneath. Amenities include twenty-four-hour room service, TV, movie selections, safe, cotton robes, hair dryer, and 110/120 volt outlets.

The Itinerary

Most of Oceania's varied selections of Mediterranean itineraries are port-intensive cultural experiences lasting from ten to fourteen days. This ten-day cruise embarks in Barcelona and heads via French and Italian ports, Malta, then eastward to Piraeus, the port for Athens.

Barcelona, now considered one of Europe's great cities for its medieval Gothic Quarter, tree-lined boulevards, museums dedicated to Picasso and Miró, and Gaudi's unusual architecture, seen in apartment buildings but especially with his unfinished but still progressing Church of the Holy Family. Consider arriving a day or two prior to the cruise.

Sailing to the coast of France, the *Nautica* docks at **Marseilles,** the once-gritty city now considered an exciting waterfront experience centered about the old port and the immediate connecting streets. Most passengers will want to go inland through the French countryside to Provence for the spectacular medieval cities of **Avignon,** Arles, and Les Baux and to the Pont du Gard and Roman amphitheater at Nimes.

Then just long the coast, visit the French Riviera from **Monte Carlo**, principality of Monaco, with its grand Beaux Arts casino, Oceanographic Museum, elegant shops, cafes, and restaurants. Nearby are seaside Nice and Cannes and up on the Grand Corniche, the hilltop village at Eze.

From the Italian port of **Livorno,** it's a short drive to the Leaning Tower of Pisa and on inland to **Florence,** straddling the River Arno. Visit masterpieces by Michelangelo and Leonardo da Vinci, the great Duomo and climb its bell tower, and the shopping mecca at the Ponte Vecchio.

Sailing down the Italian coast, Civitavecchia gives access to a day in **Rome,** and you can choose to take a tour or simply transfer and plan your own day to include such sights as the Vatican, St. Peter's Basilica, the Sistine Chapel, and the Coliseum, or explore the many beautiful piazzas and shopping streets centered at the base of the Spanish Steps.

The call at **Amalfi/Positano** means a spectacular cliffside drive with views of red-tile roof villages facing the deep blue Mediterranean. Excursions head north to Sorrento and **Pompeii** in the shadow of its destroyer, Mount Vesuvius.

Passing through the Strait of Messina between Sicily and the Italian mainland, dock at Naxos harbor then climb to **Taormina,** a nineteenth-century mountain resort, clinging to the slopes of still very active Mount Etna. The city origins date back to ancient Greece as evidenced by the Amphitheater, and the medieval period is seen in the city walls, arches, and Duomo.

Sail into **Valletta**'s Grand Harbor for a day on the island of **Malta,** a UNESCO World Heritage Site, where the architecture reflects the strategic crossroads position the city has known since ancient times. The center is easily walkable from the pier.

Following seven port calls in as many days, two nights and a day sailing eastward to Piraeus should prove a relaxing tonic to then take on **Athens** either on a tour or independently by using the local train up to stations for the Forum, Acropolis, and the Parthenon, Plaka (old city), and National Museum. The *Nautica* overnights here, and disembarkation is the second morning.

Address/Phone: Oceania Cruises, 8300 N.W. 33rd Street, Suite 308, Miami, FL 33122; (800) 531–5619 or (305) 514–2300; fax: (305) 514–2222; www.oceaniacruises.com

The Ship: *Nautica*, built in 2000 as *R5*, has a gross tonnage of 30,200, a length of 594 feet, and a draft of 19.5 feet. Sisters are *Insignia* and *Regatta*.

Passengers: 684; mostly Americans, some British, fifty and up

Dress: Casual, country-club style

Officers/Crew: European officers and mostly European crew

Cabins: 342 cabins, all but 25 outside and 232 with balconies

Fare: $$$

What's included: Cruise only, port charges

What's not included: Airfare, governmental fees, drinks, tips, shore excursions

Highlights: Beautifully run ships, excellent service, consistently good food enjoyed in a country-club-style atmosphere

Other itineraries: Besides this ten-day Mediterranean cruise, the three-ship fleet cruises in Northern Europe, Caribbean, South America, and in South, Southeast, and East Asia.

STAR CLIPPERS'
Star Clipper
French and Italian Rivieras under Sail

Designed after the mid-nineteenth-century fast clipper ships, the *Star Clipper* and *Star Flyer* are the brainchildren of Swedish yachting enthusiast Mikael Krafft. Completed in Ghent, Belgium, in 1991 and 1992, respectively, they are among the largest and tallest sailing ships ever built, with mainmasts topping 226 feet. In price and accommodations they, including the larger *Royal Clipper,* fall somewhere between the Windjammer Barefoot experience and the upscale three Windstar Cruise vessels, skewed to Windstar. As a sailing experience, they are not unlike the historic, former private yacht *Sea Cloud.*

The *Star Clipper* is generally under sail from late evening to early or mid-morning the next day. Passengers are invited to help with the lines, and some do, while most are content to sit back and look on. The 1,370-horsepower Caterpillar diesel engine kicks in when the wind dies down and is used for maneuvering in tight harbors. The social center is a sheltered deck amidships under a canvas awning, with a sit-up bar and stools around tables. The forward end opens into a lounge, where a grand piano, played by the resident pianist, is tucked under circular skylights cut into the bottom of the suspended swimming pool. Aft of the bar the Edwardian-style library has a clubby atmosphere, with a fireplace and a wall of mahogany-fronted bookcases containing a good selection of popular fiction, travel, and coffee-table books. The furniture, arranged around card tables and in conversational groupings, includes comfy chairs and sofas for a delightful retreat on a damp day.

The open sitting for all meals encourages mixing among the passengers and officers. Breakfast and lunch are served buffet style, with a generous selection of hot and cold items. Dinner, with fish, meat, and vegetarian entrees, is served by waiters. The food is of good quality and well prepared, and at dinner, passengers dress casually but not sloppily.

The moderately sized cabins, some shaped by the ship's hull, have twin beds or a queen and touches that include wood trim, electric lamps mounted in gimbals, and decorative brass counter railings to prevent items from sliding onto the floor. But the *Star Clipper* hardly lists at all; water tanks see to that. Cabins have phones and televisions that screen films, bathrooms are tiny, and there is no room service. In good weather this cruise is a shared, outdoor experience, with conversation, navigation, and sail handling providing the entertainment. At sea most passengers congregate around the wheelhouse and the two sundeck swimming pools.

The Itinerary

Leaving **Cannes** and the French Riviera behind, the helmsman sets a course for the island of **Corsica.** The first night at sea under full sail is magic, and it's difficult to leave the deck for the cabin below. In the morning the *Star Clipper* lowers its sails and motors in the yacht harbor at **St. Florent.** Some may wish to hang around and look at all the gathered boats, while others take an excursion up to Cap Corse, where medieval towers rim the cliffs.

Approaching the island of **Elba,** the captain demonstrates his considerable skill reversing into the tiny basin at **Portoferraio.** From the castle wall, you can look down onto the ship, anchored in an idyllic setting and towering over the quayside of red-tiled and pastel-colored houses. Napoleon lived in exile here for about ten months before escaping to France, and his two houses are worth visiting.

If the weather permits, the *Star Clipper* will drop anchor for a beach visit and then call at **Bastia,** a Corsican port city known for its Italianate architecture. The massive stone citadel houses the Ethnographic Museum, which tells the story of Corsican independence from Genoa, just in time for Napoleon to be born French.

Then it's overnight to the Italian coast at **Portonevere,** where it's a drive inland to see the Leaning Tower at **Pisa** or a bit farther to **Florence,** the city of art on the Arno. Sailing up the Italian coast, **Portofino** is always a favorite stop, a miniature seaside village wedged into a narrow valley, overlooked by handsome Italianate villas and the stylish Hotel Splendido. Most passengers go no farther than the town's main square for a leisurely lunch and a bit of shopping. The more energetic might take my tip and walk up to a network of paths that hug the hillside with great views down to the sea. You can continue for two hours to **Santa Margarita,** a larger old-fashioned Italian Riviera resort. For the return, the choice is a quick bus or boat ride back to Portofino.

The last call is **Monte Carlo** in the principality of **Monaco,** the domain of the rich and famous with its opulent international casino and one of Europe's finest yachting centers. On the last night, the ship sails along the French Riviera for disembarkation at **Cannes.** The order and inclusion of the ports will vary from season to season, and longer ten- and eleven-night itineraries are also available.

The *Star Clipper* is a great leveler. There are couples aboard who could buy and sell the ship and others who are working people, and it's not easy to tell one from the other. The ships cater to passengers who have done the big ships and who enjoy a working sailing ship, small ports, informality, and making friends in a relaxed setting.

Address/Phone: Star Clippers, 4101 Salzebo Street, Coral Gables, FL 33146; (305) 442–0550; reservations: (800) 442–0551; brochures: (800) 442–0550; fax: (305) 442–1611; www.starclippers.com

The Ship: *Star Clipper* was built in 1992, has a gross tonnage of 2,298, a length of 360 feet, and a draft of 18.5 feet.

Passengers: 168; all ages, including some Europeans; English is the lingua franca

Dress: Casual at all times

Officers/Crew: European officers; international crew

Cabins: 84; 78 outside and most relatively compact; no verandas

Fare: $$

What's included: Usually cruise only

What's not included: For cruise only, airfare, port charges, tips, drinks

Highlights: A terrific outdoor sailing experience; charming ports; relaxed atmosphere

Other itineraries: Besides this seven-night Western Mediterranean cruise, which operates between May and September, the *Star Clipper* offers an alternative Western Mediterranean cruise, spring and fall transatlantic positioning voyages, and two winter Caribbean itineraries. Sistership *Star Flyer* operates in the Greek islands and along the Turkish coast from May to October, then travels via the Suez Canal to cruise Malaysia and Thailand, returning through the Indian Ocean in April. The 226-passenger *Royal Clipper* also operates in the Western Mediterranean and the Caribbean and undertakes spring and fall transatlantic crossings.

SEADREAM YACHT CLUB'S
SeaDream I and *SeaDream II*
Mediterranean Living on a Yacht

SeaDream I and *SeaDream II* began life as the 116-passenger *Sea Goddess I* and *II*, two identical pioneering ships catering to the very top end of the cruise market. After a short time operating for an independent company, Cunard bought the pair, then in 2001 the two passed to Atle Brynestad, a Norwegian shipowner, to sail under the SeaDream Yacht Club banner.

If private yacht can be applied to any cruise ship, this pair deserves the term because of their size, amenities, and the pampering. The atmosphere is highly sophisticated yet casual, more relaxed than when Cunard operated them. A younger crowd, wearing good clothes but not dressing up, is drawn to the one-week itineraries in the Caribbean and the Mediterranean. Rather than days at sea, the ship is more

often found at anchor with its passengers enjoying life on deck. When the ship is docked, passengers may drift ashore to take in the local scene, such as outdoor cafe life at Calvi on Corsica, or make the short climb to the cliffs overlooking the harbor at Bonifacio at the south end of the island.

On board, wines and spirits are complimentary in the bars and at meals. Freshly prepared Mediterranean seafood and fruits are menu highlights served in the lovely main restaurant or at the partly enclosed cafe up on deck. The chef may buy from a local market, and you can join in the shopping adventure. For a private dinner, or any meal at any hour, the cabin staff will serve you course by course in your quarters, either at the raised coffee table or at a proper table supplied for the occasion. On every cruise, one dinner is served poolside, and more often there are beach-party-style lunch barbecues and picnics. Cocktail hour features caviar, smoked salmon, shrimp, and hot and cold hors d'oeuvres in the main lounge with musical accompaniment for dancing before and after dinner. A pianist plays at a grand piano in the dining room at night, and movies are shown out on deck under the stars.

The library has a good selection of books and videos and Internet access at moderate rates, and there is a small casino and open bridge policy.

Water sports and Asian spa treatments are popular activities, and while at anchor in some ports, passengers can swim, snorkel, Jet Ski, sail, or kayak from the stern marina. A golf simulator offers play at fifty championship courses, and mountain bikes may be taken ashore. For the more sedentary, the outdoor pool is always open, and soaking in the whirlpool is a social event.

On this democratic, if high-end, ship, the minisuite-size cabins are nearly identical with windows in most and portholes for others, and a number may be combined to create a separate bedroom and lounge. The blond-wood cabinetry and furnishings are all new, and the elaborate amenities include refrigerator, soft-drink-stocked bar, safe housed in a vertical enclosure, and an entertainment center with a 20-inch flat-screen TV, dataport for in-cabin e-mail, CD and DVD player, and an MP3 audio player. The beds, or bed if pushed together, are set before the window and can be curtained off from the lounge. Bathrooms have all been renewed with fresh marble tiles and glass-enclosed showers with multiple jets.

The Itinerary

The *SeaDream* pair offer several different one-week itineraries, most centered in the Western Mediterranean, and the one described here has especially good small-port

content, but there are many variations on this one embarking in Nice. Touring can be on your own from the landing, by private car, taxi, or on the cruise line's shore excursion program. Arrival and departure times are flexible depending on the weather and touring factors.

Embarkation is at the commercial port of **Civitavecchia,** a ninety-minute drive from Rome, and the ship then sails overnight to **Positano,** a picture-postcard coastal town at the south end of the **Amalfi Drive.** The narrow streets don't permit buses, so touring is by foot or private hired car to **Pompeii, Herculaneum,** or **Sorrento.** The ship then shifts across the bay to **Capri,** one of the most popular spots in all of Italy, so it is wise to take a tour by boat along the coast to one of the grottos or to a secluded beach. A good land destination is the island's second town, **Anacapri,** perched high above the sea, and from here a chairlift glides above the vineyards en route to the top of Mount Solaro for a stupendous view of Vesuvius, the Bay of Naples, Amalfi Coast, and the nearby island of Ischia.

At the north end of **Sardinia,** the stop at **Porto Servo** puts you in the world of the Aga Khan, who developed the **Costa Smeralda** beginning in the 1960s. You can visit some of the upscale resort hotels and nearby villages by bus or car. It's a short sail over to **Corsica,** where there are two scheduled port calls, the first at the medieval town of **Bonifacio,** sandwiched between steep white cliffs with a citadel to climb overlooking the harbor. Inland drives access hill towns and the rugged island's national park. On the north coast, **Calvi** is a gem of a yachting center, and the ship docks alongside a long line of cafes and restaurants.

The **Bay of Cannes** is set aside for enjoying the ship sports marina for sailing, kayaking, swimming, tubing, and boarding or simply never leaving the comfy sun lounger on deck. Shifting to **Cannes** itself, you are in a big city resort ideal for a long promenade or for taking the ship's tour inland to the sixteenth-century, fortified hill town at **St. Paul en Vence** with an attractive drive in both directions.

The port of disembarkation is Nice on the French Riviera, not far from **Monte Carlo,** in the principality of **Monaco,** a long-time playground for the rich. The *SeaDream II* will look very much at home here, so linger before you head off to other parts.

Address/Phone: SeaDream Yacht Club, 2601 South Bayshore Drive, Penthouse 1B, Coconut Grove, FL 33133; (305) 631–6100 or (800) 707–4911; fax: (305) 631–6110; www.seadreamyachtclub.com

The Ships: *SeaDream I* and *II,* built as the *Sea Goddess I* and *II* in 1984 and 1985 respectively, have a gross tonnage of 4,260, a length of 334 feet, and a shallow draft of 14 feet.

Passengers: 110; mostly Americans, some Europeans; ages thirty-five and up

Dress: Tastefully casual every night

Officers/Crew: Scandinavian officers and European and international hotel staff

Cabins: 55 one-room minisuites, all nearly identical; lowest deck cabins have portholes rather than windows. Sixteen units can be combined to provide a two-room suite.

Fare: $$$$

What's included: Cruise fare, all wines and spirits, gratuities, and sports equipment

What's not included: Port charges, shore excursions, airfare

Highlights: One of the most indulgent travel experiences possible in an atmosphere that is more private yacht than cruise ship

Other itineraries: In addition to the *Sea Dream I* and *II* making seven-day cruises throughout the Mediterranean, both ships undertake seven-night itineraries in the Caribbean, with spring and fall transatlantic crossings connecting the two seasons. Be advised that an advertised sailing may not always be available as the ships are often chartered.

STAR CLIPPERS'
Royal Clipper
Rome to Venice aboard the World's Largest Sailing Ship

On first sight, the *Royal Clipper* presents a most powerful appearance. Five tall bare poles rise above a shapely steel hull that sports a thick black stripe running its full length. Black gun-port squares below give the ship an extra sense of importance, and if one did not have a passenger ticket in hand, this ship might pass for a man-of-war, or at least a commercial cargo carrier.

The 228-passenger *Royal Clipper* is a full-rigged ship, with square sails on all five masts, while the earlier four-masters, *Star Clipper* and *Star Flyer,* are barkentine-rigged. At 439 feet, the *Royal Clipper* is 79 feet longer and qualifies as the longest and largest sailing vessel ever built, in overall size as measured in gross tons. She carries 56,000 square feet of Dacron sail, compared to 36,000 for the *Star Clipper* and *Star Flyer*. The twenty-member deck crew uses electric winches to angle the twenty-six square sails and electric motors to furl and unfurl the square sails stored in the yardarms and the eleven staysails, four jibs, and one gaff-rigged spanker.

On the Main Deck, an upward-sloping observation lounge gives a view out to the foredeck and is used for meetings, informal talks, and Internet connections. The main lounge, located amidships, has banquette, soft couch and chair seating, a sit-up bar, and a central well that looks down into the dining room two decks below. As you leave via the aft doors, the covered Tropical Bar and the paneled Edwardian library and its electric fireplace recall the earlier pair.

The handsome paneled dining room, reached via freestanding staircase from the lounge, has a large upper level surrounding a central well, the location for additional tables and the buffet. An omelet chef cooks to order at breakfast, and a carvery features roast beef, ham, and pork at lunch. Seating at tables and banquettes is open for all meals, and the lunch buffets are the biggest hit with the menu featuring such choices as jumbo shrimp, foie gras, artichoke hearts, herring, potato salad, lots of salad fixings, hot and cold salmon, meatballs, and sliced roast beef. The dining room is set low enough that in any kind of sea, the water splashes washing-machine style over the portholes. For an actual underwater view, Captain Nemo, the combination gym, spa, tiled Turkish bath, and beauty salon, has lounge seating from where one can look out for the creatures of the sea.

The deluxe suites are reached by walking along a central mahogany-paneled companionway with a thick sloping mast penetrating the corridor at the forward end. These luxurious cabins, mahogany-paneled with rose-

wood framing and molding, contrast with an off-white ceiling and the wall's upper portion. Pale gold-framed mirrors enlarge the cabin space, and brass-framed windows bring in light to bathe the corner sitting alcove. Brass wall lamps and sailing ship prints lend the distinctive feel of a ship's cabin, upward sloping at that, not the more common cruise ship hotel-style room on a hull.

A heavy wooden door leads to a private furnished teak-deck veranda with shrouds passing upward from the ship's side. Nods to upscale cruise ship amenities include the huge marble bathroom with Jacuzzi and a TV and minibar, hidden from view. There are fourteen of these 255-square-foot deluxe one-room suites, plus two even larger 320-square-foot owner's suites located at the stern, and two 175-square-foot deluxe cabins that open onto the after-deck. The most numerous standard cabins (eighty-eight) in categories 2 to 5 are 148 square feet and vary mostly by location. They have marble bathrooms with shower, TV, satellite telephone, radio channels, private safe, and hair dryers. Six inside cabins round out the accommodations. The real show takes place up on the Burma teak Sun Deck, its full length cluttered with electric winches, halyards, belaying pins, lines, shackles, ventilators, lifeboats, and, incongruously, deck chairs arranged around three swimming pools. The center pool, 24 feet in length, has a glass bottom that drops into the piano lounge and serves as a skylight to the dining room three decks below.

A hydraulic platform stages the water sport activities, and the ship offers banana boats, waterskiing, diving, snorkeling, and swimming from the 16-foot inflatable raft. An interior stairway gives access to the marina. Two 60-passenger tenders, resembling military landing craft, and two 150-passenger fiberglass tenders ferry passengers between the anchored ship and pier.

The Itinerary

The *Royal Clipper* offers two offbeat Mediterranean itineraries, a seven-day cruise calling at southern Italy's coastal and island ports and including a stop in Sicily, and the longer, innovative ten- and eleven-night cruises between **Civitavecchia,** port of Rome, and Venice, via Southern Italy, Sicily, Greece, and the Croatian coast. It is this latter more ambitious itinerary that is described here.

Sailing south overnight through the Tyrrhenian Sea, the first call is the **Isle of Capri,** the famous resort island rising high out of the sea. While stunningly lush with flowering plants, the town center is overrun with tourists, so follow some of the narrow streets and footpaths away from the main square both here and at Anacapri to appreciate the island's well-deserved reputation.

Lipari, one of the volcanic Aeolian Islands, is usually seen in passing from aboard one of the big cruise ships, with a wisp or plume of smoke rising skyward. The main town is a charming yacht haven, and from there climb up through the narrow streets to the medieval castle or head out to a secluded beach.

Next, the *Royal Clipper* will enter the Strait of Messina, the narrow passage between southern Italy and Sicily. The swift water to starboard is Scylla and the jagged rocks to part Charybdis, dangers to sailing ships in ancient times. The ship then arrives beneath mighty Mount Etna, also an active volcano and occasionally sending a scare to residents living on its slopes. The excursion climbs to **Taormina,** a mountainside resort established in the nineteenth century, where the streets parallel to the main thoroughfare will give a better glimpse into the most attractive flower-bedecked residences.

After three busy days ashore, the ship sets off, hopefully with some favorable wind to let the sails do the propelling,

around Italy's toe into the Ionian Sea with two nights and a day at sea bound for the beautiful island of **Corfu** on the west coast of Greece. Corfu town has a string of cafes and restaurants lining the principal arcaded street, back streets to explore, and the elaborate Achillion Palace, built for Austrian royalty and later used by the German kaiser.

Northward into the Adriatic Sea, the next five calls are along the Croatian coast, newly rediscovered following the ethnic wars in former Yugoslavia. The walled city of **Dubrovnik** is by far the best known, and its wartime damage has been fully repaired. If time permits, walk completely around the city center to be able to look down on the houses, narrow lanes, open squares, and church properties.

Marco Polo was born in the red-tile-roofed town on the island of **Kurcola.** Inside the Cathedral of St. Mark, paintings by Tintoretto and Titian and other Italian and Dalmatian artists are on display. Nearby **Hvar** (meaning lavender and hence the lovely smell as you tour the countryside) has been a favorite island retreat for the Romans, Byzantines, Venetians, Austro-Hungarians, and today's smart set. The town features the Cathedral of St. Stephen, a cloistered Franciscan monastery, and a Venetian arsenal.

Well up the coast, land at **Veli Losinj,** a fortified town on the island of Losinj. You can climb a sixteenth-century tower or enjoy miles and miles of beaches with water sports of all kinds offered. At **Pula** on the Istra Peninsula, the Roman Emperor Vespasian built a 23,000-seat amphitheater for gladiatorial combats and naval battles. But that is only the beginning of a whole collection of ancient arches, gates, temples, and churches to see here.

Then as a final and thoroughly noncultural event, the ship's staff will set up a beach party before sailing now virtually westward overnight to enter the Venetian Lagoon by morning, passing the Lido, Doges Palace, St. Marks Square, and the entrance to the Grand Canal. Consider staying on in **Venice** for a few days.

This itinerary also operates in the opposite direction calling at the same ports en route to Civitavecchia, the port for Rome.

Address/Phone: Star Clippers, 4101 Salzebo Street, Coral Gables, FL 33146; (305) 442–0550 or (800) 442–0551; fax: (305) 442–1661; www.starclippers.com

The Ship: The *Royal Clipper* was built in 2000, has a gross tonnage of 5,000, a length of 439 feet, and a draft of 18.5 feet.

Passengers: 228; all ages, Americans and Europeans; English is the lingua franca

Dress: Casual at all times

Officers/Crew: European captain, European officers and international crew

Cabins: 114; all but 6 outside, 14 with verandas

Fare: $$

What's included: Cruise only

What's not included: Airfare, port charges, tips, drinks

Highlights: The ultimate in a sailing ship experience; social bonding aboard

Other itineraries: Besides these two Mediterranean itineraries offered between May and September, the *Royal Clipper* makes two annual transatlantic crossings in spring and fall. Star Clippers offers other sailing ship cruises aboard the *Star Clipper* and *Star Flyer* in the Eastern or Western Mediterranean, bases two ships in the Caribbean, and in fall the *Star Flyer* sails through Suez to cruise Malaysia and Thailand, returning via the Indian Ocean in April.

WINDSTAR CRUISES'
Wind Spirit
Greek Islands and Coastal Turkey

Launched in 1986, Windstar Cruises combines the best of nineteenth-century clipper-ship design with the best of modern yacht engineering aboard its fleet of four- and five-masted sailing ships. While the *Wind Spirit*'s proud masts and yards of white sails cut an ever-so-attractive profile, the sails unfurl at the touch of a button. Windstar cruising is a top-of-the-line, ultracomfortable experience, and a no-jackets-needed policy is appreciated by the stylish, formality-eschewing guests.

On board, stained teak, brass details, and lots of navy blue fabrics and carpeting

and caramel-colored leathers lend a traditional nautical ambience. Passengers can visit the bridge at any time to watch the computerized sails at work. Intentionally, there are few organized activities offered, and the pool deck, with its hot tub, chaise longues, and open-air bar, is conducive to conversing, sunbathing, or just peaceful repose. The video library and CD collection are popular pastimes for in-cabin entertainment.

In the vaguely nautical-looking lounge, passengers congregate for port talks, pre- and post-dinner drinks, and dancing and listening to the pianist and vocalist. Local entertainment may come aboard at a port of call, and a modest casino offers slots, blackjack, and Caribbean stud poker. In addition, a tiny gym is housed in a cabin-sized room, with an adjacent coed sauna.

The food is inventive and imaginative, as reflected by an appetizer such as a corn risotto with wild mushrooms and basil, perhaps followed by an artfully presented potato-crusted fish with braised leeks and apple-smoked bacon, or a salmon tournedos with an herb crust served with stewed tomatoes and garlicky broccoli rabe. Irresistible desserts like banana pie with raspberry sauce and French profiteroles with hot-fudge sauce are beyond tempting. The once-a-week evening pool-deck barbecue is a grand party under the stars. There are two open-seating dining venues: The Restaurant, accented with teakwood trim and wood paneling and pillars wrapped in hemp, is used for dinner only; and The Veranda, a sunny, window-lined room with additional tables under umbrellas, serves breakfast and lunch.

All twin-portholed cabins are similar wood-tone outsides measuring 188 square feet and equipped with a DVD player and a flat-screen TV showing CNN and lots of movies, a CD player, a minibar, bathrobes, fresh fruit, and a compact closet. Roomy teakwood-decked bathrooms are well laid out and come with hair dryer and circular shower stalls.

The Itinerary

The weekly departures alternate between the Athenian port of **Piraeus** and **Istanbul.** When sailing from Greece, the first call is **Mykonos,** where, as in most ports, there is no need to take an organized excursion. Hop the shuttle provided by the ship and walk the town from end to end, enjoying the classic whitewashed, blue-domed chapels and maze of streets; then choose a seaside restaurant for a Greek salad and plate of calamari.

The approach to **Santorini**'s cliff rim is nothing short of spectacular, and to reach the town 1,000 feet up, hire a donkey, take the cable car, or, if fit, use the zigzagging stairs. Besides the bird's-eye views, browse the cobbled streets and sample the fresh fish and Santorini white wines. Sailing eastward to **Rhodes,** the medieval city is a short walk from the ship, and within the walls are bustling squares, cobblestone side streets leading to small shops and some wonderful restaurants, perhaps for dinner, as the ship stays until nearly midnight. One excursion visits historic **Lindos,** perched high on a steep cliff above the sea.

Bodrum, a Turkish yachting and holiday port, has a Crusader past with fortified towers dominating the town and lots of resort-style shops and fish restaurants, where you choose the fish displayed whole for cooking. Weather conditions permitting, passengers may be able to go kayaking, sailing, windsurfing, and swimming from the water-sports platform lowered at the stern. Then up the coast at **Kusadasi,** first-timers should take the tour to **Ephesus** to stand before the towering Library of Celsus and climb the steps of the great theater—but be prepared for hordes of other tourists. The pièce de résistance is the arrival in **Istanbul,** a breathtaking finale, with minarets rising up all around, with Topaki Palace and the Galata Tower adding considerable character to the skyline. Stay on a few days to take in this energetic bridge city straddling Europe and Asia.

Address/Phone: Windstar Cruises, 300 Elliott Avenue West, Seattle, WA 98119; (206) 281–3535 or (800) 258–7245; brochures: (800) 626–9900; fax: (206) 286–3229; www.windstarcruises.com

The Ship: *Wind Spirit* was built in 1988, has a gross tonnage of 5,350, a length of 440 feet, and a draft of 13 feet.

Passengers: 148; mostly American, thirty and up

Dress: Casual at all times

Officers/Crew: British officers; Filipino and Indonesian crew

Cabins: 74; all similar cabins, all outside, and no verandas

Fare: $$$$

What's included: Cruise fare, port charges, water sports, basic tips

What's not included: Airfare, governmental fees, drinks, shore excursions, extra tips

Highlights: Cuisine, ship itself, intimate atmosphere, service; Mediterranean itinerary

Other itineraries: In addition to these seven-night Eastern Mediterranean cruises, which operate between May and October, the three-ship fleet offers numerous other Mediterranean itineraries, transatlantic positioning voyages, Caribbean programs, and a one-week program in Costa Rica.

GRANDI NAVI VELOCI'S
Excelsior
To Sicily by Ferry in Style

Just the name, Grandi Navi Veloci, conjures up thoughts of extraordinary fast ships exuding Italian elegance, and these initial impressions are fully met once aboard.

The company is relatively new, having been formed in 1992 to operate the most luxurious and fastest cruise ferries in the Western Mediterranean. Until recently the company was part of the Grimaldi Genoa shipping empire, but while other investors now hold a majority stake, the Grimaldi family still retains key positions.

All but one of the company's impressive fleet of eight fast cruise ferries were built in Italy between 1993 and 2003, and the Genoa to Palermo service began with the delivery of the first ship. One of the regulars on this route is the *Excelsior*, dating from 1999. She covers the 431 nautical miles through the Tyrrhenian Sea in around twenty hours, with evening departures and

afternoon arrival times. The service operates six times weekly, increasing to daily in July and August.

The 39,739-ton *Excelsior* can carry up to 2,200 passengers in 387 cabins ranging from suites to inner four-berth cabins, and in 900 aircraft-type seats, and when completely full there is a crowded feeling. By ferry standards, the outer twins are moderately spacious, with one bed that converts to a comfortable sofa for day use. Passenger cabins occupy most of Decks 7 and 8, and the after end of both decks is given over to a glass-enclosed lido pool area furnished with wooden chairs and tables with a cafe bar serving drinks and snacks. Additional seating is out of doors.

The range of public rooms includes the attractive Belavista observation lounge and bar located on the highest passenger deck overlooking the bow. It serves as a quiet place to read during the day and have a drink in the evening. Aft on this same deck are conference facilities, card room, children's play area, and a block of the aircraft-style seats.

Deck 6 features the majority of the public rooms, starting all the way forward with a splendidly isolated quiet observation lounge, and separated by two corridors from the entertainment venue, the Magnifica Lounge. In the evening a band plays music for dancing, then the main show follows. Further aft, the open-plan Piano Bar serves drinks until late, and for serious night owls the New York Club disco on Deck 4 stays open to the wee hours.

The *Excelsior* offers two styles of dining. The Transatlantica Cafeteria, decorated with mosaic wall tiles and waist-high partitions, provides buffet-style dining, while the elegant and intimate L'Espadon a la carte serves exceptionally good food with seating for about 150. Service is attentive and prices reasonable. Recommended are the risotto and the pasta with fresh tomato sauce.

The *Excelsior* is one of four ships that operate between Genoa and Palermo at varying times of the year. She is identical to the *Excellent* and offers similar facilities to the larger *La Suprema* and *La Superba*.

The Itinerary

Boarding at **Genoa**, the birthplace of Christopher Columbus, starts two hours before the 9:00 or 10:00 P.M. departure. With spare time, visit the new maritime museum just fifteen minutes on foot from the ferry terminal or choose a harborside restaurant or cafe for a view of the port activity, with ferries sailing off to Corsica, Sardinia, Sicily, and North Africa.

Departure from Genoa is swift, and soon the ship reaches its 24-knot speed that is maintained for the next twenty hours. Restaurant service starts shortly before sailing, and beside the bars and lounge, the cinemas screen films (dubbed in Italian).

Next morning, the ship is plowing south through the Tyrrhenian Sea, and take note that breakfast in the cafeteria finishes at 9:30 A.M.

Outer deck space, while not expansive, does offer views over the stern and to port and starboard. Smoking is banned except on the decks. Daytime activities include card room board games, skeet shooting, music in the bar lounges, and a children's club. Lunch is served in both restaurants before the late afternoon arrival.

At first glance **Palermo,** Sicily's island capital set in the shadow of Mount Pellegrino, appears more industrial than Genoa. While much of the city was devastated during the Second World War, the churches, streets, and markets of the old town still display Middle Eastern influence from the time of Arab control.

There is much to see here—wonderful architecture, including the recently re-opened Massimo Theatre dating from 1897, the imposing cathedral with parts constructed in the late twelfth century, and the splendid mosaics in the Palatina Chapel, dating from 1130. Slightly out of the center the magnificent cathedral at Monreale, founded in 1172, houses some remarkable gold mosaics depicting scenes from the Old Testament.

Away from Palermo, Sicily offers an astonishing number of historical sites, some more than 2,500 years old, including Selinunte and Segesta to the southwest. On the island's east side, Taormina and its Greek theater set above the Ionian Sea has volcanically active Mount Etna as its backdrop. To the south Syracuse's fifth-century B.C. Greek theater is still used for public performances.

Attractive fishing villages are found all around the coast, while inland there is some simply stunning mountainous scenery. For touring without a car, Sicily's rail lines almost completely circumnavigate the island and buses fill in the gaps.

Address/Phone: Solbec Tours, 2116 Jean Talon Est, Montreal, Quebec H2E 1V3, Canada; (514) 729–6132; fax: (514) 729–2769. Grandi Navi Veloci has an easy-to-use information and booking site online at www.gnv.it. Click the Union Jack for the English version.

The Ships: *Excellent* and *Excelsior,* built in 1998 and 1999, respectively, have a gross tonnage of 39,739, a length of 654 feet, and a draft of 22 feet. *La Superba* and *La Suprema,* built in 2002 and 2003, respectively, have a gross tonnage of 49,270, a length of 679 feet, and a draft of 25 feet.

Passengers: 2,200 and up to 2,800 on the larger ships, mostly Italians. English is widely spoken, and onboard announcements are in English and Italian.

Dress: Casual at all times

Officers/Crew: Italian

Cabins: 387 on the *Excellent* and *Excelsior,* ranging from suites to insides with four berths. Airline-style seating is a cheap option.

Fare: $ to $$

What's included: Ferry fare and port taxes only

What's not included: Meals, drinks, tips

Highlights: Stylish ships with good food and excellent service, offering a voyage to and from one of the most interesting islands in the Mediterranean

Other itineraries: Grandi Navi Veloci ships sail from the northern Italian port of Genoa to Barcelona, Tunis, Palermo, and the Sardinian ports of Olbia and Porto Torres. Additional services operate from Livorno and Civitavecchia (port near Rome) to Palermo.

MINOAN LINES'
Ikarus Palace and *Pasiphae Palace*
A Minicruise from Venice to Greece

Few ports are more enchanting from which to sail than Venice, and following a stay in this wonderful city, consider taking a minicruise south through the Adriatic to Greece, to linger on there or come straight back. Up to six times each week, a Minoan "Palace" ferry makes the 650-nautical-mile transit, calling in at two ports en route to Patras on the Peloponnese.

Dispel from your mind any preconceptions of Greek ferries, as Minoan Lines operates one of the most modern cruise ferry fleets in the Mediterranean. This Crete-based company was founded in 1974 to link that island with the Greek mainland, later branching out to the Adriatic Sea in 1981 where seven of its ten ships operate.

The *Ikarus Palace* and her sister the *Pasiphae Palace,* the pair featured here, were built in Norway for the company in 1997 and 1998 and, with streamlined superstructures, look both sleek and fast. A third ship on the route, the 2002-built *Ariadne Palace,* is marginally smaller.

Foot passengers (those traveling without a car) board via the stern ramp and use escalators to reach the passenger accommodation on Deck 6. Most of the compact two- and four-berth cabins with private facilities are on this deck, and once you are checked in at the reception desk, a smartly uniformed steward will show you to your cabin. The full range of accommodation includes inside and outside cabins, mini-suites, aircraft-type reclining seat lounges, and even bedding down in your sleeping bag in designated areas on the open decks. Round-trip passengers might wish to consider paying the supplement for a minisuite on Deck 8, including sitting area, television, minibar, and room service.

The public rooms on Deck 7 feature an elegant self-service restaurant overlooking the bow for a wide range of freshly prepared hot and cold food at reasonable prices and a beautiful a la carte restaurant paneled with wood veneers and furnished with tasteful fabrics and wooden flooring. The restaurant on the *Ikarus Palace* may be one of the best at sea, rivaling some of the famed cruise liners for tasteful decoration. With excellent service and good food, complemented by mostly Greek wines, it's a splendid place for breakfast, lunch, or dinner. Be sure to try the shrimps saganaki, Smyrna patties, and the Greek yogurt with honey.

Just aft is the ship's main bar, arranged with pleasant alcoves in which to enjoy a quiet drink. Other places on this deck are the shopping arcade, casino, and a pub-style bar. Up on Deck 8, an observation lounge during the day becomes a discotheque at night.

Outside, spacious open decks extend over four levels, and at the stern there is a swimming pool and whirlpool, a bar serving drinks and snacks, and seating both in the open and under cover.

The Itinerary

Boarding commences two hours prior to sailing, and the ship departs **Venice** at 2:00 P.M. The route along the Guidecca Canal affords a wonderful opportunity to view the city's outstanding architecture, and in about twenty minutes, the ship passes the entrance to the Grand Canal and then Piazza San Marco, the Cathedral, and the Doge's Palace. Ahead are the Lagoon, the Lido, and the open sea. The busy waterway transit to the broad **Adriatic,** shared with ferries, launches, yachts, and freighters, takes about one hour.

Have a drink, dinner about 8:00 P.M., and then listen to some music. After you enjoy a night's rest and a leisurely breakfast, the ship will be sailing at 27 knots along the Albanian coast to pass between the island of **Corfu** and the Greek mainland before calling at the picturesque port of Corfu Town at midday. If there are other ships loading in the harbor, the apparent chaos on the quayside can be quite entertaining. The call is brief and the ship is soon underway again, heading for the Greek mainland port of **Igoumenitsa,** an hour's sailing from Corfu. A good deal of freight and some tourist traffic leaves here for the 300 road miles to the industrial city of Thessalonika, and for Istanbul, about 750 miles distant. Heading south during the afternoon through the Ionian Islands, the ferry meets a steady stream of ships bound from **Patras** to various Italian destinations, and by early evening she crosses the mouth of the Gulf of Patras to be berthed by 7:30 P.M.

Three times a week, the same ship sails again at midnight, while on other days it will be a different vessel. If booking a round-trip on the same ship, it is possible to retain the same cabin and leave luggage aboard, but disembarkation and check-in is compulsory. Consider having dinner ashore.

Sailing north, the call at Corfu is 6:30 A.M. the next morning, Igoumenitsa about 8:00 A.M., and arrival at Venice at 7:30 A.M. local time the following day. A free shuttle bus operates to the Piazzale Roma for the main bus terminus, and it's a short walk to Santa Lucia railway station.

As an alternative to returning immediately, Minoan Lines operates a connecting bus to Athens and Piraeus, but given the after-midnight arrival, a night in Patras might be preferable. Patras is a fairly modern city laid out on a grid system with some stylish shops and attractive squares, but it is also quite scruffy in parts. A good place to stay is the Astir Hotel, a slightly faded, grand hotel from the 1960s that is clean and offers good service. Ask for a room on the fifth or sixth floors overlooking the harbor. The hotel's a la carte restaurant is particularly good, and between June and September a harbor-view rooftop restaurant serves dinner.

If moving on to other destinations in Greece, the Peloponnese narrow-gauge railway takes you from Patras along the coast and over the Corinth Canal to **Athens** in four hours and to **Piraeus** in four and a half hours. The express coach is faster but travels over a less interesting route, reaching the western bus station in Athens in about three hours depending on traffic. Piraeus is a major cruise and ferry port for accessing much of the Mediterranean.

Address/Phone: Minoan Lines, Central Reservations Office 26, Akti Possidonos Street, GR 18531 Piraeus, Greece; +30 210 414 5700; fax: +30 210 414 5755; www.minoan.gr (English pages available)

The Ships: *Ikarus Palace* and *Pasiphae Palace* were Norwegian-built in 1997 and 1998 and have gross tonnages of 30,010 and 30,018, respectively, and are 656 feet long. *Ariadne Palace* was built in South Korea in 2002, has a gross tonnage of 28,007, and is 693 feet long. All ships have a draft of 21 feet.

Passengers: *Ikarus Palace* and *Pasiphae Palace* 1,500 total; *Ariadne Palace* 1,250; predominantly German, then Austrian and Italian, and other Europeans plus backpackers from all around the world. Announcements are in Greek, English, Italian, and German.

Dress: Casual at all times

Officers/Crew: Greek

Cabins: *Ikarus Palace* and *Pasiphae Palace* have 700 beds in 200 cabins; *Ariadne Palace* has 412 beds in 120 cabins

Fare: $ to $$

What's included: Cruise only including port charges; deluxe cabins (minisuites) include breakfast

What's not included: Meals, drinks, tips

Highlights: Wonderful ferry ships, excellent service, the spectacle of departing from and arriving back at Venice, great scenery from Albania all the way down to Patras

Other itineraries: Minoan Lines operate an older ship between the northern Greek port of Thessalonika and Heraklion, Crete, calling at the islands of Skiathos and Tinos (or Syros), Mykonos, Paros (or Naxos), and Santorini during the peak summer season. The company also operates modern fast ships between Piraeus and Heraklion and Patras and Ancona (Italy). Ancona is connected to the Italian State Railway system.

PACIFIC OCEAN

CAPTAIN COOK CRUISES'
Reef Endeavour
Australia's Great Barrier Reef

Captain Cook Cruises operates small cruise ships in several Australian locations and in the Fiji Islands. The closest North American equivalent in size and layout would be the *Nantucket Clipper* or the *Yorktown Clipper,* but the passenger list is an international one of all ages from North America, Europe, Australia, and New Zealand.

Public rooms include a forward-facing observation lounge, and, high up on the Sun Deck, a second, smaller observation lounge; aft are two spa pools, a sauna, a gym, and an outdoor bar. The main lounge, furnished with cane seating, has a bar and a grand piano; mouthwatering hors d'oeuvres are served here before dinner, and the room opens back onto the outdoor pool and lido area. In addition, there's a small library, a gift shop, and a self-service laundry.

The amidships dining room on D Deck runs the width of the ship, with buffet-style, open-seating breakfasts and lunches and with waiter-served, one-seating dinners. During my barrier-reef cruise, I enjoyed a seafood terrine, grilled barramundi (a local fish), and roast beef with Yorkshire pudding, accompanied by good Australian wines. Breakfast offers honeydew, rock melon, passion fruit, kiwi, mango, pawpaw (papaya), papino (pear and melon), juices, cereals, eggs to order, American and English styles of bacon, as well as sausage, toast, danish, and freshly baked croissants. One hot-and-cold lunch buffet displayed more seafood than I have ever encountered—cold whole salmon, smoked salmon, red emperor, prawns, raw oysters, curried mussels, scallops, whitebait fritters, mud crabs with huge claws, and Moreton Bay bugs (a saltwater crayfish). It would be sinful not to overeat. An outdoor deck barbecue featured steak, sausage, spareribs, chicken, and prawns.

The seventy-five similar outside cabins, arranged on four decks, fall into three categories, varying more in location than size. Most have a door opening onto the side promenade. The D-Deck cabins have portholes and open onto an inside passageway. Wooden furniture consists of a desk, a low table, a chair, two night-tables, a good-size closet, and limited drawer space. All bathrooms have showers.

The Itinerary

The *Reef Endeavour* leaves from **Cairns,** northern Queensland, twice a week on three- and four-day cruises that can be combined into a full week. The reef, located at an average distance of 40 miles from the coast, is not one continuous coral wall, but comprises 1,500 major and 1,000 minor separate living reefs ranging in age from two to twenty million years old and is home for more than 1,500 species of fish.

On the three-day cruise the *Reef Endeavour* sails south to **Fitzroy Island** for a rain-forest walk, followed by a full day anchored off **Hedley Reef** for scuba diving, snorkeling with gear provided by the ship, and viewing the undersea world from a glass-bottom boat. With the ribbon reef protection from the pounding Pacific Ocean, I saw fish as colorful as their names—clownfish, yellowtail fusilier, blue angelfish, moorish idol, surgeonfish, butterfly fish, sergeant major, sweet lip, fox-faced rabbit fish, feather starfish, blue starfish, sea cucumber, and giant clams with openings 2 or 3 feet across—in a setting of blue-tip and golden staghorn, and brain, honeycomb, boulder, and lettuce-leaf coral.

As the ship enters the beautiful **Hinchinbrook Channel,** flanked by an island and the very mountainous Queensland coast, the marine biologist talks about the nearby saltwater mangrove swamp that provides home for mud crabs, saltwater crocodiles, hammerhead and whale sharks, dugongs (similar to a manatee or sea cow), box jellyfish, and lots of fishes. In the skies above are ibis, reef herons, shags, and spoonbills. Later in the day, anchored off **Dunk Island,** a national park, a rain-forest walk might reveal bush turkeys and birdwing, tiger, and Ulysses butterflies, and a rewarding climb affords a sweeping panorama of islands, forested coastline, and seascape stretching to the far horizon.

The four-day cruise heads north to **Cooktown,** a former gold-rush site with a colorful history and architectural relics, then out to **Two Isles,** an uninhabited, except for bird life, coral cay. **Lizard Island,** location for the poshest resort on the Barrier Reef, offers a morning hike to the highest hill and a day of snorkeling and diving, and, as a finale, the best variety of sea creatures inhabit **Ribbon Reef No. 5,** at the edge of the continental shelf.

Address/Phone: Captain Cook Cruises, No. 6 Jetty, Circular Quay, Sydney NSW 2000 Australia; (011) 61–2–92–06–1100 or (888) 292–2775 for information and brochures only; fax: (011) 61–2–92–51–4725; www.captaincook.com.au

The Ship: *Reef Endeavour* was built in 1995, has a gross tonnage of 3,125, a length of 243 feet, and a shallow draft.

Passengers: 150; all ages; Australian, European, and American, with English the lingua franca

Dress: Casual at all times

Officers/Crew: Australian

Cabins: 75; all outside, most with windows and doors that open onto a promenade

Fare: $$

What's included: Cruise fare, port charges, most excursions

What's not included: Airfare, drinks, optional shore excursions such as diving

Highlights: Spending time along the Great Barrier Reef, one of the world's natural wonders; Australian hospitality

Other itineraries: The above cruise may be segmented into three or four days. The *Reef Endeavour* also makes occasional seven-day round-trips to Far North Queensland, Thursday Island, and Torres Strait. Captain Cook Cruises operates other small ships from Sydney, along the Murray River in South Australia, and in the Fiji Islands (both cruise ship and sail cruise).

SILVERSEA CRUISES'

Silver Shadow

New Zealand and Australia

Silversea Cruises operates a fleet of four ships, and the *Silver Shadow* is the first of the larger 388-passenger pair, completed in 2000. The quartet covers the globe, and from year to year the exact ship that will assume a certain itinerary will change. . Designed for the upper end of the market, Silversea ships are larger than the Seabourn trio and smaller than the newest in the Radisson Seven Seas fleet. Registered in the Bahamas, the beautiful *Silver Shadow* measures 28,258 tons, and her passenger–space ratio is among the highest afloat.

The design layout sees cabins placed forward on six decks away from the public rooms and stacked aft on seven decks, so the efficient elevators see quite a lot of use. As with the smaller pair, the show lounge faces aft and is entered from both sides at stage level via a shipwide bar and lounge. Passengers gather here before lunch and before and after dinner for drinks and dancing to a small band. Silversea attracts many nationalities who are drawn to the sophisticated European-style service; the majority, however, are American.

For viewing the coastal scenery and harbor arrivals, the Panorama Lounge affords sweeping views on three sides. For intimate places to linger and talk, the Humidor draws the cigar smokers and brandy sippers to an English club setting, and the paneled wine bar caters to the grape aficionados.

Dining is open seating, and you can ask for a table for two or join others in the large but thoughtfully laid-out main restaurant located on the lowest and most stable deck. The Terrace Café serves breakfast and lunch with a delightful covered afterdeck usually protected against the wind. Theme dinners—Italian, French, or a menu reflecting the cruising region—are by reservation but at no extra charge. Complimentary table wines are served in both restaurants at lunch and dinner. A poolside grill serves those who prefer to stay out on deck.

The small casino is located off the main lobby, and the fitness center and spa, operated by Mandara, assumes the highest position on the ship. Internet access is available in the computer center and in the suites.

Deck chairs surround the pool and whirlpools out in the open and under cover, and additional chairs ring the perimeter of the deck above.

The ship's suite accommodations put Silversea right at the top, and the smallest, called Vista suites, measure 287 square feet. The next and most numerous category, the Veranda suites, have the same interior area and add a balcony. The top accommodations fall into four more categories and range from 701 feet to 1,435 feet.

Accommodations come with sofas, cocktail tables that rise to become suitable for in-suite dining, TVs and VCRs or DVD players, refrigerators, cocktail cabinets, arched curtain dividers, walk-in closets with good storage, and two-basin marble bathrooms with tubs and stall showers, hair dryers, robes, and slippers.

Silversea provides top service, food, and accommodations on a calendar of cruises that span the world.

The Itinerary

Silversea Cruises operates several cruises a year, usually during the summer season in the Southern Hemisphere, that include Australian and New Zealand ports. Because of the distance to reach the lands down under, it is wise to take advantage of a pre- and post-cruise stay to see some more beyond the two terminal ports.

Auckland, the embarkation port for this fifteen-day cruise, is also New Zealand's largest city. Its lively inner-city neighborhoods and the Maori Collection at Auckland Museum lie a short distance from the ship and the busy waterfront. The ferry terminal is adjacent to the cruise ship pier, and boats fan out to Devonport, a nineteenth-century suburb, and to Waiheke Island with its bed-and-breakfasts, beaches, farms, and vineyards.

Sailing out of Auckland, the ship passes the city's eastern side and volcanic Rangitoto Island to sail overnight to Tauranga for the drive inland to the Maori cultural center at Rotorua, followed by a call at the art deco heritage city of Napier. Then it's two nights and a day en route to the port of Lyttleton, which gives access to **Christchurch,** located a few miles inland. This Victorian English-garden city was laid out by Anglican immigrants and offers punting on the River Avon, which flows serenely through town, superb botanical gardens, art and natural history museums, and on weekends, a bustling arts and crafts show, a flea market, and buskers (street entertainers).

Dunedin, just an overnight sail to the south, was settled by Scottish Presbyterians. Visit Larnach Castle, a Scottish-style hilltop estate, or take a nature cruise below the coastal cliffs to view seals, seabirds, and a royal albatross nesting ground.

Then enjoy a long and leisurely, and sometimes rough, sail around the bottom of the South Island and into the spectacular fjord settings of Milford, Doubtful, and Dusky Sounds, then across the **Tasman Sea** to **Hobart,** the capital of **Tasmania,** an Australian island state. The countryside is Eng-

land with a soft rural landscape, rough stone houses, and pretty parish churches. Near Hobart, **Port Arthur** at one time had the reputation of being Australia's toughest penal colony. The first prisoners, incarcerated for major crimes, established the timber industry, and eventually some 10,000 arrived. Nearby **Bonorong Wildlife Park** lets you observe such creatures peculiar to Australia as the Tasmanian devil, kangaroos, wallabies, wombats, and cuddly koalas.

Sailing around Tasmania's coast, the *Silver Shadow* crosses the Bass Strait, noted for its choppy waters, to dock at **Melbourne**'s Station Pier for two days. Located in the state of Victoria, Melbourne has an older and softer feel than fast-paced Sydney, perhaps a parallel to Boston and New York. Here you might think about buying a day transit pass and riding the famous green-and-yellow trams that glide along Collins Street, the principal center-city shopping precinct, with routes fanning out to the Victorian Arts Center, botanical gardens, smart suburbs, and seaside **St. Kilda.** An excursion includes lunch on the Colonial Tramcar Restaurant, a 1927 trolley that glides along the city streets while you dine in style.

Sailing east, it's two nights and a day to **Eden,** a port on the extreme south coast of New South Wales where there are spectacular drives to enjoy along the ocean highway.

Finally, the *Silver Shadow* sails between **Sydney**'s North and South Heads into one of the world's most magnificent harbors, cruising past the shoreline's national park, Taronga Zoo, beaches, and suburbs. The most breathtaking feature is the unfurled white sails design of the Sydney Opera House, and the ship may dock just opposite at Circular Quay or pass under the Sydney Harbor Bridge to tie up at Darling Harbor.

Whichever the berth, there is still one more night aboard with the city at your doorstep. One of the most popular outings is a harbor bridge climb, suitable even for those with mild, but certainly not severe, vertigo. Linger a few days to take in the city's energy, its cultural attractions, neighborhoods such as The Rocks, the first settlement, and **Paddington** for its display of Victorian wrought-iron bungalows and terraced houses. An excursion heads west into the Blue Mountains, the blue created by mist from the eucalyptus forests, for some spectacular scenery, waterfalls, and a steep funicular ride.

Address/Phone: Silversea Cruises, 110 East Broward Boulevard, Fort Lauderdale, FL 33301; (954) 522–4477 or (800) 722–9995; fax: (954) 522–4499; www.silversea.com

The Ship: The *Silver Shadow* was completed in 2000, has a gross tonnage of 28,258, a length of 610 feet, and a draft of 19.6 feet.

Passengers: 388; many Americans, some Europeans; forty-five and up

Dress: Formal, informal, and casual nights

Officers/Crew: Italian officers and a European and Filipino crew

Cabins: 194 spacious one-room suites, all outside, and 157 with balconies

Fare: $$$$$

What's included: Cruise fare, often a hotel stay, drinks and wines at lunch and dinner, gratuities, and usually a special shore side event

What's not included: Airfare, port charges, shore excursions

Highlights: Stylish atmosphere, unusual itinerary

Other itineraries: Besides this *Silver Shadow* warm-weather cruise in Australia and New Zealand, the Silversea four-ship fleet, including the *Silver Cloud, Silver Whisper,* and *Silver Wind,* cover virtually the entire world.

HOLLAND AMERICA LINE'S
Amsterdam
Southern California to Hawaii and Return

Holland America Line dates back to 1873, operating transatlantic passenger service for the first one hundred years, and now has one of the largest and most attractive fleets in the industry. For several years the 55,451-ton *Statendam* held down this route, but now it's the *Amsterdam*'s (featured ship) and *Zaandam*'s turn.

This larger twelve-deck ship accommodates 1,380 passengers, and the public rooms are located on Sports, Lido, Upper Promenade, and Promenade Decks. These include the Crow's Nest forward on the

Sports Deck, a delightful observation lounge during the day and an intimate nightclub in the evening. The Lido Deck offers health and fitness facilities, a large pool area (covered during cool weather by a retractable roof) amidships, and the spacious Lido Restaurant aft. Upper Promenade is anchored forward by the Van Gogh show lounge's balcony seating and the La Fontaine dining room's upper level aft. In between are shops, the Casino, the Ocean Bar for a drink and dancing, the Explorer's Lounge, and a new combination Explorations Café, Internet Center, and library. On the Promenade Deck the orchestra level of the show room and the dining room's main level bracket the front desk, and the Wajang Theater, which serves freshly popped popcorn at show time.

Carnival's influence is most apparent in the high quality of the shows performed nightly while at sea. These "Las Vegas–style" productions are full of energy, bright lights, and good staging. The show room is also the venue for popular local Hawaiian entertainment that boards in at least two ports. In the two-level dining room, the traditions of Holland America shine. The dignified Indonesian waiter service is the perfect complement to the culinary delights presented at each meal, and a Filipino band serenades at dinner. Alternative dining takes place in the Pinnacle Grill with a Pacific Northwest theme and also specializing in steaks.

The 690 cabins and suites, spread along five decks, range from 187-square-foot inside cabins to four-room penthouse suites measuring 1,126 square feet. Most cabins are outside, and two decks feature private verandas. Avoid cabins located above the theater if you retire early.

The Itinerary

By law only U.S.-registered ships may carry passengers between Hawaiian ports; hence, the Dutch-registered *Amsterdam* embarks at San Diego for the four-day ocean voyage to then call at five Hawaiian ports before sailing back to **San Diego,** a nifty combination cruise and double crossing. The days at sea are filled with traditional shipboard activities and by Holland America's lecture series, which includes such topics as finance, world politics, self-improvement, Polynesian life, Hawaiian royalty, and Hawaiian culture. One elegant evening hosts the superbly orchestrated "Black and White Ball," when all the ship's officers appear in formal white waistcoats. The crossing is a prelude to the beauty and spectacular experience of Hawaii, where, at each port, there is a wide range of shore excursions, some including lunch and a luau with traditional Hawaiian dancing.

From **Hilo** on the "Big Island" of **Hawaii,** take in the Queen Lili'uokalani Gardens or drive through the tropical forest to gaze into the Kilauea crater from Volcano House, perched right on the rim of the world's largest volcano. For a nonorganized tour rent a car or take one of the free shuttle buses to a shopping mall and the beach. Especially dramatic is the after-dark view, from the deck, of hot lava flowing down the slopes into the sea.

Sailing past Diamond Head to dock at the Aloha Tower in **Honolulu,** tour Lolani Palace, the only royal palace in the United States; drive out to Diamond Head, and shop on Kalakaua Avenue. At Pearl Harbor see the film that recalls the Japanese attack on December 7, 1941, then board a boat out to the USS *Arizona* Memorial and visit the USS *Missouri,* the battleship on which the Japanese surrendered.

At **Nawiliwili** on the garden island of **Kauai,** take a jeep safari to the rim of Waimea Canyon, the Grand Canyon of the Pacific, and a helicopter flight over the breathtaking Na Pali Coast; then enjoy a water-level view as the *Amsterdam* sails past. On **Maui** in April there is a good chance to see humpback whales up close, or ascend nearly 10,000 feet to visit Haleakala, Maui's largest volcano. At **Kona** on the far side of the "Big Island" of **Hawaii,** visit the 250,000-acre Parker Ranch, the largest single-owner cattle ranch in the United States; see Kealakekua Bay—even snorkel here—where Captain James Cook lost his life in 1779; and explore Pu'uhonua o Honaunau, a sacred Hawaiian "City of Refuge," with its sanctuary for defeated warriors, wooden carvings, and ancient temples. Following the intensive sightseeing, relax and enjoy the ship's social life on the way back to the mainland. Depending on the departure, the order of ports may vary.

Address/Phone: Holland America Line, 300 Elliott Avenue West, Seattle, WA 98119; (800) 426–0327; fax: (800) 628–4855; www.hollandamerica.com

The Ship: *Amsterdam* was built in 2000, has a gross tonnage of 61,000, a length of 781 feet, and a draft of 26 feet.

Passengers: 1,380; mostly Americans, fifty-five and up

Dress: Formal, informal, and casual nights

Officers/Crew: Dutch officers; Indonesian and Filipino crew

Cabins: 690; 557 outside and 172 with verandas

Fare: $$$

What's included: Cruise only

What's not included: Airfare, port charges, shore excursions, drinks, tips

Highlights: Attractive ship on which to spend many sea days; lots to do ashore in Hawaii

Other itineraries: In addition to these fifteen-day Hawaii cruises from San Diego, which operate January to April and October to December, other Holland America ships cruise to Alaska, the Caribbean, the Panama Canal, and South America, and the *Prinsendam* cruises around the world. Holland America's large fleet covers the globe.

COMPAGNIE POLYNESIENNE DE TRANSPORT MARITIME'S
Aranui III
Freighter Travel to Paradise

The world has shrunk to the point that most places on Earth are reached by air, but thankfully there are a few exceptions where the sea route is still paramount and the destinations remote and unspoiled. The island of St. Helena in the South Atlantic is one, and the Marquesas and Tuomotu Islands in the South Pacific are another.

The South Pacific islands have been accessible by passenger freighters named *Aranui* ("great highway" in Maori) since 1959. In 2003 a brand-new one, purpose-built, larger, and much better appointed, arrived from a Romanian shipyard located hundreds of miles up the Danube. The

200-passenger *Aranui III* then took over the sixteen-day round-trip voyages from the *Aranui II,* a general cargo ship that had been rebuilt to carry 100 passengers. The new ship carries all manner of cargo to the remote archipelago and up to 130 20-foot containers, and, because of her far greater berth capacity, she is classified as a passenger ship.

The passenger accommodations are of a high standard and include a main lounge, a library, a gym, hairdresser, small shop, laundry, and outdoor bar and lounge area by the swimming pool. A video room has a TV and a video player. An aft platform can be lowered for swimming, fishing, snorkeling, and scuba diving. On most sailings the ship carries an enrichment lecturer, and when one is not on board, a member of the crew steps in. The crew is mostly Marquesan, friendly and burly men whose bodies are colorfully decorated with tattoos.

The dining room seats up to 168, and there are normally two seatings. The food may vaguely be described as a Western-ized version of Polynesian fare, using local pork, poultry, fish, fruits and vegetables, and New Zealand beef. French wines are included with lunch and dinner. Breakfast is buffet style, and lunch and dinner are served family style. Many of the passengers are French as Polynesia is still part of France, and some American passengers complain of cultural differences that cause annoyances, often a result of the size of the group.

Cabins range from sixty-three standard moderate-size twins with portholes, shower, and toilet; to twelve windowed deluxe cabins with queen-size bed, refrigerator, and bathtub; to ten suites, eight with private balcony, highly unusual for a freighter.

The Itinerary

Most days are spent docked or at anchor off an island loading and unloading cargo, but three days are at sea. Time in port varies from a few hours to a full day, sometimes a bit more. Where the *Aranui III* does not dock, passengers need to be reasonably fit to clamber down ladders into the ship's tenders and to get out of them on shore, which might well be through the surf. But there are always strong, willing hands to assist. March through August is the dry season, though it may shower then, too, while September through February is the rainy season. Temperatures are generally in the 80s (Fahrenheit) during the day and drop to the 60s and 70s at night.

Departures from **Papeete,** the main port on the island of **Tahiti,** take place about every three to four weeks for the sixteen-day voyage that calls at two **Tuomotu Islands** and many more **Marquesas.**

At the first island call, Takapoto, the activities are watching how black pearls are harvested, swimming, and snorkeling. As you approach Ua Pou, sharp volcanic peaks pierce the clouds, with one soaring more than 4,000 feet. A delectable lunch ashore includes breadfruit, barbecued rock lobster, and something called *poisson cru,* raw fish marinated in lime juice and coconut milk.

Herman Melville fled his whaling ship and sought refuge in the Taipivai Valley on Nuku Hiva, where you board vehicles for a mountain ride to see a collection of stone tiki gods, human-like religious sculptures, and boulders strewn about carved with images of birds, fish, and turtles. The island has the only airstrip in the Marquesas, otherwise access is entirely by sea. Tahuata is simply a tiny village visit, and Fatu Hiva, a lush island formed by two extinct volcanoes, is known for its beautiful bay.

On Hiva Oa, a jeep safari takes you to see an even more important collection of tikis that recall the much larger ancient pieces on Easter Island. Paul Gauguin lived here in the village of Atuona until his death in 1903, and you can visit his gravesite, sited next to that of Jacques Brel, the Belgian songwriter who also resided here.

Ua Hika and other islands display Marquesan handicafts, and this one is also known for its 2,000-strong horse population that roams freely. For visitors, they are saddled up for a ride into the mountains.

Fakarava, the last stop, is the world's largest atoll, and the day is spent on the beach (lunch provided) snorkeling among the coral with tropical fish and parasailing.

Many of the ports visited have no other regular access, so the arrival of the *Aranui III* becomes a major event. The Marquesans are warm and friendly, a contrast to the more sullen people encountered at Papeete.

Address/Phone: For information: Compagnie Polynesienne de Transport Maritime, 2028 El Camino Real South, Suite B, San Mateo, CA 94403; (650) 574–2575 or (800) 972–7268; www.aranui.com; for bookings: TravLtips, P.O. Box 580188, Flushing, NY 11358-0188; (800) 872–8584; fax: (718) 224–3247; www.travltips.com

The Ship: *Aranui III,* completed in 2003, has a deadweight tonnage of 3,800, a length of 386 feet, and a draft of 8.8 feet.

Passengers: 200, French about 50 percent, Americans 30 percent, also Australians, British, and others; wide age range but few children

Dress: Casual at all times

Officers/Crew: Polynesian, mostly Marquesans

Cabins: 85 cabins; all outside, 8 with balconies, plus two 12-berth dormitories (male and female)

Fare: $$$

What's included: Cruise fare, all shore excursions, including meals ashore, wine with lunch and dinner

What's not included: Airfare, VAT, tourism tax and port charges, tips, drinks

Highlights: A most comfortable working ship to a beautiful remote part of the world

Other itineraries: All cruises are sixteen-day voyages year-round from Papeete, Tahiti.

RADISSON SEVEN SEAS CRUISES'
Paul Gauguin
Cruising in Paradise

The 320-passenger *Paul Gauguin* flies the French flag and is sold through Radisson Seven Seas Cruises. Overall, the ship is more French modern than South Pacific in decor, but the corridors are a gallery of intriguing photographs of turn-of-the-century Tahiti, and a small Fare Tahiti museum displays a few Paul Gauguin drawings and carved ceremonial canoe paddles, wooden flyswatters, and a trio of ironwood shark hooks. The pool is a generous size for a small ship, and deck chairs abound, but with little protection from the intense sun. For the active types the ship's marina opens up for waterskiing, windsurfing, kayaking, scuba diving, and snorkeling, but the latter two sports must be done away from the ship.

Most public rooms, including the two restaurants, are stacked aft and have wrap-around windows. On the two highest decks, two pretty observation lounges offer venues for a quiet read during the day, a formal afternoon tea with piano music, drinks before meals, private parties, a cabaret, and a late-night disco.

L'Étoile, the principal restaurant, has a high ceiling and spacious open seating for the continental dinner menu. Above, the cheery 130-seat La Veranda offers a menu and a buffet for breakfast and lunch, while dinner, by reservation, alternates between two French menus. On one night the cold starter was a dollop of Sevruga caviar set atop a charlotte of potatoes, followed by lobster ravioli in dim sum, grilled sea bass, and grilled tenderloin of beef, with crème brûlée and a Tahitian vanilla sauce for dessert. Complimentary wine accompanies both lunch and dinner. Le Grill, located outside and under cover near the midships pool, serves all three meals.

The tiered show lounge offers a wonderfully inventive multi-instrumental singing Filipino quintet and three great shows of dancing and singing islanders, from a two-year-old making her debut to teenagers and grandmothers.

Every cabin is outside, with generous-size bathrooms and tubs, and 50 percent have private verandas for enjoying breakfast and the cool early-evening breezes before dinner.

The TV comes with a VCR, and the minibar is stocked with beer, soda, tonic, and water (except for the beer, these are replenished daily without charge), as well as complimentary bottles of gin, vodka, and scotch.

The Itinerary

For ten months of the year, the 513-foot ship sails Saturdays from **Papeete, Tahiti,** on a seven-day subequatorial loop that takes in the four **Society Islands** of Raiatea, Taha'a, Bora Bora, and Moorea, with much of the week spent lazily at anchor in one gorgeous aqua-blue-water bay after another and just two nights under way. Most passengers, completely seduced by the islands' incredible beauty, seem to like it that way, and while riding at anchor, the ship gently swings about 120 degrees, revealing continually changing views of jagged mountain peaks, palm-fringed reefs, and the pounding surf just beyond.

The shore program offers a lot of variety, and because French Polynesia is an expensive region, the organized excursions are on the pricey side. At **Raiatea** a motorized outrigger canoe speeds along the coast to the Society Island chain's only river, from where it is said that the Polynesians set out to populate Hawaii, Easter Island, and New Zealand. Nearby, the seventeenth-century temple **Marae Taputapuatea** served as the center of religion and sacrifice until the Christian missionaries arrived and largely destroyed it. The ruins are being gradually pieced back to better demonstrate the island's heritage.

The adjacent island of **Taha'a** offers a jeep safari deep into the hills over a rutted road fringed by pink and red ginger, white gardenia, red hibiscus, and tiare, the fragrant flower the Polynesians wear over their ear. There's a stop to watch coconuts sliced open for sampling the sweet water, milk, dried coconut, and the mushy young meat. Another taste, a bit bland, is breadfruit, the crop that Captain Bligh and the *Bounty* had come to collect for replanting as a food crop for the West Indian slaves. Taha'a, a typical volcanic island, is surrounded by a protective reef, and palm-bedecked sandy islands called *motus* offer swimming, snorkeling, and a barbecue lunch ashore.

Anchoring off **Bora Bora,** with its fantastic pointy mountain spires, outrigger canoes head out to the fringing reef, where the guides feed the black-tipped reef sharks and stingrays ranging close by (in shallow waters stingrays, if fed, do not mind being stroked). A jeep ride leads to terrific island views and locations where World War II American cannon point to sea. Author James Michener was stationed here in 1942, and his *Tales of the South Pacific* refer to Bora Bora as "the most beautiful island in the world."

Moorea may be the favorite island of most visitors, but it's a close call. Snorkeling brings the sight of picasso triggerfish and butterfly, angel, surgeon, and parrot fish. On land, plantation agriculture shows fields of pineapples, mangos, papaya, guava, bananas, taro, vanilla, melons, and avocados. Days can be hot and humid, but the water is always nearby, and on clear nights the sky reveals the Southern Cross, False Cross, Orion's Belt, and Castor and Pollux.

At the end of the cruise, visit Tahiti's fine museum, with its displays of sailing craft, tiki sculpture, and maps of Polynesian immigration and European exploration. Another museum is dedicated to Paul Gauguin's life rather than his artistic works. Even after a short visit, it is easy to see how one might be taken over by the islands' incredible lure and the genuine friendliness of the local Polynesians.

Address/Phone: Radisson Seven Seas Cruises, 600 Corporate Drive, Suite 410, Fort Lauderdale, FL 33334; (954) 776–6123 or (800) 285–1835; brochures: (800) 477–7500; fax: (954) 722–6763; www.rssc.com

The Ship: *Paul Gauguin* was completed in late 1997, has a gross tonnage of 18,800, a length of 513 feet, and a draft of 17 feet.

Passengers: 320; age forty and up, mostly Americans

Dress: Casual at all times

Officers/Crew: French officers; European and Filipino crew

Cabins: 160; all outside, 80 with verandas

Fare: $$$

What's included: Cruise, wine at meals, stocked minibar, tips

What's not included: Airfare, port charges, shore excursions, drinks at the bars

Highlights: Cruising among some of the most beautiful islands in the world; sophisticated yet relaxed onboard ambience

Other itineraries: In addition to the above seven-night cruise aboard the *Paul Gauguin,* which operates most of the year, the ship also makes ten-, eleven-, and fourteen-night cruises to the Marquesas Islands. The line operates the 490-passenger *Seven Seas Navigator,* the 720-passenger *Seven Seas Mariner,* and *Seven Seas Voyager* as well.

AFRICA AND THE
MIDDLE EAST

ST. HELENA LINE'S
RMS *St. Helena*
Into the Remote South Atlantic via Royal Mail Ship

In 1978 Curnow Shipping of Falmouth, Cornwall, began operating a passenger, mail, and cargo service under a contract with the British government between Britain, the Canary Islands, Ascension, St. Helena, and Cape Town to replace the one hundred years of liner service operated by the Union-Castle Line. Now Andrew Weir Shipping holds the five-year contract.

Purpose-built in a Scottish shipyard in 1990 to serve the islands, the present RMS (for Royal Mail Ship), as she is affectionately known, undertakes occasional sailings from Portland, Dorset, to the island and makes many more additional sailings north from Cape Town, offering the comfortable facilities of a small liner for 128 passengers and a British and St. Helenian crew of sixty-five.

The homey public rooms include a two-section forward observation lounge with a bar, a video for screening films, and a reading area. Aft the Sun Lounge looks onto the open lido with outdoor pool, and a light breakfast and lunch are served here daily. The dining room, on a lower deck, operates with two reserved sittings at dinner, and the food is good British fare, such as tasty soups, lunchtime curries, dinner roasts, and well-prepared fish. The plainly furnished cabins are outside, with windows or portholes, twin beds, uppers and lowers, and private shower and toilet. Budget accommodations, reserved for the "Saints"—a people of mixed British, South Asian, East Indian, and Madagascar origin—are sometimes available for nonisland passengers.

The Itinerary

While the majority of voyages sail round-trip from Cape Town, calling at Luderitz and Walvis Bay, Namibia, en route to St. Helena and a week ashore, the classic liner voyage described here has no equal.

The ship embarks at Portland, Dorset, on the south coast of England for the two-week voyage to St. Helena, and following a week on the island, onward passage to Cape Town, South Africa. On our voyage, among the passengers were the Saints, who make up about half of the complement—students returning from university, persons on leave from jobs abroad, and others planning to resettle in their island home. The visitors came from Britain, Germany, France, South Africa, and the United States. Stored below decks were ninety-three bags of mail and parcels, refrigerated and frozen food, medical equipment and drugs, planks of a West African wood resistant to white ants, educational textbooks, nine automobiles, and one-fifth of a ton of stamps, one of the island's few sources of income.

During the cycle of gradually warming days, we established a daytime routine of reading and socializing on deck, visiting the bridge, and taking a swim or playing deck tennis with the officers atop the forward cargo hatch. In the evening the purser had an uncanny knack of getting everyone involved in creative activities: frog racing, quizzes, and pantomime, all old-fashioned shipboard fun. Such is the atmosphere aboard a purposeful ocean liner.

After a six-hour call at **Tenerife,** the Canary Islands, the RMS leaves the main shipping lanes for the remote South Atlantic. The sea remains placid and quite empty, erupting occasionally when flying fish and porpoises break the surface. A dozen days after leaving England, **Ascension** comes into view, a desolate and forbidding volcanic island rising 2,800 feet above sea level from the mid-Atlantic ridge. The ship anchors to take on passengers while the purser gives a tour ashore, weather permitting.

Two days later, **St. Helena** spreads across the horizon beneath a low cloud clinging to the mountain peaks. Brown at the edges and green in the center, the island's steep cliffs provide a natural fortress. The RMS anchors off Jamestown, a pastel-colored nineteenth-century Georgian town, sandwiched into a deep valley that slices inland to the island's incredibly beautiful central highlands.

Through passengers get the bonus of a week on the island while the RMS discharges her cargo and makes a passenger run to Ascension and back. Most visitors stay at two small hotels in Jamestown, whereas others choose a bed-and-breakfast or self-catering cottages up in the hills, which means hiring a car and negotiating twisting, one-lane tracks and blind hairpin curves for touring and grocery shopping.

Napoleon spent six years here from 1815 until his death in 1821, and Longwood, his permanent residence and gardens, is open to visitors; nearby, Deadwood Plain is home to the island's indigenous wirebird. Transit passengers may be invited for a tour of Plantation House, a handsome 1791-built mansion and grounds that is home to a giant Seychellois tortoise named Jonathan, who is reputed to be about 175 years old. There are miles of walking trails around the coast and down to secluded bays, with rewarding mountain vistas and seascapes of pounding surf. Jamestown offers a small museum, a pretty Anglican church, a few shops, and a couple of restaurants, but the main attraction is Main Street, the island's social center, where everyone gathers to talk.

After a week the RMS returns and embarks passengers for **Cape Town** via Walvis Bay and nearby Swakopmund, former German settlements retaining their colonial architecture and important bird-watching centers, and Luderitz, a more remote German colonial port town and historic diamond mining region. Just short of four weeks after departing England, the little ship sails into Table Bay as dawn breaks behind Table Mountain. Loading fresh food, supplies, cement, and coal takes three days; then the ship returns northward.

Address/Phone: St. Helena Line, Andrew Weir Shipping Ltd., Dexter House, 2 Royal Mint Court, London EC3N 4XX, England; (011) 44–20–7575–6480; fax: (011) 44–20–7575 6200; www.rms-st-helena.com

The Ship: RMS *St. Helena* was built in 1990, has a gross tonnage of 6,767, a length of 344 feet, and a draft of 19.6 feet.

Passengers: 128 in all berths. Passengers of every age travel in the ship, with St. Helenians, British, and South Africans predominating, plus Europeans and some Americans.

Dress: Jacket at dinnertime only

Officers/Crew: British and St. Helenian officers; St. Helenian crew

Cabins: 49; mostly outside with two to four berths, plus a few inside without facilities sold at subsidized fares for St. Helenians

Fare: $$

What's included: Sea fare only unless you purchase an air-sea package

What's not included: Shore excursions, tips, drinks, and the hotel or cottage stay on the island, which must be arranged in advance through the line or done independently by fax or e-mail

Other itineraries: In addition to the one-month southbound voyage described here, the RMS *St. Helena* makes similar northbound trips and round-trip voyages that sail from Cape Town to St. Helena via Luderitz and Walvis Bay, Namibia, where passengers go ashore for the week while the ship sails to Ascension and returns via St. Helena to embark passengers for Cape Town. Once a year, the ship also makes a two-week round-trip voyage to the even more remote island of Tristan da Cunha, located about halfway between South Africa and South America. This one sells out well in advance.

ABERCROMBIE & KENT'S
Sun Boat III
Egypt's Nile Valley

Abercrombie & Kent, one of the top expedition tour companies, operates an Egyptian program that uses luxury-level riverboats and forms groups for touring on land that do not exceed twenty-four participants. Well-educated Egyptologists, whose biographies appear in the brochures, provide a clear and highly palatable enrichment program that ferrets out a highly complex country's incredibly long history.

The *Sun Boat III,* one of the smallest on the Nile with just thirty-six berths, is a sleek-looking, well-maintained, four-deck riverboat with lots of outside space, both awning covered for reading, socializing, and taking in the riverbank sights and open for sunbathing and dipping in the Sun Deck pool. Tower Deck houses a lounge for lectures and showing videos, a separate lounge and bar for drinks, space for a barbecue lunch, and a comfy covered afterdeck with cane furniture. Additional amenities include a small gift shop, gym, massage room, card and board games, and laundry facilities.

The window-lined, no-smoking restaurant on Promenade Deck offers spectacular Nile views, so you miss nothing during meals. Seating is open and unassigned, and the menu includes excellent Egyptian/Middle Eastern dishes and nights with French and Italian themes. Fresh fruit is in abundance, and excellent local beer and palatable light wines are complimentary. Breakfast is an American-style buffet with eggs to order, lunch is a buffet, and dinner is served. The Egyptian staff is attentive and experienced.

The roomy, well-appointed cabins, located forward on three decks, are all windowed outsides with individually controlled air-conditioning, minibars, TVs, CD players, music channels, internal and international phone access, and bathrooms with showers and hair dryers. The lounges and cabins are delightful retreats after a long and sometimes hot day exploring the archaeological sites.

The Itinerary
The fourteen-day cruise tour described here, more comprehensive than most, sails downriver to Dendera and allows extra time in both Aswan and Luxor. When the number of passengers exceeds twenty-four, the

group is split into two for the land tour portion and shore excursions. The initial **Cairo** stay visits the Egyptian Museum of Antiquities and includes a drive across the Nile to Memphis and the Step Pyramid at Sakkara, the Great Pyramids, Sphinx, and the Solar Boat Museum.

Leaving Cairo, the flight south lands at **Abu Simbel** for a visit to the Temple of Rameses II, four 65-foot statues flanking the entrance where inside, vivid reliefs depict Rameses' battle triumphs. Adjacent is the equally impressive Temple of Nefertari, Rameses' favorite wife.

Boarding the *Sun Boat III* at **Aswan,** the vessel becomes a hotel moored at the riverbank, with plenty of time for browsing ashore and shopping at both Aswan and Luxor. A boat boarded from a landing behind the Aswan High Dam heads to the island Temple of Philae with a stop to see an enormous unfinished obelisk lying on the ground. Leaving Aswan, the *Sun Boat III* first makes a stop to see **Kom Ombo**'s unique features— double portals and double sanctuaries containing mummified crocodiles and a painted ceiling panel with the wings of Horus in a fine state of preservation. Farther downstream at **Edfu,** horse and carriage clip-clop out to the Temple of Horus, the falcon god, with its remarkable storytelling reverse reliefs. The entry to a passageway is decorated with two guardian Horuses.

Sailing on, the small temple at **Esna,** located in the middle of a lively town, is 30 feet below grade and is threatened by the rising water table, one of the many (and this time negative) consequences of the **Aswan Dam.** Unfortunately, it can't be moved; every inch of its twenty-four columns is covered with wonderful inscriptions and topped by unique capitals, several with stone frogs perched, peering over the edges.

At **Luxor,** visits are made to the **Temple of Karnak** with its great hypostyle hall, a forest of 134 high columns that rise 70 feet. On the Nile's West Bank opposite Luxor, the tombs in the Valleys are constantly being opened and closed, but you will see the Colossus of Memnon, the Rameseum and the mortuary Temple of Hatshepsut. In the **Valley of the Kings,** our group saw the burial chambers for Rameses III and VI, the latter with vividly painted scenes in a remarkable state of preservation. Our energetic guides got their groups to the ticket kiosk early enough to get the very limited number of first-come, first-served tickets for the tomb of Tutankhamon. The dramatic story of its discovery lost nothing in the retelling at the site.

The **Temple of Dendera,** up the map and down the Nile north of Luxor, is isolated at the edge of the desert, and the Roman-era structure, unique because of its intact roof and excellent overall condition, has a depiction of Cleopatra. There's even graffiti from a 1799 Napoleonic expedition. A morning is spent at Abydos, the holy city dedicated to Osiris, Lord of the Netherworld. The boat then returns to Luxor for visits to the Temple of Luxor, and to the excellent Luxor Museum for statuary found in the area and the mural from the Temple of Aton.

Returning by air to **Cairo,** the sightseeing encompasses Old Cairo's Coptic Christian Church, the Ben Ezra Synagogue and Hanging Gardens, and a nighttime Sound and Light performance at the Pyramids and Sphinx. Then on the last day, it's Islamic Egypt, with visits to the medieval Citadel of Salah-el-Din and Mohammed Ali's Mosque, and modern Egypt with a foray into the Khan el-Khalili bazaar.

It's a full program, but if one comes reasonably well informed, interest is not likely to flag, especially when the guides are as good as they usually are. Aboard ship, in the coaches, and at the sites, security was both conspicuous and unobtrusive. A shorter cruise tour is also available.

Address/Phone: Abercrombie & Kent, Inc., 1520 Kensington Road, Oak Brook, IL 60523; (800) 554–7016 or (630) 954–2944; fax: (630) 954–3324; www.abercrombiekent.com

The Ship: *Sun Boat III* was built in 1993 and has a shallow draft.

Passengers: 36 passengers; Americans and British, forty-five and up

Dress: Casual at all times

Officers/Crew: Egyptian

Cabins: 18 cabins; all outside, 14 are doubles and 4 are suites

Fare: $$$$

What's included: A complete package, including hotels; meals on land; transfers; excursions; beer, wine, and soft drinks at meals; tips at hotels and on the riverboat

What's not included: International and internal Egyptian airfares, bar drinks, and tips to Egyptologists

Highlights: Seeing some of the greatest sights in the Ancient World, with terrific guides, and accomplished in considerable comfort

Other itineraries: Besides this fourteen-day Nile cruise, plus a land portion that includes Cairo and area and Abu Simbel, which operates between mid-September and the end of May, A&K operates the larger eighty-passenger *Sun Boat IV* on shorter five-day Nile cruises plus land packages. In addition, A&K operates expedition-style cruises and tours worldwide.

SOUTHEAST ASIA
AND THE FAR EAST

STAR CLIPPERS'

Star Flyer

Thailand's Islands in the Andaman Sea

Seemingly a vision from the past, the tall ship *Star Flyer* faithfully re-creates the lure and romance of sailing on a true clipper ship. Cruising the idyllic and virtually undiscovered Andaman Sea islands off Thailand, passengers enjoy a delightfully social week of sailing and water sports without sacrificing too many cruise ship comforts.

It is impossible to prepare yourself. No matter how many pictures you've seen, your first glimpse of the *Star Flyer,* with her graceful bow stretching into a lengthy bowsprit and her three masts stretching 226 feet into the air, will literally send shivers down your spine.

Launched in 1991, this 360-foot vessel is one of the most beautiful sights on the ocean and delights both sailing purists and those seeking a reasonably priced alternative, ages apart from the Caribbean megaships. The culmination of a lifelong dream by Star Clippers owner Mikael Krafft, the *Star Flyer* is infused with the owner's zeal for sailing, and passengers take an active interest in their ship, often chatting with the captain on the bridge or listening to his morning navigational talks.

While not as luxurious as the Windstar vessels or as party-oriented as Windjammer Barefoot Cruises, these ships fall neatly in between and are the most authentic of the sailing cruise lines. Make no mistake—these are true sailing ships. Walk around and marvel at the myriad of rigging stretching skyward like a vertical spiderweb. Winches, cleats, and lines are scattered on all open decks, and whenever possible, the sails are used as the vessel's main propulsion.

Passengers come from around the world, with Americans often representing 10 percent or less of those onboard when in Asia. The spoken language is English, and most passengers are in their forties and fifties, with several honeymooners on each trip. As is common on a small ship, meeting and bonding with others on board becomes a valued and integral part of the experience.

Life on board is low-key, unplanned, and casual, with a heavy emphasis placed on a popular water-sports program. Upon anchoring offshore in the morning, a flotilla of boats and kayaks is dispatched to the beach, and a Zodiac takes divers directly from the ship to the dive spot. Toward sunset, everyone mingles around the open-air bar and chats with the ship's resident parrot before heading one deck up to watch the sails being set and the ship begin to heel to the breeze.

Happily, Star Clippers still lets passengers roam almost anywhere, including the bowsprit stretching 30 feet forward of the bow with its hammocklike netting suspended over the ocean, affording probably the most unique and delightful setting on any cruise ship afloat. Passengers are also given the opportunity to climb into a harness and scramble up the ratlines to a platform partway up the mast. It is an amazing experience, to be lost high up amidst the sails, looking at your ship below being driven through the waves by the wind.

Although rarely used, the ship's public rooms are pleasantly nautical and offer a nice respite for those who have had too much sun. The Piano Bar is centered underneath one of the two splash pools and is comfortable with round banquettes and sailing ship paintings and prints hung on the bulkhead. Aft of the outdoor bar is a small Edwardian-style library, complete with faux fireplace, where the cruise director may hold nightly talks on sailing history.

Nightlife tends to be a bit hokey, with the water-sports staff often putting on a fashion show or organizing silly deck games. Although hardly sophisticated, it does gather everyone outdoors by the bar after dinner, with dancing and socializing sure to follow until 1:00 A.M. or so. Occasionally, a movie will be shown on deck, and passengers might stop by the open bridge and enjoy the quiet sounds of rustling canvas found only on a ship under sail at sea before retiring to their cabin.

Breakfast and lunch are served buffet style in the restaurant, and all meals are open seating without an assigned table or set time. Service, while always friendly, can be rushed and occasionally forgetful, and the food could stand to be somewhat improved. Still, passengers come for the casual sailing atmosphere, not luxury, and hence rarely complain about anything. In keeping with the casual atmosphere, a Polo shirt is sufficient for dinner, with passengers donning a button-down shirt for the captain's dinner.

Cabins themselves are attractive and atmospheric and, with some shaped by the hull's curvature, can be authentically cozy, with the smallest accommodations measuring only 97 square feet. Although the bathrooms are generally tight, the cabin layout makes the rooms feel homey rather than cramped.

For those eager for a social, unique week at sea, there are few more appealing or invigorating cruise experiences available. Spotting your ship at anchor each day, you will be amazed that such a sight still exists and then feel privileged to be lucky enough to experience it.

The Itinerary

Star Clippers tends to shun the larger, more developed ports, and on the northern **Andaman Sea** itinerary, the *Star Flyer* is the only foreign commercial vessel allowed to stop at some islands. Sailing from the resort city of **Phuket, Thailand,** the *Star Flyer* sails north to the **Surin Islands** near the Burmese border, anchoring offshore of this national park around noon. Other than the local Thai families staying at the campground and the sea gypsies that still live on a neighboring island, you can expect a deserted island and great diving.

The next day the ship sails south to the **Similan Islands,** another uninhabited cluster of islands also known for their fantastic diving and tranquil beaches. Snorkeling, diving, waterskiing, and hiking to the top of the island round out another day in the sun.

The rest of the cruise continues this pattern—sailing for a few hours in the morning before anchoring off a beach until sunset. Although the islands farther south, Ko Rok Nok, Langkwai (Malaysia), and Phi Phi, have become slightly more discovered with day tourists from Phuket, there are hardly crowds to speak of. With beautiful islands strung closely together, the Andaman Sea seems to be the Caribbean long before it was discovered by the megaships—or even before chartered sailboats—and at a fraction of the cost.

The only disappointment with this itinerary is the lack of a consistent breeze, and although the crew will put on a brave face and often sail out of anchorages under sail alone, the engines come on at night far more frequently than on Caribbean or Mediterranean sailings.

The last day is spent sailing amidst the mesmerizing rock formations of **Phang Nga Bay.** Climbing into Zodiacs, you'll set off to explore sculpted, colored rock masses jutting straight out of the sea before returning to circle and photograph the ship under full sail. Having seen a sight you won't soon forget, you'll climb back aboard and settle in for one last night of being rocked to sleep before arriving in Phuket the next morning.

Address/Phone: Star Clippers, 4101 Salzebo Street, Coral Gables, FL 33146; (305) 442–0550 or reservations: (800) 442–0551; fax: (305) 442–1661; www.starclippers.com

The Ship: *Star Flyer* was built in 1991, has a gross tonnage of 2,298, a length of 360 feet, and a draft of 18.5 feet.

Passengers: 168 double occupancy; all ages, including Americans and Europeans; English is the lingua franca.

Dress: Casual at all times

Officers/Crew: European officers and international crew

Cabins: 78 of 84 are outside and most are relatively compact; no verandas

Fare: $$

What's included: Usually cruise only, although cruise tour rates will include air, hotels, some meals, some sightseeing, and transfers

What's not included: For cruise only, airfare, port charges, shore excursions, tips, drinks

Highlights: The ship is very much the destination, making one feel adventurous and recalling the sailing ship past; exotic itinerary for an exotic ship cruising with new-found friends

Other itineraries: Besides two seven-night alternating itineraries from Phuket, Thailand, along the west coast of Thailand and Malaysia, and seven-day trips between Phuket and Singapore, which are offered between November and March, the *Star Flyer* returns through the Indian Ocean to cruise the Greek islands and the Turkish coast from May to October. Between May and September, the *Star Clipper* and larger *Royal Clipper* offer alternative Western Mediterranean cruises, spring and fall transatlantic positioning voyages, and winter Caribbean itineraries.

SEABOURN CRUISE LINE'S
Seabourn Spirit
Coastal Vietnam Sojourn

The *Seabourn Spirit,* one of three roughly 10,000-gross-register-ton, 200-passenger sisters, provides the ultimate in quiet, luxurious shipboard living, albeit at a high price. Passengers are well-traveled couples or friends traveling together, and few will be making a first cruise. Socializing is a major part of life aboard. Decorated in an understated Scandinavian style, the Club, a glass-partitioned complex, includes a

lounge, a cocktail bar, and a casino. Drinks with music take place here before and after dinner, plus dancing and a cabaret show. During the days at sea, in the Amundsen Lounge, guest lecturers will give talks relating to East Asian history, relations with the United States, and economic issues.

With open seating for all meals, one has the choice of sitting alone or sharing a table. The menus are designed to encourage sampling five or six courses, and big eaters can order larger portions. The cold soups, rack of veal, saddle of venison, and broiled salmon were particularly memorable entrees, and, overall, the food and service are some of the best afloat. Poured wines are complimentary, as are all drinks. The Veranda Café offers both indoor seating and a single line of tables under a canvas awning at the stern, and breakfast time is a particularly friendly hour to meet other passengers. A chef takes special orders for eggs Benedict, Belgian waffles, and blueberry pancakes. Lunch is also served here and even more informally at the Sky Bar above the pool. The Veranda Café serves dinner by reservation, with an Italian, French, or Oriental theme.

Most passengers occupy similar 277-square-foot, one-room suites loaded with amenities with a large sitting area next to a picture window. Thirty-six suites have been refitted with French balconies, in place of the large windows. Amenities are minibar and refrigerator, flat-screen TV and DVD player, radio, walk-in closet with a safe, and marble bathroom with double sinks and a tub.

On a warm-weather cruise, the lido provides protection from the sun and two popular Jacuzzis for cooling off after a steamy day ashore, plus an awkwardly sited outdoor pool. The spa offers an exercise room, two saunas, steam rooms, and a masseuse.

The Itinerary

On this cruise, the *Seabourn Spirit* embarks in Singapore and Hong Kong, reversing the order of ports. Sailing north into the Gulf of Thailand, the ship's first call is at Bangkok, followed by the island of **Ko Kood,** and then a full day at sea. Sailing out of the South China Sea into the broad Mekong Delta, the ship follows the Saigon River channel to **Saigon,** now officially **Ho Chi Minh City.**

During the overnight stay docked next to the city center, visits include the former South Vietnamese presidential palace. Legacies from nineteenth-century French colonial days are Notre Dame Cathedral, the General Post Office, and the former City Hall. At the National Museum, a repository of Vietnamese and Chinese art, the Vietnamese water puppet show has unseen performers who maneuver colorful representations of fish, serpents, frogs, and humans.

A two-hour drive takes you to the Cu Chi Tunnels, a maze of underground passages and chambers started after World War II; from their well-concealed entrances, the Viet Cong sniped at the enemy and quickly retreated underground, where they could remain for weeks at a time. Several hundred feet of tunnels at three levels have been enlarged to allow tourists to explore, though it's not recommended for the claustrophobic.

Following two nights and a day at sea, the ship calls at **Danang.** From here a three-hour scenic drive north along Route 1 crosses the Cloud Pass and descends to hug the low coastline into **Hue.** The city, located along the Perfume River, offers a glimpse at what formerly was a grand imperial palace virtually leveled during the 1968 Tet Offensive.

For the visit to **Hanoi,** this cruise calls at **Hongai,** but other cruises may use **Haiphong Harbor.** Regardless, the drive inland passes through a timeless landscape of rice paddies. Hanoi, a low-rise city built around Chinese-style lakes, presents a far slower pace than Saigon. A somber mausoleum, guarded by smartly uniformed soldiers, holds the embalmed body of Ho Chi Minh, the country's much-loved patriot who died in 1969. There may be time to explore the Quarter of 36 Streets, each block specializing in some commodity such as paper goods, silver, silk, flowers, or hardware.

Entering **Halong Bay,** a national park made up of 3,000 towering limestone islets, you cruise through a fantastic natural wonder, similar to the conical peaks that dot the River Li at Guilin in China. After a final day at sea, the ship sails into **Hong Kong** harbor. Most visitors stay a few days to ride the incline railway for the view from Victoria Peak, or cross the island to seaside Repulse Bay and Aberdeen's typhoon shelter. On the **Kowloon** side there are visits to a Taoist temple, the jade and bird market, and Nathan and Canton Road shops.

Address/Phone: Seabourn Cruise Line, 610 Blue Lagoon Drive, Suite 400, Miami, FL 33126; (305) 563–3000 or (800) 929–9391; fax: (305) 463–3070; www.seabourn.com

The Ship: *Seabourn Spirit* was built in 1989 and has a gross tonnage of 9,975, a length of 440 feet, and a draft of 17 feet.

Passengers: 204; mostly Americans, some Europeans, age fifty and up

Dress: Formal and casual nights

Officers/Crew: Norwegian officers; mostly European crew, plus some Filipinos

Cabins: 102; all outside suites, the majority identical except for location; six with verandas. Thirty-six French balconies (window-type double doors set before a railing) have been added to some suites in the place of sealed windows.

Fare: $$$$$

What's included: Cruise, port charges, wine and drinks, tips, and a special Seabourn shore excursion

What's not included: Airfare, governmental fees, transfers, shore excursions

Highlights: A luxurious and enriching way to visit Vietnam

Other itineraries: In addition to this fourteen-day cruise tour between Singapore and Hong Kong, Seabourn offers global itineraries, including *Seabourn Pride* in South America.

VICTORIA CRUISES'
Victoria Star and *Victoria Queen*
Cruising the Yangtze

In 1994 Victoria Cruises, a Sino-American joint venture, brought international standards to Yangtze River travel when the 154-passenger *Victoria I* entered service, followed by *Victoria II, III, V,* and *VI,* and six additional ships. First-time visitors to China will want to visit several destinations such as Beijing, Shanghai, Suzhou, Xian, and Guilin, so Victoria Cruises concentrates on the Yangtze's most scenic portion, the 870 miles between Wuhan and Chongqing, a trip of four nights downstream and five nights upstream.

Victoria Cruises has introduced a new generation of larger and more sophisticated ships for more than 200 passengers with the addition of three vessels in 2004—the rebuilt *Victoria Star,* the *Victoria Queen,* and the brand-new *Victoria Katarina*—and three more rebuilt—the *Victoria Empress, Victoria Rose,* and *Victoria Prince.*

The *Victoria Katarina,* completed in 2004 and the company's largest vessel, has 133 cabins (119 standard rooms and 14 suites to take up to 266 passengers). All cabins are roomy and have bathtubs, balconies, and closed-circuit films. The ships have atriums with chandeliers and walls of gleaming woods; overall decor features European influences and Asian accents.

The single-seating Dynasty Dining Room serves American breakfasts and lunch buffet style and serves dinner banquet style with both Western and Chinese fare. The Yangtze Club, with a small and the only smoking section on the ships, hosts cultural presentations, fashion shows, and traditional Chinese music. Additionally, Tai-chi, calligraphy, Chinese language, and kite flying lessons are offered. Additional amenities and services are a beauty salon, traditional massage, facials and acupuncture, fitness room, library, and gift shop. Outdoor space is generous for viewing the sometimes outstanding scenery.

The Itinerary

The **Yangtze** is south China's principal highway, and tugs, barges, cargo ships, ferries, passenger steamers, and cruise boats maneuver along the constantly shifting channel. This cruise shows the many aspects of this complex country and includes a visit to the world's largest dam.

At the smoky industrial town of **Yichang,** the boat passes through the Gezhouba Dam, China's largest, rising 65 feet in a single lock. This dam is nothing compared to the 600-foot-high **Three Gorges Dam** just upriver at **Sandouping,** which is beginning to flood many historical sites. If everything goes as planned, by 2009 a reservoir will stretch back 370 miles, submerging 1,500 towns and villages and 72,000 acres of agricultural land, forcing the resettlement of 1.3 million people. The project is expected to supply 15 percent of China's electricity, control flooding, facilitate navigation by eliminating rapids, and boost national pride.

During the stop at **Wushan,** make your way up a lively main street of shops and food stalls to high ground overlooking the junction of the Yangtze and **Daning** Rivers. At the far end of town, you board longboats that sputter up through the Daning River rapids into the **Three Little Gorges,** and when the strong currents threaten to stop progress, two men pole mightily to maintain headway.

The main event, the passage through the **Three Gorges,** extends over two days. The 47-mile **Xiling Gorge** at one time was considered the most dangerous of all. Numerous steamers came to grief in the rock-strewn rapids before a safe channel was blasted through in the 1950s. A temple, built 1,500 years ago, is silhouetted against the sky. The 35-mile **Wu Gorge**'s sheer cliffs rise to green-clad limestone peaks often enshrouded in swirling mists, and the highest, Goddess Peak, resembles a woman kneeling in front of a pillar. **Qutang Gorge** is dramatically flanked by 4,000-foot mountains that squeeze the river into a narrow canyon, inhibiting two-way traffic.

Beyond the attractive walled city of **Fengjie,** where stone steps lead up from the river landings to Ming Dynasty gates, hundreds of porters load coal into baskets and with rapid steps file down to ships at the water's edge. At **Fengdu,** known as the City of Ghosts, a temple complex, which dates back to the Han Dynasty (206 B.C. to A.D. 220), has undergone extensive reconstruction. Disembarking at **Chongqing,** passengers will see that the city is usually enveloped in fog, a natural phenomenon exacerbated by industrial pollution.

Address/Phone: Victoria Cruises, 57-08 39th Avenue, Woodside, NY 11377; (800) 348–8084 or (212) 818–1680; fax: (212) 818–9889; www.victoriacruises.com

The Ships: *Victoria Star* and *Victoria Queen*, rebuilt in 2004, are 4,587 gross tons, 289 feet in length, and have drafts of 8.5 feet. The other vessels are similar in size and standards.

Passengers: 206; age range is forty and up, Americans mostly on China tours; also many Chinese Americans, Chinese from all over Asia, and some Europeans

Dress: Casual

Officers/Crew: All Chinese, plus American cruise and enrichment staff

Cabins: 103 cabins; all outside with balconies, 93 standard rooms, and 10 suites

Fare: $$

What's included: For independent travelers (those not part of a tour), the cruise fare includes port charges and tea, coffee, and soft drinks with meals

What's not included: Airfare, tips, drinks not served at meals, and shore excursions

Highlights: The Three Gorges, plus a terrific insight into rural and industrial China

Other itineraries: In addition to the above cruise between Wuhan and Chongqing, which is offered between March and December, the company operates longer Yangtze River trips between Shanghai and Chongqing, nine days up and seven days downstream. The best travel months are May and June and September and October; July and August are unpleasantly hot and humid; fog descends on the river in winter. Several of the tour operators that include the Yangtze in their programs are Pacific Delight Tours, (800) 221–7179, www.pacific delighttours.com; Travcoa, (800) 992–2003, www.travcoa.com; and Uniworld, (800) 360–9550, www.uniworld.com.

POLAR REGIONS

CLIPPER CRUISE LINE'S
Clipper Adventurer
Cruising the White Continent and the Falklands

St. Louis–based Clipper Cruise Line, in business since 1983, operates four small ships, one of which is the 122-passenger *Clipper Adventurer,* introduced in 1988. Rebuilt from the Russian-flag *Alla Tarasova,* the ship operates in the style of a seagoing club and is a graceful, stabilized beauty within and without.

The public rooms, paneled with mahogany-wood grain, include a forward lounge and bar, seating all passengers for talks, films, and light breakfast and lunch buffets. The Clipper Club, a second bar with card tables and settees, leads aft to an open-seating restaurant with wraparound windows. The menus feature grilled salmon, sea bass, roasted duckling, prime ribs, tasty wild mushroom and roasted pepper soups, fresh salads, and freshly baked cakes and pies. The library, one deck above, is a warm and quiet retreat for readers, puzzle addicts, and board-game players. With an open-bridge policy, the ship provides passengers with another popular social center, and it's just a few steps down to the forward observation deck.

The all outside cabins (portholes or windows) fall into seven categories and have parallel or L-shaped twin beds, good closet space, and bathrooms with showers. Promenade Deck cabins look through two sets of glass to the sea.

The Itinerary

The Antarctic continent is the most pristine and least populated place on earth, and an international treaty signed in 1959 aims to keep it that way. Antarctica's wildlife is the tamest and least fearful of humankind, and its scenery, seen through the clearest air, presents a breathtaking combination of majestic mountains draped by massive glaciers and rugged islands spread across a seascape peppered with icebergs longer than a football field. Include the Falkland Islands, and the nimble *Clipper Adventurer* will take on an adventure cruise in a thoroughly professional manner. Some departures include South Georgia, adding six days to the itinerary.

The group meets in **Buenos Aires,** the most European of all South American cities, and with the devaluation of the local currency, now far more reasonably priced to enjoy. The architecture is outstanding, borrowing from classical and flamboyant styles found in London, Paris, and Madrid, and the street life energetic, especially after dark. Visit Eva Perón's mausoleum in Recoleta Cemetery, the antique district, the city's restaurant row for an Argentinean steak restaurant and the tango.

A flight south to the southern Argentinean port of **Ushuaia** leads to a half-day tour of a small corner of mountainous Tierra del Fuego before embarking in the *Clipper Adventurer.* Orientation talks are scheduled during the two nights and a day en route to the **Falklands,** the British islands invaded by Argentina in 1982, resulting in a nasty war between the two countries that Britain eventually won.

The first wet Zodiac (inflatable craft) landing visits a cliffside rookery of nesting rockhopper penguins, black-browed albatross, and blue-eyed cormorants. Seated on a nearby rock, wearing rubber boots and parkas provided by the ship, I watched a well-ordered line of 2-foot-high penguins literally hop their way up the steep path from the beach, bellies full of fish and krill (shrimp-like crustacean) for regurgitating into the mouths of their fluffy chicks. A second landing provided a gentle 3-mile walk through a hillside colony of burrowing Magellanic penguins that pop up to have a look as we pass. **Port Stanley,** the island capital, is a sleepy bit of old England transferred to the South Atlantic with the world's most southerly Anglican cathedral and an eccentric museum packed with historic and natural history exhibits overlooked by a delightful curator.

During the forty-eight-hour crossing of the **Drake Passage,** which can be extremely rough or mercifully calm, the naturalists might help spot Wilson's storm petrels, Antarctic terns, and the huge wandering albatross boasting a wing span of up to 9 feet. Landings on the Antarctic Peninsula and South Shetland Islands may vary from cruise to cruise because of high winds and weather, but you will see colonies of Adélie, chinstrap, and gentoo penguins in several locations such as **Half Moon** or **Paulet Islands** and **Paradise Bay.** When going ashore, stay as long as you can to enjoy their antics. The Antarctic summer comes with almost twenty-four hours of daylight and temperatures that may rise into the fifties, and they can plunge quickly when the weather changes.

Cruising into the drowned caldera of **Deception Island,** the *Clipper Adventurer* drops anchor for a walk among the eerie ruins of a whaling station and British research base, quickly abandoned just prior to a volcanic eruption in 1969. Steam and the smell of sulfur percolate through the black sand.

Continuing south into the **Lemaire Channel,** towering icebergs with fantastic shapes and shades of blue and green often generate their own strong winds even when it otherwise seems calm. Other landings add the sight and smell of molting young elephant seals, weighing up to 4,000 pounds; minke whales; and crabeater seals; and a call at a working Ukrainian research station.

At **Port Lockroy,** go ashore to a once closed and now reopened British base, where whale bones from a century ago litter the beaches, and from the Zodiacs leopard seals may be seen lazily lying about on ice floes.

Elephant Island, named after the elephant seals that live here, is also home to fur seals and thousands of penguins. For some four months the main part of Ernest Shackleton's pioneering party lived here after their ship, the *Endurance,* was crushed by ice. Shackleton and five men set off in a small boat to get help, which eventually came after landing on South Georgia some 800 miles away.

Northbound, hold on for a second crossing of the **Drake Passage,** understandably feared by the legendary Cape Horners battling monstrous seas for days on end, until the ship reaches the lee of **Tierra del Fuego,** finally docking at **Ushuaia.** A charter flight transfers you to **Santiago, Chile,** for an evening, overnight, and city sightseeing before then returning home.

Address/Phone: Clipper Cruise Line, 11969 Westline Industrial Drive, St. Louis, MO 63146; reservations: (800) 325–0010; brochures: (800) 282–7245; fax: (314) 727–6576; www.clippercruise.com

The Ship: *Clipper Adventurer,* built in 1975 as the Russian-flag *Alla Tarasova* and rebuilt in 1998, has a gross tonnage of 4,575, a length of 330 feet, and a draft of 16 feet.

Passengers: 122; age fifty and up, nearly all American

Dress: Casual at all times

Officers/Crew: Scandinavian; Filipino officers; American bar staff; Filipino waitstaff, deckhands, and cabin stewardesses

Cabins: 61; all outside, average size

Fare: $$$$

What's included: Cruise, port charges, all shore excursions, gratuities, charter flights to and from the ship, hotel nights in Buenos Aires and Santiago

What's not included: Airfare between home and South America, drinks

Highlights: Incredible beauty of Antarctica, icebergs, many types of penguins, remote research stations, British colony of the Falklands, excellent enrichment program

Other itineraries: In addition to this sixteen-day Antarctica and the Falklands winter cruise itinerary, several longer cruises also include South Georgia. The *Clipper Adventurer* offers late spring and summer trips in the Mediterranean, Northern Europe, Iceland, Greenland, and Eastern Canada; and in fall south along the U.S. East Coast to South America and the Amazon. The *Yorktown Clipper* cruises California's river and Alaska, and the *Nantucket Clipper* cruises the East Coast.

LINDBLAD EXPEDITIONS'
National Geographic Endeavour
Antarctica, Falklands, and South Georgia

Originally built for the North Sea fishing industry, the *National Geographic Endeavour* is an extremely well-built and well-maintained expedition ship that was very recently refitted. The Scandinavian officers and Filipino crew provide a disciplined yet happy ship, and they mix well with the older, well-traveled, and mostly American passengers. The ship has an open-bridge policy, a very popular feature. With a hull hardened for ice and a deep 21-foot draft, she can take the pounding seas of the South Atlantic and upon occasion has seen the worst weather that nature can produce.

On the Bridge Deck, a small, large-windowed library offers comfortable seating and lots of books on history, ecology, geography, and fauna and flora, plus twenty-four-hour coffee- and tea-making facilities. Aft is a cluster that includes a small gym with treadmills, bikes, a sauna, and an e-mail station. The Veranda Deck below houses the spacious lounge and bar where evening recaps take place; plus the lecture program—up to three on a sea day—that often includes slides and videos screened on flat-screen TV monitors.

One naturalist is a diver who will show footage taken that same day of undersea marine life such as shrimp, octopus, dolphins, and acrobatic seals. A professionally produced ninety-minute trip video, with music and commentary, is available for purchase at the end of the cruise.

Forward on the Upper Deck, the restaurant has an open-seating policy, with tables for two to eight, buffet-style meals for breakfast and lunch, and table service from a menu for dinner. The food gets good marks for variety, preparation, and presentation.

The cabins are comfortable, all outside with windows or portholes, and most have beds placed athwartships to minimize rolling. The cabin radio airs announcements and music, and the closet and drawer space is adequate for a casual cruise. There is a lock drawer. As on Lindblad's other ships, there are no cabin keys. Viewing is excellent from the forward observation deck, the bow, the bridge wings, and the port and starboard sides and aft. Some of the deck space is sheltered.

The Itinerary

For the whole nine yards, this granddaddy of an itinerary includes it all, the Antarctic Peninsula, the Falklands, South Orkneys, and South Georgia. Other shorter departures cover all but the roundtrip to South Georgia, and the shortest, fifteen days, just Antarctica.

The complete twenty-five-day cruise begins in **Santiago, Chile,** with a night's hotel stay in a residential section and hosted sightseeing. The city combines Spanish colonial with European and modern architecture, and two of specific sights will be the presidential palace and the vast cathedral square area. Not far away, the central market must be one of the world's largest with some curious eatable shellfish, including huge barnacles, from the Humboldt Current waters off the Chilean coast.

Then fly south to **Ushuaia,** South America's southernmost city, located on the island of Tierra del Fuego, to board the *Endeavour.* During the two-night passage east to the Falkland Islands, the expedition staff will introduce their many subjects of expertise and prepare you for your first landings.

Going ashore by Zodiac at a combination sheep farm and nature preserve in the **Falklands,** there is a slight climb to a cliffside rookery of nesting rock-hopper penguins, black-browed albatross, and blue-eyed cormorants with all the smells and sounds associated with such colonies. The most enjoyable to watch are the rock-hoppers leaping from ledge to ledge as they make their way back from the sea to feed their chicks with fish and krill (shrimp-like crustacean). A second landing may include a walk across a sloping meadow, home of the burrowing Magellanic penguins, who at the sound of feet will pop up to see what's what.

Port Stanley is the only Falklands community of any size, and the locals of English descent have an accent all their own. One topic will likely be the nasty 1982 war precipitated by Argentine forces landing on British soil in South Georgia. While there is no evidence of damage in Port Stanley, the surrounding fields are still full of plastic mines, and anyone venturing off the main paths should have a map issued by the Ministry of Defense. The quiet town offers a museum collection of historic and natural history exhibits, a small cathedral, and the chance to buy wonderfully warm handmade woolen sweaters.

Between the Falklands and South Georgia, Shag Rocks, cone-shaped protrusions rising from the sea, swarm with bird life, and here on one cruise eight Wright whales were sighted. The *Endeavour* will then make numerous landings on **South Georgia** at such places as **King Haakon Bay** on the west coast where Ernest Shackleton landed after an 800-mile, open-ocean crossing in a 22-foot boat from the Antarctic Peninsula, and **Peggotty Camp** where he began his march across the island to his rescue. At **St. Andrews Bay,** on the lee side of the island, passengers may have a beach reception committee of literally thousands of king penguins, plus a herd of elephant seals that deserve a wide berth.

At **Grytviken,** an abandoned whaling station, naturalists offer a 2-mile hike over mountain. The settlement has a museum of South Georgia island history, remnants of the whaling activities, and the cemetery where Shackleton is buried.

En route to the Antarctic Peninsula, the *Endeavour* will pause at the seldom-visited **South Orkney Islands** for Zodiac excursion to watch penguins and leopard seals float past on icebergs, pintado and snow petrels fly overhead, and sheathbills or a lone wandering albatross staying with the ship for hours, and the latter sometimes for several days.

Arriving at the **Antarctic Peninsula,** the four days devoted here require a completely flexible schedule that depends on the wind and weather and ice conditions. The captain keeps watch to see that the ship does not get caught in pack ice should a change of wind direction cause the ice to shift. One likely landing will be **Elephant Island,** where in 1916 Ernest Shackleton and his crew made their longest stay, after having to abandon the expedition ship *Endurance.* He and a handful of men then set out in the small boat for South Georgia.

The *Endeavour* sails into **Deception Island**'s water-filled extinct volcano, where a now abandoned whaling station once employed one hundred men. It's an eerie place littered with ruined buildings and machinery surrounded by lava flows and black volcanic sand underfoot.

In **Lemaire Channel,** known as Iceberg Alley, chunks of ice from small bergy bits up to cathedral-size masses float by exhibiting blues and greens and wondrous shapes under a sky that can be as clear as any you will ever see or one that is gray and threatening with the coming of winter.

Still, most landings during the Antarctic summer will be warmer than you might have expected, especially when the sun, during the twenty-four hours of daylight, is reflecting off the ice and snow. Besides orcas and minke whales, likely to be seen are leopard and Weddell seals, and hundreds of Adélie, chinstrap, and gentoo penguins.

Following four days on the Antarctic Peninsula, the return passage across the Drake Passage can be mild or stormy.

This is the ultimate in a deep South Atlantic cruise, and the passengers who come aboard are in for the best that Lindblad has to offer—the fine ship, its personnel and the staff of naturalists who share their knowledge and enthusiasm at informal presentations, meals, in Zodiacs, and ashore.

Address/Phone: Lindblad Expeditions, 96 Morton Street, New York, NY 10014; (212) 765–7740 or (800) 397–3348; fax: (212) 265–3370; www.expeditions.com

The Ship: *National Geographic Endeavour* was originally built in 1966 for the fishing industry. It was rebuilt as a cruise ship and renamed *North Star* and *Caledonian Star* before taking on the current name. The gross tonnage is 3,132, the length is 295 feet, and the draft is 21 feet.

Passengers: 110, mostly Americans, age fifty-five and up

Dress: Casual

Officers/Crew: Scandinavian officers; Filipino crew

Cabins: 62; all outside, twin beds, no verandas

Fare: $$$$

What's included: Cruise, port charges, airfare between Santiago and the ship, shore excursions

What's not included: Airfare between home and Santiago, tips, drinks

Highlights: In-depth tour of Antarctica, the Falklands, and South Georgia; Shackleton connections, naturalist staff, ambience on board

Other itineraries: Apart from this twenty-five-day cruise to Antarctica, the Falklands, and South Georgia, the *Endeavour* also makes fifteen-day cruises to Antarctica between November and February, sails along the South America coast, and in Northern Europe and the Mediterranean. The *Polaris* and *Islander* cruise within the Galápagos, and the *Sea Lion* and *Sea Bird* cruise to Alaska, along the Columbia and Snake Rivers, along California rivers, and in the Sea of Cortez. The *Sea Voyager* cruises in Central America.

CIRCUMNAVIGATIONS
AND LONG VOYAGES

HOLLAND AMERICA LINE'S
Prinsendam
Voyaging to Seven Continents

The *Prinsendam,* Holland America's new world cruiser, has a past dating back to 1988, when she entered service for the Royal Viking Line as the *Royal Viking Sun.* The ship was designed to bring back roominess and space, which had been lost when the original early-1970s 22,000-ton Royal Viking trio had midsections inserted and tonnage increased to 28,500 and passenger capacity got upped to 750. The *Royal Viking Sun* carried 758 passengers within a ship of 37,845 gross tons. When Royal Viking was disbanded, the *Royal Viking Sun* became the *Seabourn Sun* for Cunard's Seabourn division, an awkward fit as she was so much larger than the original Seabourn trio and the Sea Goddess pair. Then in May 2002 she was transferred to Holland America and, after a makeover, reemerged as the *Prinsendam* to cruise Alaska and make a global voyage, taking over the latter role from the *Amsterdam* and *Rotterdam.*

With a roomy passenger space ratio of 47.6, she has taken on many familiar Holland America Line features, yet with half the passenger capacity of the rest of the fleet, she has a clubby atmosphere and is distinctive and well suited to take on ambitious worldwide itineraries. The officers are European, and the crew includes some Dutch but mostly Indonesians and Filipinos.

Approaching the ship, she sports a blue hull and once aboard, a curved double staircase rises through the five-deck atrium, decorated with handsome glass bas-reliefs, tubular glass sculpture, and Dutch maritime art. Promenade Deck is Grand Central, and from the atrium public rooms, renamed to coincide with the HAL fleet, range fore and aft.

Forward, the Queens Lounge, the ship's 424-seat show room, mounts five new productions each cruise on a new stage. Walking aft past the Erasmus Library, furnished with four leather chairs, the angled corridor becomes a shopping arcade leading to the one-hundred-seat Wajang Theater, used to screen films and host lectures. The clubby Java Bar and Cafe connects to the Oak Room, a largely original smoking lounge with electric fireplace, and to the moderately small casino, offering roulette, poker games, blackjack, dice, and slot machines. On the starboard side, the former Compass Rose has been freshly transformed into the Explorer's Lounge, a walk-through piano bar furnished with tan leather chairs, dark veneer paneling, and a patterned wine-red carpet. The artwork is a traditional-style Dutch maritime painting on aluminum and a set of drawings touting early Dutch exploration.

Lower Promenade features a continuous wraparound walking deck where four laps equal a mile and the width permits easy passing, but not a line of lounge-style deck chairs as with the rest of the fleet. Within are the restaurants, and it is here that there are significant changes.

The main restaurant aboard the ship as built could handle all passengers at one seating, but to match the rest of the fleet, it has been downsized for two seatings. Most passengers will want to secure a table in the after big-window section rather than the starboard side passage. Tables are set with Rosenthal china and Holland America–embossed silverware, and for dinner the chairs are covered with a white drapery, giving the otherwise handsome room a sterile look.

The former midships section of the restaurant has been converted into Holland America's trademark Ocean Bar, the ship's social center. The fore-aft varnished wood deck passage runs through the lower lounge section parallel to the promenade deck windows and to the bar, dance floor, and bandstand recessed on the raised interior portion.

The pièce de résistance is this ship's Pinnacle Grill, formerly the Odyssey Restaurant, an alternative dining venue offering a Pacific Northwest menu at an extra charge. It looks out onto the Lower Promenade, and it offers just forty-eight seats in a lovely paneled setting with Murano glass wall sconces set against a wine red and pale yellow fabric, the rich colors also matching the carpet. Suite passengers get the first shot at reservations.

Moving to an altogether different part of the ship, the Crow's Nest high up on Sports Deck is a lovely blue, green, and aquamarine observation lounge, bar, and piano bar. Its scale is much more intimate and better arranged for viewing than the vast three-sectioned Crow's Nests on the bigger ships.

The outdoor spaces are many, including cozy fore and aft sections on several decks and the standard lido-style pool deck. This ship does not have a Magrodome, and the oversize whirlpool is almost as large as the small swimming pool. A larger pool is tucked aft behind the spa, gym, and beauty salon complex. The lido restaurant is designed with double lines, plus a terrace grill, ice-cream bar and sit-up bar, and a most attractive awning-covered seating area aft. Other spaces are an eleven-station Internet Cafe, meeting and card rooms, art gallery, practice tennis, volleyball/basketball court, and golf driving range.

There are 398 cabins in seven categories, including just twenty-five insides and 145 with private verandas. A new block of ten poorly designed balcony cabins are in a cluster aft in a private section of promenade deck. Eight have balconies that those on the deck above can look down into, and two have smoked glass enclosures jutting out onto the aft deck. The Midnight Sun Lounge was sadly sacrificed to up the passenger capacity. The nineteen suites on Sports and Lido Decks have use of the Neptune Lounge with veranda for reading, snacks, and concierge services. All cabins have telephones with computerized wake-up service, multichannel music system, and closed-circuit television. All but the insides have full tub baths.

Holland America's *Prinsendam* shows how an outclassed dowager can be transferred into a clubby world cruiser.

The Itinerary

The *Prinsendam* has held down the world cruise for the last few years, substituting for the *Amsterdam* and *Rotterdam*. The January into April itinerary is revamped every year to keep the loyalists coming back, and in 2006, for example, the route is not a complete circumnavigation but nonetheless a highly creative selection of ports to all seven continents.

The 105-day cruise begins at **Fort Lauderdale** in early January, and passengers making the complete voyage may disembark in either Fort Lauderdale or New York, the latter adding another three days. With all due speed the ship heads south with several sea days to settle into a routine before calling in at **Barbados** and **Devil's Island**, a former French penal colony. Then the cycle of ports begins in earnest with a sail into the

Amazon and coastal stops in Brazil, Uruguay, and Argentina, the major destinations being **Rio de Janeiro** and **Buenos Aires,** each for two days.

Nature takes precedence with a sail through the Beagle Channel and past Cape Horn then across the Drake Passage to the **Antarctic Peninsula** to cruise among the ice and islands, but there is no landing with such a large ship. Remoteness continues with calls at **South Georgia** and **Tristan da Cunha,** both tiny outposts of the British Empire.

Cape Town rates three days for inland trips to the wine country and the Garden Route, then it's up the South Africa coast via game park safaris to **Madagascar,** the **Comores, Zanzibar,** and **Mombasa** for another three-day call. Travel up the coast to Arab-influenced Lamu and inland to Kenya's famous game parks in the shadow of Mount Kilimanjaro. Crossing the Indian Ocean, there's a call in the tropical **Seychelles** then onto India with a call at **Cochin,** a city with Chinese, Arab, British, and now Indian influences. Three days are spent docked at **Mumbai** (Bombay) for tours to **Rajasthan, New Delhi, Agra,** and the Taj Mahal.

Recrossing the Indian Ocean then into the Red Sea, the destination is **Egypt,** the Nile Valley, Cairo and the Pyramids, and a **Suez Canal** passage. In the Mediterranean, there is a rapid succession of calls in **Turkey, Greece, Libya, Sicily, Italy, Corsica,** and **Spain** then out into the Atlantic to **Madeira** and transatlantic to **Fort Lauderdale** and north to **New York.**

As with all global voyages, many choose to do just a two- or three-week segment such as Cape Town to Mumbai or Mombasa to Rome. The *Prinsendam,* built for long ocean voyages, is an ideal world wanderer.

Address/Phone: Holland America Line, 300 Elliott Avenue West, Seattle, WA 98119; (800) 426–0327; fax: (206) 281–7110; www.hollandamerica.com

The Ship: *Prinsendam* was completed in 1988, originally sailing as the *Royal Viking Sun,* then *Seabourn Sun.* She now measures 37,845 gross tons, has a length of 674 feet, and a draft of 23.6 feet.

Passengers: 794, mostly Americans, fifty-five and up on the world cruise

Dress: Formal, informal, and casual nights

Officers/Crew: Officers are Dutch and European, and the crew is Indonesian and Filipino

Cabins: 398, of which 368 are outside and 145 have balconies

Fare: $$$

What's included: Cruise fare only

What's not included: Airfare, port charges, tips, drinks, shore excursions

Highlights: Sailing aboard a ship built for world cruising

Other itineraries: Besides this world cruise that operates between January and April, the *Prinsendam* operates to Alaska in the summer, and the combined Holland America fleet covers North and South America and Europe plus some long circle Pacific cruises.

DISCOVERY WORLD CRUISES'

Discovery

From Northern Europe to the South Pacific

The 650-passenger, 20,216-ton *Discovery* began her sea life in 1972 as the *Island Venture* then in a few short years became the *Island Princess*, one of the original Love Boats operating for many years under the Princess Cruises' banner. After a short career taking tourists from South Korea to a sacred mountain site in North Korea, Gerrod Herrod, who started Ocean Cruise Lines and Orient Lines, bought and impressively refitted her for a relaunch in mid-2003. The *Discovery* is one of the last ships to be designed with upward sheer, that graceful curve to the decks that is so pleasing to the eye, and coupled with streamlining, gives her an ocean liner profile. With a strong hull and deep draft her sea-keeping abilities are good, and her small size is key to exploring out-of-the-way places.

The line prides itself by offering intriguing itineraries, well-planned shore excursions, good guest lecturers, and local cultural entertainment brought on board wherever possible, all at a moderate price. The ship operates under the double banner of the British firm Voyages of Discovery and the American subsidiary Discovery World Cruises, and she draws British, Americans, Australians, and New Zealanders, a kind of English-speaking Union.

On my voyage embarking at Fort Lauderdale for England, I found the atmosphere low-key and traditional. The sea days offered enrichment lectures, films, deck games, gym and spa facilities, afternoon tea, reading, and lots of socializing.

Navigating the ship with its moderate size and organized layout is relatively simple. Public rooms stretch the length of

Riviera Deck with naturally lighted side galleries providing an enclosed promenade. A view of the sea is never far away.

A retractable dome allows for all-weather use of the pool and two whirlpools and provides a well-protected space to enjoy buffet breakfasts and lunches. Outdoor deck space is generous and wind-protected.

Colorful furniture patterns give a cheerful atmosphere, especially where natural light streams in. Several public rooms have forward or aft-facing views, and they lend themselves to reading, quiet contemplation, and conversation during the day, and take on a more social buzz in the evening.

The Discovery Lounge and adjoining Explorer Bar have a wide swath of two-deck-high glass looking out onto aft pool deck. Passengers gather inside for drinks and dancing before and after dinner. The curved mezzanine above holds the card room. On the starboard side amidships, the Palm Court serves as a connecting gallery, reading room, and the main location for afternoon tea with light streaming in through the promenade deck-style windows.

The forward-facing Carousel Show Lounge provides gently terraced semicircular seating for specialty lectures, one of the line's strengths, and evening entertainment such as classical concerts, singers, comedians, crew shows, and local folkloric acts. Additional venues are an impressive book library; smallish casino with four roulette, blackjack, and poker gaming tables and three-dozen slot machines; a cinema; night club; gym; spa and beauty salon; Internet Center; Photo Gallery; boutique; and an impressive two-deck-high reception lounge with mezzanine.

The 351 average-size cabins and suites include 222 outsides (windows or portholes) and none with private balconies. Seventeen cabin categories are spread over five decks, and furniture arrangements often vary further from room to room at the same rate. Bed arrangements include twin or double beds (some in L-shaped configuration), direct-dial telephones, TVs, safes, and built-in hair dryers. All categories have some cabins with a third upper berth or a sofa bed, and a few can accommodate four. A large number are set aside for single travelers.

For dining, the Seven Continents Restaurant handles passengers at two sittings (6:30 P.M. and 8:30 P.M.) at assigned round and banquette tables for four to eight, low down in the ship for stability and with not much of a view. It's a sprawling room, partly divided by low partitions and slightly raised at the sides. The food is good international fare, well-prepared and varied, and the polite Filipino service of a very high standard.

The eighty-seat Yacht Club, a high-up observation venue, serves as the alternative restaurant on most nights offering varied Asian, East-meets-West, Italian, and South Pacific menus, geared to the cruising region. Reservations are required, and there is no extra charge. If you dine early, you will get a sweeping view of the sea ahead.

Aft on the same deck, the Lido Buffet serves breakfast and lunch in an open setting, under cover of the lido deck overhang or inside in the Yacht Club. At lunch, the pasta station serves a daily special, and occasional elaborate barbecues include chicken, lamb chops, steaks, grilled fish, sausages, and hamburgers. In fine weather, outdoor evening feasts take place here. This ship more than fills the bill for spending blissful sea days en route to faraway places with strange-sounding names.

The Itinerary

No single itinerary would do this ship justice as the *Discovery* sails widely from above the Arctic Circle in the North Hemisphere to as far south as most ships go in the Antarctic waters of the Southern Hemisphere. The itineraries are mostly nonrepeating and designed for an English-speaking clientele. The cruises last from two to three weeks, and they may be combined for longer vacations such as the complete trans-Pacific voyages between South America and New Zealand.

At the start of the year, the *Discovery* offers one of the very few moderately priced cruises to the **Antarctic Peninsula,** and she lands her passengers, subject to weather and ice conditions, at King Georges Island, Hope Bay, Paradise Harbor, and Half Moon Island. Not all passengers go ashore at once, and while some are on terra firma or shuttling to and from the ship, others will be attending informal talks about the region's natural history. The longer trips include either a call in the British-owned **Falklands** or sail into the **Chilean fjords.**

Following the Antarctic season the *Discovery* heads across the open **South Pacific** to parallel the route of Captain Cook's explorations and the *Bounty*'s infamous and ultimately mutinous voyage. Calls are made at **Easter Island, French Polynesia,** and **Fiji** en route to New Zealand.

Two-island **New Zealand** is an ideal region for cruising as so much of interest is close to the coastline. Ports offer city life at **Auckland** and **Wellington,** art deco architecture at **Napier** and Victorian in **Christchurch,** beautiful vineyards producing prized wines near the north end of the

South Island, majestic fjords in **Doubtful, Dusky,** and **Milford Sounds,** and sheep everywhere. In fact the four-legged population far exceeds the number of Homo sapiens.

Returning back across the Pacific via **Pitcairn Island,** the *Discovery* is one of the few non-Ecuadorian–registered ships allowed to land passengers in the **Galápagos,** one of nature's most amazing repositories of animal, bird, and undersea life such as marine iguanas and blue-footed boobies. Then the ship transits the **Panama Canal,** making calls in **Central America** en route to **Nassau.** The Atlantic Ocean crossing calls at **Bermuda** and the **Azores** en route back to **England,** and this voyage usually offers a maritime history theme for the many sea days.

By late spring the *Discovery* is back in North Europe for a season of cruises to the northern isles, **Norway,** and the **North Cape** and **Baltic** ports east to **St. Petersburg.** British passengers predominate as many cruises depart from England. Then later in the summer, the ship sails via **Portugal** and **Spain** into the Mediterranean for calls in **France, Italy, Malta, Croatia, Greece, Turkey,** the **Middle East,** and along the **North African** coast. As the late fall weather arrives, the ship completes its circuit by sailing from Europe and into Atlantic for **South America** and another Antarctic season.

Address/Phone: Discovery World Cruises, 1800 S.E. Tenth Avenue, Suite 205, Fort Lauderdale, FL 33315; (866) 623–2689 or (954) 761–7878; fax: (954) 761–7768; www.discoveryworldcruises.com

The Ship: *Discovery*, completed as the *Island Venture* in 1982 and for many years carried the name *Island Princess*, has a gross tonnage of 21,186, a length of 554 feet, and a draft of 25 feet.

Passengers: 610; British, American, and only English speakers, fifty-five and up

Dress: Formal, informal (jacket with or without a tie) or casual

Officers/Crew: British and international; Filipino crew

Cabins: 351 of moderate size, 222 outside and none with balconies

Fare: $$

What's included: Cruise fare and port charges

What's not included: Transportation to and from the ship, shore excursions, drinks, tips

Highlights: A traditional cruise liner with a genteel, low-key atmosphere

Other itineraries: The *Discovery* cruises in Europe and across the Atlantic to South America and in the South Pacific. For Antarctic cruises, the passenger capacity drops to 450, making her an affordable alternative to the high-tariff expedition ships.

PETER DEILMANN'S
Deutschland
A National Flagship in the European Tradition

The name of this handsome German flagship, *Deutschland,* simply means Germany. Unlike the multinational crews found aboard most ships today, the *Deutschland*'s 260-member crew, and most of the passengers, are largely from the German-speaking countries of Germany, Austria, and Switzerland. The staff's standard of speaking English is as good or even better than on many internationally crewed ships catering to North American passengers.

Within, the *Deutschland* is, without qualification, absolutely beautiful, extremely well designed, and has a public-room layout that suits many different occasions and moods. The decor is richly Edwardian, with art nouveau and art deco flourishes. Public rooms are varied and spacious with never a feeling of crowding, and they run the gamut from light and airy with large windows to one that opens onto side galleries to another that's cozy and enclosed for late-night conversation.

The materials are high quality and carry off the effect better than I have seen on any ship—real marble and faux marble; real wood, wood veneers, and faux burled paneling; some real brass that tarnishes and needs constant polishing and some metal that is brass in color; molding and pilasters that appear to be plaster; excellent Tiffany-style stained glass especially in the ceilings; and very tasteful furnishings.

For quiet reading, playing games, and having afternoon tea, the Lido Terrace, an observation lounge, provides a wonderful light-filled atmosphere with views outside to the surrounding open decks. The furnishings

are comfortable white and tan wicker chairs with green and gold patterned cushions.

For a drink before meals, with music provided by a trio, the Lili Marleen Salon, dedicated to Marlene Dietrich, is a cozy space with polished medium-dark paneling, a beamed ceiling with plaster decoration, opaque cut-glass globes, and additional indirect lighting from stately floor lamps. Zum Alten Fritz replicates a dark paneled taverna with its etched glass mirrors and button leather curved banquettes. It offers live music, hot snacks such as bratwurst (frankfurters) and weiss wurst (white veal sausage), and beer by the stein.

The deck space is so good and varied that one needs a very long voyage to enjoy all the outdoor, covered, and enclosed venues furnished with high-quality varnished wooden deck chairs and royal blue cushions. Happily, the ship offers extended cruises.

Dining takes place in a two-sitting main restaurant, the Berlin, in the more private Vierjahreszeiten (Four Seasons) with reservations but no extra charge, and the Lido Gourmet, a buffet offering indoor and outdoor seating, The menus are continental with German specialties, and the preparation is good to excellent.

Some of the courses that we enjoyed were air-dried beef with fresh horseradish; mild French goat cheese with grape seed oil and a baguette; cream of asparagus with baby shrimps; black noodles with lobster and scallops; grilled lemon sole with lime sauce; veal loin with morels and dates in a cream sauce; and white chocolate mousse with basil.

The lunchtime buffets offer hot and cold meats, a fair variety of salad fixings, lots of cheeses, and excellent desserts. From the grill, one could order freshly prepared shrimp, lamb chops, rib eye steaks, and chicken. At breakfast, the menu caters to European and American tastes. The service in the main dining room is relaxed and professional, and in the Vierjahreszeiten, the dinner sessions are scheduled for up to three hours.

The Kaisersaal is an extraordinarily opulent cabaret lounge furnished in a 1920s bordello style, with comfortable chairs, small table lamps, and a mezzanine with tables for two set next to the railing. Of the 286 cabins, 224 are outside and seventeen outside are singles, and all have white wood-tone paneling, handsomely framed reproduction oil paintings, decent closets, storage, and counter space, color TVs, radios, safes, and stocked refrigerators with charges for their use. Most cabins are moderately sized with less attention paid to elaborate decorative details than in the public rooms.

The prevalence of smoking is as you would find in any European setting. Any American who likes European travel or more specifically travel to Germany will find this ship a most appealing and certainly a most distinctive experience.

The Itinerary

The *Deutschland* is continuously exploring most of the world's seas, following the warm weather whenever possible, so one specific itinerary would not do the itinerary planners justice.

Beginning in 2006, the ship will be positioned in the **Indian Ocean** en route to the South African coastal ports between **Richard's Bay** near **Durban** and **Cape Town,** nestled beneath Table Mountain, thence up

to **Luderitz** and **Walvis Bay** in Namibia, which was once German Southwest Africa. Returning to South Africa, the *Deutschland* sails up the East African coast via **Madagascar** to **Zanzibar** and **Mombasa** and the Arab-settled **Lamu** in Kenya, then eastward to three beautiful **Seychellois** ports and northward to the Arabian Peninsula and into the Persian Gulf as far as the boom-town port of **Dubai.**

The seldom-visited Arabian Peninsula ports include **Abu Dhabi** in the United Arab Emirates; **Muscat** and **Salalah** in Oman; and **Aden** and **Hodeidah** in Yemen; **Aqaba** for **Petra** in Jordan; Egyptian ports of **Sharm-el-Sheik** on the Sinai Peninsula, **Safaga** for the Nile Valley, and Suez and Port Said for **Cairo.**

Entering the Mediterranean Sea in late March, the ship calls at **Cyprus,** several ports in **Turkey,** and makes a circuit of Black Sea ports in **Ukraine, Romania,** and **Bulgaria.** Returning to the Mediterranean, the track is westward into the Adriatic, then into the Western Mediterranean, out into the Atlantic, and northward to Northern Europe for the summer. Following a fall season in the Mediterranean, the *Deutschland* sails transatlantic to the Caribbean for two winter cruises, then in early 2007 circumnavigates South America via Panama, West Coast ports, Cape Horn, and East Coast ports. She returns to the Mediterranean in March 2007.

The above itineraries are sold in fourteen- to sixteen-day segments that may also be combined as many of the German passengers do. Many of the cruises have classical music, garden, or gold themes. Deilmann air-sea packages can also include hotel stays in embarkation and disembarkation ports.

Address/Phone: Peter Deilmann Cruises, 1800 Diagnoal Road, Suite 170, Alexandria, VA 22314; (703) 549–1741 or (800) 348–8287; fax: (703) 549–7924; www.deilmann-cruises.com

The Ship: *Deutschland* was completed in 1998. It has a gross tonnage of 22,400, a length of 574 feet, and a draft of 18.4 feet.

Passengers: 513, age forty-five and up; German-speaking, plus some Americans on some cruises (inquire when booking)

Dress: Formal, informal, and casual nights

Officers/Crew: German officers; largely German-speaking crew with a good facility of English

Cabins: 286, with 224 outside; 17 outside and 50 inside singles

Fare: $$$

What's included: Cruise fare only

What's not included: Airfare, port charges, shore excursions, tips, and drinks

Highlights: Splendid art nouveau and Edwardian decor; German-speaking European atmosphere

Other itineraries: The *Deutschland* travels all over the world. Deilmann riverboats cruise European waterways.

APPENDIX

SHIPS BY SIZE

Small Ships take up to 400 passengers, double occupancy, and include all the expedition-style vessels, riverboats (except the two largest Mississippi stern-wheelers), and coastal cruise vessels and most of the super luxurious boutique ships:

Midsize Ships, taking from 400 to 1,000 passengers, are relatively few in number and include some of the ferry liners (total passenger capacity) and a few of the top luxury ships:

Large Ships carrying more than 1,000 passengers include most of the megaships that also appear in the City at Sea category, those that will appeal to families, and several of the largest Scandinavian ferry liners. The largest, including more on order, exceed 2,500 passengers when all berths are occupied, and a few even top 3,000 (not including crews numbering 1,000).

TYPES OF CRUISES

Expedition-Style Cruises

Some of the best destination-oriented cruises take place aboard small expedition vessels offering what are often called soft adventure or naturalist cruises. These explore remote and exotic parts of the globe such as the Arctic, Antarctica, the Upper Amazon, and Australia's Great Barrier Reef. Some incorporate a distinctive interest in the local culture, and often the lines invite experts in natural history, ecology, anthropology, and wildlife to give enrichment talks aboard ship and to accompany passengers ashore.

Cultural Enrichment Cruises

While a number of expedition-style cruises carrying a lecture staff have some cultural orientation, the list here includes those that emphasize the region through which they are sailing, with onboard experts in the fields of history, politics, and archaeology.

Cruising under Sail

Sailing ships often draw people who would not otherwise take a standard big ship cruise. These ships also operate with diesel engines when winds are not favorable and for maneuvering in port.

Super Luxury

Some high-end ships offer all-suite accommodations and the very best food and service afloat. Most are relatively small and take 300 passengers or fewer, but there are exceptions in the midsize category and aboard the Queen Elizabeth 2 when booking grill-class accommodations.

Cruising with Children

Families traveling with children can enjoy a wide variety of activities, including separate supervised areas catering to several age levels. Most lines provide babysitting services, and some British ships have matrons to look after very small children and an early sitting for supper. Overnight ferry cruises are fun for children, offering informal dining and playrooms and games arcades aboard Scandinavian ships. A few soft adventure-type cruises are included for their orientation toward water activities.

Cruising with Foreigners

Sailing with different nationalities can be an enriching experience, especially in European waters. On a few ships, Americans may be in the minority, but all languages will be equally catered for. Some ships, as indicated, may carry mostly British or German-speaking passengers, and a few may be English-speaking unions (ESU) of Americans, British, Australians, New Zealanders, and South Africans.

Cities at Sea

The largest ships afloat are virtual urban centers with many activities, varied entertainment, large casinos, shopping malls, acres of deck space, several outdoor pools and whirlpools, elaborate health and fitness spas, and multiple dining options.

No Mal de Mer

Seasickness does affect some passengers and is a worry for others, so we are listing those ships navigating rivers and inshore waters that are less likely to cause any upset stomachs. Those marked * also offer some itineraries with short open sea stretches.

American Eagle* 41
American Glory* 45
American Queen 53
Arca 137
Canadian Empress 73
Columbia* (ferry) 33
Delta Queen 49
Emita II 39
Frederic Chopin 188
Grande Caribe* 38
Grande Mariner* 48
Infinity* 20
Katharina von Bora 188
Kawartha Voyageur 75
Litote 191
Malaspina* (ferry) 33

Matanuska* (ferry) 33
Mississippi Queen 56
Mozart 181
Nantucket Clipper* 43
Norwegian Star 17
Queen of the North* (ferry) 36
Queen of the West 68
Queen of Prince Rupert* (ferry) 36
Reef Endeavour* 216
Rio Amazonas 137
River Explorer 60
Sapphire Princess* 15
Sea Bird 65
Sea Lion 65
Seven Seas Mariner* 22
Spirit of Endeavour* 122
Spirit of '98* 27
Sun Boat III 230
Taku* (ferry) 33
Victoria Star and Victoria Queen 238
Viking Europe and Viking Spirit 180
Viking Neptune 184
Wilderness Adventurer 31
Yorktown Clipper 62

INDEX

ABOUT THE AUTHOR

Theodore W. Scull has spent more than four years plying the seven seas on ocean liners, cruise ships, expedition vessels, sailing ships, riverboats, barges, and overnight ferries. His first voyages were both stylish trips and student travel on some of the great and not so great Atlantic liners. Once a passion for ships and European travel took hold, there was no turning back.

Besides *100 Best Cruise Vacations,* he has also had seven other books published on travel, transportation, and New York topics. He writes as contributing editor for every issue of *Cruise Travel* magazine. He also writes for U.S. newspaper travel sections and cruise industry publications; British cruise magazines; and Web sites. On the lecture circuit, he talks on travel, maritime, and New York subjects aboard ships and to general and special-interest groups. He and his wife, Suellyn, homeport in Manhattan, now and forever.